THE GLOBAL LIVES OF THINGS

The Global Lives of Things considers the ways in which 'things', ranging from commodities to works of art and precious materials, participated in the shaping of global connections in the period 1400–1800. By focusing on the material exchange between Asia, Europe, the Americas and Australia, this volume traces the movements of objects through human networks of commerce, colonialism and consumption. It argues that material objects mediated between the forces of global economic exchange and the constantly changing identities of individuals, as they were drawn into global circuits. It proposes a reconceptualization of early modern global history in the light of its material culture by asking the question: what can we learn about the early modern world by studying its objects?

This exciting new collection draws together the latest scholarship in the study of material culture and offers students a critique and explanation of the notion of commodity and a reinterpretation of the meaning of exchange. It engages with the concepts of 'proto-globalization', 'the first global age' and 'commodities/consumption'. Divided into three parts, the volume considers in Part One, Objects of Global Knowledge, in Part Two, Objects of Global Connections, and finally, in Part Three, Objects of Global Consumption. The collection concludes with afterwords from three of the leading historians in the field, Maxine Berg, Suraiya Faroqhi and Paula Findlen, who offer their critical view of the methodologies and themes considered in the book and place its arguments within the wider field of scholarship.

Extensively illustrated, and with chapters examining case studies from Northern Europe to China and Australia, this book will be essential reading for students of global history.

Anne Gerritsen is Associate Professor in the Department of History at the University of Warwick. Her previous publications include *Ji'an Literati and the Local in Song-Yuan-Ming China* (2007).

Giorgio Riello is Professor in the Department of History at the University of Warwick. In addition to several edited collections, he is the author of *A Foot in the Past* (2006) and *Cotton: The Fabric that Made the Modern World* (2013).

THE GLOBAL LIVES OF THINGS

The material culture of connections in the early modern world

*Edited by Anne Gerritsen
and Giorgio Riello*

Routledge
Taylor & Francis Group

LONDON AND NEW YORK

First published 2016
by Routledge
2 Park Square, Milton Park, Abingdon, Oxon OX14 4RN

and by Routledge
711 Third Avenue, New York, NY 10017

Routledge is an imprint of the Taylor & Francis Group, an informa business

British Library Cataloguing in Publication Data
A catalogue record for this book is available from the British Library

Library of Congress Cataloging-in-Publication Data
Names: Gerritsen, Anne. | Riello, Giorgio.
Title: The global lives of things : the material culture of connections in
    the early modern world / edited by Anne Gerritsen and Giorgio Riello.
Description: London : Routledge, 2015. | Includes bibliographical references.
Identifiers: LCCN 2015019553 |
Subjects: LCSH: Material culture—History. | Globalization—History. | Social
    networks—History. | Commerce—History. | Colonies—History. | History,
    Modern. | Economic history.
Classification: LCC GN406 .G56 2015 | DDC 306.4/6—dc23
LC record available at http://lccn.loc.gov/2015019553

ISBN: 978-1-138-77666-1 (hbk)
ISBN: 978-1-138-77675-3 (pbk)
ISBN: 978-1-315-67290-8 (ebk)

Typeset in Bembo
by Apex CoVantage, LLC

MIX
Paper from
responsible sources
FSC
www.fsc.org   FSC® C013604

Printed and bound by CPI Group (UK) Ltd, Croydon, CR0 4YY

CONTENTS

Figures, maps and tables   *viii*
Preface   *xi*
Contributors   *xiii*

The global lives of things:
material culture in the first global age   1
Anne Gerritsen and Giorgio Riello

PART I
Objects of global knowledge   **29**

1   Itineraries of materials and knowledge in
    the early modern world   31
    Pamela H. Smith

2   Towards a global history of shagreen   62
    Christine Guth

3   The coral network: The trade of red coral to the
    Qing imperial court in the eighteenth century   81
    Pippa Lacey

PART II
Objects of global connections 103

4 Beyond the *kunstkammer*: Brazilian featherwork
in early modern Europe 105
Mariana Françozo

5 The empire in the duke's palace: Global material
culture in sixteenth-century Portugal 128
Nuno Senos

6 Dishes, coins and pipes: The epistemological
and emotional power of VOC material
culture in Australia 145
Susan Broomhall

7 Encounters around the material object:
French and Indian consumers in
eighteenth-century Pondicherry 162
Kévin Le Doudic

PART III
Objects of global consumption 181

8 Customs and consumption: Russia's
global tobacco habits in the seventeenth
and eighteenth centuries 183
Matthew P. Romaniello

9 Sugar revisited: Sweetness and the environment in the
early modern world 198
Urmi Engineer

10 Coffee, mind and body: Global material
culture and the eighteenth-century
Hamburg import trade 221
Christine Fertig and Ulrich Pfister

Afterword: How (early modern) things travel 241
Paula Findlen

Afterword: Objects and their worlds 247
Suraiya Faroqhi

Afterword: Things in global history 253
Maxine Berg

Index 259

FIGURES, MAPS AND TABLES

Figures

Figure 0.1	Antonio de Pereda, *Still Life with an Ebony Chest*	2
Figure 0.2	*Interior of a shop,* Netherlands, 1680–1700	7
Figure 0.3a	Crow's cup, produced in Jingdezhen, 1600–1625	9
Figure 0.3b	Porcelain cup produced in China with silver-gilt mount applied in England, *c.*1585	9
Figure 0.3c	Porcelain cup, produced in Jingdezhen, China, before 1613	9
Figure 0.4	Astronomical clock. Wood, metal and glass, China, 18th century	15
Figure 0.5	Knife, *c.*1660–1680	17
Figure 0.6	*Pineapple,* drawing by John White, 1585–1593	20
Figure 1.1	Handstein with mine scene and crucifixion	34
Figure 1.2	*Speculum metallorum* (1575), fol. 56v, the blood of Jesus on the Cross forming minerals in the earth	35
Figure 1.3	Native silver (dendritic formations), Freiberg District, Erzgebirge, Saxony, Germany	36
Figure 1.4	Hans Leinberger, *c.*1510–1520, Mass for the victims of a mine accident, limewood	37
Figure 1.5	Drops of Jesus's blood painted in vermilion (Psalter and Rosary of the Virgin), *c.*1490	39
Figure 1.6	Martin Schongauer, *The Flight into Egypt*, *c.*1470–1490	41
Figure 1.7	Frederick II, Hohenstaufen, *De arte venandi cum avibus*	45
Figure 1.8	'Molino Ewer', *c.*1450–1500	46
Figure 1.9	Two mandarins of Ming dynasty court, silk painting by unknown artist	50
Figure 1.10	Deep red cinnabar stone	51
Figure 1.11	Zolfatara di Pozzuoli	52
Figure 1.12	Chart to illustrate the multi-focal origins of proto-chemistry	54

Figure 2.1   Japanese lacquer coffer with domed lid (*Kamaboko-bako*)   67
Figure 2.2a Rayskin shield with lacquer ornament, Japan *c*.1580 (front)   69
Figure 2.2b Rayskin shield (back)   69
Figure 2.3   Illustration of sword hilt décor from *Kōi seigi* (1785)   70
Figure 2.4   Knife with handle of sheet silver stamped to resemble
             shagreen and a case made of shagreen   72
Figure 3.1   Plate with scene of offering coral trees to the Emperor   82
Figure 3.2   Portrait of the Qianlong emperor as a young man,
             unidentified artist, 19th century, Qing dynasty   83
Figure 3.3   Foreigners presenting Coral Trees to an *Arhat*. From an Album
             of Six Buddhist Arhats and Worshippers by Liu Luohan
             (or Lu Lengjia), *c*.730–760 CE   85
Figure 3.4   Raw harvested unprocessed coral branches,
             Torre del Greco, Italy   87
Figure 4.1   *Portrait of Sophie of the Palatinate*, by Louise
             Hollandine of the Palatinate   106
Figure 4.2a Cape. Rio de Janeiro, America, sixteenth century,
             Tupinambá (front)   108
Figure 4.2b Cape. Rio de Janeiro, America, sixteenth century,
             Tupinambá (back)   108
Figure 4.3   Tupinambá dance in Theodor de Bry,
             Dritte Buch Americae, 1593   112
Figure 4.4   Images 'La Bresilienne' and 'Le Bresilien', in François Deserps,
             Recueil de la diversité des habits, 1564   114
Figure 5.1   Portrait of Duke D. Teodósio I of Bragança, print, *c*.1755   129
Figure 5.2   Ducal Palace of Vila Viçosa   129
Figure 5.3   Mother-of-pearl casket, India, Gujarat   131
Figure 5.4a Saucer dish (front) with the armillary sphere of King
             Manuel I and the 'IHS' monogram   135
Figure 5.4b Saucer dish (back)   135
Figure 5.5   Gujarati tortoiseshell casket   138
Figure 6.1   Dirck Hartogh dish, *c*.1600–16.   146
Figure 7.1   Veranda of the Lagrenée de Mézières hotel, last third of
             the eighteenth century   167
Figure 7.2   Louis XVI style settee, late eighteenth–early
             nineteenth century   168
Figure 7.3   Excerpt from Pierre Le Gardeur de Repentigny's probate
             inventory, 1776   169
Figure 7.4   Pair of statuettes of parrots perched on rocks   172
Figure 7.5   Torch-bearing angel, Coromandel Coast, India,
             c.1680–1700   174
Figure 7.6   French and Indian product consumption,
             according to product origin   175
Figure 8.1   Johann Gottlieb Georgi, *Russia: Or, A Compleat
             Historical Account of All the Nations
             which Compose that Empire*   185

Figure 8.2 'Paramoshka at Savoska's house', woodcut   189
Figure 9.1 Representation of deforestation in Barbados, *c.*1646   204
Figure 9.2 'Impoverished Sugar-Estates, Barbados', 1898   205
Figure 9.3 Erosion and deforestation along the Haiti/Dominican
            Republic border   206
Figure 9.4 Plan of the city of New Orleans and adjacent
            plantations, 1875   209
Figure 9.5 'A heap of odd water receptacles, collected out of yards', 1909   212
Figure 9.6 'Sugar barrels on the landing dock in
            St Pierre, Martinique', 1898   213
Figure 9.7 'A New Orleans yard and cistern', 1912   215

Maps

Map 1.1 Al-Rāzī in Bukhara, Rayy and Baghdad   53
Map 3.1 The coral network map   86
Map 7.1 Pondicherry in the late eighteenth century   164
Map 9.1 Global spread of sugar cultivation and the plantation complex   200

Table

Table 10.1 Real import quantities of colonial commodities through
            Hamburg (yearly average of index values, 1736–1742=100)   227

PREFACE

The Global Lives of Things is a joint effort of several scholars working at the inter-section between global history and material culture. Their papers were presented and discussed at several events organised as part of an AHRC-funded International Network on 'Global Commodities' active between 2011 and 2013 and coordi-nated by the Global History and Culture Centre at the University of Warwick. The Victoria and Albert Museum (Glenn Adamson and Marta Ajmar), the Pea-body Essex Museum in Salem, Massachusetts (Karina Corrigan), Bilgi University, Istanbul (Suraiya Faroqhi) and our colleagues at Warwick, Maxine Berg and Luca Molà helped us organise a series of events that took place in London, Warwick, Istanbul and Salem. These meetings and a large conference that took place at the University of Warwick in December 2012 allowed us to develop a series of conversations with an increasingly large number of colleagues interested in exploring the ways in which objects – be they traded commodities, gifts, rari-ties, artworks or everyday mundane artefacts – came to shape the lives of people across the globe and at the same time created new and sometimes unpredictable connections.

The papers included in this volume only represent a small part of these con-versations, and it is not possible to mention all of our partners. A few people shine through their absence here, but deserve special mention. Dana Leibsohn has been an inspiration from the earliest beginnings of this project. Even if cir-cumstances conspired against her, her support and critical commentary has been invaluable for us. Michael North delivered the keynote lecture at our Global Commodities conference, and his work on transcultural mediation, especially of Netherlandish art and material culture was and remains important to us. Several contributions delivered at our workshops and conferences have appeared in the volume *Writing Material Culture History* edited by Gerritsen and Riello, whilst others will appear in a forthcoming book entitled *Global Gifts: The Material Culture of Diplomacy in Early Modern Eurasia* edited by Zóltan Biedermann, Anne Gerritsen and Giorgio Riello.

Anne Gerritsen and Giorgio Riello,
September 2015

CONTRIBUTORS

Maxine Berg, FBA, is Professor of History at the University of Warwick. Recent books include *Goods from the East: Trading Eurasia 1600–1800* (Palgrave, 2015), *Writing the History of the Global: Challenges for the 21st Century* (Oxford, 2013), *Luxury and Pleasure in Eighteenth-Century Britain* (Oxford, 2005), *Luxury in the Eighteenth Century: Debates, Desires and Delectable Goods* (Palgrave, 2002), *Consumers and Luxury in Europe 1650–1850* (Manchester, 1999), *Technological Revolutions in Europe 1760–1860* (Edward Elgar, 1997), *The Age of Manufactures* (Routledge 1985, new edition 1994). *Markets and Manufacture in Early Industrial Europe* (Routledge, 1990, new edition 2012), has appeared in a recent updated edition.

Susan Broomhall is Professor of Early Modern History at the University of Western Australia and specialises in the history of women and gender, emotions, material culture, as well as the role of scholarly histories in heritage tourism and arts industries. Recent publications include (with Jennifer Spinks) *Early Modern Women in the Low Countries: Feminising Sources and Interpretations of the Past* (2011) and (with Jacqueline Van Gent) *Dynastic Colonialism: Gender, Materiality and the Early Modern House of Orange-Nassau* (Routledge, 2016). She was a Foundation Chief Investigator in the Australian Research Council Centre of Excellence for the History of Emotions where her published research explored the interpretation of pre-modern objects in the history of emotional processes and practices and in modern museum contexts. She is an Advisor to the AHRC Research Network 'Gender, Power and Materiality in Early Modern Europe, 1500–1800' (2015–17).

Kévin Le Doudic completed his first degree in Art History and Archaeology and is currently completing his PhD thesis on the history of the French in India in the eighteenth century. His research focuses on material culture and the connection between the object and cultural identity studied through the use of notarial records. His research is conducted in close collaboration with the Museum of the East India Company (Lorient, France), the Museum of Decorative Arts of the Indian Ocean (Reunion Island, France), and, in Pondicherry, with the French Institute and the French School of Asian Studies (École française d'Extrême-Orient).

Urmi Engineer is Postdoctoral Fellow at the World History Center of the University of Pittsburgh. She approaches world history from an ecological and cross-cultural perspective. Her research focuses on disease and ecology in the Atlantic, and draws connections between the southern United States, the colonial Caribbean, and South Asia.

Suraiya Faroqhi completed her studies at the universities of Hamburg and Istanbul, as well as at Indiana University/Bloomington, before embarking on a long career at Middle East Technical University (Ankara, 1971–87). She was later professor at the Ludwig-Maximilians-Universität in Munich (1988–2007). After retirement, she has joined Istanbul Bilgi University, where she is currently teaching. Her field is Ottoman social history, with a special interest in artisans. She is a co-editor of the four-volume *Cambridge History of Turkey* (2006–13).

Paula Findlen is Ubaldo Pierotti Professor of Italian History at Stanford University. Her research concerns the relationship between collecting, curiosity, science, and material culture. Publications include *Possessing Nature: Museums, Collecting and Scientific Culture in Early Modern Italy* (1994), *Merchants and Marvels* (2002, co-edited with Pamela Smith) and, most recently, *Early Modern Things: Objects and Their Histories, 1500–1800* (2013) and the English translation of Renata Ago's *Gusto for Things: A History of Objects in Seventeenth-Century Rome* (2013).

Christine Fertig holds a PhD in history from the University of Münster (2012), with a study on families and social networks in northwestern German rural society, entitled *Familie, verwandtschaftliche Netzwerke und Klassenbildung im ländlichen Westfalen (1750–1874)* (2012). She is currently working at the University of Münster on a new project about exotic substances in German trade and the development of knowledge in eighteenth- and nineteenth-century specialist literature.

Mariana C. Françozo is Assistant Professor of Museum Studies at Leiden University and associate researcher at the National Museum of Ethnology, Leiden. Her research focuses on the circulation of Amerindian material culture between Brazil and Europe and on the production of ethnographic knowledge, with particular emphasis on the early modern period. She is the author of *De Olinda a Holanda: a coleção de curiosidades de Nassau* (2014).

Anne Gerritsen is Associate Professor in the Department of History at the University of Warwick, and holds the Kikkoman Chair in Asia-Europe Intercultural

Dynamics with special attention to material culture, art and development at the University of Leiden. Her previous publications include *Ji'an Literati and the Local in Song-Yuan-Ming China* (2007) and *Writing Material Culture History* (co-edited with Giorgio Riello, 2015).

Christine Guth is a Senior Tutor in Asian design in the V&A/RCA postgraduate History of Design Programme. She has written widely about aspects of transnational cultural exchange from the early modern to the modern eras. Her publications include *Art, Tea and Industry: Masuda Takashi and the Mitsui Circle* (1993); *Art of Edo Japan: The Artist and the City 1615–1868* (1996; 2010); and *Hokusai's Great Wave: Biography of a Global Icon* (2015).

Pippa Lacey is Postdoctoral Researcher in the School of Art History and World Art Studies, Sainsbury Institute for Arts, and Academic Co-ordinator, Guides' Training Course at the Sainsbury Centre for Visual Arts, University of East Anglia. Her research explores the construction of identity and status through material culture, with a focus on coloured materials.

Ulrich Pfister holds a PhD in history from the University of Zürich (1984). He is currently Professor of Economic and Social History at the University of Münster (since 1996). His earlier research covers the history of regional export industries (proto-industries), of rural societies, of religious practices as well as historical demography. His present research interests centre on the aggregate development of the German economy, *c.*1500–1871.

Giorgio Riello is Professor of Global History and Culture and Director of the Institute of Advanced Study at the University of Warwick. He is the author of *A Foot in the Past* (2006) and *Cotton: The Fabric that Made the Modern World* (2013) and has published extensively on the history of fashion, design and consumption in early modern Europe and Asia. He is the co-editor of *Shoes* (2006; 2011); *The Spinning World* (2009; 2012); *Global Design History* (2011); *Writing Material Culture History* (with Anne Gerritsen, 2015) and other volumes.

Matthew P. Romaniello is Associate Professor of History at the University of Hawaii at Manoa. He is the author of *The Elusive Empire: Kazan and the Creation of Russia, 1552–1671* (2012) and the co-editor of *Tobacco in Russian History and Culture: From the Seventeenth Century to the Present* (2009).

Nuno Senos earned his PhD at the Institute of Fine Arts, New York University (2006). He is now based at the Universidade Nova de Lisboa (Lisbon, Portugal) where his work focuses on the early modern age and on the arts and the Portuguese expansion. He publishes on architecture in Portugal and Brazil and on the global art trade in the Portuguese world.

Pamela H. Smith is Seth Low Professor of History and Director of the Center for Science and Society at Columbia University where she teaches courses in early modern European history and history of science. Her books include *The Business of Alchemy* (1994); *Merchants and Marvels* (2002, co-edited with Paula Findlen); *The Body of the Artisan* (2004); *Making Knowledge in Early Modern Europe* (2008, co-edited with Benjamin Schmidt); *Ways of Making and Knowing* (2015, co-edited with Amy R.W. Meyers and Harold Cook); and *The Matter of Art* (2015, co-edited with Christy Anderson and Anne Dunlop). She has published numerous articles on early modern European artisanal knowledge and culture, and, in current research, she is directing a large collaborative research and teaching initiative, The Making and Knowing Project, to reconstruct the vernacular knowledge of early modern craftspeople from a variety of disciplinary perspectives.

THE GLOBAL LIVES OF THINGS

Material culture in the first global age[1]

Anne Gerritsen and Giorgio Riello

In 1652, the Spanish painter Antonio de Pereda (1599?–1678?) completed a large canvas entitled *Still Life with an Ebony Chest* (Figure 0.1).[2] The painting depicts a group of objects on a surface covered in a red velvet cloth. In the centre stands the ebony chest that gives the still life its name, a woven cloth hanging down from the top drawer. Five different vessels stand on the top of the chest, including two red ceramic vessels decorated with small pieces of quartz from Mexico, a gourd-shaped vessel with silver mounts, a transparent glass vessel, and an Italian bowl.[3] The chest is flanked by a chocolatière with a wooden implement to stir the chocolate on one side, and a two-handled Talavera pottery jar on the other.[4] In the foreground, we see round wooden boxes containing chocolate, and breads, biscuits and cheeses, and on the left hand side, three cups and a spoon on a silver tray. The three cups on the tray are all different: a small blue-and-white Delftware cup on the left, a small lusterware bowl from Manises on the right, and a taller cup with spreading, damaged mouth rim and a fine underglaze blue decoration. The wide variety of shapes, sizes, materials, textures and colours is lovingly depicted, and the signs of use in the broken biscuits, the crumpled cheese paper, and the chipped porcelain cup all serve to enhance the tangible qualities of what is displayed.

Art historians have described this as one of De Pereda's masterpieces, displaying his 'visual acuity and technical accomplishment'.[5] Art historians have tended to view this painting first and foremost *as painting*, paying close attention to aspects such as the brushwork, the use of light, the theme of the painting, and its significance in De Pereda's wider oeuvre. But the painting invites multiple types of viewing, both today, in the present, as it did in the past. The tangible quality of the objects in the painting, for example, suggests stories of use: of chocolate stirred, food eaten, jugs poured, and drawers opened and shut.[6] Of course this painted juxtaposition of objects has complex meanings, but if we focus briefly on the objects

FIGURE 0.1 *Still Life with an Ebony Chest*, by Antonio de Pereda. Spain, 1652. 80 × 94 cm. State Hermitage Museum, Saint Petersburg, inv. no. GE-327. © 2015. Photo Scala, Florence.

themselves, then we can ask questions about their origins: when, where and how did De Pereda acquire these objects, and what did they mean to him?

Arguably, the meanings of the objects depend on their 'social life', as Arjun Appadurai would have it. Before these objects were selected and placed together on a single canvas by the artist, they each circulated in 'specific cultural and histori-cal milieus' in which 'desire and demand, reciprocal sacrifice and power interact to create economic value in specific social situations'.[7] These 'things', then, have value, meanings, and trajectories. The publication of Appadurai's 1986 edited volume, *The Social Life of Things*, and the writings of other anthropologists, archaeologists and art historians encouraged social and economic historians to look at 'things'. In the wake of *The Social Life of Things*, scholars in a variety of fields turned to artefacts. Material culture, materials and materiality, making things, and desiring things had all been studied before, but gained newfound importance from the 1980s onwards.

A decade after Appadurai's study, the intellectual landscape changed again through what we might call 'the global turn', linked to the publication of several key works in the field of history, the ongoing growth of globalization in our con-temporary socio-political, cultural and educational environment, and the decreasing significance of political and cultural boundaries.[8] Across the disciplines, the word 'global' started to appear in titles of research proposals, projects, articles, and books.[9] Of course the particular interpretation of the word varied and continues to vary widely, but its application generally implied a challenge to national approaches to history. Since the global turn, cross-border connections and interactions take precedence over the boundaries and narratives that seek to suggest the importance of separate nations. We ask different questions, and our eyes have been opened to the interactions of people, ideas, and things across cultural and geographical zones. The 'things' we see in De Pereda's still life, then, are not just things with social lives, but with global trajectories.

Luxuries and global trade

The objects De Pereda depicted form only the tip of a vast iceberg of objects that were exchanged and commodities that were traded throughout the early modern world. From Chinese traders in the Southeast-Asian archipelago and merchant communities stretching across the Indian Ocean in the thirteenth century, Islamic merchants exchanging goods across the Silk Roads in the fourteenth century, the first explorations initiated by the Portuguese crown in the late fifteenth century, the Spanish ventures into the Americas in the sixteenth, the arrival of the Dutch and English trading companies in the Asian seas in the seventeenth, to the global annexations and colonizations of the eighteenth and nineteenth centuries, goods moved across vast distances.[10] Trade and exchange was far from new of course; goods were traded across significant distances in the ancient and medieval worlds, too. Roman commentators were allured and appalled by 'oriental' luxuries such as spices, precious stones, silks and cottons.[11] The so-called 'Silk Roads' that traversed Eurasia continued to be a major thoroughfare of all sorts of luxury goods moving over short and long distances.[12] Spices such as cinnamon, cloves, nutmeg and pepper originated in Asia, were traded across Central Asia via the Levant by caravan, and formed part of the European medieval kitchen.[13] Other goods that were traded across vast distances and circulated widely throughout Europe included indigo, lapis lazuli and other ingredients required for dyestuffs and painters' pigments, Chinese silks, and of course precious stones and metals.[14]

Janet Abu-Lughod's work has shown us that already as early as the thirteenth century, goods, people and ideas circulated in what she designated as nine separate zones of interaction.[15] These included, for example, a zone that reached from Beijing in the north, along the eastern seaboard of the Chinese (Mongol-Yuan) empire into the South China Sea and connected the rich commodities of the Southeast-Asian island kingdoms with the seats of imperial power in China, Japan and Korea. Other zones included one that incorporated most of the Indian Ocean, another that connected the extremities of the Silk Roads, and areas in Central Asia, Northern Africa, the Mediterranean, northern Europe, and so on. But the trade in goods across distances moved a significant step towards becoming truly globe-encompassing with the 1572 establishment of the Spanish colonial outpost of Manila in the Philippines.[16]

From the late sixteenth century onwards, then, we see not only the long-distance trade in high-value luxury goods for the elite markets, but ever-growing regular flows of commodities traded in bulk across vast distances.[17] Within the Ottoman realm, for example, the consumption of exotic luxuries and tradable commodities used in everyday life flourished. The Safavid Empire in what is now Iran was also one of the most important nodes in the global flows of commodities. Europe, too, received substantial quantities of Asian goods through the trade of a series of chartered companies including the English (est. 1600), the Dutch (est. 1601), the French (est. 1664), and the smaller Swedish, Danish and Ostend companies.

The silver tray on the table in De Pereda's painting points to the Spanish silver that started to flow across the globe from the late sixteenth century onwards. It was silver that had facilitated the earliest exchanges of goods between Europeans and traders from far-flung locations, for example in the Levant. However, silver was only mined in a few places, and until the sixteenth century, remained a rare precious metal.[18] With the expansion of the Spanish empire into the Americas, the colonisers were able to exploit local resources, including the silver-rich mines of Potosí in what is now Bolivia.[19] The silver mined in Potosí was shipped in Spanish galleons to Europe, to Manila, into the South China Seas and the Indian Ocean. Chinese demand for silver was high, especially because of the new requirement to make all tax payments in silver rather than in kind (mostly silk and grains) in the Chinese empire from the late sixteenth century onwards.[20] In return, the Europeans bought vast quantities of commodities and goods manufactured in Asia. The silver tray, then, betrays a vast global system of trade and exchange, with Habsburg Spain and late Ming-early Qing China as dual centres.

The ebony chest that lends its name to the still life also points to the global connections of the early modern world. Precious woods like ebony, mahogany, rosewood and cedar were valued by cabinetmakers for their hardness, colour and shine, and used in cabinets and chests of various kinds, picture and mirror frames, musical instruments, and religious objects.[21] Some hardwoods were native to Europe, but in the mediaeval era, ebony was imported via Venice and the Levant from East Africa and Southeast Asia, and after the establishment of colonial outposts in the East and West Indies, brought to Europe by ship.[22] The marquetry decorations on the small chest of drawers may well be ivory or another contrasting wood transported across vast distances before being made into this elegant, lockable chest.[23]

Apart from silver and precious woods, ceramic vessels, and especially porcelain vessels, are objects that signal global connections.[24] The global variety in ceramics production is impossible to capture in a few lines, but some broad generalizations could be made. On the whole, Chinese, Korean and later Japanese potters preferred thinner vessels with monochrome or underglaze blue decorations fired at high temperatures, referred to as porcelain, while in the Islamic world and in the Mediterranean regions, brightly coloured pigments were applied to a tin-glazed surface, producing ceramics known as majolica or faïence. Ceramics were also traded and exchanged between these zones of preference and taste, and out of these exchanges and contacts emerged new forms and designs, such as, for example, blue-and-white Delftwares, and blue-and-white Puebla wares.[25] The vessels depicted in De Pereda's painting provide examples of several of these different ceramic traditions.

The colourful bowl on the right-hand corner of the ebony chest, for example, is an Italian majolica bowl, decorated in shades of red, green, cream and brown, with flowers, leaves, medallions and a winged, crowned human figure. The two-handled jar to the right of the chest is, similarly, made of stoneware, covered in a cream-coloured tin-glaze, and decorated with red and green pigments. Another example of this type of pottery is visible in the small bell-shaped cup with red decorations on the silver tray. This type of ceramics was manufactured throughout the Islamic world, the Mediterranean, and the technology spread northwards from there to Antwerp, Delft and the British potteries in the sixteenth century.[26] These, then, exemplify the local tradition of ceramics manufacture.

Several of De Pereda's vessels, however, exemplify the global trade in ceramics. The red vessels decorated with quartz flowers standing on the chest, for example, were brought to Spain from Mexico. The tall cup with the cracked rim standing behind the others on the tray, has a thin body and a fine light-blue landscape design, and most likely represents a piece of imported Chinese porcelain. Both the Portuguese and the Spanish purchased vast quantities of porcelain in Asia and delivered these to consumers in the Americas, along the African coasts, and in Europe. Once the Dutch, English, French and Swedish trading companies also established themselves in various locations throughout Asia, the quantities of traded ceramics rose substantially, leading to speculations about the overall quantities of porcelain shipments that number in the millions. The small blue-and-white cup on the left-hand side of the silver tray, finally, exemplifies the blends of traditions that emerged from the contacts and exchanges in ceramic traditions and styles. It is a tin-glaze object, possibly made in Delft, in a colour scheme and decorative pattern that appropriates ideas of the Chinese porcelain tradition.

Textiles, too, were traded in vast quantities throughout the early modern period. De Pereda shows at least three types of cloth in his painting: a deep red velvet; what looks like a small piece of linen to wrap the biscuits; and a small cloth probably of American origin. Whilst the velvet and linen are clearly European (though velvet was mastered only in the thirteenth century by Europeans in imitation of Chinese velvets), the small American cloth takes us back to a pre-Columbian design tradition. It provides us also with a counter-narrative as it is a 'global thing' that did not achieve global success. It was the textiles of the East Indies (India) and not those of the West Indies (the Americas) that became commodities with a global appeal. Chintzes, calicoes and other textiles produced in India found markets across and beyond the Indian Ocean well before the arrival of the European trading companies. Textiles had been the most common traded commodities since antiquity with the best silks coming from China and the best cotton textiles from India. The artist's choice of an American cloth might have been an aesthetic preference though at the time he was painting, Indian cotton textiles were still rare in Europe. Only in the second half of the seventeenth and during the eighteenth century did they become extremely popular and fashionable, not just among European but also among African and American consumers.[27]

The choice of an American cloth might have been partly motivated by the fact that it matched well a series of implements for the preparation of drinking chocolate, a very American commodity that was slowly finding success in Europe.[28] De Pereda captures one of the elements of what Alfred Crosby has defined as the 'Columbian exchange', the exchange between the Americas and Afro-Eurasia following the 'discovery' of the New World.[29] A series of plants, animals and diseases from the Americas found their way to Europe, Asia and Africa and vice versa. The European diet was revolutionized from the sixteenth century onwards by new foods, not just cocoa, but also the nutritious potato, corn, the indispensable tomato as well as peppers, beans and pumpkins. The turkey was one of the animals transplanted from the Americas though its provenance – at least in the English language – was often confused with that of other fowls of Turkish origin. A series of plants from the Afro-Eurasian continent arrived in the Americas as well: these include common fruit such as the banana, grapes, peaches, pears and oranges and vegetables such as onions and olives. Animals such as horses and cows made their first appearance in the new world in the sixteenth century.[30]

Chocolate is here representative not just of a commodity from the Americas new to Europeans but of a larger category of beverages unknown to Europeans before 1500 that include also coffee from the Arabian Peninsula and tea from China.[31] These have in the course of the past five centuries become global commodities that are cultivated and consumed around the world.[32] Key to their success was not simply their transplantation to other continents but their potential to be cultivated in plantations. This is the case for sugar, an Old World sweetener that started to be mixed with the bitter cocoa beans to suit the European palate.[33] Sugar changed the landscape and the economy and social structure of several areas of the Americas.[34] By the seventeenth century it was grown in large plantations through the exploitation of slave labour from Africa. Crops therefore, perhaps more than manufactured goods, had a profound effect on the relationship between different continents, on people's habits and on the lives of millions of Africans.[35]

From global things to the global lives of things

From the early sixteenth century onwards, then, the world of trade began to transform the world of goods. This was true not only in Europe, but also in East and Southeast Asia, the Islamic empires of Safavid Iran, Mughal India and the Ottomans, along the African coasts, in the Americas, and in Australasia. The interior of this imaginary shop (Figure 0.2), painted in Europe, only gives a small inkling of the vast diversity of goods that became available to consumers with the growth of global trade connections.

A very different range of luxury items than we saw in De Pereda is for sale here: lacquered chests, cabinets and boxes, screens, picture frames, tall wooden stands, a variety of Chinese porcelains ranging from delicate little bowls and lidded jars to

FIGURE 0.2 *Interior of a shop.* Netherlands, 1680–1700. Gouache on paper, mounted on wooden panel. H 26.3 cm × W 43.6 cm. Victoria and Albert Museum, P. 35–1926.

large vases and bowls, red earthenwares, Indian chintzes, Persian paintings, small ivory devotional sculptures and an array of folded fans. There are groups of customers in the shops, seated and standing by the pieces of furniture, testing the fabrics, and selecting fans, dressed in a wide range of what seem to be Asian costumes. The objects are foregrounded, literally, by standing in the foreground of the painting, but also by filling every part of the surface, right to the top of the painting, to the point of sacrificing the sense of physical space in the shop. The viewer sees an abundance of objects, in rich variety of materials, colours, textures and designs. The viewer also sees a variety of markers and identifiers: styles of clothing and headdress depicted in the portraits and paintings but also in the clothing of the shop's customers make it difficult to locate the shop within a single cultural context. Equally, the flora and fauna that grace the paintings, textiles, porcelains and pieces of furniture suggest an extra-European world without determining a specific cultural or geographical context.

The absence of a clear pathway for the viewer to enter and inhabit the space of the shop, and the lack of a consistent viewing perspective of the objects on display, mean that the viewer remains on the outside of the world depicted, unsure of the physical location of the space he or she views. Beyond the European architecture of the shop, there are few markers to suggest where the shop is located or who its imagined consumers are, leaving the objects to speak for themselves. But the objects also raise questions: Where have these objects come from? Where will they go from here? What do the objects mean, for whom, and why? The painting presents a world of global goods, but suspends these objects in an undefined space, urging us to ask further questions. In order to make sense of the world of goods depicted in this painting we need to make an analytical move; viewing objects as traded commodities that have been moved from A to B is not enough; in order to understand what is on display here, we need to identify the 'things' as global things and trace their trajectories, so that we see the accumulation of meanings that objects acquire as they travel. To see the objects as things with global lives, we need a repertoire of disciplinary, methodological and conceptual tools, so as to draw on a variety of insights, ranging from art history, archaeology and anthropology to literature and historical studies, especially global history.[36]

The study of things

We have started with examples of 'things' that are represented via the medium of a painting, but also two-dimensional works such as prints, drawing and etchings. For historians of European art, the fine arts, especially the art of painting, have always had pride of place. The fine arts, in this classification, revealed the imagination, the eye and the hand of a great master.[37] The decorative arts, such as ceramics, glass, furniture, carved stones, wood, ivory and gems, metalwork, and textiles, in contrast, were not produced by an individual master, but in a workshop context.[38] The emphasis on the process of making things (e.g. in a workshop), and thus the emphasis on precious materials, designs, modes of manufacturing and practical application, often absent in the study of fine arts, are crucial for the study of the decorative arts. The object, in that context, is seen as the artistic outcome of a combination of specifically selected and prepared materials, finely tuned skills and craftsmanship, and the designs and decorative schemes shaped by taste, fashion and use. Each of these has the power to elevate an object into the realm of the decorative arts; a high quality material, exquisite skill or extraordinary design can lift an object from its ordinary object-ness to the level of an artistic object.

Histories of art, the decorative arts and museum studies have come to question the prominence given to outstanding 'works of art'. What happens, for example, when we move from the aesthetic consideration of a painting as in Figure 0.1 to the physical form of one of the objects represented? Figure 0.3a is a small Chinese porcelain cup of the Ming dynasty. It is not the one represented in the painting but it is not dissimilar. This cup is not in any sense a 'work of art'. In fact it was one of the hundreds of thousands such things produced in the kilns of Jingdezhen in Jiangxi province, China, and traded to Japan, the Middle East, India, Europe and already by the early seventeenth century to the European settlements of North America.[39] Like the gourd-shaped vessel with silver mounts in De Pereda's painting, Chinese cups and other porcelain arriving in Europe in the sixteenth century were expensive and rare and as such deserved to be mounted either in silver or gold (Figure 0.3b).[40] The best Chinese porcelains were treasured as items of collecting by the European, Persian, Indian and Ottoman elites from the sixteenth century onwards. They were often arranged into collections: assemblages of artefacts that were not appreciated merely as 'works of art' or as simple commodities for consumption but as representations of an expanding world of wonder. The so-called

FIGURE 0.3a Crow's cup, produced in Jingdezhen, 1600–1625. H 8.1 cm. Rijksmuseum AK-R-BK-14772-A.

FIGURE 0.3b Porcelain cup produced in China with silver-gilt mount applied in England, *c.*1585. Gilbert Collection © The Rosalinde and Arthur Gilbert Collection on loan to the Victoria and Albert Museum, London.

FIGURE 0.3c Porcelain cup, produced in Jingdezhen, China, before 1613. H 8.2 cm. This bowl was part of the cargo of the VOC ship *Witte Leeuw*. Rijksmusem NG-1978–127–8859-W

kunstkammer (or cabinet of curiosity) was a form of collecting in the early modern period. Many of the famous cabinets of curiosity also laid the foundations for museum collections, including science museums and ethnographic collections.[41] A further approach is therefore based on thinking about objects beyond their classifications and individual characteristics. Early modern collections combined natural and man-made products into a single unifying system, raising important questions on the distinction between natural things and artefacts.[42]

For our purposes here, it is crucial to recognise the contribution of the critical scholarship on collecting and the histories of collections and museums, especially the value of seeing how, why and where things were put together, understanding the construction of histories and meanings of objects that occurs when creating collections, and recognising the explicit and implicit value judgements about things that always emerge when objects are situated within collections.[43] But with a few notable exceptions, the emphasis in much of this work has been on the European context of collecting and (museum) collections.[44] Moreover, the shift in this scholarship towards context and away from things means that we tend to focus on the collection as a whole, and lose sight of the specific trajectories of objects before they entered such collections, or indeed after they became part of the collections.

For archaeologists, objects also exist in collections, the so-called 'assemblages' in which they were excavated. Especially, though not exclusively, for the prehistoric archaeologist, the material remains form the primary material connection with the past and the only access route into this world, and the approach to objects is, thus, far more inclusive.[45] All of the material remains of the past that reveal traces of human activity, referred to as artefacts, are considered part of the assemblage of material culture, including food remains, waste piles, and the traces of architectural structures.[46] Excavated artefacts, then, are more readily studied in their wider context, and it is the context that is mobilized to make sense of the artefacts and their trajectories, use and meaning. By mobilising every single trace of evidence that the site and its artefacts yield, a wealth of information can be unearthed. An example might be some of the recent discoveries in maritime archaeology. One of the largest findings to date is the cargo of the Dutch East India Company's vessel *Witte Leeuw* that was lost off the island of St. Helena on 13 June 1613. It was part of the VOC convoy on its way back to the Netherlands when it was attacked by two Portuguese carracks. The vessel was found only in 1977 when seven of the ship's 25 cannons, large quantities of pepper and beautiful porcelain were recovered in a large-scale maritime archaeology enterprise (Figure 0.3c).[47] Often funded by commercial companies making a profit from the sale of the found treasures, this 'digging of the sea' is indicative of the varied biographies of things.[48]

Anthropologists might question things as signs with social and cultural significance, but archaeologists and anthropologists share some of their approaches to objects.[49] Both are interested in all objects as evidence of human practices and in the cultural contexts in which those practices emerged, in contrast to the selective practices of the art historians and historians of collections. Anthropologists interested in history would likely question the relationship between people and artefacts. In the case of our three porcelain cups, anthropologists might wish to understand why, how and through which processes such objects were used; why they survived intact rather than ending up broken or shipwrecked; what was their meaning not just in elite practices of collecting but in the everyday lives of millions of people. They might question why early modern Europeans thought of enhancing the value of Chinese porcelain by setting them in precious metal, a practice alien to many other cultures. They might ask whether such a cup would have been better placed to be an item of gifting (many ambassadorial gifts included mounted porcelain) than the more simple (one might say untouched) cup and whether the latter retained stronger connections to its place of origin than one manipulated, reshaped and mounted.

One understands the importance that anthropology has had in the study of material culture – past and present. If the history of collecting questions the boundaries between natural and artefactual, anthropology challenges the long-standing 'common-sense opposition between the person and the thing'.[50] It advocates a more profound understanding of things so as to achieve deeper insights into us as human beings. The investigation of the everyday through a close analysis of its material forms has been a methodology championed since the mid-1980s by a variety of scholars, first among whom is Daniel Miller. With Miller and Appadurai, the historical study of things changed thoroughly. Since the publication of *Material Culture and Mass Consumption* (1987) and *The Social Life of Things* (1986), 'history can unabashedly begin with things'.[51] Things have been transformed from objects that stand in the background, to subjects that take centre stage. As Appadurai's mobilization of Marx' ideas about fetishism and the value of materials, and Simmel's ideas about the importance of exchange for the value of things has made clear, things, which he refers to as commodities, have economic value 'in motion', as they circulate in social life.[52]

Things in history and global history

Historians, on the whole, readily borrow terms and methods from across a whole spectrum of disciplines. That is why history often refers interchangeably to objects, artefacts and things. Generally, the historian has seen the analysis of texts and documents as a mark of his or her craft. When historians have focused on things, it has often been from a quantitative perspective.[53] The shift from objects to goods, and from qualitative to quantitative approaches that we see in much of this work is captured by the term consumption. Over the years, the study of (the history of) consumption has grown into a vast field. Early key figures in this field include Neil McKendrick and John Brewer, as we see in the 1982 publication of *The Birth of a Consumer Society: The Commercialization of Eighteenth-Century England*, and the research project led by John Brewer, entitled 'Culture and Consumption in the Seventeenth and Eighteenth Centuries', which led to the publication of the famous *Consumption and the World of Goods*.[54] Almost without exception, the studies discussed in this large tome dealt with European goods, and especially English and Anglo-American goods. There are references to France, the Netherlands, and to the European consumption of Asian goods, but consumption is seen as a largely European phenomenon, and one related to the emergence of a peculiarly European early modernity.[55] On the whole, then, the consumption of goods in other parts of the world was not part of this wave of academic production.

Two related developments had a very important impact on this state of affairs. One was the emergence of global history, and the other the improved communication between area studies and disciplinary fields such as (art) history and literary studies. To begin with the second point, it is important to note that when the group of contributors to *Consumption and the World of Goods* first gathered in the late eighties and early nineties, the scholarship of area studies specialists was hardly read outside of the specialized fields like Islamic Studies, Latin American Studies, or Chinese and Japanese Studies. The journals they published articles in, the publishing houses that produced their books, and the conferences they attended were all focused on the specialized field and catered only for an audience of experts. A small group of individuals, who not only read the work of scholars well beyond the boundaries of their own fields but also wrote for readers from a much wider spectrum of disciplinary and geographic specialisations made a key difference. With the publication of their work, which straddled several disciplines and theories and drew on wider and comparable methodological studies, it gradually became less acceptable to address only the narrowest of area studies specialists, and more common to expect scholarly studies to draw on such traditionally 'area studies' materials.

By the late 1990s some historians started to question the Euro-centred perspective of much of the literature on consumption. They did so by investigating similar phenomena in different areas of the world including the Ottoman Empire, Ming and Qing China, Edo Japan, Latin America and East Africa.[56] This extra-European literature came to challenge the very notion of a consumer revolution by highlighting how similar processes were in place elsewhere in the world in the seventeenth and eighteenth centuries. European historians too started to acknowledge that the local or national scale of investigation of consumption was ill suited to explain the ways in which a possible European consumer revolution relied on commodities coming from elsewhere in the world, the type of world captured by De Pereda in his still life. But it was not just about consumption: Maxine Berg proposed the idea that Asian commodities such as porcelain and textiles caused a material transformation in Europe and sparked the imagination of consumers and producers alike. She showed how European manufacturing came to be reshaped by Asian products through processes of imitation and innovation that eventually led to what we call the Industrial Revolution.[57]

A second important change of direction came not from academia but from the museum world. An exhibition such as Encounters, held at the V&A in 2003, showed the value of thinking about different commodities ranging from porcelains, to carpets, cotton and silk textiles, tiles, decorative artefacts and maps, within larger historical explanations that could capture not just their specific historical meaning but also their changing values across time and space.[58] This was just the first of a number of 'global' (both in scope and in audience) exhibitions sometimes tackling specific geographic areas in new and unexpected ways. This was the case of the exhibition entitled 'Turks' at the Royal Academy in London in 2005.[59] This shift towards wider geographies was beautifully represented in the British Museum's series entitled 'A History of the World in 100 Objects', presented by the museum's director Neil McGregor.[60] More recently, similar approaches have been adopted in new ways of presenting textiles as in the case of the 2013 'Interwoven Globe' exhibition at the Metropolitan Museum in New York.[61]

In conjunction with these developments, the field of history itself changed direction, away from narrowly-focused national histories and towards studies that focused on border and contact zones, and away from studies that presumed a European or Western priority towards studies that took seriously the developments and transformations that occurred within different context and periodization throughout the world. For some, it became crucial to refer to this new field as global history, others attached these developments to the field of world history, with its long-standing devotees in US academia, and for others still, a more inclusive and less nation-based approach began to characterize their practice, even without the term global or world history. What matters for us is the impact of all these developments on the historical study of objects. Instead of merely studying Western goods, or focusing on consumption in Western contexts, this global turn meant that historians began to see objects as part of wider stories that crossed geographical and chronological zones.

The global turn transformed the ways in which historians studied objects. They began to see the connected histories that led to the circulation of objects throughout the various parts of the world. Very few geographical spaces stayed outside the reach of the connections forged by the global circulation of goods, although the extent, intensity and variety of global goods changed significantly depending on the space and time. This transformation in the approach and outlook of the scholarly community led to the production of a wide variety of studies that featured goods that were termed 'global' in one way or another. To stay close to home, the editors of this book have in different ways addressed a global dimension through the analysis of specific 'global things'. Giorgio Riello in his work on cotton explains the complex web of design, material, economic and technical factors that connected producers in India and consumers across the Indian Ocean and beyond.[62] Whilst his work addressed the macro picture and argued for the materiality of things as one of the major aspects of a so-called first phase of globalization, Anne Gerritsen, in her work on Jingdezhen's porcelains, investigates the relationship between the local and the global. Production for global markets also has a significant impact on the centre of production itself, and on the regional consumption of such global commodities.[63]

Several further developments, however, are important for explaining the pieces that are part of this particular volume of papers, and the choice of title, which includes not only the word 'global' but also the word 'lives'. We are not only interested in trajectories that span time zones and geographical variations, but we are concerned to explore the transformative impact of these trajectories on the goods themselves. Individual objects, composite objects, and complements of goods bear the traces of their lives in different contexts, spaces and times, like the marks of age on a face, the creases of wear in an item of clothing, or the cracks in the spine of a well-read book.

Objects of global knowledge

Things have always played a key role in the creation of knowledge, be it knowledge of natural and cultural phenomena or the more formalized ideas that constitute science and technology. After all, new instruments made new observations and measurements possible, which in turn led to the development of new hypotheses and theories. According to Toby Huff, the Dutch invention of the telescope in 1608, and the subsequent possibility of observations of both the minute (microscopy) and the remote (astronomy) eventually led to Newton's insights about the force of gravity, which form the basis of modern Western science.[64] Toby Huff's telescope, but also things like the steam engine and the spinning jenny, clocks, wheels and levers all form part of the rich repertoire of the historian of science and technology.

To study scientific instruments *as things*, however, is a reasonably new development, and emerged as part of a reconceptualization of what 'science' and its history might be.[65] Rather than thinking of science as the outcome of a linear trajectory that began with the enquiries of great men within Western civilisation, scholars have begun to investigate the multiple trajectories of what we might refer to as scientific culture. That shift in focus opened our eyes to the important contributions of women in science, of global connections, interactions and exchanges in the development of European science, and of the importance of collecting, understanding and displaying *things* for scientific development.[66] It is because of these developments that we now speak of cultures of knowledge.[67]

The astronomical clock (Figure 0.4) is a good example of the entangled histories of scientific objects. This astronomical clock was probably manufactured in eighteenth-century Canton, where merchants and manufacturers from various parts of China and Europe mingled. The clock's movement was made in China, by a clockmaker who seems to have worked with a late eighteenth-century English model. Several unusual choices and creative adaptations suggest the Chinese clockmaker integrated notes or drawings of the English example with his own expertise to make an entirely new creation. It combines an ornate wooden stand, which would not look out of place in any wealthy Chinese household, a large round clock face with a chart that shows the stars as they are visible from southern China, joined into traditional Chinese constellations, and surrounded by a thin circle, divided into the twelve Chinese zodiac signs. Beyond that are two metal brass rings the show the seasons, the quarter hours and the minutes, making it possible to tell the time in both Chinese and European fashion. The only other known astronomical clock like this was made one hundred years later in Suzhou, China, and is now in the Forbidden City. The flows and cross-currents of objects, materials, people and ideas that form

FIGURE 0.4 Astronomical clock. Wood, metal and glass. China, eighteenth century. H 82cm, W 38 cm. The Oriental Museum, Durham. Gift from Sir Charles Edmund Hardinge. DUROM.1960.880. Reproduced by permission of Durham University Museum.

part of the global life of this object, include its acquisition by Charles Edmund Hardinge (1878–1968), and its arrival in Durham in the United Kingdom.

The first part of this book dedicated to 'Objects of Global Knowledge' investigates the specific topic of materials and materiality in the early modern world. The three papers included in this section emphasise the properties, meanings and knowledge embodied by different materials. Part of the attractions of commodities ranging from porcelain to cotton and lacquer rested on their material properties. But such material properties created also global exchanges of knowledge and came to influence notions of manipulation of materials and, as Pamela Smith argues, the bodily and conceptual interventions on the natural world. Smith sets the context by considering artisanal practices in the vast space of Eurasia and focuses on the properties of mercury and sulphur. She argues that material fluxes were created and in turned reshaped systems of knowledge, thus integrating history of science within the study of material culture and global exchange. What she proposes is to see knowledge not as bounded within a particular cultural context, but built on the shared foundations that emerge from the global exchange of things and people.

Christine Guth's chapter on shagreen is another example of global knowledge. Shagreen is a leather made from shark and rayskin, with very specific practical and aesthetic properties: it is waterproof but not slippery, strong but malleable, and attractive because of its textured variegations. As Guth's study shows, throughout early modern Europe and America, the Ottoman and Persian empires, India, South-east Asia and Japan, shagreen became desirable, but only because interactions through trade brought increased knowledge about this material. Sites of shagreen production and consumption were local and global at the same time: local, because the material formed part of different cultural repertoires that assigned meanings to the material, but global, because the material depended upon the global knowledge that emerged through networks of trade and the circulation of exotic goods in the early modern world.

Similarly, Pippa Lacey's material, coral, has global and local iterations shaped by the emergence of global knowledge during this period. Like shagreen, coral forms part of very different repertoires of knowledge and meaning, but because it grows naturally in only a few sites, it could only circulate in and out of those repertoires through global networks of trade and knowledge. Lacey refers to this as the 'coral network', which connects the eighteenth-century Chinese court with the Mediterranean, and Chinese imperial desire for its colour and 'curiosity' with the East India Company merchants' desire for tradable goods and financial profit. Very different knowledge systems, then, are connected through the properties of the material: the ways in which it was grown and harvested, preserved and transported, measured, assessed and valued, transformed into other goods and represented in art and visual culture. All three pieces show the interconnected nature of knowledge, shaping and shaped by the exchange of commodities and materials over vast distances.

Objects of global connection

Connectivity has been a key concept in recent global histories. Yet the shaping and articulation of connections in the early modern world was far from being either unilateral or univocal. A great deal of the history of trade – focusing as it does on large categories of traded commodities – has tended to portray commercial connections as the movement of goods from places of production to places of consumption. This type of easy material connection (from 'A' to 'B') is problematic as it rarely reveals the complex linkages across spaces, how often connections broke down, the shifting meanings that artefacts assumed within and between these spaces and the fact that mobility often reshaped artefacts physically and changed the very cultures entering into contact through exchange. Artefacts are a good way to consider the processes of connections affecting the early modern world. An example can be found in a rather prosaic object such as the late seventeenth-century knife in Figure 0.5. It is an object that captures the connection between early seventeenth-century India and England in its material shape. The slight curve and rounded blade was a typical product of the metal production of the city of Sheffield in England, though it is stamped with the dagger mark used by the Cutlers Company of London.[68] The handle however was made in India, probably in Goa, and represents a lady dressed in Indian costume, a motif that was particularly fashionable in late-seventeenth century Europe.[69] These types of ivory carvings were made by Goanese craftsmen specifically for the European market.

An object like this hints at the commercial connection between England and India via the English East India Company, but also shows how craftsmen engaged in steel-blade making in England and carvers of ivory objects in Southern India unwittingly came to cooperate in the production of an object specifically destined for European consumers. It also shows the processes of acquisition of meaning of objects, especially if we think that neither of the producers probably saw the finished artefacts. Indeed, the Goanese craftsmen might have had little understanding of the final usage of what they carved. This object – by virtue of taking shape in

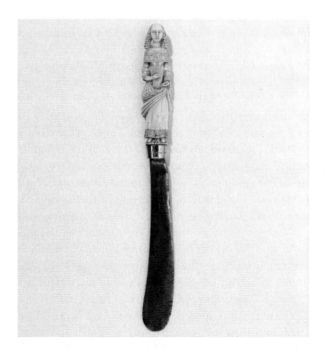

FIGURE 0.5 Knife, *c.*1660–1680. The blade was probably made in Sheffield, England, whilst the carved handle was produced in Goa, India. Steel, with ivory handle. Victoria and Albert Museum 522–1893 (currently on display in the British Galleries, room 56e, case 1).

space, literally moving across continents – shows how meaning is created in layers and how different actors might only temporarily appropriate objects.

It must be said that this knife was not intended for dining, but was probably treasured within the space of a cabinet of curiosities. This is a topic considered by Mariana Françoso in her analysis of early modern South American feathers and featherwork. These were some of the most prized and sought-for items in European collections of curiosities. Once made for ritual use by Tupi societies of Brazil, after the first contacts with Europeans these indigenous peoples started manufacturing feather ornaments to be traded with foreigners. While this fact points to a possible categorization of such artefacts as global commodities, Françoso's paper argues that their meanings and values can only be understood locally: the appreciation and categorization of featherwork varied according to different reception contexts. By considering the *Ballet de la Carmesse* that took place in The Hague in 1655, and comparing it with other contemporaneous festive events where South American featherwork was displayed and used, Françoso investigates the performative display of these objects. *Kunstkammer* pieces were not necessarily 'museified' but found practical use as well. This in turn allowed for the incorporation of the New World into the symbolic language of Northern European court festivities and court diplomacy.

Nuno Senos expands the analysis of the purchase and collecting of 'exotic' objects by concentrating on a specific space. This is the palace of one of the wealthiest aristocrats in sixteenth-century Portugal, D. Teodosio, duke of Braganza, the son of a hero of the war in Morocco, brother to a viceroy of India, who died in 1543. An impressive probate inventory of more than 1,600 pages was produced. This is the largest inventory to have survived from sixteenth-century Portugal and one of the largest in Europe, providing a unique view of the contents of the duke's palace. Senos' paper focuses on the various entries that reflect the duke's interest in the objects from different parts of the Portuguese empire ranging from chronicles, maps and nautical instruments, to bezoar stones, mounted coconuts and Chinese porcelain. Reference is also made to the ways in which these goods were kept and used or displayed in the palace as Senos questions the concept of 'collection' as a pertinent one to understand the duke's relationship with these objects.

Susan Broomhall takes us to the opposite side of the world and explores how objects were used, or expected to be used, in the development of relations between Dutch East India Company officials and the indigenous peoples they encountered in what is now Australia. By using the extensive documentation of the Company, her contribution explores the nature of objects that the Dutch expected would be useful for building and sustaining fruitful economic, practical and emotional relationships between their cultures. In particular, it considers the historical and archaeological evidence of the objects that Dutch East India officials did employ as they negotiated with indigenous peoples on the north and west coasts of Australia. She thus proposes a provocative argument in claiming that objects, bound in complex relationships with emotions and expectations, profoundly shaped the nature of Dutch encounters with the landscapes and peoples of Australia, creating unanticipated geographies, histories, and connections in the process.

The final paper of this section by Kévin Le Doudic considers instead the confined space of one Indian port city: Pondicherry. By using probate inventories, surviving artefacts and a number of other 'ego-documents', Le Doudic considers the consumption patterns of both local Indian inhabitants and the small but influential French community resident in Pondicherry. His paper analyses through the buyers' origin (nationality, social and professional position) how commodities played a role of interface and became nodes in the construction of the commercial, social and cultural relations between two distinct groups of people: Europeans and Asians. The well-known notions of exoticism and hybridity are here questioned. He argues that the two cultures came together around the same goods but without sharing the same stylistic references, perception of space, or relations to material culture on a broad sense (which define the cultural and financial values of the objects).

The papers in this second section of the volume thus provide a variety of ways of interpreting connection in the so-called first global age. They consider both commercial and cultural connections and critique established ideas that see Europe as a key node of global connectivity in this period. They focus instead on rather distinct spaces of connection that range from the interior of a palace to the structure and life of a port city to the wider connections between the Americas and Europe but also between the Americas and Asia, Europe and Asia and Europe and Australasia. Rather than focusing on 'anonymous exchange' and tracking the movement of goods to and from different points of the globe, the chapters here included emphasize the interlocked material and cultural complexity of exchange across continents and cultural zones. They show that notwithstanding the long-distance networks of early modern trade, exchange was often not anonymous at all. It might involve networks of gifting and collecting; purposeful reinterpretations of the meanings associated with specific objects; or even the material re-shaping and transformation of objects through processes of customisation, alteration, and re-combination.

Objects of global consumption

As we have already seen, consumption has been a key way of approaching material culture. An interest in the ways in which novel forms and patterns of consumption emerged in early modern Europe led to important research on the ways in which non-European goods came to be part of the consuming habits of rich and poor alike. This strand of research has been particularly important for the eighteenth century when, it has been argued, exotic and novel objects came to reshape material expectations, manufacturing methods and social practices.[70] Yet such a history should not be taken to be solely about Europe's engagement with other continents and the ways in which non-European commodities impacted on European consumption. The last decade – in line with what we said in the previous section – has seen a proliferation of studies in which the consuming habits of people in different parts of the world were reshaped by artefacts, commodities and technologies from other world areas or continents.

Take for instance this image of a fruit well known to us all: a pineapple (Figure 0.6). It was drawn in the late sixteenth century by John White, an English artist and early settler in North America. In 1585 White was commissioned to draw the inhabitants of the New World during his time at Roanoke Island. He compiled a beautiful album that is now at the British Museum in London, containing among the many this image of a pineapple. The pineapple was indigenous to the area between southern Brazil and Paraguay. Its cultivation spread throughout Latin America, eventually reaching the Caribbean, Central America and Mexico. What Columbus called *piña*

FIGURE 0.6 *Pineapple*, drawing by John White. Watercolour over graphite, touched with white, 1585–1593. © The Trustees of the British Museum Prints & Drawings 1906, 0509.1.41.

de Indes (pine of the Indians) was one of the many American plants that found its way to Europe and eventually Asia in what Alfred Crosby called 'the Columbian exchange'.[71] It was introduced into India by the 1550s and via the Pacific to Hawaii and the Philippines. Still a rarity in Europe in the late sixteenth century, it is unclear whether White had seen a pineapple before arriving on the shores of the Americas.[72]

The pineapple is a fruit whose cultivation spread across the globe. Today not many people would be able to recognise it as an American plant and fruit as we mostly associate it with the Pacific and Hawaii in particular. Its global impact might have been less profound than that of other American crops such as maize, tomatoes and potatoes that after 1500 revolutionized both diets and the cuisines of different areas of Asia, Europe and Africa. Yet, the pineapple shares with other crops a truly global reach.

The final part of this book focuses on raw commodities rather than manufactured products. A great deal has been written on tropical commodities (cocoa, sugar, tea and coffee) but far too often these beverages and sweeteners have been considered only in relation to changing consuming habits in Europe, or to be more precise in North-western Europe. The papers included in this section of the book challenge this narrative and consider new geographies such as that of Russia and its engagement with tobacco, or the global shift of sugar cultivation. They also complicate narratives of consumer desire according to which novel products are sought after by consumers. The papers included here show instead that novel products were sometimes contentious, were opposed or subject to outright bans. In other cases they found acceptance but did not trickle down the social ladder, remaining instead at the reach of a smaller elite. The cultivation of new commodities on a large scale had also profound environmental consequences as Urmi Engineer details. All of them came with a baggage of knowledge about their properties and effects on well-being that influenced their acceptance and success among consumers.

An example of a commodity that was much debated and fought against (in the past as much as in the present) is tobacco. Tobacco was fought against in Europe as much as it was in Mughal India. Matt Romaniello considers instead the trajectory of tobacco in seventeenth-century Russia. Here too, the Tsar implemented the empire's first prohibition against tobacco sales in the 1620s. By 1649, the government instituted a ban against all consumption, a restriction that would last for another fifty years until it was reversed by Peter the Great. What was the world's longest tobacco embargo did not hinder the success of this new substance. Russia's imperial subjects adopted the tobacco habit, though a combination of smuggling and regional trade networks created distinctive consumption customs. In European Russia, tobacco was first introduced as leaf for pipes and early cigars by English and Dutch merchants, before a transition to snuff that began in the eighteenth century in a conscious adoption of contemporary European elite culture. In western Siberia, the indigenous Ostiaks preferred instead to smoke tobacco in water-pipes, adopting the custom from their primary suppliers in Safavid Iran and Mughal India. In eastern Siberia, Chinese ball tobacco for pipes became the regular habit among the Chukchis and Kamchadals. The Russian Empire's tobacco habit, therefore, was supplied by Western European empires, the Middle East, South Asia, East Asia, and, eventually, directly from the Americas. Romaniello argues that the spread of this global product did not unify the Russian Empire with a common habit, but instead revealed strong regional distinctions that remained largely unaffected by increasing consumption.

The idea that the trade in raw commodities had consequences beyond the creation of new consuming patterns is also embraced by Urmi Engineer's analysis of sugar. The significance of sugar as a global commodity has been explicated by Sidney Mintz in his seminal work, *Sweetness and Power* published in 1985.[73] Literature on the history of sugar focuses on labour issues, cultural aspects of consumption, and issues related to health and nutrition. Engineer's contribution examines instead the ecological consequences of sugar from a global perspective. Such a perspective is often adopted in analysis of commodity chains and commodity production in the twentieth century. Here Engineer makes an argument for extending such a methodology back at least to the seventeenth century. The establishment of large-scale sugar plantations in the Caribbean, she argues, had profound ecological and environmental consequences, which resulted in widespread deforestation and soil erosion. This is especially evident in the transformation of tropical forests in Saint-Domingue/Haiti and Cuba, as well as in the swamp country of Louisiana. Moreover, sugar plantations also required the draining of wetlands, and the building of canals and irrigation ditches. These alterations in the landscape transformed the region's ecology, as the construction of sugar plantations and port cities attracted *Aëdes aegypti* mosquitoes, which served as a vector for yellow fever transmission. Because sugar plantations depended on West African slave labour, West African diseases, including yellow fever and malaria, became part of the Caribbean disease environment.

A final paper by Christine Fertig and Ulrich Pfister brings us back to the relationship between trade and consumption in Europe. Their paper however focuses on an area such as Germany that only in recent years has been researched in its global connections. Fertig and Pfister connect the trade in coffee and other tropical produce to new notions of well-being. By considering the toll registers of the port of Hamburg in the period 1733–98, they show the strong and steady growth of the coffee trade to become the second most important item in Hamburg's maritime imports at the end of the eighteenth century. They argue that coffee consumption made it easier for lower-class households without land to subsist on progressively meagre rations of grain. They thus challenge Jan de Vries's notion of a consumer revolution by showing that notwithstanding the increase of consumer items in Hamburg's toll registers, the phenomenon remained restricted to small elite groups. The final part of their contribution focuses on commodities that were considered to aid bodily well-being and serve medical purposes. The growth and differentiation of this trade suggest globalization of expedients to physical well-being. Overall, then, these studies show the complex trajectories of these commodities, contentious in past and present due to their addictive nature and yet ubiquitous in many parts of both the early modern and modern worlds.

Conclusion

The Global Lives of Things seeks to make a contribution to a new field, where global history and material culture intersect. It considers how in the early modern period, the social lives of things were global: they transcended the cultural and political boundaries of nations and even continents. This book does not claim to cover all material manifestations, but focuses on the small but crucial portion of material culture that contributed to the creation of long-distance social and economic connections. Methodologically, contributions included in this volume do not limit themselves to the analysis of broad social processes and phenomena of classes of objects over the *longue durée*. They often embrace a micro-methodology reminiscent of the 'cultural biography' approach and focus on the individual experiences of specific commodities/artefacts. Taken together, the complex trajectories of these objects reveal a world of movement and interaction, shaped by raw and manufactured commodities that in themselves told tales of other places and unknown lands. The global lives of things help us tell the stories of these interactions.

Notes and references

1. The research and writing of this introduction has been possible thanks to the support of the AHRC International Network 'Global Commodities: The Material Culture of Global Connections' led by Gerritsen and Riello and by the Philip Leverhulme Prize and the Leverhulme Network 'Luxury and the Manipulation of Desire: Historical Perspectives for Contemporary Debates' led by Riello.
2. Antonio de Pereda's dates are unclear. He was born in Valladolid in 1599 or 1611, and died in Madrid in 1669 or 1678.
3. See Figure 76 in *Treasured Possessions from the Renaissance to the Enlightenment*, ed. Victoria Avery, Melissa Calaresu and Mary Laven (London: I.B. Tauris, 2015), 74–75. For a description of the painting and a detailed identification of all the objects in the painting, see Cinta Krahe, 'Chinese Porcelain and other Orientalia and Exotica in Spain during the Habsburg Dynasty' (Unpublished PhD Thesis, University of Leiden, 2014), 241–242. A gourd cup very similar to the one depicted here is in the Távora Sequeira Pinto Collection in Porto (Portugal), and appeared in the exhibition entitled 'Luxury for Export: Artistic Exchange between India and Portugal around 1600' held at the Isabella Stewart Gardner Museum in Boston in 2008. The authors of the catalogue identify the Porto cup as 'probably Goa'. Pedro Moura Carvalho, *Luxury for Export: Artistic Exchange between India and Portugal around 1600* (Pittsburgh, PA: Gutenberg Periscope Publishing, 2008), 50–1. The gourd depicted in the painting has also been described as 'a lacquered gourd bowl of the type imported from Mexico'. William B. Jordan and Peter Cherry, *Spanish Still Life from Velázquez to Goya*. Exhibition catalogue, National Gallery, London (London: The National Gallery, 1995), cat. no. 30, p. 88.
4. The jar is identified as made in Talavera in Jordan and Cherry, *Spanish Still Life*, 88. On chocolate and its implements, see Marcy Norton, *Sacred Gifts, Profane Pleasures: A History of Tobacco and Chocolate in the Atlantic World* (Ithaca: Cornell University Press, 2008).
5. Jordan and Cherry, *Spanish Still Life*, 87.
6. It has been suggested that Pereda owned at least some of the luxury objects depicted in his still lifes, as they appeared in several of his paintings. Jordan and Cherry, *Spanish Still Life*, 87.
7. Appadurai, 'Introduction: Commodities and the Politics of Value', in *The Social Life of Things: Commodities in Cultural Perspective*, ed. Arjun Appadurai (Cambridge: Cambridge University Press 1992), 4.

8. One of these key works is undoubtedly Kenneth Pomeranz, *The Great Divergence: China, Europe, and the Making of the Modern World Economy* (Princeton: Princeton University Press, 2000). Other titles that could be mentioned are Jared Diamond, *Guns, Germs, and Steel: The Fates of Human Societies* (New York: Norton & Co, 1998); Maxine Berg, 'In Pursuit of Luxury: Global History and British Consumer Goods in the Eighteenth Century,' *Past and Present* 182 (2004): 85–142; Chris Bayly, *The Birth of the Modern World, 1780–1914* (Oxford: Blackwell, 2004); Bruce Mazlish, *The New Global History* (New York: Routledge, 2006); Kevin O'Rourke and Jeffrey G. Williamson, *Globalization and History: The Evolution of a Nineteenth-Century Atlantic Economy* (Cambridge, Mass.: MIT Press, 1999); and Timothy Brook, *Vermeer's Hat: The Seventeenth Century and the Dawn of the Global World* (London: Bloomsbury Press, 2007). For a brief overview see: Lynn Hunt, *Writing History in the Global Era* (New York and London: W.W. Norton & Co., 2014), esp. ch. 2.

9. *Writing the Global: Challenges for the 21st Century*, ed. Maxine Berg (Oxford: British Academy and Oxford University Press, 2013).

10. There is now a vast literature on each of these subjects. Three general overviews might provide a helpful starting point to this literature. Robert Marks, *The Origins of the Modern World: A Global and Ecological Narrative* (Lanham, MD: Rowman & Littlefield, 2002); Geoffrey C. Gunn, *First Globalization: The Eurasian Exchange, 1500 to 1800* (Lanham, Md.: Rowman & Littlefield, 2003); Charles Parker, *Global Interactions in the Early Modern Age, 1400–1800* (Cambridge: Cambridge University Press, 2010).

11. Grant Parker, 'Ex Oriente Luxuria: Indian Commodities and Roman Experience', *Journal of the Economic and Social History of the Orient* 45.1 (2002): 42.

12. Valerie Hansen, *The Silk Road: A New History* (Oxford: Oxford University Press, 2012); Liu Xinru, *The Silk Road in World History* (Oxford: Oxford University Press, 2010); and Susan Whitfield, *Life Along the Silk Road* (Berkeley: University of California Press, 1999), for a few examples.

13. Johanna Maria van Winter, *Spices and Comfits: Collected Papers on Medieval Food* (Totnes: Prospect Books, 2007).

14. On the medieval trade in the ingredients for painters' pigments, see: *Trade in Artists' Materials: Markets and Commerce in Europe to 1700*, ed. Jo Kirby, Susie Nash, and Joanna Cannon (London: Archetype Publications, 2010), especially the study by Wendy R. Childs, 'Painters' Materials and the Northern International Trade Routes of Late Medieval Europe', 29–41.

15. Janet L. Abu-Lughod, *Before European Hegemony: The World System A.D. 1250–1350* (New York: Oxford University Press, 1989).

16. The studies by Dennis O. Flynn and Arturo Giráldez have done a great deal to clarify the global impact of the founding of Manila. See, for example, the collection of their articles in Dennis O. Flynn and Arturo Giráldez, *China and the Birth of Globalization in the 16th Century* (Farnham, Surrey: Ashgate Variorum, 2010).

17. Ina Baghdiantz McCabe, *A History of Global Consumption, 1500–1800* (Abingdon and New York: Routledge, 2015).

18. C.C. Patterson, 'Silver Stocks and Losses in Ancient and Medieval Times', *Economic History Review* 25.2 (1972): 205–233. For mining in Saxony, see Adolf Laube, *Studien über den erzgebirgischen Silberbergbau von 1470 bis 1546; seine Geschichte, seine Produktionsverhältnisse, seine Bedeutung für die gesellschaftlichen Veränderungen und Klassenkämpfe in Sachsen am Beginn der Übergangsepoche vom Feudalismus zum Kapitalismus* (Berlin: Akademie-Verlag, 1974).

19. See, for a general introduction: John E. Wills, *1688: A Global History* (New York: Norton, 2001), esp. ch. 1, 'The Empire of Silver,' 13–31. For an art-historical study, see: Pedro Querejazu and Elizabeth Ferrer, *Potosí: Colonial Treasures and the Bolivian City of Silver* (New York: Americas Society Art Gallery in association with Fundación BHN, La Paz, 1997). For a story of the ecological impact of this mining, see: Nicholas A. Robins, *Mercury, Mining, and Empire: The Human and Ecological Cost of Colonial Silver Mining in the Andes* (Bloomington: Indiana University Press, 2011).

20. For a discussion of the monetary system of the Ming dynasty, and the influx of foreign silver, see: William Atwell, 'Ming China and the Emerging World Economy, *c.*1470–1650', in *The Cambridge History of China. Vol. 8: The Ming Dynasty, 1368–1644. Part 2*, ed. Denis Twitchett and Frederick Mote (Cambridge: Cambridge University Press, 1998), 376–416. The centrality of China in the global flows of silver during this period is highlighted by Andre Gunder Frank in his *ReOrient Global Economy in the Asian Age* (Berkeley: University of California Press, 1998). For the impact of the influx of silver on the culture of the late Ming, see Timothy Brook, *The Confusions of Pleasure* (Berkeley: University of California Press, 1998).

21. See Madeleine Dobie, 'Orientalism, Colonialism, and Furniture in Eighteenth-century France', in *Furnishing the Eighteenth Century: What Furniture Can Tell us about the European and American Past*, ed. Dena Goodman and Kathryn Norberg (New York: Routledge, 2007), 13–36.

22. Jennifer L. Anderson, *Mahogany: The Costs of Luxury in Early America* (Cambridge, Mass.: Harvard University Press, 2012).

23. For an introductory piece about early modern global trade in ivory, see: Martha Chaiklin, 'Ivory in World History – Early Modern Trade in Context', *History Compass* 8.6 (2010): 530–542.

24. The literature on ceramics and global connections is extensive. A good starting point is Robert Batchelor, 'On the Movement of Porcelains: Rethinking the Birth of Consumer Society as Interactions of Exchange Networks, 1600–1750', in *Consuming Cultures, Global Perspectives: Historical Trajectories, Transnational Exchanges*, ed. John Brewer and Frank Trentmann (Oxford: Berg, 2006), 95–121. See also Robert Finlay, *The Pilgrim Art: Cultures of Porcelain in World History* (Berkeley: University of California Press, 2010). See also the various studies in 'Global China: Material Culture and Connections in World History', special issue of *Journal of World History* 23.1 (2012) edited by Anne Gerritsen and Stephen McDowall.

25. Aileen Dawson, *English & Irish Delftware 1570–1840* (London: British Museum Press, 2010); George Kuwayama, *Chinese Ceramics in Colonial Mexico* (Los Angeles: Los Angeles County Museum of Art, 1997); Marion S. van Aken-Fehmers, Titus Eliëns, Suzanne Lambooy, Erik Hesmerg, and Janey Tucker, *Het Wonder van Delfts Blauw – Delft Ware Wonderware* (Den Haag: Gemeentemuseum Den Haag, 2012).

26. A few examples of the vast scholarship on these topics might include *Tamerlane's Tableware: A New Approach to the Chinoiserie Ceramics of Fifteenth- and Sixteenth-century Iran*, ed. Lisa Golombek, Robert Mason and Gauvin Bailey (Royal Ontario Museum: Mazda Publishers, 1996); C. Dumortier, *Céramique de la Renaissance à Anvers* (Bruxelles: Édition Racine, 2002); *Majolica and Glass: From Italy to Antwerp and Beyond: The Transfer of Technology in the 16th–Early 17th Century*, ed. Johan Veeckman (Oxford: Oxbow Books, 2002).

27. Giorgio Riello, *Cotton: The Fibre that Made the Modern World* (Cambridge: Cambridge University Press, 2013). See also *How India Clothed the World: The World of South Asian Textiles, 1500–1850*, ed. Giorgio Riello and Tirthankar Roy (Leiden: Brill, 2009); and *The Spinning World: A Global History of Cotton Textiles, 1200–1850*, ed. Giorgio Riello and Prasannan Parthasarathi (Oxford: Oxford University Press and Pasold Research Fund, 2009).

28. McCabe, *A History of Global Consumption*, 65–68.

29. Alfred W. Crosby, *The Columbian Exchange: Biological and Cultural Consequences of 1492* (Westport, Conn.: Greenwood Press, 1972). See also Christopher Cumo, *The Ongoing Columbian Exchange: Stories of Biological and Economic Transfer in World History* (Santa Barbara, CA: ABC-CLIO, 2015), and Jeffrey M. Pilcher, *Food in World History* (New York, NY: Routledge, 2006).

30. John F. Richards, *The Unending Frontier: An Environmental History of the Early Modern World* (Berkeley: University of California Press, 2005).

31. Kate Loveman, 'The Introduction of Chocolate into England: Retailers, Researchers, and Consumers, 1640–1730,' *Journal of Social History* 47.1 (2013): 27–46.

32. Ross W. Jamieson, 'The Essence of Commodification: Caffeine Dependencies in the Early Modern World', *Journal of Social History* 35.2 (2001): 269–294.

33. Marcy Norton, 'Tasting Empire: Chocolate and the European Internalization of Meso-american Aesthetics', *American Historical Review* 111:3 (2006): 660–691.
34. Sucheta Mazumdar, *Sugar and Society in China: Peasants, Technology, and the World Market* (Cambridge, MA: Harvard University Asia Center, 1998); and Sidney Mintz, *Sweetness and Power: The Place of Sugar in Modern History* (New York, NY: Viking, 1985).
35. Charles C. Mann, *1493: Uncovering the New World Columbus Created* (New York: Knopf, 2011).
36. Anne Gerritsen and Giorgio Riello, 'Introduction: Writing Material Culture History', in *Writing Material Culture History*, ed. Anne Gerritsen and Giorgio Riello (London: Bloomsbury, 2015), 1–13.
37. For an introductory text on such matters, see: Babette Bohn and James M. Saslow, *A Companion to Renaissance and Baroque Art* (Chichester, West Sussex: Wiley-Blackwell, 2013).
38. Isabelle Frank, *The Theory of Decorative Art: An Anthology of European and American Writings, 1750–1940* (New Haven: Yale University Press, 2000).
39. John Carswell, *Blue & White: Chinese Porcelain around the World* (London: British Museum Press, 2000); and Finlay, *Pilgrim Art*. For Chinese porcelain in the Americas, see: Kuwayama, *Chinese Ceramics in Colonial Mexico*; and Jean McClure Mudge, *Chinese Export Porcelain in North America* (New York: C.N. Potter, 1986).
40. Stacey Pierson, 'The Movement of Chinese Ceramics: Appropriation in Global History', *Journal of World History* 23.1 (2012): 9–39.
41. A good (but by no means the only) example is the Tradescant collection that formed the starting point for the Ashmolean Museum in Oxford, one of the oldest museums in the world. *The Origins of Museums: The Cabinet of Curiosities in Sixteenth and Seventeenth-Century Europe*, ed. Oliver Impey and Arthur MacGregor (Oxford: Clarendon Press, 1985). See also: Gabriele Bessler, *Wunderkammern: Weltmodelle von der Renaissance bis zur Kunst der Gegenwart* (Berlin: Reimer, 2012).
42. See the opening editorial statement, *Journal of the History of Collections*, 1.1 (1989): 1–2.
43. Susan M. Pearce, Alexandra Bounia, and Paul Martin, *The Collector's Voice: Critical Readings in the Practice of Collecting*, 4 vols. (Aldershot: Ashgate, 2000).
44. One important exception is the PhD dissertation by Anna Grasskamp, 'Cultivated Curiosities: A Comparative Study of Chinese Artifacts in European kunstkammern and European Objects in Chinese Elite Collections' (unpublished PhD dissertation, University of Leiden, 2013).
45. Charles E. Orser, Jr., 'Beneath the Material Surface of Things: Commodities, Artifacts, and Slave Plantations', *Historical Archaeology* 26.3 (1992): 95–104.
46. *The Archaeology of Food and Identity*, ed. Katheryn C. Twiss (Carbondale, Ill.: Center for Archaeological Investigations, Southern Illinois University Carbondale, 2007).
47. *The Ceramic Load of the 'Witte Leeuw'*, ed. Christine L. van der Pijl-Ketel (Amsterdam: Rijksmuseum, 1982); Julia B. Curtis, 'Perceptions of an Artifact: Chinese Porcelain in Colonial Tidewater Virginia', in *Documentary Archaeology in the New World*, ed. Mary C. Beaudry (New York: Cambridge University Press, 1988), 25–27.
48. An example is the so-called 'The Wanli Shipwreck'. See the website maintained by Sten Sjostrand, http://www.thewanlishipwreck.com/ (last consulted on 10 March 2015). For the catalogue, see Sten Sjostrand and Sharipah Lok Lok bt. Syed Idrus, *The Wanli Shipwreck and its Ceramic Cargo* (Kuala Lumpur: Ministry of Culture, Arts and Heritage, Malaysia, 2007).
49. Amiria J. M. Henare, Martin Holbraad, and Sari Wastell, *Thinking Through Things* (London: UCL, 2005).
50. Daniel Miller, *Stuff* (Cambridge: Polity Press, 2010), 5.
51. Bill Brown, 'Thing Theory', *Critical Inquiry* 28.1 (2001): 2.
52. Appadurai, 'Introduction', 9.
53. For a different argument, see: Leora Auslander, 'Beyond Words', *American Historical Review* 110.4 (2006): 1015–1044.

54. Neil McKendrick, J.H. Plumb and John Brewer, *The Birth of a Consumer Society: The Commercialization of Eighteenth-Century England* (London: Europa, 1982); and *Consumption and the World of Goods*, ed. John Brewer and Roy Porter (London: Routledge, 1993).

55. For a forceful statement of this perspective, see: Craig Clunas, 'Modernity Global and Local: Consumption and the Rise of the West', *American Historical Review* 104.5 (1999): 1497–1511.

56. Craig Clunas, *Superfluous Things: Material Culture and Social Status in Early Modern China* (Honolulu: University of Hawaii Press, 1991); Suraiya Faroqhi, *Pilgrims and Sultans: Hajj Under the Ottoman* (London: I.B. Tauris, 1994); S.A.M. Adshead, *Material Culture in Europe and China, 1400–1800* (New York: Palgrave Macmillan, 1997); Susan B. Hanley, *Everyday Things in Premodern Japan: The Hidden Legacy of Material Culture* (Berkeley: University of California Press, 1997); Brook, *Confusions of Pleasure*; *Consumption Studies and the History of the Ottoman Empire, 1550–1922: An Introduction*, ed. Donald Quataert (Albany: CUNY, 2000); Suraiya Faroqhi, 'Moving Goods Around and Ottomanists Too: Surveying Research on the Transfer of Material Goods in the Ottoman Empire', *Turcica* 32 (2000): 435–466; Arnold J. Bauer, *Goods, Power, History: Latin America's Material Culture* (Cambridge: Cambridge University Press, 2001); Craig Clunas, *Empire of Great Brightness: Visual and Material Cultures of Ming China, 1368–1644* (London: Reaktion, 2007); Jeremy Prestholdt, *Domesticating the World: African Consumerism and the Genealogies of Globalization* (Berkeley: University of California Press, 2008); Suraiya Faroqhi, *A Cultural History of the Ottomans* (London: I.B. Tauris, forthcoming 2016).

57. See in particular: Berg, 'In Pursuit of Luxury' and her other work on luxury: *Luxury in the Eighteenth Century: Debates, Desires and Delectable Goods*, ed. Maxine Berg and Elizabeth Eger (London: Palgrave, 2002); and Maxine Berg, *Luxury and Pleasure in the Eighteenth Century* (Oxford: Oxford University Press, 2005). See also John Styles, 'Product Innovation in Early Modern London', *Past and Present* 168 (2000): 124–169.

58. Anna Jackson and Amin Jaffer, *Encounters: The Meeting of Asia and Europe, 1500–1800* (London: V&A Publications, 2004).

59. David J. Roxburgh, *Turks: A Journey of a Thousand Years, 600–1600* (London: Royal Academy of Arts, 2005).

60. Neil MacGregor, *A History of the World in 100 Objects* (London: Allen Lane, 2010).

61. *Interwoven Globe: The Worldwide Textile Trade, 1500–1800*, ed. Amelia Peck (London: Thames & Hudson, 2013).

62. Riello, *Cotton*.

63. Anne Gerritsen, 'Fragments of a Global Past: Ceramics Manufacture in Song-Yuan-Ming Jingdezhen', *Journal of the Economic and Social History of the Orient* 52.1 (2009): 117–152.

64. Toby E. Huff, *Intellectual Curiosity and the Scientific Revolution: A Global Perspective* (Cambridge: Cambridge University Press, 2011).

65. Lorraine Daston, *Things That Talk: Object Lessons from Art and Science* (New York: Zone Books, 2004). See also Laura J. Snyder, *Eye of the Beholder: Johannes Vermeer, Antoni Van Leeuwenhoek, and the Reinvention of Seeing* (New York: Norton, 2015).

66. *The Contest for Knowledge: Debates Over Women's Learning in Eighteenth-Century Italy*, ed. Maria G. Agnesi, Rebecca M. Messbarger and Paula Findlen (Chicago: University of Chicago Press, 2005); Paula Findlen, *Possessing Nature: Museums, Collecting, and Scientific Culture in Early Modern Italy* (Berkeley: University of California Press, 1994); Lorraine Daston, *Things That Talk: Object Lessons from Art and Science* (New York: Zone Books, 2004); Dagmar Schäfer, *The Crafting of the 10,000 Things: Knowledge and Technology in Seventeenth-Century China* (Chicago: The University of Chicago Press, 2011).

67. *Cultures of Knowledge Technology in Chinese History*, ed. Dagmar Schäfer (Leiden: Brill, 2012). See also: *The Material Culture of Enlightenment Arts and Sciences*, ed. Adriana Craciun and Simon Schaffer (London: Palgrave, forthcoming 2015).

68. The improper use of London marks was not uncommon in the sixteenth and seventeenth centuries. In 1624 a Sheffield cutler working in London had some of his knives confiscated because 'they had the dagger counterfeited upon them being Sheffield

knives'. http://collections.vam.ac.uk/item/O77653/knife-vigo/ (last consulted 23 June 2015).

69. Costume was one of the ways in which Europeans understood and analysed the non-European world. This was done through a number of costume books – collections of images of the dress of different parts of the world that were popular in Europe since the second half of the sixteenth century. They also represented the costumes of the people of different parts of the world on maps, prints and drawings, on artefacts such as porcelain and in carvings such as that decorating this knife. Kristen Ina Grimes, 'Dressing the World: Costume Books and Ornamental Cartography in the Age of Exploration', in *A Well-fashioned Image: Clothing and Costume in European Art, 1500–1850* ed. Elizabeth Rodini and Elissa B. Weaver (Chicago: David and Alfred Smart Museum of Art, 2002), 13–21; Odille Blanc, 'Ethnologie et merveille dans quelques livres de costumes français', in *Paraître et se vêtir au XVIe siècle. Actes du XIIIe Colloque du Puy-en-Velay*, ed. Marie Viallon (Saint-Étienne: Publications de l'Université de Saint-Étienne, 2006), 77–91; Gabriele Mentges, 'Pour une approche renouvelée des recueils de costumes de la Renaissance. Une cartographie vestimentaire de l'espace et du temps,' *Apparence(s)* 1 (2007), 1–21; Chandra Mukerji, 'Costume and Character in the Ottoman Empire: Dress as Social Agent in Nicolay's *Navigations*', in *Early Modern Things: Objects and their Histories, 1500–1800*, ed. Paula Findlen (Basingstoke: Routledge, 2013), 151–169.
70. Berg, *Luxury and Pleasure*.
71. Crosby, *Columbian Exchange*.
72. Kaori O'Connor, *Pineapple: A Global History* (London: Reaktion Books, 2013).
73. Mintz, *Sweetness and Power*.

PART I
Objects of global knowledge

1

ITINERARIES OF MATERIALS AND KNOWLEDGE IN THE EARLY MODERN WORLD

Pamela H. Smith

In the production of things, and, more generally, in all human acts of making, materials – which possess particular properties that enable a certain range of manipulations by the human hand – undergo a series of transformations, first into the 'raw materials' of human use by means of specialized practices and technologies, then into objects and things, and, finally (or, rather, concurrently), humans assign meanings to these things by integrating them into systems of knowledge and belief (or, 'theories'). This is a reciprocal rather than linear process, and this chapter seeks to follow this complex and often partially obscured itinerary of materials, techniques, and ideas as they travel across geographic and epistemic space in Eurasia to form an 'amalgam' or 'assemblage' that I will label a 'material complex'.

In the first part of the chapter, I develop a picture of the interaction of humans and materials; in the second part, I provide a case study of a material complex in Europe. The chapter continues by giving a cursory and somewhat eclectic overview of the movement of such material complexes across Eurasia; and in the final part, I suggest an itinerary through which the material complex treated in part two formed.

Humans and materials

In the reciprocal process between matter, hand, cognition, and intellect, natural materials and the human body mingle. Indeed, tool use and the acquisition of skills can perhaps ultimately be viewed as evolutionary processes of interaction between humans, the human body, and the environment.[1] An example can be found in the ancient human activity of wood cultivation and management, in which the matter of made things is *grown* by practices like pollarding every year for narrow poles, by coppicing every five to seven years, for larger poles every twenty years, and fostering the decades-, sometimes centuries-long growth of individual tall trees for ships' masts, and house frames. Joiners and carpenters employed the properties of living wood in their practices also; for example, in splitting wood along its growth rays, or in making a join strong by inserting pins of dry wood into holes of green wood. As the green wood dried, it gripped the pin ever tighter.[2] The still-living wood is part of the process of making. Where in these practices of wood cultivation does growing end and human making begin?

The human body is an integral part of this continuum of growing and making. Consider its uses in the early modern workshop: the body functioned as a tool in myriad ways – for warming, blowing, handling, manipulating, sensing, tasting, and providing force and dexterity, just to name a few of its functions. The human body was also a source of substances employed in manufacture – including urine (the urine of pre-pubescent children possessed different properties from that of adults – again growth is important), excrement, blood, ear wax, and saliva; and the body was a model for natural processes – for the fermentation, digestion, concoction, purging, and excretion of the human body provided a conceptual framework for the transformation of materials in nature. Moreover, the quotidian stuff that sustained growth in the human body – including bread, butter, eggs, milk, honey, figs, and garlic – was also employed on a daily basis in workshop practices. And it was by means of the body and its learned gestures and techniques that the embodied and collaborative knowledge of craft was produced and reproduced, passed on from one generation to the next.[3]

European craft recipes measured in proportion to the human body, expressing volume in terms of 'four drops of spittle', or 'two-fingers wide'.[4] Time in craft practices was measured by reciting pater nosters, which, together with the admixture of holy water, could also be viewed as a prophylactic. A lock of hair was used to measure the temperature of material being heated,[5] and human touch could measure whether an object was 'cool enough to be held for a short time in your hand', before being subjected to the next process.[6] All five bodily senses were fully employed in the workshop: vitriol could be identified by its biting, sharp-to-the-taste, pungent-to-the-tongue, astringent nature, while rock alum had 'a bitter taste with a certain unctuous saltiness'.[7] Other measurements relied upon hearing: 'Put your cuttlefish bone very close to the fire, if you hear little cries it means that your bone is dry enough',[8] and, in another, 'If the tin cries very much it means you added enough lead and not too much'.[9] In a process for hardening mercury, the material in the crucible was supposed to sound a loud bang to sign that it had had enough of the fire.[10] The purity of tin was tested by biting to see whether it made cracking sounds, 'like that which water makes when it is frozen by cold'. Good iron ore could be indicated by presence of a red, soft, fat earth that made no crackling noise when squeezed between the teeth.[11] In a dramatic account of casting bells, a medieval metalworking text advises the caster to 'lie down close to the mouth of the mold' as the metal is poured into the bell mould, 'and listen carefully to find out how things are progressing inside. If you hear a light thunderlike rumbling, tell them to stop for a moment and then pour again; and have it done like this, now stopping, now pouring, so that the bell metal settles evenly, until that pot is empty'.[12]

An anonymous goldsmith's treatise advises the assayer to make certain that an acid bath has dissolved all available silver in an alloy by listening carefully to see if the glass vessel makes a 'bott, bott, bott' sound when tapped.[13]

The workshop functioned as an extension of the capacities and products of the human body. But the body was more than a tool in production – it was also implicated in the work: the bodies of metalworkers and the very matter upon which they laboured interpenetrated each other: bad breath could prevent the adhesion of metal gilding, and, conversely, metal fumes were known to shorten the lives of metalworkers, and records of their practice give evidence that they wore masks and ate bread and butter before starting work. Why? Because bread was viewed as a perfectly tempered food that filled the stomach and prevented the subtle metal vapours from being drawn into the body. At the same time, the hot, wet qualities of butter counteracted the miasmic exhalations of the minerals and metals rising up from the ground or billowing out from the smelting furnace. In eating butter, these artisans operated within the Greco-Roman-Arabic health worldview based on an Aristotelian framework of the four elements and qualities. In this scheme, butter was hot; metal vapours were cold.[14] This was also the framework for mine manager and author of *De la Pirotechnia* (1540), Vannoccio Biringuccio's explanation for what happened when bronze was poured into a cold mould – the cold, moist mould overcame the nature of bronze and turned it back to its primordial earthy-watery state.[15]

The human body and natural materials shared many properties. To take one example from metalworking: The idea of *temper* was crucial in the mental world of early modern Europeans. 'Temper' meant to balance by mixing, and a person's temperament was determined by a balance of the four qualities – hot, wet, dry, cold – and their instantiation in the humours: black bile, phlegm, blood, and yellow bile. Each individual's unique combination of the four qualities and humours could be tempered by diet, exercise, purging, and so on (the six non-naturals), and this process of tempering was crucial to human health. Metals too partook in this system and their balance of qualities could be rectified by tempering, as steel was tempered (sometimes using the urine of pre-pubescent boys), and copper was given temper and tone by adding tin in making the alloy, bronze. Minerals and humans alike received their temper from the movements of the heavens, for the sun was a source of growth for all living things – gold grew better along riverbanks warmed by the sun and in south-facing veins, and, in the common understanding of health and identity in early modern Europe, the celestial spheres and bodies determined the temperament of human beings at their conception and birth, just as they did for metals. This was a theological vision as well as a cosmological one, and it was codified in objects (Figure 1.1), as well as images and texts (Figure 1.2), and it gave rise to all manner of practices, such as praying before going down in a mine, a practice that continued into the twentieth century, baptizing mines and invoking God and the saints before a bronze pour.[16]

Metalworkers viewed the matter they worked as capable of growth. They daily employed processes in the production of goods that we conceptualize as typical of organic growth, such as in a pigment recipe for a gold colour that calls for mixing

FIGURE 1.1 Handstein with mine scene and crucifixion. Bohemian, mid-sixteenth century, silver, gilding, wood, mineral specimens, including proustite, argentite, marcasite, lautite, malachite, quartz, fluorite. H. 27.1. Kunsthistorisches Museum, Vienna KK 4167.

mercury with a fresh hen's egg and then putting it back under the hen to heat slowly,[17] or the use of constant slow heat produced by thermophilic bacteria in putrefying horse manure for the slow heat needed for some metalworking procedures.[18] Formations brought out of the *veins* in the body of the earth, such as the pure strands of native silver, were self-evident proof for the growth and ripening of metals in the earth (Figure 1.3).

Artisanal manuals and recipe collections mixed procedures for grafting and growing plants, fermenting liquids, and healing humans and animals with instructions

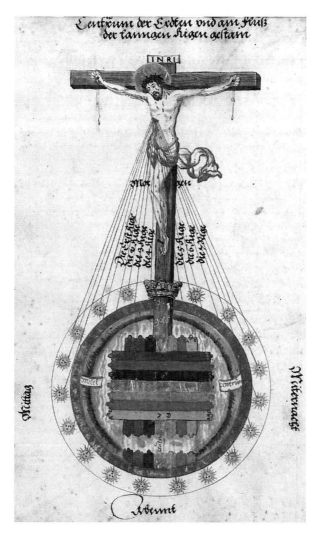

FIGURE 1.2 *Speculum metallorum* (1575), fol. 56v, the blood of Jesus on the Cross forming minerals in the earth. Stadtarchiv Calw, Germany.

for producing objects from ingredients we would now call inorganic because they were viewed as operating according to the same principles. Blood and metal were related as well, and blood appears among the ingredients and operations of numerous metalworking recipes: the blood of goats, oxen, foxes, rams, of a menstruating woman, and of the dragon tree – a red resin.[19] The colour red appears to have been seen as possessing many of the attributes of blood, and it too is mentioned frequently in both medicinal and metalworking recipes.[20]

This entanglement of the human body with matter is especially clear in the labour of mining and metalworking, in which the bodies of miners and smelters

FIGURE 1.3 Native silver (dendritic formations), Freiberg District, Erzgebirge, Saxony, Germany. Houston Museum of Natural Science. Wikimedia. Courtesy of the Houston Museum of Natural Science.

are penetrated by the very matter upon which they laboured. Their bodily striving underground brought the materials to the earth's surface and then drew out the metals from the matrix of their ores, but in this process, the spirits and humours of the metals and minerals mixed with those of the metalworkers, and they affected and shaped each other in distinctive ways. Grounding his account on German physician Daniel Sennert's work, Joannes Jonston wrote in 1657 that 'the Flux of Veins hath somthing proportionable to vegetable nature; ... in the Lungs of such

FIGURE 1.4 Hans Leinberger, *c.*1510–1520, Mass for the victims of a mine accident, limewood, Bode Museum, Berlin. The heads and the feet of the victims are visible at the lower left.

as use to dig in Mines, their bodies being opened when they are dead, you shall find the same Mettals grown hard, wherein they laboured being alive . . '.[21] A vivid emblematic evocation of the co-penetration of human body and the material of the earth can be seen in an early sixteenth-century altarpiece relief commemorating a mine accident that shows the limbs and a head of dead miners protruding from the mass of rock and earth of the collapsed shaft (Figure 1.4). This representation shows the endpoint of the struggle with matter that shaped the bodies of miners. Like other craftspeople, their specific bodily labour formed their musculature and posture, and the matter they worked marked their bodies by distinctive diseases.

A case study: vermilion in Europe

The interpenetration of environment, making, and knowing, as these examples illustrate, was especially clear in mining and metalworking. One of these processes of metalworking – the production of the deep red pigment, vermilion, from sulphur and mercury, used by artists to imitate blood – indicates not just the role of the body in working materials, but can also shed light on the crisscrossing flows of matter, practices, people, and knowledge – not just within Europe, but across all of Eurasia in the middle ages and early modern period. In this sense, it shows how knowledge is made both across space, and also between social groups, in a kind of 'epistemic' movement back and forth among vernacular practitioners and text-oriented scholars in their diverse practices of producing and reproducing knowledge about natural things.

In the medieval and early modern period, red pigment was produced by grinding red ochre clay or by boiling, drying, and grinding madder root, or through mashing kermes beetles from Poland and Armenia;[22] but a much more saturated red could be produced by grinding cinnabar (HgS, or mercury sulphide), mined since Roman times in Almaden, Spain; or, after the 1520s, by drying, compressing, then grinding the red cochineal beetle, which lived on Central and South American cacti.[23] Finally, from at least the eighth century in Europe, sulphur and mercury were heated together to produce a 'synthetic' cinnabar which yielded a bright vermilion pigment. The making of vermilion is dramatic – mercury and sulphur are heated together until they become a black paste, then this paste turns dark blue on the outside and silver on the inside, and eventually forms a vapour that condenses as a bright red cake on the walls of the crucible. This powder is scraped off to form the pigment.[24] More than other red pigments employed in medieval and early modern Europe, it was viewed as possessing powerful properties associated with blood and regeneration. Red substances in general were associated with blood. Red coral, for example, had a variety of valuable qualities, as a thirteenth century author wrote:

> It is good against any sort of bleeding. [. . .] worn around the neck, it is good against epilepsy and the problems of menstruation, and against storms, lightning, and hail. And if it is powdered and sprinkled with water on herbs and trees, it is reported to multiply their fruits. They also say that it speeds the beginning and end of any business.[25]

Vermilion was often employed by painters to depict deep red blood, and it was especially associated with the redeeming blood of Christ (Figure 1.5). Especially telling in this regard, is the practice of scribes and illuminators, who marked the places where vermilion was to be used in their manuscripts with a cross, standing for Jesus's blood poured out at the crucifixion.[26]

In vernacular practices and high theology, blood possessed overlapping and contradictory meanings, signifying vitality, fertility, the material of conception and the spirit of life, but at the same time, blood poured out could indicate death, and of course that shed by Jesus signified death, life, and redemption, all at the same time.[27]

FIGURE 1.5 Drops of Jesus's blood painted in vermilion, *Psalter and Rosary of the Virgin*, *c.*1490. British Library, Egerton Ms 1821, ff. 1v–2. The pages have probably been touched and kissed, which accounts for their abrasion.

Blood was also regarded as an extremely powerful agent by metalworkers and jewellers: it was often listed in recipes as the only means to soften or cut hard gemstones such as diamonds. Most such recipes called for the blood of a male goat or a ram:

> If you want to carve a piece of rock crystal, take a two- or three-year-old goat and bind its feet together and cut a hole between its breast and stomach, in the place where the heart is, and put the crystal in there, so that it lies in its blood until it is hot. At once take it out and engrave whatever you want on it, while this heat lasts. When it begins to cool and become hard, put it back in the goat's blood, take it out again when it is hot, and engrave it. Keep on doing so until you finish the carving. Finally, heat it again, take it out and rub it with a woolen cloth so that you may render it brilliant with the same blood.[28]

Recipes, such as this one for rendering solid substances malleable, and for the inverse processes of 'fixing' liquid or volatile materials, are to be found in overwhelmingly large numbers in European recipe collections up through the seventeenth century. Some do cause changes of state, such as dissolution in acid, or heating, or even tempering of steel, but many of them, such as this goat's blood recipe, are repeated over and over again, despite the fact they could not possibly have functioned as intended. It may be that the origin of this recipe was to crack crystals in order to allow dye penetration.[29] However, it seems more likely that such recipes instead were reiterated because they reinforced the philosophical framework of the Hippocratic-Aristotelian-Galenic view of nature in which opposites must be combined (or 'tempered') in order to bring the four elements/humours/qualities into equilibrium, which denoted good health.

All kinds of red substances and blood appear among the ingredients and operations of metalworking recipes, as noted above. Additionally, blood and gold were viewed as possessing analogous properties in medicine: blood acted as the carrier of life heat, while gold was seen as heating up the body and stimulating rejuvenation when prepared as the medicinal 'potable gold' or even when worn on the body as jewellery.[30]

Red components, such as the pigment vermilion, were often ingredients in recipes to produce gold pigment,[31] even when they had no practical effect on the actual chemical reaction. And, gold was used to produce red colour in the techniques of producing red lustreware glaze and ruby glass, for example. Red seems to have been considered an essential ingredient in processes that sought to generate, transform, especially related to the noble metal gold.[32] The materials of vermilion, sulphur and mercury, also often appear in recipes for gold pigments, such as that for mosaic gold (tin or stannic sulphide, SnS_2), a sparkling golden pigment that imitated pure gold. At the end of the fourteenth century, Cennino Cennini lists one such recipe, which calls for 'sal ammoniac [ammonium chloride], tin, sulphur, quicksilver, in equal parts; except less of the quicksilver'.[33] Art conservators have determined that the mercury in this recipe is not necessary to produce the gold pigment and instead appears to refer back to the homologies between red and gold.[34]

This correspondence between blood, red, and gold in the worldview of early modern metalworkers from at least the twelfth through sixteenth centuries also involves another unexpected component: lizards and salamanders, which are included as ingredients in some metalworking recipes.[35] For example, a 1531 text that includes pigment-making and metalworking recipes, titled *Rechter Gebrauch der Alchimei,* contains several recipes for making noble metals through a process of catching, feeding, and burning lizards and salamanders.[36] These creatures were associated more generally with processes of putrefaction, generation, and regeneration: they appear seemingly spontaneously from putrefying matter (Figure 1.6), informing the commonsense principle that generation involved a process of decay. Furthermore, lizards regenerated their tails when severed, and lizards emerged fully grown from their places of hibernation after freezing winters.[37] This nexus of meaning around materials and practices involving red, blood, gold, and lizards forms a 'vernacular science'[38] of matter and transformation, a relational web of interlinked homologies among red, blood, gold, and lizards that underlay artisanal practices and techniques, and that generated meaning in their world.[39]

This knowledge system was not a theory in the sense that it could be formulated as a set of propositions, rather it was sometimes practised and lived and sometimes

FIGURE 1.6 Lower left: Lizards climb the 'Dragon Tree' from which a healing red resin 'Dragon's Blood' is obtained. Martin Schongauer, *The Flight into Egypt*, *c.*1470–1490, h 255 mm × w 169 mm. Rijksmuseum, Amsterdam RP-P-OB-998.

expressed in writing. It related making practices to knowing nature, and it gave access to the powers of nature, transformation, and generation.

Vermilion possessed further layers of meaning because its production involved sulphur and mercury, metals understood to be respectively hot and cold, and to impact the workers' bodies in contrary ways, necessitating remedies of their opposites. In addition, in its manufacture, vermilion goes through a process of transformation which resembles the description in early modern European texts of alchemy, in which metals are transmuted from a base state to a noble one. The metal mass is described as black in the putrefaction stage and bright red just before it turns gold. Some alchemical writers believed that it might be possible to derive a substance which could cause this purification of base metals instantaneously. This 'philosopher's stone', which was theoretically capable of transmuting a mass of base metal into shining gold through a dramatic series of colour changes, was often described as a red powder, like vermilion.

As a component of alchemical theory, vermilion making also interested medieval European scholars such as Albertus Magnus (1206–1280), separated from the metalworkers just discussed by both social and intellectual distance. Albertus was part of the generation of European scholars intensely involved in assimilating the ancient Greek and Latin corpus of texts entering Europe after the Crusades and through Islamic Spain. He was especially eager to obtain a full view of Aristotle's works. At the end of Book III of the *Meteorologica*, Aristotle had promised a detailed account of metals and non-metallic minerals, but did not write it. Albertus was convinced, however, that Aristotle had written such a text, and he searched for years, but when he found nothing, he took matters into his own hands, saying: 'we shall make additions wherever books are incomplete, and wherever they have gaps in them, or are missing entirely – whether they were left unwritten by Aristotle or, if he did write them, they have not come down to us'.[40] In order to remedy this troubling lacuna in Aristotle's corpus, Albertus made, as he said, 'long journeys to mining districts, so that I could learn by observation the nature of metals. And for the same reason I have inquired into the transmutations of metals in alchemy, so as to learn from this, too, something of their nature and accidental properties'.[41] He had much opportunity for such observations during his extraordinarily wide travels throughout Europe in various church administrative positions. One of the practices he observed on his travels was vermilion making.[42]

Vermilion was especially interesting to Albertus, as he had also just come into contact with Arabic alchemical theory which taught that the 'principles' of sulphur and mercury form the underlying substratum of all metals (recall that vermilion is manufactured by heating mercury and sulphur together). This theory of metals had only just arrived in Europe in the twelfth century via the books of alchemy translated from Arabic into Latin. Before the eleventh and twelfth centuries, European scholars knew of recipe collections such as the *Mappa clavicula* (A Small Key of Handiwork) for operations using gold, precious stones, and gems. Although these recipes contained fragments from earlier Greek alchemical writings, these mysterious interpolations had been detached from any sort of conceptual framework. In the twelfth century, however, books of alchemy began to be translated from Arabic into Latin. Alchemical theory, based on Aristotle's four elements, stretched back to a conglomeration of Greek matter theory and Gnostic spiritual practices found in texts of second- and third-century CE Hellenistic Egypt, but the sulphur-mercury theory of metals was an innovation of Arabic alchemical writers, worked into the older Hellenistic texts and appearing for the first time in the Latin West as an entirely new field of knowledge.[43] Albertus's enthusiasm for this new theory of metals was the outcome of an extraordinary movement of texts and translators in a process that resulted from a kind of philological jigsaw puzzle.[44]

By the time Albertus avidly took up Arabic alchemical theory – as codified in writing – in the thirteenth century, European craftspeople had already been combining mercury and sulphur to produce a red powder for at least four centuries.[45] Indeed, the practice of vermilion production – its materials of sulphur and mercury, its dramatic colour changes, its red powder form – everywhere pre-dated the articulation in texts of the alchemical theory of metals which included these same components. It appears probable, then, that the sulphur-mercury theory of metals emerged from the practices of making vermilion – from the work of craftspeople and their productive activity. In other words, one of the most pervasive and enduring metallurgical theories of matter and its transformation – the alchemical sulphur-mercury theory – flowed from the making of a valuable material. Here is an instance of knowledge moving across 'epistemic distance', in which matter and craft practices shaped and informed the theories of text oriented scholars. European metalworkers oriented their practices through the red of vermilion and blood, and they believed lizards to be a key to transformation. At the same time, Albertus Magnus, relying upon the Arabic alchemical works that had come to him along a tortuous path of translation and compilation, and setting out to observe miners and metalworkers, found the same idea in the workshops that red was at the heart of the transformation of matter, and he found confirmation for his core theory that mercury and sulphur were central components of such transformation.

Some itineraries of material complexes in Eurasia

Besides illustrating the epistemic movement of knowledge between social groups and knowledge systems in Europe, vermilion manufacture also gives insight into the movement of knowledge in the more conventional sense of motion over geographic distance. We get the first hint of this from a fourteenth-century book of secrets. This book contains many 'secrets' for lighting a house, one of which calls for cutting off the tail of a lizard and collecting the liquid that bleeds from it, 'for it is like Quicksilver', and when it is put on a wick in a new lamp 'the house shall seem bright and white, or gilded with silver'.[46]

Here again mercury, lizards, and noble metals are related, but this recipe also transports us to the other end of Eurasia, where lizards and red also appear to have had significant powers ascribed to them. In the early twentieth century, anthropologists recorded recipes using reptiles to produce light in the oral culture of illiterate South Indian villagers.[47] In China, too, lizards are implicated in transformation, indicated even by the very characters in which they are expressed, which signify transformation. Red pigment and lizards are also related in the third-century CE text by Zhang Hua (232–300 CE), which includes a recipe for pounding lizards and cinnabar together to form a substance that when dotted on the emperor's concubines indicated whether they had had sex, thus it was known as 'guard chamber'.[48] This conjuncture of red and lizards, embedded in systems of practice and meaning that explained generation and transformation across these tremendous spans of time and space – from third-century CE China to thirteenth-century Europe appears at first glance remarkable.

To gain perspective on this conjuncture, let us shift our gaze from the local space of European workshops and Chinese philological investigations to a more expansive view over the long-term and long-distance flows of goods, knowledge, texts, practices, and peoples across the 'Afro-Eurasian ecumene'.

Following these flows of materials shows how some moved with particular speed, especially those related to weapons technology, whether it was the alloying of copper and tin to create the tough and pourable copper alloys (including bronze) in the fourth millennium BCE for weapons, or the horse chariots that spread throughout Middle Eurasia from about 4000 BCE,[49] taking the shape of war chariots from ca. 1600 BCE,[50] or the stirrup (widespread in China from the fifth century CE, then found in Persia and throughout the Islamic world by the seventh century and in Europe from the eighth),[51] or the gunpowder weaponry that shaped the Ottoman, Safavid, and Moghul 'Gunpowder Empires' of the fourteenth to seventeenth centuries, and influenced the mining of copper and tin throughout Eurasia.[52] Like the physical instruments of power and destruction, the trappings, ceremonies, and techniques of staging power, such as the royal hunt carried out with noble animals and raptor birds also spread very extensively throughout Afro-Eurasia (Figure 1.7).[53]

Perhaps related to the noble pastime of the hunt, mathematical problems of pursuit, which contain calculations about the relative speeds of one animal (or planet) chasing another, are also found in China in the first century, in India in the seventh century, and in Latin in their simplest form in the ninth.[54]

But less deadly objects and techniques also flowed across this space: food crops probably travelled as swiftly as weapons, although our primary evidence for this comes from the period when New World foods entered into already well-established trade routes at the eastern end of Eurasia. But a few examples indicate just how fast such crops could spread: the peanut, cultivated in the Chaco region of South America, could already be found growing as a food crop near Shanghai at the latest by the 1560s or 70s; sweet potatoes arrived in China at least by the 1560s; New World maize was established in China in 1555 where it had been brought by Turkic frontiersmen, and along the Euphrates by 1574.[55] Food plants travelled in advance of recorded contact between peoples, carried by sailors and other anonymous intermediaries, and their cultivation in new soils must have occasioned much experimentation by their growers both in the field and at the dinner table.

While food and weapons – the means of survival – seem to have travelled around the Afro-Eurasian ecumene most rapidly, luxury goods also moved along the same routes: rock crystal vessels from India and dancing elephants from Khotan, red parrots and single white cockatoos all arrived as tribute into eleventh-century Song China,[56] all manner of *materia medica* including the dragon's blood was brought in

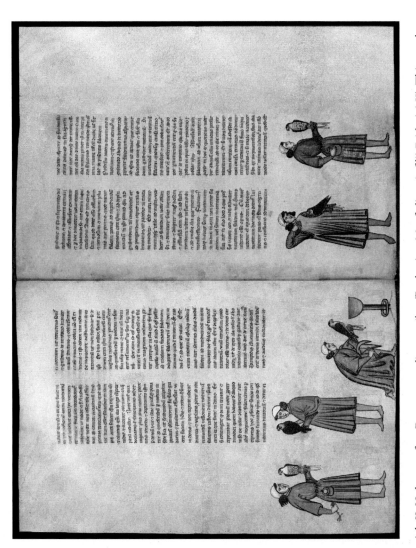

FIGURE 1.7 Frederick II, Hohenstaufen, *De arte venandi cum avibus* (Redaction Manfedi regis filii Friderici II). Thirteenth century. Biblioteca Apostolica Vaticana, Rome, Ms. Pal. Lat. 1071, fol. 82v and 83v.

to treat infantile fits in the Southern Song (1127–1279),[57] and large quantities of sulphur flowed by the ton into Tang China from Indonesia and Japan between the seventh and tenth centuries CE. This sulphur went to concoct fireworks and to temper the constitution, as the minister of state Yuan Cai aimed to do when he 'took his *hot* viands from porcelain utensils floating in cool water, [and] ate and drank *cold* preparations from sulphur bowls, aiming at the perfect balance between hot and cold influences thought to be necessary for bodily health'.[58] This flow of objects and materials included Chinese porcelain of the eleventh century that can still be found today in the treasury of Venice's San Marco, looted in 1204 from Constantinople, and, late in the period, the Molino Ewer which, like other goods, travelled both ways in its making (Figure 1.8).[59] All these rarities, as well as the staples

FIGURE 1.8 'Molino Ewer', *c.*1450–1500. Brass ewer made in Flanders or Germany. The ornament on the lid includes the coat of arms of the Molino family of Venice, and the decoration was probably executed in Egypt or Syria. It seems that a member of the Molino family sent the ewer to Syria to be decorated in an Islamic style. It was then returned to Italy. Victoria and Albert Museum, Gift of Dr W.L. Hildburgh, FSA, M.32–1946.

of silk and cotton textiles, glass ingots, ceramics, tea, salt, spices, aromatics, medicinal herbs, gold, and silver, created pathways along which, as Robert Hartwell noted, '[t]echniques, ideas and institutions flowed in a constant stream'.[60]

Sometimes this stream included organized exchanges of technologies and peoples, such as the Chinese physicians sent to Koryo in the eleventh century to educate Korean doctors, or the forced migrations of craftspeople by the Mongols, as well as informal exchanges such as prisoners of war, always viewed as valuable transmitters of techniques. An eleventh-century Persian scholar writing in Arabic reported that Chinese prisoners passed on the practices of paper-making when they were captured by Islamic forces in the Battle of Talas in 751.[61] Another Arabic author feared the potential for technology transfer by means of prisoners:

> As for the flammable oils, they [the Franks] do not know [the technique of], [fitting gunpowder and explosive devices to weapons], nor do they know the [flying fire] arrows, or the composition of the fuses . . . If one is taken prisoner by them, God forbid, he must not give them any information because they will then ruin everything.[62]

Chinese institutional forms of the Song Dynasty (960–1279) spread widely to Korea, Vietnam, Baghdad, and even Norman Sicily, which all adopted some elements of Chinese institutions such as the examination system, the relay postal system, granaries, famine relief, and techniques for managing fiscal monopolies. Roger II (r. 1132–1154) of Norman Sicily gathered information and informants from all parts of the world, and his plan for training members of the court in three stages of education may have been based upon his knowledge of Chinese practices.[63]

Particularly intense periods of exchange occurred during the Bronze Age (ca. 3500–800 BCE) as societies fiercely competed for and exchanged the tin and copper to produce valued metal; and again from about the sixth century BCE when, in a dynamic that would occur repeatedly, greater exchange across Eurasia unfolded concurrently with the emergence of greater differentiation in culture and religion.[64] It was during this period that the four dominant core regions began to produce corpuses of texts in Greek, Chinese, Sanskrit, and early Persian, which would come to form the principal bases for remarkably durable identities.

Trade and exchange also peaked during the simultaneous expansion of the Roman and Han empires;[65] during the period of the Tang (618–906 CE) as the empire conquered lands to the west and the court revelled in the luxuries brought across Central Asia; again during the remarkable efflorescence of technological invention during the Song period; across the extraordinary reach of the Abbasid Empire and its successor states; from the eighth century; during the so-called *Pax Mongolica* of the thirteenth and fourteenth centuries; and again in the sixteenth through eighteenth centuries as western Europe and the Americas entered into these well-established connective pathways. From about 1500 BCE to about 1500 CE, much of the exchange across Eurasia was knit together by the web of land routes, known confusedly since the nineteenth century as the 'Silk Road', confusing because it was neither a single road, nor was silk by any means the primary good that travelled over it. The 'Silk Road' has overshadowed an even earlier eastward flow of furs along a northerly 'fur route'.[66] Such flows continued further east and west around the globe as the Americas were forcibly incorporated within the Afro-Eurasian ecumene.

Shared patterns of consumption emerged which placed great value on unique, rare, and unusual objects that could make real and tangible qualities of distant parts of the realm. The simultaneously social, moral, and exchange economy in which such wonders were embedded extended downward and outward through the courts of regional nobles.[67] At the same time, the consolidation of the major religions, with their similar practices of prayer, sacrifice, and pilgrimage by which devotees pursued the signs and sites of the god scattered throughout the world, brought into existence a large infrastructure of transport, food, credit, and international trade to support their practices of devotion and their extensive systems of pilgrimage (spice for incense and Brahminical food restrictions, for example, and salted fish for Catholic fasting).[68] The individuals traversing these various pilgrimage and trade routes shared both a common view of health and a common range of medicines. Central medical concepts, such as 'life-breath', common to ancient Chinese, Greco-Roman, and South Asian medical writers (*qi*, *pneuma*, and *prāna*) informed care of the body throughout Eurasia. Both the Greco-Roman-Islamic system of the four humours and the Chinese system of *qi* and *yin/yang* had their origins in an overarching notion of balance and tempering contrary forces in order to bring the body to a healthy state.[69]

Moreover, a person's individual constitution was viewed throughout Eurasia as influenced by the heavenly bodies, and many of the remedies by which bodies could be tempered and balanced were transported over very long distances via the same trade routes by which weapons and rarities also travelled. Spices (wholly integrated into the health framework), medicinal plants (such as dragon's blood), animal parts (like rhinoceros horn), precious stones (for example, turquoise for eyesight; red coral to stop blood flow), and mineral-based concoctions (sulphur and mercury) all possessed medicinal virtues and commanded high exchange values throughout Afro-Eurasia. A literature on 'wonders', which began to codify and canonize these objects' marvellous qualities and simultaneously to stimulate desire for them, grew up around this exchange in rarities and medicines. In this literature, India was identified as the primary location of wonders and marvels, as well as the source of precious stones (which, along with Sri Lanka, it actually was).[70] A tenth-century writer in Arabic Buzurg ibn Shahryar in his *Kitab 'ajayib al-Hind* (The Wonders of India, *c*.960) recounts marvels of all sorts purportedly told to him on board merchant ships, including many involving fearsome snakes,[71] future-divining lizards as well as lizards with double sexual organs,[72] and especially crayfish, for example[73] crayfish that fell into the Sea of Senf, turned into stones, and were subsequently 'carried into Iraq . . . and used in making an ointment to cure eye complaints'.[74] Such travellers' reports and sailors' yarns (best known perhaps are those of Sinbad the Sailor) spread exceedingly widely, forming the stuff of 'folk tales' across Afro-Eurasia,[75] and merit investigation as the possible generators of the reptile stories of both the fourteenth-century European books of secrets and the oral culture of illiterate South Indian villagers in the early twentieth century.

Even this brief and cursory survey of the dense pathways of exchange that coursed across Afro-Eurasia since prehistoric times shows that the flows of goods and of the people who mined, produced, transported and consumed them helped to constitute the social, cultural, and medical complexes of belief that both structured and fostered this exchange. In this reciprocal process, the mundane production of material things (involving the manipulation of materials) informed and transformed theoretical formulations of knowledge; the transfer of practical techniques across space fostered new ways of controlling both nature and other people; and the motion of goods and their trade gave rise to people telling oral tales, some of which were compiled, written down (only *sometimes* by identifiable authors), and translated into various vernacular and learned languages in texts that also moved across great distances and themselves stimulated the movement of yet further travellers, objects, and ideas.

We should not perhaps be astounded, then, at the similar meanings and powers held by the materials cinnabar, mercury, vermilion, and lizards at opposite ends of Eurasia.[76] For, when viewed against the continuous flow of materials, people, technologies, practices, texts, and ideas back and forth across the continent, it is entirely plausible that the complex of ideas and practices surrounding lizards, vermilion, metals, and generation spread with the trade in pigments, *materia medica*, and health practices, and informed both metalworkers' vernacular beliefs and learned scholars seeking the lost books of Aristotle or the elixir for eternal life.

This breathless account of movement across Eurasia does not sufficiently take into account blockages, barriers and constraints to the movement of objects and technologies, including natural and political barriers, social hierarchies that prevent learning and transfer, and cultural predispositions such as those which kept lapis lazuli and quantitative representations of the world out of China,[77] or, in Thomas Allsen's account, the 'filtering' effect that impelled the Mongols to adopt only parts of the cosmology and astrology of China.[78] Perhaps the focus here on speed of movement also creates a flattened picture of the differences and particularities of the importance of the materials and the material complex in the various places through which they travelled.

Itinerary of the material complex around vermilion

One of the materials moving around China was medicinal cinnabar and its artificially-produced substitute vermilion. From at least the fourth century BCE, the pigment derived from cinnabar had come, on the one hand, to convey the power of the emperor in the bright red ink employed on particularly important documents of state and in the robes of imperial officials (Figure 1.9),[79] and on the other to symbolize transformation. The *Baopuzi* (The Master Embracing Simplicity) of 320 CE by Ge Hong for example, lists recipes for making artificial gold with red substances,[80] the same mosaic gold made by painters such as Cennino Cennini

FIGURE 1.9 Two mandarins of the Ming dynasty court wearing bright red robes. Silk painting by unknown artist. Chinese, fifteenth century. Topkapi Museum Istanbul. Photo Credit: The Art Archive/Topkapi Museum Istanbul/Gianni Dagli Orti Reference: AA366347.

and metalworkers in Europe.[81] Ge Hong believed that the essence of cinnabar generated gold.[82]

A hoard of *materia medica* from between 741 and 756 CE containing cinnabar, red coral, gold powder, and gold leaf uncovered recently[83] indicates again the connections between red and gold, but also points to the widespread use in China of cinnabar in medicines and particularly in elixirs concocted to prolong life.[84] Cinnabar is listed in tribute texts back to the fifth century BCE, and these texts themselves go back to an oral tradition three hundred years older. The oldest text in Chinese that definitively places cinnabar within a medical framework is from the second century BCE, and the use of cinnabar in this text is embedded in ritual practices.[85] Over time, this literature on the medicinal uses of cinnabar swelled into a veritable flood. In it, cinnabar was viewed as far more efficacious for prolonging life than plant substances, but it could also be employed for seemingly contrary uses, to cause abortions,[86] pointing to the ambiguous place of this powerful transformative substance. Like lizards, cinnabar was implicated in death and putrefaction as well as regeneration.[87] When struck with miners' tools, cinnabar sheds tears of mercury;[88] when heated and refined, cinnabar runs with living 'quicksilver', and this mercury could revert again to cinnabar in the process of vermilion manufacture (Figure 1.10).[89] Much was made of mercury's quickening qualities in texts of the third century BCE, and, in the same period, channels in tomb chambers were constructed to run with liquid quicksilver. Indeed, one imperial tomb depicted the lands over which the emperor had ruled by means of a relief map, in which the rivers and streams flowed with liquid mercury, just as the emperor's veins had once flowed with blood.[90] Texts on Chinese alchemy from at least the eighth century CE focus on the refining of cinnabar to mercury and mercury back to vermilion powder, prescribing repeated cyclical transformations both to produce valuable elixirs of life and at the same time to foster higher spiritual understanding in the adept.[91]

Now, it seems obvious that this complex of ideas about gold, mercury, sulphur, and red must have originated in China and spread via the Islamic empires to European scholars, for Arabic alchemy incorporates both elixirs and the central place of mercury and sulphur – which are the heart of Chinese medical and alchemical practice. But there is no evidence of textual transmission of Chinese alchemy to Arabic scholars. We do possess, however, material evidence, for the meeting of Islamic and Chinese forces at the Battle of Talas River in 751 CE brought forth

FIGURE 1.10 Deep red cinnabar stone. Author's photo.

a trade in material goods. First, the movement of *materia medica* gives evidence of this flow from matter to ideas, for the remedies recorded in the Arabic and Persian pharmaceutical writings incorporated a hugely expanded range of medicinals from 'China, Southeast Asia, the Himalayas, and Southern India'.[92] Second, another material, sal ammoniac (ammonium chloride), an important export from Central Asia to China since the first millennium CE, emerged after the Islamic inroads into this region as an essential material of Arabic alchemical and industrial practices and a central component of the Arabic alchemical theory of salts and acids in the ninth century.[93] This salt was collected at the mouths of vents in 'solfatoras' near Urumqi in Chinese Turkestan, and from burning coal seams in other Central Asian borderlands (Figure 1.11), and used to colour metals, as a flux to clear metal surfaces for tinning, silvering, or gilding, as well as in dyeing and pharmacology.[94] References to sal ammoniac in many Arabic sources date knowledge of ammonium chloride to c. 850 CE and ammonium carbonate (sometimes labelled interchangeably 'sal ammoniac') to c. 875 CE, as well as chloride from sublimation using dung and soot in 900 CE. Sal ammoniac was in constant use by the early tenth century.[95]

Ali b. 'Abbas al-Majusi (d. 994) saw salts as one of four basic categories of drug preparation, and Abulcasis al-Zahrawi (*c.*936–1013) devoted one-third of his medical compendium, *al-Tasrif*, to the preparation and purification of substances including sal ammoniac, antimony, and cinnabar.[96]

FIGURE 1.11 Zolfatara di Pozzuoli with brightly coloured mineral concentrations deposited by the vapours. Wikimedia Commons. Author: Mentnafunangann (2 November 2014) licensed under CC by 4.0.

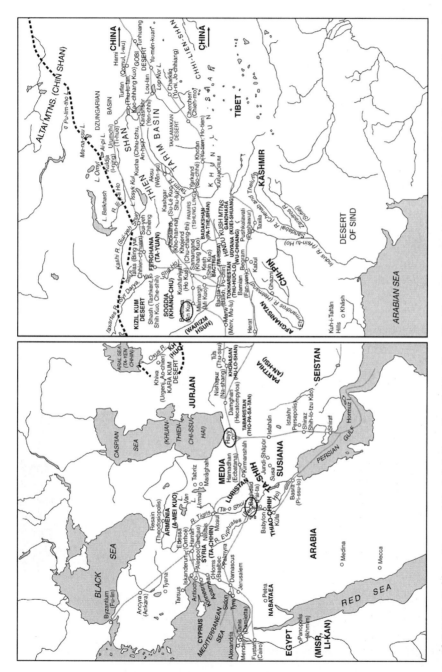

MAP 1.1 Al-Rāzī in Bukhara, Rayy and Baghdad. From Joseph Needham, Ho Ping-Yü, Lu Gwei-Djen, *Science and Civilisation in China*, vol. 5, pt. 4 (Cambridge: Cambridge University Press, 1980), pp. 406–7.

Techniques travelled too, as can be seen from the existence of an early ninth-century 'how-to' manual in Arabic which includes glue for broken porcelain, instructions on how to construct 'Chinese saddles' (apparently an object of interest, as we also know that several were taken at the Battle of Talas River), a 'Chinese cream' for polishing mirrors, and other technical recipes.[97] Such a how-to manual offers further evidence that it was by means of the motion of objects and techniques that new complexes of knowledge emerged in the contact zones of China and the lands of Islam.[98]

Finally, ninth and tenth-century Arabic alchemical scholars Jābir ibn Hayyan (*ca.* 722–*ca.* 812) and his followers, especially Abū Bakr al-Rāzī (*ca.* 864–925), discuss in detail the process of vermilion making and other operations with mercury. Al-Rāzī mentions sal ammoniac in his *Book of the Secret of Secrets* (*Sirr al-Asrār*).[99] He also notes the luxury trade in good Chinese mirrors made with mercury amalgamate, objects that might have provided both a stimulus to imitation and experimentation as well as information about their manufacture when 'reverse-engineered' by practised craftspeople and scholar-experimenters like al-Rāzī.[100] Al-Rāzī was born and died in Rayy, Persia, and he directed hospitals in Rayy and in Baghdad, as well as serving at the Central Asian Sāmānid court in Bukhara where Chinese mirrors would undoubtedly have been available. All three cities in which he worked were important trading zones between China and Central Asia (Map 1.1).

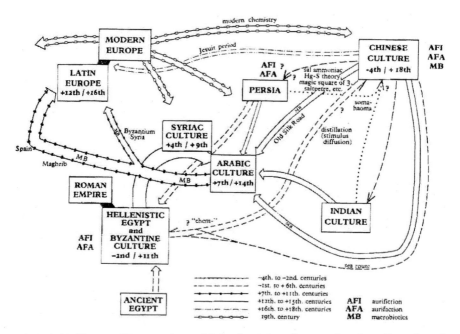

FIGURE 1.12 Chart to illustrate the multi-focal origins of proto-chemistry. From Joseph Needham, Ho Ping-Yü, Lu Gwei-Djen, *Science and Civilisation in China*, vol. 5, pt. 4 (Cambridge: Cambridge University Press, 1980), p. 504. This chart gives a sense of the pathways of the material-textual complex that is alchemy.

These movements of materials and things from China to writers in Arabic thus provide clues for the transfer of ideas about sulphur and mercury. By the twelfth and thirteenth century, as noted above, the texts of Jabir, al-Rāzī, and others that provided a textual container for the material complex of vermilion-making would enter Europe (although our knowledge of this process is limited by the fact that scholars have only recently once again made serious efforts to study Arabic alchemical texts), (Figure 1.12).[101]

Even so, as Robert Halleux notes, 'everyone admits today that Latin alchemy from the Middle Ages is all founded on Arabic heritage, [but] the transmission mechanisms have not yet been studied. The translations are not all discovered yet; their Arabic model is not always identified, their manuscript tradition is not known; the translator is only mentioned in a small number of cases'.[102] In the meantime, vermilion-making itself had already arrived in Europe by at least the eighth century,[103] practices moving, as usual, ahead of the written word.

Conclusion

This paper began by tracing the reciprocal processes by which materials and humans interact in the artisan's workshop. Workshop practices mingled the senses and materials, employed bodily fluids, natural processes of fermentation, and the generative power of materials. Such bodily interaction with materials produced not just things, but also knowledge about the nature and behaviour of materials, and about growth and life – a 'material complex'. One such complex formed around the material vermilion. The properties of sulphur and mercury enabled the manufacture of this prized red by a laborious process that marked the bodies of its makers and came to have a significant place in European culture. This paper has attempted to trace the itinerary across Eurasia over which some of the components of this material complex came together.

More generally, this paper has argued that any knowledge system should be understood from the ground – or, rather, so to speak, from the materials – up, and through this, we can follow the struggle of the human body with materials, and the processes of bodily labour and embodied reasoning by which the properties of materials come to be known and material things emerge. From this, we can begin to understand how human intervention – both bodily *and* conceptual interventions – in the flows of materials comes to constitute scientific knowledge.

Notes and References

1. See Raymond Tallis, *The Hand: A Philosophical Inquiry into Human Being* (Edinburgh: Edinburgh University Press, 2004); and especially Tim Ingold, *The Perception of the Environment: Essays in Livelihood, Dwelling and Skill* (London and New York: Routledge, 2000).
2. Robert Tarule, *The Artisan of Ipswich: Craftsmanship and Community in Colonial New England* (Baltimore: Johns Hopkins University Press, 2004), ch. 1.
3. For a discussion of craft practices such as these, see: Pamela H. Smith, *The Body of the Artisan* (Chicago: University of Chicago Press, 2004).

4. *The Strasburg Manuscript. A Medieval Painters' Handbook,* translated by Viola and Rosamund Borradaile (London: Alec Tiranti, 1966).
5. Anonymous, *Rechter Gebrauch der Alchimei / Mitt vil bissher verborgenen, nutzbaren uund lustigen Künsten / Nit allein den fürwitzigen Alchmisten / sonder allen kunstbaren Werckleutten / in und ausserhalb feurs. Auch sunst aller menglichen inn vil wege zugebrauchen* (No publisher noted, 1531), ix verso.
6. Theophilus, *The Various Arts. De Diversis Artibus,* ed. and trans. C.R. Dodwell (Oxford: Clarendon, 1986), 181.
7. Vannoccio Biringuccio, *The Pirotechnia,* trans. Cyril Stanley Smith and Martha Teach Gnudi (New York: Basic Books, 1943), 95–98.
8. Bibliothèque Nationale, Paris, Ms. Fr 640, Anon., probably late sixteenth century, f. 145v.
9. Ms. Fr 640, f. 131v.
10. Anonymous, *Rechter Gebrauch der Alchimei,* iiii.
11. Biringuccio, *Pirotechnia,* 60–67.
12. Theophilus, *Various Arts,* 173.
13. H.G., *c.*1604, 'The Goldsmith's Storehouse'. V.a. 179. Folger Library, ff. 22v–24r.
14. For a fuller statement of and references to the foregoing discussion, see Pamela H. Smith 'Making as Knowing: Craft as Natural Philosophy', in *Ways of Making and Knowing: The Material Culture of Empirical Knowledge,* ed. Pamela H. Smith, Amy R.W. Meyers and Harold J. Cook (Ann Arbor: University of Michigan Press, 2014), 17–47.
15. Biringuccio, *Pirotechnia,* 250.
16. For these practices, see my discussion in Smith, 'Making as Knowing'.
17. Anon., *Kunstbüchlein* (Augsburg: Michael Manger, 1538), f. 19v.
18. The warmth of dung, approximately equal to a hen brooding an egg, was classified as the first degree of heat by the medical and chemical systematiser, Herman Boerhaave (1669–1738). See John C. Powers, 'Measuring Fire: Herman Boerhaave and the Introduction of Thermometry into Chemistry', *Osiris* 29 (2014), issue on 'Chemical Knowledge in the Early Modern World', ed. Seymour Mauskopf, Bill Newman and Matthew Eddy.
19. On different sorts of blood, see for example the recipes in the collection written down in the Monastery of Tegernsee in the fourteenth and fifteenth centuries: Anna Bartl, Christoph Krekel, Manfred Lautenschalger, Doris Oltrogge, *Der 'Liber illuministarum' aus Kloster Tegernsee* (Stuttgart: Franz Steiner Verlag, 2005), and especially the discussion by Christoph Krekel and Manfred Lautenschlager, 'Bearbeitung von Glas, Edelstein, Bein und Horn', 675.
20. I treat this in Pamela H. Smith 'Vermilion, Mercury, Blood, and Lizards: Matter and Meaning in Metalworking', in *Materials and Expertise in Early Modern Europe: Between Market and Laboratory,* ed. Ursula Klein and Emma Spary (University of Chicago Press, 2010), 29–49.
21. Joannes Jonstonus, *A History of the Wonderful Things of Nature* (London: John Streater, 1657), 92. My thanks to Daniel Margócsy for this reference.
22. 'Kermes' comes from the Arabic/Persian word for red or carmine, *qirmiz,* derived from the Sanskrit *krimija,* meaning 'worm-made', indicating the widespread significance and movement of this colour. Most red dye in India and Southeast Asia was produced from the lac beetle. Elena Phipps, 'Cochineal Red: The Art History of a Color', *The Metropolitan Museum of Art Bulletin* 47.3 (2009), 8–9.
23. Kermes and cochineal are members of the same superfamily of the Coccoidea beetle, Phipps, 'Cochineal Red', 14 and 17.
24. Daniel V. Thompson, Jr., 'Artificial Vermilion in the Middle Ages', *Technical Studies in the Field of the Fine Arts* 2 (1933–1934): 62–70.
25. Albertus Magnus, *Book of Minerals,* thirteenth century, trans. Dorothy Wyckoff (Oxford: Clarendon Press, 1967), 81.
26. John Gage, 'Colour Words in the High Middle Ages', in *Looking through Paintings: The Study of Painting Techniques and Materials in Support of Art Historical Research (Leids*

Kunsthistorisch Jaarboek XI), ed. Erma Hermens (Baarn, The Netherlands: Uitgeverij de Prom, 1998), 39.

27. See Caroline Walker Bynum, *Wonderful Blood: Theology and Practice in Late Medieval Northern Germany and Beyond* (Philadelphia: University of Pennsylvania Press, 2007), esp. chs. 7 and 8.
28. Theophilus, *The Various Arts*, 189–190. The recipe strives for a tone that would indicate that the practice comes out of experience even when it in fact goes back millennia more or less unchanged at least to Pliny, *Natural History*, book 37 (The Natural History of Precious Stones), ch. 15 (Adamas). Berthold Laufer, *The Diamond: A Study in Chinese and Hellenistic Folk-Lore*, Anthropological Series, vol. 15.1 (Chicago: Field Museum of Natural History, 1915), pub. 184, 16n1, 23–5, recounts the philological evidence for this story passing from Pliny to the Physiologus (second to fourth century CE) to India and from there to Fu-nan and from Fu-nan to China, where it is recorded by the fourth-century Daoist adept Ge Hong.
29. Kurt Nassau, *Gemstone Enhancement* (London: Butterworths, 1984), 10.
30. Albertus Magnus, *Libellus de alchimia*, fourteenth century (first printed 1561), trans. Virginia Heines, S.C.N. (Berkeley and Los Angeles: University of California Press, 1958), notes on p. 19 that gold stimulates heat and life.
31. Just one example comes from the anonymous 'Goldsmith's Storehouse', *c.*1604, f. 55r: ch. 25.
32. For examples of pigment recipes in which red and gold are associated, see Spike Bucklow, 'Paradigms and Pigment Recipes: Vermilion, Synthetic Yellows and the Nature of Egg', *Zeitschrift für Kunsttechnologie und Konservierung* 13 (1999), 145–147.
33. Cennini, *Il libro*, 'Mosaic gold', 101–2.
34. Arie Wallert, 'Alchemy and Medieval Art Technology', in *Alchemy Revisited*, ed. Z.R.W.M. von Martels (Leiden: Brill, 1990), 158–159.
35. See Smith 'Vermilion, Mercury, Blood, and Lizards'.
36. Anonymous, *Rechter Gebrauch der Alchimei*, f. 13. See also Theophilus, *Various Arts*, 119–120. There is a great deal of discussion of this recipe by historians of alchemy. The most recent contribution to this debate is Robert Halleux's view that it is based on Arabic recipes, perhaps part of the Jabirian corpus. Robert Halleux, 'The Reception of Arabic Alchemy in the West', in *Encyclopedia of the History of Arabic Science*, ed. Roshdi Rashed (London: Routledge, 1996), vol. 3, 887–888.
37. See Pamela Smith, *Body of the Artisan*, 117–123. Modern scientists are still interested in lizards: geckos, which can amputate their own tails at will in order to distract predators, are now being studied for the insight that they give into neurons that make up central pattern generators in the spinal cord. 'The Tail of a Gecko Has Life of Its Own', *New York Times*, 9 September 2009. The all-female species of whiptail lizards can reproduce without males and maintain a high level of genetic variation, 'Puzzle Solved: How a Fatherless Lizard Species Maintains Its Genetic Diversity', *New York Times*, 23 February 2010, D3.
38. Such a vernacular science has also been discussed as an 'indigenous knowledge system' and a '*savoir prolétaire*'. For example, *Indigenous Knowledge Systems and Development*, ed. David Brokensha, D.M. Warren, and Oswald Werner (Washington, DC: University Press of America, 1980); Helen Watson-Verran and David Turbull, 'Science and Other Indigenous Knowledge Systems'. For savoir prolétaire, see: Florike Egmond, 'Natuurlijke historie en savoir prolétaire', in *Kometen, Monsters en Muilezels. Het Veranderende Natuurbeeld en de Natuurwetenschap in de Zeventiende Eeuw*, ed. Florike Egmond, Eric Jorink, and Rienk Vermij (Haarlem: Uitgeverij Arcadia, 1999), 53–71. See also Clifford Geertz, *Local Knowledge. Further Essays in Interpretive Anthropology* (New York: Basic Books, 1983), 73–93; and Steven Shapin, 'Proverbial Economies: How an Understanding of Some Linguistic and Social Features of Common Sense Can Throw Light on More Prestigious Bodies of Knowledge, Science for Example', *Social Studies of Science* 31.5 (2001): 731–769.

39. Some of what follows is drawn from Pamela H. Smith, 'Knowledge in Motion: Following Itineraries of Matter in the Early Modern World', in *Cultures in Motion*, ed. Daniel Rogers, Bhavani Raman, Helmut Reimitz (Princeton: Princeton University Press, 2014), 109–133.
40. Quoted in Albertus, *Book of Minerals*, xxviii.
41. Albertus, *Book of Minerals*, 153.
42. Albertus, *Book of Minerals*, 212: the 'manufacturers of minium [by which he means cinnabar] make it by subliming sulfur with quicksilver'. Albertus never travelled to the Iberian peninsula, and his remarks about the extraction of mercury from cinnabar ore (a process he might have observed in the Iberian mines) are not derived from first-hand observation. Ibid., 207–208.
43. Another translator added a preface to his text, which announced, '[A]s your Latin world does not yet know what alchemy is and what its composition is, I will clarify it in the present text'. Halleux, 'Reception of Arabic Alchemy', 890–891.
44. See Georges C. Anawati, 'Arabic Alchemy', in *Encyclopedia of the History of Arabic Science* (New York: Routledge, 1996), ed. Roshdi Rashed, vol. 3, 853–885, and Halleux, 'Reception of Arabic Alchemy'.
45. A point made by Wallert, 'Alchemy and Medieval Art Technology', 155.
46. Albertus Magnus, *The Book of Secrets of Albertus Magnus of the Virtues of Herbs, Stones and Certain Beasts. Also A Book of the Marvels of the World*, late thirteenth-century, 1530 English translation, ed. Michael R. Best and Frank H. Brightman (Oxford: Clarendon Press, 1973), 104.
47. Edgar Thurston, *Omens and Superstitions of Southern India* (New York: McBride, Nast & Co., 1915). My thanks to Robert Goulding for this reference and for allowing me to read his lecture 'Snakes in a Flame', in manuscript.
48. With deep thanks to my colleague Dorothy Ko. ''Xi yi 蜥蜴 are also called yan yan 蝘蜓. If you keep it in a vessel and feed it cinnabar (*zhu sha*), its body will turn all red. After it has ingested seven *jin* of cinnabar, pound it into a pulp by ten thousand smashes with a pestle. Dot it on a woman's limbs and body and it will glow without extinguishing. If she has sexual intercourse, then it would extinguish. Therefore, it is called *shou gong* 守宮 (guard chamber)'.
49. Marshall G.S. Hodgson, *Rethinking World History*, ed. Edmund Burke (Cambridge: Cambridge University Press, 1993), 17.
50. A how-to manual on horse training for chariot use exists in cuneiform on a clay tablet from the fourteenth century BCE. *Beyond Babylon: Art, Trade, and Diplomacy in the Second Millennium B.C.*, Metropolitan Museum exhibition catalogue, 18 November 2008–15 March 2009, ed. Joan Aruz, Kim Benzel and Jean M. Evans (New Haven: Yale University Press, 2008), 158.
51. Joseph Needham, Ho Ping-Yü, Lu Gwei-Djen, and Wang Ling, *Science and Civilisation in China.* Vol. 5, Part 7: *Chemistry and Chemical Technology. Military Technology* (Cambridge: Cambridge University Press, 1986), 17. See also Nanny Kim, 'Cultural Attitudes and Horse Technologies: A View on Chariots and Stirrups from the Eastern End of the Eurasian Continent', in *Science Between Europe and Asia*, ed. Feza Günergrun and Dhruv Raina (Heidelberg: Springer, 2011), 57–73.
52. Arnold Pacey, *Technology in World Civilisation: A Thousand-Year History* (Cambridge, MA: MIT Press, 1991), 73. See also, Christopher Cullen, 'Reflections on the Transmission and Transformation of Technologies: Agriculture, Printing and Gunpowder between East and West', in *Science Between Europe and Asia*, 18–21. The source of much information about gunpowder remains Needham, Ho, *et al.*, *Science and Civilisation, Vol. 5, Part 7*.
53. Thomas T. Allsen, *The Royal Hunt in Eurasian History* (Philadelphia: University of Pennsylvania Press, 2006).
54. Andrea Bréard, 'Problems of Pursuit: Recreational Mathematics or Astronomy?', in *From China to Paris: 2000 Years of Transmission of Mathematical Ideas*, ed. Yvonne

Dold-Samplonius, Joseph W. Dauben, Menso Folkerts, Benno van Dalen (Stuttgart: Franz Steiner Verlag, 2002), 57, 65–67.

55. Alfred W. Crosby, *The Columbian Exchange: Biological and Cultural Consequences of 1492* (Westport, CT: Praeger Publishers, [1st edn 1972] 2003), 199 (peanut); 200 (sweet potato); and 189 (maize).

56. Robert M. Hartwell, 'Foreign Trade, Monetary Policy and Chinese Mercantilism', in *Collected Studies on Sung History Dedicated to James T.C. Liu in Celebration of His Seventieth Birthday*, ed. Kinugawa Tsuyoshi (Kyoto: Dohosha, 1989), 469 and 474. My thanks to Nicola di Cosmo for this reference.

57. Hartwell, 'Foreign Trade', 479, records dragon's blood for this purpose rendered as tribute during the Southern Song; and Schafer states that during the Tang it was used as an astringent drug and prescribed for hemorrhages. Edward H. Schafer, *The Golden Peaches of Samarkand: A Study of T'ang Exotics* (Berkeley: University of California Press, 1963), 211.

58. Schafer, *Golden Peaches of Samarkand*, 219.

59. http://collections.vam.ac.uk/item/O69504/ewer-unknown/ (accessed 7 January 2015).

60. Hartwell, 'Foreign Trade', 458.

61. Tha'ālibī, *The Book of Curious and Entertaining Information: The Latā'if al-ma'ārif of Tha'ālibī*, trans. with introd. and notes C.E. Bosworth (Edinburgh: Edinburgh University Press, 1968), 140. Jonathan Bloom argues persuasively that Tha'ālibī's paper-making genealogy cannot be true because paper had already been employed before 751 in Central Asia, but this does not change the fact that prisoners were regarded as valuable repositories of technique. A single line of diffusion need not be established for this and other techniques. Jonathan Bloom, *Paper Before Print: The History and Impact of Paper in the Islamic World* (New Haven: Yale University Press, 2001), 8–9, 42–43.

62. Quoted in Ahmad Yousif Al-Hassan, 'Chemical Technology in Arabic Military Treatises', in *From Deferent to Equant: A Volume of Studies in the History of Science in the Ancient and Medieval Near East in Honor of E.S. Kennedy*, ed. David A. King and George Saliba (New York: New York Academy of Sciences, 1987), 153–166.

63. Hartwell, 'Foreign Trade', 466–468.

64. Another example of this dynamic is around 1500, when racialized hierarchies of caste and *casta* emerged together with truly global linkages and exchange. C.A. Bayly, '"Archaic" and "Modern" Globalization in the Eurasian and African Arena, *ca.* 1750–1850', in *Globalization in World History*, ed. A.G. Hopkins (London: Pimlico, 2002), 55.

65. In 1937–9, a French expedition to Begram, in the lands of ancient Bactria, unearthed two walled-up storerooms of transit trade goods, probably seized by the Kushan kings before 250 CE. The stores included Indian ivory objects and Chinese lacquer-ware going west and bronze and glass vessels of Syria and Alexandria going east. Joseph Needham, Ho Ping-Yü, Lu Gwei-Djen, *Science and Civilisation in China. Vol. 5, Part. 4: Spagyrical Discovery and Invention: Apparatus, Theories and Gifts* (Cambridge: Cambridge University Press, 1980), 414–15 note h.

66. See Daniel T. Potts, 'Technological Transfer and Innovation in Ancient Eurasia', in *The Globalization of Knowledge in History*, ed. Jürgen Renn (Berlin: Edition Open Access, 2012), ch. 4.

67. Bayly, '"Archaic" and "Modern" Globalization', 50–51.

68. Bayly, '"Archaic" and "Modern" Globalization', 52–53.

69. Joseph Needham and Lu Gwei-Djen, *Science and Civilisation in China. Vol. 6, Part 6: Medicine*, ed. Nathan Sivin (Cambridge: Cambridge University Press, 2000), 38–45. See also Geoffrey Lloyd and Nathan Sivin, *The Way and the Word: Science and Medicine in Early China and Greece* (New Haven: Yale University Press, 2002). Lloyd and Sivin see great differences in basic concepts used to articulate ideas about nature in ancient Greece and China, stating that the Greeks focused on 'nature and the elements, the Chinese on *ch'i*, yin-yang, the five phases, and the Way'. Ibid., 6.

70. The trade in precious stones was carried on as far back at the very least as 4000 BCE, when a gem market is recorded in Babylon. India has exported diamonds, sapphires, and

rubies at least since 400 BCE. The alluvial deposits of Sri Lanka and Madagascar have also long been a source of precious gems: Webster Anderson, *Gems: Their Sources, Descriptions, and Identification* (Washington DC: Butterworths, 4th edn 1983). Berthold Laufer argues that the view that wonders originated in India emerged out of an aristocratic Arabic-Persian milieu (Laufer, *The Diamond*, p. 11). Muzaffar Alam and Sanjay Subrahmanyam, *Indo-Persian Travels in the Age of Discoveries, 1400–1800* (Cambridge: Cambridge University Press, 2007), note that medieval travel literature the world over includes 'wonders' or 'aja'ib', which are marvels, astonishing things or 'mirabilia' (p. 4), most often told in first-person narrative. For the European literature on wonders, see Lorraine Daston and Katherine Park, *Wonders and the Order of Nature, 1150–1750* (New York: Zone Books, 1998), in which they recount that the very first of 129 wonders which Gervase of Tilbury lists in his 1210 *Otia imperialia* is the magnet, 'an Indian stone', with the property of attracting iron (p. 21). William of Auvergne (*ca*.1180?–1249) wrote that 'in parts of India and other adjoining regions, there is a great quantity of things of this sort [i.e., wonders], and on account of this, natural magic particularly flourishes there'. Ibid., 75.

71. Buzurg ibn Shariyar, *Kitab 'ajayib al-Hind*, Arab text with French trans. L. Marcel Devic (Leiden: Brill, 1883–1886), pp. 47 ff and 120 ff.

72. ibn Shariyar, *Kitab 'ajayib al-Hind*, 157 and 173.

73. ibn Shariyar, *Kitab 'ajayib al-Hind*, 7–8.

74. ibn Shariyar, *Kitab 'ajayib al-Hind*, 171. Muhammad ibn Ahmad Bīrūnī's (973?–1048) *Kitab al-Hind* (Book of India) has a very different tone than these books of wonders. Although he mentions oddities, such as 'in shaking hands they grasp the hand of a man from the convex side', and 'they spit out and blow their noses without any respect for the elder ones present, and they crack their lice before them', and 'in playing chess they move the elephant straight on' (vol. 1, 182), and he relates several examples of charms, but concludes that 'most of their charms are intended for those who have been bitten by serpents', about which he says 'I, for my part, do not know what I am to say about these things, since I do not believe in them' (vol. 1, 194). And, about the people in India in general: 'in all manners and usages they differ from us to such a degree as to frighten their children with us, with our dress, and our ways, and customs, and as to declare us to be devil's breed, and our doings as the very opposite of all that is good and proper. By the bye, we must confess, in order to be just, that a similar depreciation of foreigners not only prevails among us and the Hindus, but is common to all nations towards each other' (vol. 1, 20). Edward C. Sachau, *Alberuni's India*, 2 vols. (London: Trübner & Co., 1888. Facs. repr. Elibron Classics, Adamant Media, 2005).

75. Berthold Laufer's pioneering philological research on folk beliefs, such as *The Diamond*, and 'The Story of the Pinna and the Syrian Lamb', *Journal of American Folk-Lore*, 28 (1915): 103–128; and 'Asbestos and Salamander', *T'oung Pao*, 2nd series, 16.3 (1915): 299–373 shows just how ancient some of these tales are, as well as tracing the remarkable accretions which they acquired as they moved over time and space. The three mentioned here trace 'exotic' concepts and objects back to the Hellenistic-Roman East, whence, he argues, they spread throughout Eurasia. Aesop's fables were told along the Silk Roads.

76. Dagmar Schaefer has pointed out to me that in asserting the similarities in value and meaning of red and vermilion in Europe and China, it is easy to overstate the importance of the red/gold/lizard complex in China. The most important symbol of transformation may not have been this quasi-alchemical complex, but rather the silk worm.

77. 'To certain Ming thinkers, "number" was diminished by its constant propensity to act as a stable referent, guaranteeing fixed meanings for visible phenomena. It thus claimed to figure a world at a level unworthy of serious philosophical or aesthetic attention'. Craig Clunas, 'Number and Numerology in China in the Fifteenth and Sixteenth Centuries', in *History of Science, History of Text*, ed. Karine Chemla (Boston: Kluwer Academic, 2004), 118.

78. Thomas T. Allsen, *Culture and Conquest in Mongol Eurasia* (Cambridge: Cambridge University Press, 2001), 176–211. Cullen, 'Reflections on Transmission and Transformation', also provides insight into structural constraints that determined technology use and movement.

79. Needham and Lu, *Science and Civilisation. Vol. 5, Part 3*, 6.
80. Needham and Lu, *Science and Civilisation. Vol. 5, Part 2*, 69.
81. Mosaic gold was being made in China at the time Ge Hong wrote. Needham and Lu, *Science and Civilisation. Vol. 5, Part 2*, 271.
82. Needham and Lu, *Science and Civilisation. Vol. 5, Part 2*, 67. For this reason gold could be found below cinnabar deposits.
83. Needham and Lu, *Science and Civilisation. Vol. 5, Part 2*, fig. 1335, plates.
84. Needham and Lu, *Science and Civilisation. Vol. 5, Part 3*, 3.
85. Fabrizio Pregadio, *Great Clarity: Daoism and Alchemy in Early Medieval China* (Stanford: Stanford University Press, 2006), 30. He also makes clear that the earliest alchemical texts show that the performance of rites is part of alchemical practices from their earliest recorded mention. Ibid., 31.
86. Needham and Lu, *Science and Civilisation. Vol. 5, Part 2*, 286.
87. Indeed, in *c.*800 CE, mention is made of mercury and cinnabar being used to fabricate gold vessels, but these are regarded as poisonous. Does this perhaps indicate the influence of Arabic books on poisons? Needham and Lu, *Science and Civilisation. Vol. 5, Part 2*, 243.
88. Needham and Lu, *Science and Civilisation. Vol. 5, Part 13: Mining*, ed. Peter Golas (Cambridge: Cambridge University Press, 1999), 149.
89. Needham and Lu, *Science and Civilisation. Vol. 5, Part 3*, 128.
90. Needham and Lu, *Science and Civilisation. Vol. 5, Part 3*, 4–5.
91. Needham and Lu, *Science and Civilisation. Vol. 5, Part 3*, 126. Pregadio, *Great Clarity*, makes clear that alchemy was never just about producing materials, but always aimed at higher enlightenment through the process of producing these materials.
92. Emilie Savage-Smith, 'Exchange of Medical and Surgical Ideas', 35.
93 Needham, Ho and Lu, *Science and Civilisation. Vol. 5, Part 4*, pp. 437 ff. And see various other parts of Volume 5 for the use of salts in gunpowder, glaze production, etc.
94. Ibid., 438–39, who relies upon Julius Ruska, 'Der Salmiak in der Geschichte der Alchemie', *Zeitsch. für angewandte Chemie*, 41 (1928), 1321, and *Forschungen and Fortschritte* 4 (1928), 232.
95. Ibid., 435–436.
96. Sami K. Hamarneh, 'Arabic-Islamic Alchemy – Three Intertwined Stages', *Ambix* 29 (1982), 79. See this article for further examples of Chinese influence on Arabic alchemy, and its relationship to Europe up through the sixteenth century.
97. Needham, Ho and Lu, *Science and Civilisation. Vol. 5, Part 4*, 452.
98. Needham, Ho and Lu, *Science and Civilisation. Vol. 5, Part 4*, make this point in their section on China and the Arabic world, 388 ff. See also, *Chau Ju-Kua: His Work on the Chinese and Arab Trade in the Twelfth and Thirteenth Centuries, entitled* Chi-fan-chï, trans. and ed. Friedrich Hirth and W.W. Rockhill (Amsterdam: Oriental Press, 1966). The earliest Arab narratives about trade with China date from the ninth century. Ibid., 15.
99. Needham, Ho and Lu, *Science and Civilisation. Vol. 5, Part 4*, 398.
100. Pacey, *Technology in World Civilization*, emphasizes the importance of stimulus, response, and dialogue in the dynamics of technology 'transfer'.
101. In common with George Sarton's attempt to show the ecumenical origins of modern science, nineteenth and early twentieth-century scholars such as Julius Ruska undertook extensive study of Arabic alchemy.
102. Halleux, 'Reception of Arabic Alchemy in the West', 886.
103. Thompson, 'Artificial Vermilion'.

2

TOWARDS A GLOBAL HISTORY OF SHAGREEN

Christine Guth

Between 1600 and 1800 the allure of shagreen – leather made from shark and rayskin – had a significant impact on material culture in many parts of the world. Both practical and decorative, it satisfied the need for a material that was easily graspable and waterproof, but also had visual appeal. Although fish leather had been used since ancient times, this era saw a surge in its application to a new range of goods including weapons, scientific instruments, lacquered chests, luggage, eyeglass and watch cases, and other personal accessories.[1] Today, ongoing global demand for shagreen, a legacy of the cachet it first assumed during the early modern era, has resulted in many species of ray becoming endangered, their future uncertain. This chapter explores the trade in shark and, especially, rayskin, drawing particular attention to the way this commonplace natural product was positioned globally as a luxury commodity as a consequence of the flourishing of trade across the Atlantic, Indian and Pacific Oceans. My chief reference point is Japan, a major importer of the skins, producer of luxury goods using them, and, as I will argue, catalyst for their fashionable new applications in Europe.

What is at stake here is not simply a question of supplementarity, adding information about a previously overlooked commodity and the goods crafted from it, but rather an understanding of the complex commercial, material, and symbolic networks in which shagreen's circulation was implicated. Shark and rayskin were commodities fished expressly for sale in distant markets, and Dutch entry into the lucrative Japanese market stimulated massive and systematic harvesting of the most desirable species at various points along their trade route, but especially along the east coasts of India and Thailand. It also brought the Dutch into competition with Chinese merchants who had previously dominated the regional trade. But most significantly for this study, building on the Portuguese trade in exotic Japanese lacquerwares made using rayskin, the Dutch drew attention to the physical properties and aesthetic attractions of this material in Holland, England and France, setting in place fashion for its use that continues to this day. In proposing this study as a global history, I am painfully aware that there remain many gaps in the written and material record. While Dutch and Japanese sources are richly informative regarding the trade, crafting and uses of shark and rayskin, documentation for other parts of the global network is much sparser. In seeking to impose global coherence on this study, however, my aim is not to suggest that shagreen was used uniformly everywhere but rather to provide a framework for examining it as a nexus of a complex multi-directional network involving both intensive and extensive global development with significant local variations.

Ray and sharkskin were not materials that could simply sell themselves. As Igor Kopytoff observed in his essay on the cultural biography of things:

> commodities must be not only produced materially as things, but also culturally marked as being a certain kind of thing. Out of the total range of things available in a society, only some of them are considered appropriate for marking as commodities. Moreover, the same thing may be treated as a commodity at one time and not at another. And finally, the same thing may at the same time, be seen as a commodity by one person and something else as another.[2]

These points are worth keeping in mind in mapping the history of shagreen. Aquatic leather was not just a global commercial phenomenon, but the product of specific communities that brought highly variable local cultural values to its crafting, applications, and consumption. People the world over have a complex range of symbolic relationships with the natural world that may have little to do with its material reality. The fact that consumers in many parts of the world found shagreen desirable during the same period does not mean that they did so for the same reasons. There were, to be sure, functional continuities, since aquatic leather was invariably adopted as a means of covering, protecting, and/or embellishing a substrate, but local circumstances dictated the techniques, forms, styles, fashions and symbolism with which it became associated. In every instance, however, the exchange value of fish leather involved its reconceptualization as a cultural rather than a natural product, a process inextricably bound up with the language used to describe it. Prejudices owing to the physical properties of rays and sharks meant that it was especially important to distinguish their skins through the representational processes of language, craftsmanship and design.

Shark, ray and shagreen

Shark and ray, along with skate, are cartilaginous fish distinguished by a tough outer skin made up of collagenous fibres rather than a bony skeleton.[3] They further differ from bony fish in that they breathe in water through a special hole just behind each eye, instead of through the mouth, and they breathe it out again through gills on each side of the head. Bottom feeders, their mouth is not at the end of the snout but beneath it. Rather than flat scales, their skins, rough enough to use in sandpapering wood and grating horseradish, are covered with small projections known as dermal denticles, since they are formed from the same pulpy centre and enamel covering as teeth. The connective fibres of ray and shark skin are long and densely interwoven, like fabric, making it easy to work with when wet. Leather made from it is thick yet flexible, and much more durable than that made from quadrupeds.[4] More significantly, it is waterproof, and its grainy surface makes it more easily grasped, and therefore well suited to the protective covering of instruments and containers used in battle, for food, and at sea.

To prepare the leather, the fish skin was soaked in warm water for several days, the flesh removed, and then dried, a process described in detail in the *Kōi Seigi* 鮫皮精義 or *Discourse on the Spirit of Shagreen*, an eighteenth-century Japanese text by Inaba Tsūryū, an Osaka merchant.[5] Beyond this basic preparation, however, the skins could be treated in various ways. In Japan, the projecting nodules were left intact when the skin was intended for covering sword and dagger hilts, but ground down when it was to be embedded in lacquer. The nodule-like denticles were also removed altogether and sprinkled decoratively on the surface of wet lacquer in the same manner as the gold and silver particles used in making decorative pictorial *makie*. This sprinkled technique, known as *togidashi samenuri*, was the norm in the manufacture of so-called Namban coffers made for export to Europe in the late sixteenth and early seventeenth centuries. The leather was not usually dyed in Japan, although it was sometimes bleached to bring out its whiteness.[6] In Europe the projecting nodules were ground down by mechanical means to reveal the distinctive dermal pattern formed by the triangular or rhomboid shapes of the denticles. The size and shape of the dermal pattern is age- and species-specific and may be brought out by dyeing. As the hard cartilaginous residue of the denticle and the softer collagenous skin absorb pigment differently, the surface takes on an attractively variegated appearance. Green mineral pigment made from *terre verte* (glauconite) was probably used for this purpose, and this was sometimes covered with a layer of lacquer (*vernis martin*) to heighten the sheen.[7] The appeal of shagreen in Europe was closely bound up with the way the translucent skin absorbs colour, but in Japan, its whiteness was the measure of value.

Predatory shark and ray are part of the marine eco-systems of all oceans. A woodcut illustration and the accompanying text in Pierre Belon's book on fish about the species of shark known as *chien de mer, rousette* or in English, dogfish, testifies that by 1550 the skin of this common Atlantic species was already known as both an abrasive in furniture making and as a protective covering for swords and daggers.[8] Later, however, craftsmen in both Europe and Japan sought the skins of non-native species, especially those of ray most populous in the Red Sea, Indian and South Pacific Oceans. Views on the species favoured in each region vary widely. In his *Industries of Japan* (1889), J.J. Rein asserts that several species of the *rhinobatus armatus* were employed for *samegawa-nuri*, the generic Japanese term for lacquer to which rayskin has been applied.[9] Charles Stevenson, author of a standard source on the utilization of the skins of aquatic animals, asserts that Parisian manufacturers used a species of Malabar shark, Turkish craftsmen the skin of the angel shark found in the Mediterranean, and the makers of German swords diamond sharks common in the

North Sea.[10] Whitehead, meanwhile, asserts that true French shagreen, or galuchat as it came to be known, was made from the skin of *dasyatis sephen*, a stingray with a range from the Red Sea to the Indian Ocean distinguished by its size and very tight pattern of nodules, although other rays, sharks and dogfishes were also used.[11] There are many varieties within the *dasyatis* family, but the *daysatis sephen* is the largest, sometimes weighing 250 kilos and measuring 1 metre 75 across. In Japan, accord-ing to Kanako Morinaka, the preferred species for sword hilts was the *trigon sephen*, whose skins were imported from South-east Asia.[12] All these claims need to be read with caution, however, since once the skins have been treated, species identification is extremely difficult, even under magnification.[13]

Linguistic ambiguity further compounds the problems of identification because in Europe and Japan alike, textual references do not always distinguish clearly between shark and ray or their skins. This is partly due to the fact that on the basis of observation alone it is sometimes difficult to distinguish between these two carti-laginous fish. In Japan the term *same* (or *fuka* in the region around Kyoto and Osaka) has commonly been used for both.[14] The same homology is true of shagreen, and its Dutch and French variants *segryn* and *chagrin*. The origins of the term shagreen, by which the treated fish skin has been known since at least the seventeenth cen-tury, add a further level of epistemological complexity. It derives from the Persian *saghari* or the Turkish *sagri*, which refers to a type of untanned horse leather into which mustard seeds have been pressed to produce an attractively granular texture that somewhat resembles treated shark and rayskin. In the Persian and Ottoman worlds, this was commonly dyed green and used to make footwear. The decora-tive border of green equine shagreen or its imitation in footwear worn in Central Asia and China well into the nineteenth century may be a legacy of this tradi-tion.[15] The Turkish scholar Esin Atul has suggested that *sagri* developed in imitation of sharkskin on the basis of three unusual examples of embroidered sharkskin – on a Koran binding, a large rectangular box, and a tankard – all likely to have been made in the same mid-sixteenth-century Istanbul studio that served the court of Suleyman. These elaborately embroidered objects in the Topkapi collection are unique, however, and do not resemble the kind of blue-green horsehide commonly designated as *sagri* or shagreen in Europe.[16] Nonetheless, I concur with Atul's sug-gestion that the catalyst for this Ottoman experimentation with sharkskin was the introduction of decorative goods from South and East Asia, a development that speaks to the way global trade in this commodity and the artefacts made from it in the sixteenth century spurred production of distinctive local products.

The introduction to Europe of the term *shagreen* seems to have been one of the inadvertent results of the conjunction of two products with physical similarities. Given that fine leather goods of many kinds from the Ottoman world were in circulation in Europe before the development of trade with South and East Asia in the second half of the sixteenth century, it is likely that the term shagreen first came into use to refer to imported equine leather and was only later applied to its aquatic counterpart. The diaries of English travellers to the Ottoman and Per-sian empires testify to the former usage. Abel Pincon, the companion of Anthony Sherley, a well-known English traveller to Persia, writing around 1600, refers to a town about ten days' distance from Tabriz where artisans made 'the best shoes in the whole country out of segrin [shagreen] in green, white and other colours', and later references as well as extant examples of green shoes make clear that this was a grainy horse leather.[17]

The material and linguistic relationships established through multidirectional global trade transformed expectations, uses, and understandings of shark and rayskin in many regions, in ways that shaped and reflected the economic agendas of each particular consumer community. Whether by accident or design, European adoption of the term shagreen to refer to fish leather, as well as the practice of dyeing it green, seems to have capitalized on the cachet of an already established import with similar textural qualities. This exotic nomenclature, which became widespread in the eighteenth century, may have helped to mitigate prejudices against shark and ray. Not only are these fearsome fish predatory bottom feeders, they are also marine scavengers. Another factor that might have contributed to an aversion to them is the ammoniac smell the dead flesh emits, a consequence of the breakdown of the chemical substance, urea, that fish of this family use to control osmotic balance (water leaching out from their bodies and vice versa).[18] Such powerful sensorial factors may explain the slower take-up of fish shagreen in Europe, where leather made from quadrupeds being readily available, there was a choice of resources. This situation was in contrast to Japan, where necessity dictated the use of shark and ray-skin since ancient times; its application to sword hilts reputedly followed Chinese precedent, dating from the second century CE.[19] In either event, while initially craftsmen in both Europe and Japan seem to have been content with local sourcing, interregional and global trade in the late sixteenth and seventeenth centuries vastly expanded their options.

Portuguese trade goods

Shagreen first became a marker of luxury not in its semi-processed natural state, but through its application to lacquerwares imported from Japan, and introduced to Europe in the late sixteenth century by Portuguese traders. Both the look and feel of lacquer meant that European consumers were willing to go to great lengths to acquire goods made of it. Initially, the circulation of lacquer goods made to Portuguese taste (commonly referred to as Namban, 'southern barbarian' style) was restricted to Europe's aristocratic elite and the churches they patronized. Of these goods, only a small percentage incorporated shagreen into their décor.[20] These lacquers are in the form of domestic furnishings whose shapes and functions were familiar but whose décor satisfied the fashion for the exotic that had come to occupy an increasingly important place in the lifestyles of the European elite. One prevalent type in the late sixteenth and early seventeenth centuries is a large rectangular coffer with domed lid probably intended to hold clothing or bedding. Because the container resembles *kamaboko*, a kind of fish paste sausage with that shape, it has come to be referred to in the scholarly literature by the Japanese term *kamaboko-bako* (Figure 2.1). Another is a smaller cabinet with hinged doors and inset drawers known in Portuguese as

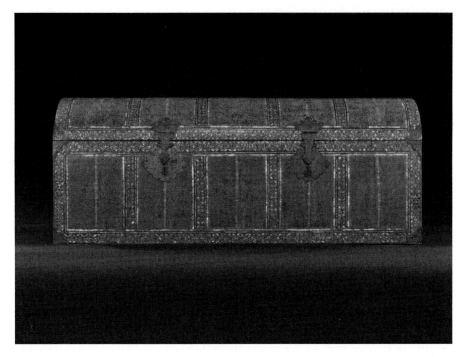

FIGURE 2.1 Japanese lacquer coffer with domed lid (*Kamaboko-bako*), early seventeenth century. Lacquered wood with rayskin and mother of pearl with gilt metal mounts. H. 58 cm; L. 144.5 cm; W. 50.5 cm. Private collection. Photo courtesy Jorge Welsh.

vento thought to have been intended for jewellery and other precious objects.[21] Both were equipped with handles for portability. Production of shagreen-covered chests seems to have ceased in the 1640s, when the Dutch secured a monopoly on European trade with Japan, possibly because this style of furniture fell out of favour, or for the economic reasons discussed below. An eighteenth-century cabinet mounted on a stand now in the Rijksmuseum made from lacquered shagreen panels that were recycled from a coffer speaks to the way that such valuable but outmoded styles might be refashioned to suit changing tastes.[22]

Whatever its size or shape, such furniture was formed from a wood substrate covered with layers of lacquer and other materials to reinforce and create surface uniformity. Because of its durability and high gloss, lacquer was the medium of choice in Japan for home furnishings of many kinds, and craftsmen readily adapted their techniques to the demands of foreign ones. While lacquer impregnated with black and polished to a high sheen was appreciated on its own terms in Japan, *makie*, the finest quality lacquerware, was generally embellished with pictorial and geometric motifs fashioned from a variety of precious materials including gold and silver, and other metals as well as mother of pearl. There is no evidence that shagreen was applied to Japanese domestic furnishings, although it had a long tradition of use in weaponry. Its adaptation for export goods likely came about in response to practical and economic considerations. Furniture made for export tended to be larger in size than those articles used in the Japanese context, and using sprinkled rayskin denticles was less labour intensive and costly than the pictorial décor and sprinkled gold of *makie*, whose shimmering effects the *togidashi samenuri* technique mimicked. Japanese craftsmen and the merchants who mediated the sale of goods for export developed a keen understanding of their market and tailored their goods accordingly. European consumers arguably would have been willing to accept this variant style since their expectations were not based on extended familiarity with the particular styles associated with the lacquer medium within Japan. Indeed, it is entirely possible that initially European consumers were not even aware that rayskin was used in the fabrication of Japanese lacquers. The appearance of the term *same* in the Portuguese–Japanese dictionary of 1603, and reference to its use for the sword hilts or scabbards, however, testifies that the Portuguese traders who commissioned these products were familiar with this material and may have had a role in negotiating its adoption.[23]

Although specific artisans cannot be identified, it is likely that the *kamaboko bako* and *vento* commissioned for Portuguese consumption were collective products of workshops rather than of an individual hand. Late sixteenth- and early seventeenth-century lacquer workshops are known to have been concentrated in Kyoto, but there is also evidence of regional production in the Ryukyu Islands.[24] The substitution of a local marine product for imported gold and silver powders may have first developed there. Such a possibility is supported by recent investigations carried out by conservator Ulrike Korber on a lacquer-covered leather shield in the Kunsthistorisches Museum, Vienna first mentioned in the 1596 estate inventory of Archduke Ferdinand II, making it the earliest documented example of an artefact using rayskin imported to Europe from Asia (Figures 2.2a and 2.2b). The shield's exact provenance has long puzzled scholars, but based on the formal language of its décor, which combines animal and floral motifs in gold, as well as the composition of the lacquer itself, it is now thought that the wood and leather support was made in India or Ceylon, then shipped for lacquering to China or the Ryukyu Islands, an archipelago strategically located between Japan's southernmost island of Kyushu and Taiwan. Portuguese contact with goods from the Ryukyu Islands likely began after the capture of Malacca in 1511, and continued into the seventeenth century.[25] The shield's multi-sited manufacture underlines the hybridity of Portuguese trade goods.

The functional and decorative impulses materialized in this shield exist in uneasy tension with one another, and it was likely intended as a display piece rather than an actual weapon. The shield recently featured as an example of the kind of ethnographic material that was collected and displayed by European rulers in their Kunst- and Wunderkammer as evidence of their power and knowledge.[26] However, Mughal miniatures as well as Japanese screen paintings of the arrival and departure of Portuguese ships show figures with such round lacquered shields in

FIGURE 2.2a Rayskin shield with lacquer ornament (front). Japan, *c.*1580. Wood covered with rayskin and decorated with black and gold *makie* lacquer. 54 cm. Kunsthistorisches Museum, Vienna.

FIGURE 2.2b Rayskin shield with lacquer ornament (back).

hand.[27] Although the tough grainy rayskin may have had apotropaic connotations, the sprinkled denticle technique reveals a more aesthetic sensitivity.

This use of the *togidashi samenuri* technique is similar to the styles of decorative treatment of sword and dagger hilts described in detail in the *Kōi seigi*. The simplest kind of material alteration was to add individual denticles to enhance the natural line formed by the skin's dorsal ridge, which was aligned vertically with the length of the sword (Figure 2.3). The decorative pattern could be improved upon further still by the addition of similar nodules formed from bone or other material. The accents in the vertical décor at the centre of the five panels in the coffer illustrated in Figure 2.1 (p. 67) are formed by the addition of mother-of-pearl inserts. Thus the decorative technique in which natural denticles were enhanced by the addition of nodules made from other materials seems to have been shared in the manufacture of both domestic weaponry and export lacquer wares.[28]

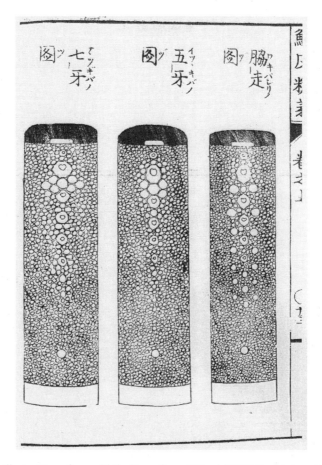

FIGURE 2.3 Illustration of sword hilt décor from *Kōi seigi* (1785), vol. 1, p. 13.

Shagreen in England, Holland and France

The application of shagreen to a range of new articles in the late seventeenth and eighteenth centuries by craftsmen in England, Holland, and France created an expanded, and socially diverse consumer base, and this process intertwined with the construction of larger sets of cultural values and meanings. This new discursive context formed chiefly around its use for scientific instrumentation, for domestic culinary implements, curiosities, and brand name goods. One significant consequence of this development was heightened awareness of shagreen's materiality and tactility.

Shagreen's tactility lent itself well to the growing need for scientific precision while at the same time evoking curiosity about the new worlds that could be explored with both hand and eye. A significant number of microscopes and telescopes had drums covered with shagreen, a protective waterproof coating that also made delicate adjustments with the hand easier to carry out while also transforming a functional instrument into an *objet de vertu*. Aquatic leather seems to have been especially common on those made in London by Edmund Culpeper in the 1720s, but the fashion extended to Holland as well.[29] Even as the display of a shagreen-covered microscope or telescope in the study or library signified the new observational realms of the gentleman naturalist or traveller in the age of enlightenment, so too, shagreen-covered cutlery in the dining room signified the growing instrumentalization of the domestic sphere. Under 'plate' [silver], the inventory of all the household goods belonging to Sir Isaac Newton upon his death in 1727 itemizes the following: '3 silver dishes, 3 salvers, 3 salts, 2 soup spoons, 3 casters, one coffee pot, a pair of candlestick snuffers and pan, seven spoons and forks, 2 silver urinals, and a shagreen case with 12 knives, forks and spoons as well as 12 ivory-handled knives', the total value of which was assessed on the basis of its weight at £101.19.[30] Place settings of the kind owned by Newton were significant personal possessions at a time when table manners were changing and forks rather than fingers were becoming *de rigueur* among the social elite for conveying food from plate to mouth.

Recognition of the advantages of cutlery led to the production of individual knives or knife and fork sets with shagreen-covered handles and sheaths so they could be safely carried during travel. The numerous eighteenth-century examples of such sets made in England, Holland as well as France housed in museum collections today speak to the spread of this manner of eating. A Dutch example in the Victoria and Albert Museum made around 1700 is noteworthy for the way the silver sheet metal used to form the knife handle was stamped to resemble the granulated shagreen of its sheath (Figure 2.4).[31] This doubleness, by mutually intensifying visual and haptic awareness of two very different materials, one mineral and the other animal, underscores the importance of the sensate body in the use of instruments. It also speaks to the way the sensuous feel of shagreen became familiar both as a material and texture across gender, a development further underscored by the introduction in 1714–1715 of broad silk fabrics woven and dyed to resemble shagreen leather.[32] This migration of a functional yet pleasing texture and its connotations from one medium to another has continued into the twenty-first century: in 2006,

Wedgwood introduced a line of dinnerware named Shagreen with a grainy looking pale green border décor inspired by the fashion for and palette of shagreen in Art Deco home furnishings and accessories. In the early modern era, a similar process of translation of the cachet of shagreen to ceramics also occurred in Japan in the form of a glaze known as *samekawa*. It was revived by Shimizu Uichi (d. 2004), a potter known for his experiments in recovering traditional glazes.[33]

Shagreen also took other popular commodified forms. The auction catalogue of all the curiosities and stock in trade of the 'late ingenious Mr. Peter Parquot, Toy Man and Virtuoso' held in London in February 1727–8 includes shagreen pocket books, shagreen scissors, looking glass and razor cases, along with cornelians, agates, onyxes and all sorts of coloured stones and other articles made of gold, silver, ivory, amber, and fine woods.[34] Their classification as curiosities, a term that played upon the connection with the elite cabinet of curiosities, suggests that these were metonymic objects that the public related to through the lens of the exotic. It was not so much regional origin that was at stake here but the perceivable strangeness of the natural material, which lent itself both to aesthetic appreciation and to the pursuit of knowledge. This explosion of enticing, small, and reasonably affordable articles that could be used in daily life made clear that in the eighteenth century, a material that formerly had been a signifier of the rare and elite could be purchased by most anyone.

The popularization of shagreen involved recognition that it could be used to advantage over other forms of leather, but craftsmen also had to design, make, and sell the articles to which it was applied. An entry in *The London Tradesman* indicates that by 1747 shagreen work was a recognized profession in England that 'affords reasonable profits to the maker and salary of 15–16 shillings a week', continuing, 'it requires neither much strength, nor any previous Education; a Youth may be bound to it about Fourteen Years of Age'.[35] The fashion for shagreen also crossed the

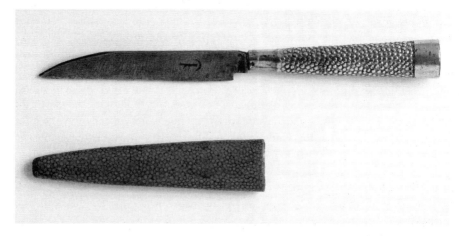

FIGURE 2.4 Knife with handle of sheet silver stamped to resemble shagreen and a case made of shagreen; knife 5.5 in.; *c.*1700; Holland. Victoria and Albert Museum, London. Given by J.H. Fitzhenry 1072&A-1902.

Atlantic: in 1767, a shagreen maker who had set up shop in New York, advertised his services in a local newspaper as follows: 'John Clark, shagreen case maker from London . . . makes and sells all sorts of shagreen cases for knives and forks, both in shagreen and mahogany, and cases for Plate, Lady's Dressing-Boxes, Necklaces and Jewel Cases, Buckle cases and Razor Cases of all Sorts'.[36]

Comparable work was carried out by *segrynwerkers* in Holland and *gaisniers* in France.[37] The latter, however, came to enjoy a prestige that their counterparts elsewhere did not. In France, Galuchat became a brand name that displaced the generic designation shagreen, leaving its French equivalent *chagrin* with only its early connotations as an abrasive, an image that Balzac later evoked in the title of his novel *Peau de Chagrin*. This development owed largely to the success of the Galuchat workshop and, especially, Jean-Claude Galuchat (aka Galluchat; d. 1774), whose family operated a 'boutique de gaisnier' or box covering shop, on the Quai des Morfondus (later Quai de l'Horloge) in Paris. There are no signed or surviving works securely attributed to him, but royal patronage by Madame de Pompadour, mistress to Louis XV, led the name Galuchat to become an index of aristocratic taste and privilege. Noted for her taste for luxury and the exotic, she owned many small etuis and other containers covered in green polished shagreen.[38] Announcements for lost articles in gazettes from the 1760s and 1770s testify that the fashion for shagreen containers for personal possessions such as toothpicks, pencils, and sewing implements went beyond the highest levels of the French aristocracy.[39]

The Galuchat workshop gained a reputation both for skill in dyeing and covering its wares in *vernis martin*. This resurfacing of a material that already assured a protective covering with another transparent layer of varnish set off shagreen's natural qualities with a glossy sheen resembling Japanese lacquer, which also enjoyed status as a fashionable luxury at the time owing to Madame de Pompadour's and, later, Marie Antoinette's fondness for it. This transfer of the cachet of shagreen onto the family who crafted it, gave it a stylistic edge it did not have elsewhere in Europe. In England such a promotional culture did not develop in conjunction with shagreen as it did with ceramic production, such as Wedgwood. Although craftsmen in France, England, and Holland used the same material to manufacture many of the same products, those in France sought to promote theirs as embodying a higher standard of craftsmanship and elegance. Attempts to counteract the anonymity of the craftsman by making Galuchat a brand name and his products exemplary of French style were strategies that helped to secure for France recognition and authority as an international taste-setter.

The skin trade

The market for rayskin was characterized by a network of transnational relations that are only partially visible through available records. As noted above, Japanese lacquerers employed it as part of the decorative language of export goods in the sixteenth and early seventeenth centuries, but no records of Portuguese shipments of shagreen during that period have yet come to light. Research into the VOC records by Dutch historian Mathieu Willemsen has disclosed only occasional shipments of shagreen to Holland and objects covered in the skin are not mentioned after 1645.[40] Is this because it made more commercial sense for the VOC to sell the skins in Japan than consuming it themselves? Scattered indications of the value of such cargo, such as an act of Dutch piracy against a Chinese ship with a cargo of 677 rayskins, and a shipment of sappanwood, deerskins, and rayskins, white raw silk, black lacquer, and buffalo horns valued at 34,529 guilders that arrived on the *Nassau* in 1641 would support such an interpretation.[41] If so, the question remains: by what routes was this commodity reaching Europe? One possibility is that craftsmen were relying on local ray, *leucoraja fullonica*, found the Atlantic as far north as Iceland and south as the Madeira Islands.[42] Another possibility is illicit trade, but this alone is unlikely to have been sufficient to meet the demand. The answer may lie in yet-unexamined records of the British East India Company, which was well-positioned to purchase skins on the Coromandel Coast, in other Indian ports, or in China. A French source from the end of the eighteenth century indicates that England supplied the French market.[43]

While it is difficult to map the circulation of rayskin in Europe, there is no doubt that the markets in England, Holland and France were informed by mutual dependency with the market in Japan. The VOC developed a highly organized trade system in an expansionist frame geared to maximizing the value of their capital, and their trading decisions in one market were made in response to transactions in another, and these in turn were influenced by those in still another. It was the management of these commodity chains critical to global trade that made the Dutch East India Company so successful. Although the global economic impact of aquatic skins was minor compared to silver, copper, tea, porcelains, cottons and silks, the very sizable transactions carried out by the VOC indicate that these occupied a particularly significant place in interregional trade between the Coromandel Coast of India, Thailand and Japan.[44]

The VOC's commercial success followed from their knowledge of the goods desirable throughout the regions where they traded, and recognition of the high cultural appreciation for rayskin in Japan led them to open a highly lucrative trading post in the Ayutthaya kingdom in modern Thailand expressly for procuring raw materials to exchange in Japan. In addition to rayskin, these included deer hides (used for making shoes), sappanwood (used for red dye), raw lacquer, elephant tusks (for carving netsuke and other decorative articles, buffalo horn (for medicinal purposes), and silk. According to George Vinal Smith, one of the few scholars to have followed this commodity, between 1633 and 1663, when the VOC had a near monopoly, exports from the Ayutthaya office to Japan included 464,126 rayskins, representing 9.4 percent of the total, but between 1664 and 1694 this declined to a mere 500 pieces.[45] This dramatic change reflected diminishing returns owing to competition from Chinese merchants and careful 'weighing of the potential profits of Thai goods against those of other areas'.[46]

Rayskin was also trans-shipped for sale in Japan from São Tomé, a port on India's Coromandel Coast. This was a very risky business, however, since worms and water damage could reduce the value of the cargo or lead to outright rejection. Japanese buyers were extremely sensitive to the quality of rayskins. In 1731, for instance, the diary of the head of the Dutch trading post on the island of Deshima noted 'only 919 ray skins out of a total of 9,000 have been selected to serve as presents for the shogun'.[47]

The registers and diaries of Dutch merchants residing in Japan suggest that ray-skin arrived in the cargo of most ships entering the port of Nagasaki between the 1640s and 1800.[48] Japanese public awareness of this trade as well as of its economic and social value is underscored in passages from Ihara Saikaku's novel *Nihon Eitaigura* (The Japanese Family Storehouse; 1688):

> Nagasaki, first city of Japan for fabulous treasure, is a busy sight when the autumn shipping calls and bidding starts for the bales of raw silk, rolls of cloth, medicinal herbs, shark skin, aloes wood, and curios of all kind. Year after year there is a mountain of merchandise, and not a thing is left unsold.[49]

The reason shagreen was so valuable in Japan was its criticality in the manufacture of sword hilts and scabbards. During the Pax Tokugawa that extended from 1615 to 1867, the sword was more important as a symbol than as a weapon, and display of lavishly decorated swords and suits of armour became symptomatic of the increasingly conspicuous and competitive way that feudal lords defined their pre-eminence. Since each sword or dagger required the skin of one ray to create the distinctive ridged line of dorsal denticles running vertically down the centre of the hilt, and members of the samurai elite prided themselves on large collections, consumption levels were extraordinarily high. As noted in the quote from the Dutch records cited above, the shogun sent an inspector to Nagasaki to choose the finest skins as tribute, since Japan's relationship with the Dutch and their envoys (the VOC) was understood within a lord-vassal framework.

In Japan, as in Europe, shagreen work was a recognized profession. The activities of *sameshi* are first portrayed in pictorial inventories of craftsmen published in the seventeenth century. These also advertise shops in Osaka and Kyoto.[50] The status connotations of handling this material are clear from another passage from Saikaku's *Nihon Eitaigura*.

> The correct appearance for a shop differs according to type. If you are dealing in ray skin, books, perfumery, or silks, your shop should be decorated tastefully and have an air of spaciousness. But if you run a pawnbroker's or a grocery store, a cramped interior and a suggestion of disorder is more suitable.[51]

This text linking the value of shagreen work to its presentation in the store suggests that Japanese craftsmen had a good understanding of the world into which they were sending their products: the setting in which goods were presented and sold as well as the circumstances of their sale were recognized to be important constituents of the construction of luxury value.

There is a good deal of uncertainty about the inherent value of rayskin in Europe, but in Japan, each skin was discussed and graded like a work of art. The opinions of expert inspectors (*mekiki*) were relied upon, but there could still be room for interpretation based on age, condition, size, and especially provenance. Thus, cultural elaboration was required to lift rayskin from both the aquatic and commodity realms. In his *Kōi seigi*, Inaba offers an extraordinarily detailed account of the process through which this was carried out. It is likely that the rules and procedures for selecting skins, like the guide to dressing and applying them to weaponry, were intended primarily for the craftsmen whose products helped to package the ideals and aspirations of the warrior class.

> How to judge (*mekiki* 目利き) *same* is very difficult to explain in writing, but the important points are as follows: When one wishes to judge accurately it is best to study new *same* 鮫, distinguishing its quality in three grades: upper, middle, and lower . . . The best quality costs 1,000 ryō, so that the important thing is to give readily one's opinion of the quality. Of course, it is not only so with rayskin but with other *objets d'art* (*dôgu* 道具) in which the price varies greatly. . . . Generally very white *same* is preferred on sword handles, but those qualities which are very white but dull, like dead bone, are no good. Though we prefer brilliant *same*, that which is too brilliant looks like fried tofu (*aburage* 油揚) and is not good . . . whatever the colour, it must have a good surface . . . the colour is the most important point, more so than the regular grain.[52]

Of particular note here is the degree to which rayskin became the object of connoisseurial appreciation comparable to ceramics and other *objets d'art* used in ritual tea drinking (*chanoyu*). Recognition of its qualities, moreover, was premised on an intricate system of classification that required considerable experience. *Same* skins, like tea ceremony utensils, were evaluated on the basis of highly subjective sensorial qualities, including colour and texture, using language that relied heavily on analogies with other materials and substances such as bone and fried tofu. Like tewares also, provenance was a further consideration in its appraisal. Skins from Champa and São Tomé (on the Coromandel coast) were the most prized, but those from Kabochiya (Cambodia), Shamur (Siam) and Kōchi (Cochin, northern Vietnam) were also admired. Of rayskins from Tōguchi, literally, 'mouth of China' (Hainan?), however, Inaba warns: 'the quality is very inferior and worthless because there is no active appearance in it, generally people admire *same* of active appearance (*ikioi* 勢い); this term is quite impossible to explain, but in such a case one would understand gradually when studying with care for some time'.[53] *Ikioi* is a resonant term meaning energy, military strength, authority, and sexual power that highlights the magical life-force that ownership of a rayskin-sheathed sword hilt promised to its owner.

This account speaks to the way that even as the prestige of rayskin was underwritten by the social and political power of the sword, the visceral apprehensions and uncertainties of the warrior were also projected onto it.

Conclusion

Materials are first adopted because they meet a particular need and because they are at hand, but over time their use is determined by cultural context. Rayskin's exchange value in the early modern era depended on its unusual texture, its exotic origins, the craftsmanship brought to its use, and its application to fashionable emblems of individual and social identity. It was assimilated into the material language of power through military might and scientific knowledge but also into the domestic everyday through home furnishings and forks and knives. In both Europe and Japan, it also became a signifier of a pleasantly textured, grainy surface that gave exotic distinction to familiar artefacts. Japan generated and focused sustained domestic and international demand for this material between 1600 and 1800, but thereafter it declined, only to be revived at the end of the nineteenth century in Britain by members of the arts and crafts movement, and in the 1920s in France by Art Deco style luxury furniture makers.[54] Within Japan, the abolition of the samurai class and of sword bearing after the fall of the Tokugawa shogunate in 1867 led to a decline in the local market for rayskin, from which it has never recovered.

The dynamics of the markets, uses, and meanings of shagreen speak to globalization as a localizing process that involves both nature and culture, materials and language. Although fashioned into a range of goods premised on culturally specific value systems, the simultaneous domestication and exoticization of aquatic leather shares an underlying logic involving the mobilization of materials as signifiers of otherness to fulfil social and cultural aspirations. The coded language used to create the seductive fantasy spaces *sagri*, shagreen, and *same* came to occupy through their complex migrations, was as important as the tangible reality of the materials and crafted goods they evoked. Nomenclature develops from historically produced relationships, and the logic of these coinages is coextensive with Portuguese and Dutch trade, but not narrowly confined to it. Shagreen is a term that produces different readings in different locations, but readings that became conflated through global trade. It would not have come into circulation without the integrating forces of the transfer of commodities, capital, and cultural exchanges that came about through the development of global trade between the 1550s and 1800. Shagreen thus maps a historically complex and mutually constitutive socio-cultural and economic web connecting Europe, America, the Ottoman and Persian empires, India, South-east Asia and Japan both materially and symbolically.

Notes and references

1. For general studies of shagreen, see Jean Perfettini, *Le Galuchat: un matérieu mystérieux, une technique oubliée* (Paris: Editions H. Vial, 1988); and Lison de Caunes and Jean Perfettini, *Galuchat* (Paris: Les editions d'amateur, 1994).
2. Igor Kopytoff, 'The Cultural Biography of Things: Commodification as Process,' in *The Social Life of Things: Commodities in Cultural Perspective*, ed. Arjun Appadurai (Cambridge: Cambridge University Press 1986), 64.

3. See Paul Budker and Peter James Palmer Whitehead, *The Life of Sharks* (London: Weidenfeld and Nicholson, 1971), 187–193. For a conservator's perspective on the material see Rudi Graemer and Marion Kite, 'The tanning, dressing and conservation of exotic, aquatic and feathered skins,' in *Conservation of Leather and Related Materials*, ed. Marion Kite and Roy Thompson (Amsterdam: Elsevier, 2006), 170–183.
4. Budker and Whitehead, *Life of Sharks*, 190–191.
5. *The Sword Book in Honchō gunkikō and the Book of same Kōhi sei gi of Inaba Tsūrio*, trans. Henri L. Joly and Inada Hogitarō (Reading: Privately printed 1913), 23–25. For the original text, see Inaba Tsūryō, *Kōi seigi* (Osaka: 1785), vol. 2, 1–3.
6. *The Sword Book*, 14; Inaba, *Kōi seigi*, vol. 1, 15.
7. Mathieu Willemsen, 'Shagreen in Western Europe: Its Use and Manufacture in the Seventeenth and Eighteenth Centuries,' *Apollo* 145/419 (1997), 37.
8. The text and illustration from Belon's *Livre des poissons* (1550) is reproduced in Perfettini, *Le Galuchat*, 12.
9. J.J. Rein, *The Industries of Japan: Together with an Account of its Agriculture, Forestry, Arts and Commerce* (London; Hodder & Stoughton, 1889), 363.
10. Charles H. Stevenson, *Utilization of the Skins of Aquatic Animals* (Report of the US Fish Commission for year ending 30 June 1902), 347.
11. Budker and Whitehead, *Life of Sharks*, 189.
12. Kanako Morinaka, 'A Study on Samekawa: Skin from Ray and Shark as Material for Japanese Decorative Arts' (unpublished paper 2004), 2.
13. Personal communication, Oliver Crimmen, senior curator of fish, Natural History Museum, London, October 2011.
14. Terashima Ryōan, *Wakan sansai zue* Toyo bunko 471 (Tokyo: Heibonsha, 1987) vol. 7, 217–218.
15. The Victoria and Albert Museum has a number of pairs of nineteenth-century embroidered shagreen boots and boots with a shagreen border. Their exact provenance is uncertain. They may be from Central or West Asia. They include T.40cd-1956; and 2074; 2084. They are not yet searchable on the public website. My thanks to Helen Persson for this information.
16. Esin Atul, *The Age of Suleyman the Magnificent* (Washington: National Gallery of Art and New York: Harry N. Abrams, Inc., 1987), 61.
17. *Sir Anthony Sherley and his Persian Adventure including some contemporary Narratives relating thereto*, ed. Sir E. Denison Ross (London: George Routledge and Sons, Ltd. 1933), 153. My thanks to Carol Maver for directing me to this reference. The OED, under the heading shagreen, also records similar usage in 1677 by Tavernier, another traveller to Persia. www.OED.com (accessed 30 May, 2014). The Bata Shoe Museum in Toronto has a pair of seventeenth-century equine shagreen high-heeled Persian riding shoes. For a discussion and reproduction of these see http://www.bbc.co.uk/news/magazine-21151350 (accessed 30 May, 2014).
18. Although the unpleasant odour dissipates with cooking, historically, neither shark nor ray (unlike skate) was regarded as a choice fish in early modern Europe or Japan. In Japan shark seems to have been used primarily to make a kind of fish paste sausage known as *kamaboko*.
19. *Sword Book*, 7; Inaba, *Kōi seigi*, vol. 1, 1.
20. For a comprehensive discussion and reproduction of examples of *samegawa-nuri* see: *After the Barbarians: An Exceptional Group of Namban Works of Art* (London and Lisbon: Jorge Welsh Oriental Porcelain and Works of Art, 2003), 22–28. See also, Oliver Impey and Christian J.A. Jorg, *Japanese Export Lacquer, 1580–1850* (Amsterdam: Brill, 2005), esp. 122, 150–153.
21. For an example, see *After the Barbarians*, 194–197.
22. The accession number is BK-1979-21. For illustration, see https://www.rijksmuseum.nl/en/search/objecten?q=BK-1979-21&p=1&ps=12&ii=0#/BK-1979-21,0 (accessed 30 May, 2014).
23. Leonor Leiria, 'The Art of Lacquering According to the Namban-jin Written Sources,' *Bulletin of Portuguese/Japanese Studies*, 3 (2001), 21.

24. For a discussion of Ryukyu lacquer production, see: James C.Y. Watt and Barbara Brennan Ford, *East Asian Lacquer: The Florence and Herbert Irving Collection* (New York: The Metropolitan Museum of Art, 1991), 329–371.
25. Ulrike Korber, 'Reflections on Cultural Exchange and Commercial Relations in Sixteenth-century Asia: A Portuguese Nobleman's Lacquered Mughal Shield,' in *Portugal, Jesuits, and Japan: Spiritual Beliefs and Earthly Goods*, ed. Victoria Weston (Boston: McMullen Museum of Art, Boston College, 2013), 27.
26. See *Encompassing the Globe: Portugal and the World in the 16th and 17th Centuries*, ed. Jay A. Levenson (Washington DC: Arthur A. Sackler Gallery, Smithsonian Institution 2007), 118–119.
27. Korber, 'Reflections,' 22–23.
28. See *After the Barbarians*, 326–331.
29. See Gerard L'Estrange Turner, *Collecting Microscopes* (London: Christie's Collectors Series, 1981), 39–42. I am also grateful to the helpful email exchanges on this subject with Dr Alexi Baker, Research Associate, National Maritime Museum, London, 17/11–23/12/2014.
30. http://www.isaacnewton.org.uk/ntheman/NTMinv (accessed 30 May, 2014).
31. The V&A accession number is 1072+A-1902. See http://collections.vam.ac.uk/item/O110611/knife-and-case-unknown/ (accessed 1 June, 2014).
32. See entry on shagreen in the OED. www.oed.com (accessed 30 May, 2014).
33. The Guimet Museum in Paris has a nineteenth-century jar with a *samekawa* glaze, accession number MG2740. A teabowl with this glaze by Shimizu Uichi is in a private London collection.
34. *A Catalogue of Curiosities and Stock in Trade of that Late Ingenious Mr. Peter Parquot, Toy Man and Virtuoso deceased*, February 1720–1737, 3, 4, 6, 7, 10, 17, 22, 29. My thanks to Kyongjin Bae for drawing this source to my attention.
35. R. Campbell, *The London Tradesman* (London: 1747), 255. http://books.google.co.uk/books?id=nNoHAAAAQAAJ&pg=PA255&lpg=PA255&dq=the+london+tradesman+shagreen&source=bl&ots=6zkgmP-z-X&sig=5ZqVOa6SDhk7_9Dorj4YYvs3#v=onepage&q=the%20london%20tradesman%20shagreen&f=false (accessed 30 May, 2014).
36. Cited in Esther Singleton, *Social New York under the Georges, 1717–76* (New York: Appleton, 1902), 167.
37. Perfettini, *Le Galuchat*, 20 reproduces a page from an almanac of 1769 listing *gaisniers* among the professions.
38. de Caunes and Perfettini, *Galuchat*, 15.
39. de Caunes and Perfettini, *Galuchat*, 16.
40. VOC stands for Vereenigde Oost-Indische Compagnie (United East India Company). One shipment of 900 skins arrived in Amsterdam in 1661. Willemsen, 'Shagreen,' 35–36.
41. The VOC's piracy is discussed in Adam Clulow, *The Company and the Shogun: The Dutch Encounter with Tokugawa Japan* (New York: Columbia University Press, 2014), 179. For the arrival of the *Nassau* see: *The Deshima Dagregisters*, ed. Cynthia Viallé and Leonard Blussé (Leiden: Institute for the History of European Expansion, 2001), vol. 11. 1641–1650, 71.
42. http://www.sharktrust.co.uk/en/factsheets/63/shagreen-ray.html (accessed 30 May, 2014).
43. Willemsen, 'Shagreen,' 36 citing B.G.E. de la Ville de la Cépede, *Histoire naturelle des poissons* (Paris, 1798–1803), Part 1, 139.
44. Rayskins were also transshipped from the Coromandel Coast by VOC; these are likely to be the ones described as 'San Tome' in Japanese sources. See Els M. Jacobs, *Merchant in Asia: The Trade of the Dutch East India Company during the Eighteenth Century* (Leiden: CNWS Publications 2006), 103.
45. George Vinal Smith, *The Dutch in Seventeenth-Century Thailand*. Center for Southeast Asian Studies Special Report 16, 1977 (Northern Illinois University, 1977), 80.
46. Smith, *Dutch in Seventeenth-Century Thailand*, 80.

47. The Diary of Opperhoofd P. Boocksteijn; August, 1731, in *The Deshima Diaries: Marginalia 1700–1740* (Tokyo: Japan-Netherlands Institute, 1992), vol. 1, 386.

48. This assertion is based on my survey of the entries in *The Deshima Dagregisters* from 1600–1641 and *The Deshima Diaries* from 1700 to 1740.

49. Ihara Saikaku, *The Japanese Family Storehouse or the Millionaire's Gospel Modernized*, trans. G.W. Sargent (Cambridge: Cambridge University Press, 1969), 106. I have altered the translation of *samegawa* from sharkskin to rayskin. For the Japanese text I consulted *Gendaigoshaku Saikaku Zenshu, vol. 9: Nihon eitaigura*, trans. Teruoka Yasutaka (Tokyo: Shogakkan, 1977), 137.

50. *Jinrin kinmō zui*, Toyo bunko 519, comp. Asakura Haruhiko (Tokyo: Heibonsha 1990), 147.

51. Ihara Saikaku, *The Japanese Family Storehouse or the Millionaire's Gospel Modernized*, 131; *Gendaigoshaku Saikaku Zenshu, vol. 9: Nihon eitaigura*, 168.

52. Translation adapted from *Sword Book*, 14–15; Inaba, *Kōi seigi*, vol. 1, 14–15.

53. *Sword Book*, 11; Inaba, *Kōi seigi*, vol. 1, 10–11.

54. See N. Natasha Kuzmanovic, *John Paul Cooper: Designer of the Arts and Crafts Movement* (Gloucestershire: Sutton Publishing, 1999), 69–92 and de Caunes and Perfettini, *Galuchat*.

3

THE CORAL NETWORK

The trade of red coral to the Qing imperial court in the eighteenth century[1]

Pippa Lacey

Most studies of global commodities trace the flow of exotics into Europe. Mediterranean red coral, *Corallium rubrum*, was one of the few European commodities to find ready markets in eighteenth-century Asia. This paper reconstructs the nodes of what we might call the early-modern 'coral network' from the Mediterranean Sea to Qing China (1644–1911) via the English East India Company (EEIC) records. This allows us to understand some of the mechanisms through which red coral, a highly sought-after Chinese 'curiosity', reached the Qing imperial court.[2] This coral network linked Italian coral fishermen with London diamond merchants, English naval captains with Chinese officials and Guangdong craftsmen with their Manchu rulers, the Qing emperors. Each link in the coral network combined to effect the transformation of red coral from natural raw material to precious imperial treasure; from Italian *coralli* to Chinese *shanhu*.[3] South Asia, with its lucrative English coral-for-diamonds exchange, was a vital node in the coral network; nevertheless, the trade for red coral in China operated under a very different dynamic to that of the South Asian exchange.[4] Once it had been unloaded in Guangzhou (Canton), red coral became known as *shanhu*; here it entered into a complex system and was ascribed with an assortment of Chinese cultural associations.

In eighteenth-century China red coral was accorded both spiritual and courtly significance and incorporated into countless imperial artefacts from miniature landscapes (*penjing*) that decorated palace rooms (Figure 3.1) to court necklaces (*chaozhu*) draped around imperial shoulders (Figure 3.2). *Shanhu* was codified in the *Huangchao liqi tushi* (Illustrated Precedents for the Ritual Paraphernalia of the Imperial Court), the sumptuary code of the Qianlong emperor (1735–1796), promulgated in 1759.[5] Coral was the prescribed red gemstone for the Imperial ritual necklace and belt (*chaodai*) to mark the celebration of the annual Prayers to the Morning Sun held at Spring Equinox;[6] red coral beads complemented the red ritual robes worn for the occasion. Red coral was combined with freshwater pearls, known as Eastern Pearls (*dongzhu*), and placed around the necks of the emperor, his empress and the empress dowager in their imperial court jewels. (In Figure 3.2, the young Qianlong emperor wears a necklace of coral and jade).

In addition, *shanhu* denoted high rank when worn as a coloured button (*dingzhu*) on the Qing court-hat (*chaoguan*).[7] The specification of red coral in Qing sumptuary codes suggests an assurance of supply for courtly purposes, along with Qianlong's desire to control and order Manchu-ruled China through precious coloured

FIGURE 3.1 Plate with scene of offering coral trees to the emperor. Qing dynasty, Yongzheng period (1723–1735). Porcelain plate with coloured enamels on biscuit from Jingdezhen. Dimensions: H 9.2 cm × D 55.6 cm. Metropolitan Museum of Art 61.200.72. Bequest of John D. Rockefeller Jr, 1960. This colourful plate features an imagined scene in which five female courtiers stand in a courtyard offering plates and vases of red coral to the emperor who receives them from a raised open-sided pavilion. On an altar behind the emperor's head is a further branch of coral arranged in a tall vase. Two of the proffered coral offerings are whole large branches, or trees, which are borne in tall-necked vases. Two further trays, or plates, contain what appear to be shaped flames, possibly also made from coral, possibly modified as part of a miniature landscape display. The scene has echoes of a Tang dynasty image showing foreigners offering a tray with coral trees to a Buddhist holy man (*see* Figure 3.3) The image attributed to Lu Lengjia (*c.*730–760 CE) is now in the Palace Museum, Beijing. It indicates that the tradition of important figures receiving coral branches had venerable and spiritual associations in imperial China.

FIGURE 3.2 Portrait of the Qianlong Emperor as a Young Man, Unidentified Artist, nineteenth century, Qing dynasty. Hanging scroll, ink and colour on silk. Dimensions: 161.3 × 77.5 cm. Metropolitan Museum of Art 42.141.8. Rogers Fund, 1942. The young emperor is depicted on a throne. Around his neck is a court necklace (*chaozhu*). Unlike the imperial *chaozhu* which has eastern pearls together with coral separators, this necklace is made from beads of red coral with large green jade separator beads. The accessories that hang from the emperor's belt are decorated with red coral beads and eastern freshwater pearls. On the emperor's head is a hat topped with eastern pearls and a shaped ruby button.

materials.[8] The expectation of a supply of valued materials such as red coral is important for two key reasons. It underlines the authority of the imperial court at the centre of the Middle Kingdom to attract the most precious materials. Further, it is integral to the colour coding and marking of hierarchies through colour and dress that was an intrinsic part of Chinese court practice. Vollmer says 'Ritual and ceremonial clothing were regarded as absolutely necessary to maintaining the proper hierarchical order in society.'[9] Courtly society was organised and regulated according to colours and through the use of selected materials. In his introduction to the *Illustrated Precedents*, the Qianlong emperor reaffirms the importance of hats and dress (including jewellery) for the very survival of the dynasty.[10] In other words, he believed that prescribed textiles and accessories ensured the smooth running of the empire. In order to gain insights into some of the influences concerning the selection of red coral in the self-fashioning by the eighteenth-century Qing emperors, I explore briefly some ancient Chinese precedents for coral as a valued coloured material. Coral is examined within a broader Chinese context through a consideration of foreign tribute networks, imperial workshops and some of the physical and cultural associations. This process allows an understanding of some of the layers of complexity ascribed to red coral in the Qing imperial universe and demonstrates that these have venerable associations.

National treasures

Red coral has a long history in China. One of the earliest historical references to coral is in a political debate, which took place at the Western Han dynasty court of Emperor Zhao (87–74 BCE), in 81 BCE, recorded in the *Discourses on Salt and Iron*. Lord Grand Secretary Sang Hongyang said:

> Mules, donkeys and camels enter the frontier in unbroken lines . . . The furs of sables, marmots, foxes and badgers, coloured rugs and decorated carpets fill the imperial treasury, while jade and auspicious stones, corals and crystals become national treasures.[11]

This speech illustrates something of the longevity of a coral trade to China. The early trade route was overland, via the plains and mountains of Eurasia. It indicates the high economic and cultural value placed on a variety of imported materials. Such imports were not everyday items; they were rare, luxurious commodities enclaved, or reserved, for the Chinese elite as 'national treasures'.[12] Ideas, as well as goods, moved along international trade routes. For instance, Roman notions about coral fishing found their way into Chinese texts.[13] The Buddhist religion itself was an import from India, popularised during the Han dynasty, AD 58–75.

An image in the style of the late Southern Song (1127–1279) or early Yuan dynasties (1271–1368), attributed to Tang dynasty artist Lu Lengjia (active

*c.*730–760 AD), is entitled: *Foreigners Presenting Coral Trees to an Arhat* (Figure 3.3).[14]
The large album leaf, one of six in the collection of the Palace Museum, Beijing,
depicts a seated Buddhist holy man (*arhat* or *luohan*) giving audience to two possibly Persian men – one kneeling, one standing. The men are shown presenting
the *arhat* with bowls of treasures; miniature landscapes with red coral 'trees' and
tall rocks. The scene involves an interesting conceit. The *arhat* is Buddhist, while
Persians paying homage are likely to have been Muslim or Zoroastrian. This suggests that coral may have been associated with particular modes of spirituality and
that, as a pictorial motif, it had ancient roots. Some of these modes were clearly
foreign – as witnessed by the 'Persians' – but others, such as coral, became encul-
turated into Chinese ways.

Echoes of this earlier Chinese practice of presenting coral to powerful leaders
can be seen in a decorative Yongzheng plate (1722–1735), now in the Metropolitan Museum of Art (Figure 3.1). In an imagined historical scene, several young
female courtiers offer the emperor large trees of red coral on trays and vases. Similarly through the displays of *penjing* incorporating precious red coral and gemstones
in their eighteenth-century palaces, the Qing emperors were tying themselves to
revered and much earlier Chinese Buddhist practices. I shall return to the idea
of treasures and preciousness; potent concepts giving special status to a material,
a symbol or an idea. First, I retrace the stages of the coral network to follow the
physical transformation of red coral.

FIGURE 3.3 Foreigners presenting Coral Trees to an *Arhat*. From an Album of Six
Buddhist Arhats and Worshippers attributed to Tang dynasty artist, Liu Luohan (or
Lu Lengjia) (*c.*730–760 CE). Two foreign figures present gifts to a seated Buddhist
luohan or *arhat*. The kneeling man offers a bowl of treasures: a miniature *penjing*
landscape with red coral 'trees' and tall rocks. Palace Museum, Beijing. Ink and
colour on silk. University of Oregon Visual Resources collection. http://
oregondigital.org/u?/artimages,55034.

From North Africa to Northern China

The eighteenth-century coral network began in the waters of the Mediterranean Sea off the coast of North Africa and modern-day Italy (Map 3.1). Coral fishing grounds were highly prized. Across the centuries, many nations and city-states – Phoenician, Carthaginian, Ottoman, French, Venetian, Sicilian and Genoese – vied for the rights to harvest the marine crop. The ambiguous nature of coral and its distinctive red colour enhanced its attraction. For example, Greek mythology drew a connection between red coral and blood; it was said that red coral was petrified blood of the Gorgon Medusa, beheaded by the hero Perseus. For centuries, coral

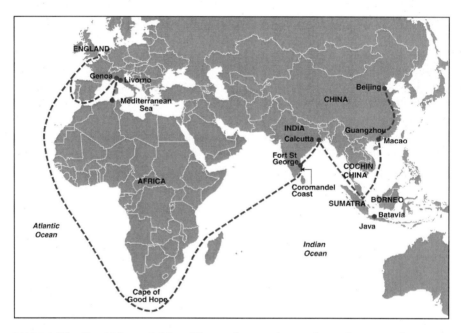

MAP 3.1 The Coral Network Map. The coral network map shows the route taken by raw coral, from the shores of the southern Mediterranean, off North Africa and Italy, via Livorno or Genova, and England, en route to China, and ultimately the Qing imperial court in Beijing. In the early modern period English East India Company China Ships plied the route between the Thames Estuary, near London and the Pearl River to the port of Guangzhou, China. South Asia was a vital node in the coral network with its lucrative English coral-for-diamonds exchange, centred at Fort St George, on the Coromandel Coast. Here, China Ships restocked before continuing on to the South China Sea. Foreign ships were unable to enter the southern city of Guangzhou and were required to anchor at Whampoa, an estuarine island in the Pearl River near to the southern city of Guangzhou. Once in China, coral and other precious goods were transported north to the capital Beijing, via the Hangzhou-to-Beijing Grand Canal; a journey of several weeks. As coral moved along the network the terminology associated with it shifted, from crop, to commodity, to curiosity, to national treasure. *Cartography*: Gilly Thomas, Visual Impact Graphics.

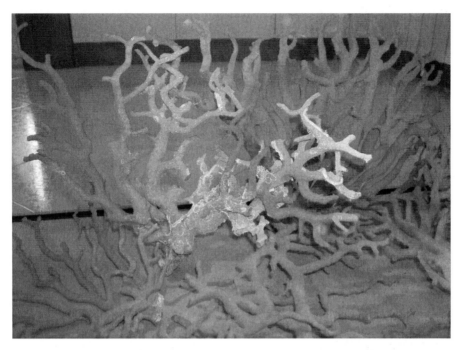

FIGURE 3.4 Raw harvested unprocessed coral branches, Torre del Greco, Italy.
Image: Pippa Lacey.

was thought to be a plant that hardened to stone on human contact.[15] In fact, coral is the skeleton of tiny marine polyps. Its hue varies from pale pink to deep blood-red, depending on the depth, temperature and location in which it grows.

The finest Mediterranean *Corallium rubrum* was found off Sicily, Algeria and Tunisia, with key ports at La Calle and Tabarca.[16] Jean-Baptiste Tavernier, the seventeenth-century French jeweller and traveller, however, reported that the 'best and the most beautiful of all' came from Arguerrel, off western Sardinia.[17] Coral fishing was a difficult and dangerous occupation requiring the co-ordinated work of teams of strong-armed men. At the end of each gruelling season, raw *corallo* was transshipped north to Livorno[18] or Genoa to be cleaned and semi-processed.[19] Here, coral became a commodity; the harvested coral crop entered the market to be bought and sold internationally.[20] London agents purchased raw pieces, shaped beads or whole coral trees. 'Deepe red' *grossezze* coral was preferred.[21] According to Feuchtwanger: '*Pallini althorn* . . . are principally [sent] to China, where the favourite colour is rose-red and the most perfect kind.'[22] English East India Company (EEIC) records indicate the need for careful packaging to ensure that this brittle cargo did not spoil during its long sea-journey. For example, an EEIC letter to Leghorn agents, Messrs Balle, Gosfright and Company, dated 15 June 1677, suggests that the Company purchased coral from a local Jewish merchant, named Abraham Mocarto. It details the type (*Grezio, Ricadutti*),[23] size (large) and forms (beads, branches) of coral, as well as payments and packaging instructions: '. . . Each chest not to exceed three hundred pounds [in weight], the large branches to be packed in a box by themselves and put in the middle of every chest . . .'[24] The specific attention paid to the transportation of large coral branches demonstrates that the agents were keen that the precious commodity arrived in prime condition. It also suggests that they anticipated high return on their speculative investment.

Until the early seventeenth century, the Company purchased coral directly. However, each autumn after 1635, the EEIC issued licences for the transport of coral mainly to India, as 'private trade'.[25] London-based bankers, diamond merchants and tea traders would apply individually or collectively, to dispatch consignments of coral, amber, silver and plate to the East Indies on Company ships.[26] On 19 December 1764 for instance, the following entry was made in the EEIC Court Book:

> Order'd that Mr George Challoner be allowed to send to the East Indies the value of £2,000 in Coral Beads for the purchase of Diamonds and £3,000 to China in the like article, on condition he pays the produce thereof into the Company's Cash at Canton.[27]

Crates, barrels or tubs of coral marked with the owners' brand and initials were dispatched by sea to the Thames Estuary, for loading onto ships bound for India and China.[28] The long-distance China Ships were also loaded with broadcloth, armaments, silver and other goods. They would return laden with tea, silks, porcelain, spices and diamonds. China Ships set sail from England in the late autumn reaching southern China the following autumn. They frequently called at Fort St George, Madras, on India's Coromandel coast, or Calcutta, Bengal, en route.[29] India was a vital node providing both an impetus and an *entrepôt*. Indian commodities – spices and cloth – were taken on board for inter-Asian trade. The English had developed a lucrative coral-for-diamonds exchange centred at Fort St George, in the period between 1700 and 1770, in what today would be a multi-million pound business.[30] English bankers and merchants carried the risk of these transactions. Frequently, they were Jewish businessmen with familial connections in London, Italy and Amsterdam.[31]

In addition to issuing licences to merchants, the Company sanctioned another form of 'private trade' to China. Senior EEIC officers were permitted an allowance for personal speculation. Much of this trade was in luxuries known as *singsongs*, i.e. *objets d'art*, jewellery, coral and mechanical clocks destined for the Chinese court via local officials.[32] Guangzhou was the main gateway into China from the eighteenth century.[33] Foreign ships were required to drop anchor at the estuarine island of Whampoa in the Pearl River.[34] The ship's log of the *Hawke*, captained, in 1766, by John Cotton, was bound for 'Whampoa, China'. Ships' logs are long on weather and short on trade details. It contains a brief entry: 'Wednesday 8th January 1766 – Gravesend . . . Re'd on board on Acc't of Peter and Richard Musilman, 1 box Coral.'[35] Eleven months later, the *Hawke's* log merely states: 'Whampoa – 3rd Nove[mber] 1766 loaded a chop with private trade.'[36] From this we see that small but important licensed private trade consignments of coral were being loaded on board EEIC ships in Gravesend, England. Eleven months later, when ships reached the Chinese mainland private trade boxes entered into a new cultural, economic and political sphere.

Once they had berthed, foreign supercargoes (cargo officers) liaised with the Hoppo, Guangzhou's imperial customs superintendent. The Hoppo was responsible for the collection of customs duties. His office measured incoming ships and issued contracts to the *Co-hong* (guild of merchants, 1760–1771) and interpreters who worked directly with the Europeans. As such there was a monopoly over the distribution of goods within China. John Misenor's 1755 diary and correspondence of the English factory (i.e. trading post) gives an insight into the system:

> On the arrival of the ships from Europe, the said shops are permitted to deal with private people but not in any goods imported for account of the Companies Contracts belonging properly to the Hongist Securities as well as Curiosities of value, such as Pearl, Coral, Chrystal [*sic*], True Amber, &c, all of which being for the Emperor's Use, no Shops shall presume to Interfere.[37]

As this account indicates, incoming 'curiosities' were officially destined for the Emperor. Having landed and been taken into the care of the authorities, *shanhu*, as coral was now known, was no longer considered merely a 'trade commodity'. As a prized 'curiosity' reserved for imperial consumption, *shanhu* did not appear on the open market, instead it entered into a complex local dynamic, known as the Canton System (1757–1842). China attempted to maintain monopolistic control over all trade entering the country through its southern port of Guangzhou via local Hongs, or merchants.

The English were not the sole suppliers of Mediterranean coral to China. An EEIC archive headed: 'Foreign Imports brought over at Canton, 18th October, 1764' records that 8.38 *peculs* of coral beads were among the cargo of the 'Four French' ships, and '1.76 *peculs*' of small coral pieces were brought by 'Two Danes'.[38] Nevertheless, the English EIC accounted for nearly half of the European trade to China in the late-eighteenth century.[39] Increasing numbers of independent private or country traders also brought goods via Asia.[40]

The sea journey from north Africa via Italy, England and India to Guangzhou were the first stages in the coral network. The focal point of the coral network was the Qing court in northern China. I now consider the domestic Chinese mechanisms by which *shanhu* moved from the southern port to the imperial court in Beijing.

Palace presentation lists

As part of the customs duties, taxes and fees levied on imports were annual gifts, due to the imperial court; these helped to oil the 'giant economic wheel' of the Chinese economy.[41] Each province presented local tributes to the imperial court, thus marking and reinforcing the centrality of the emperor within the Qing polity and as a means of acknowledging and reinforcing the ties and connections between the periphery and the imperial centre.[42] As guardians of the main portal for European goods, senior officials in Guangdong Province had access to the choicest imports and were required to send an allowance to court. Historian Paul van Dyke describes this as follows:

> After the signing of the bond, the Hoppo would request to see the 'sing-songs' (mechanical gadgets such as clocks or music boxes) or mirrors and other luxury items [such as coral] the foreigners had brought with them. These would supply the presents the Hoppo was expected to offer to his superiors each year for the privilege of his office. After selecting the best items, the Hoppo would ask the Chinese security merchants to purchase them . . . As the number of foreign ships increased, Hoppos became more selective as to which would come under their personal supervision (those with the rarest and most precious cargoes, of course).[43]

As customs inspector, the Hoppo was able to secure the cream of the foreign imports. He was required to offer these as payment for his position. Further, he was able to acquire these at a highly discounted price via the merchants he favoured with contracts.

Surviving eighteenth-century Palace presentation lists (*jindan*) and tribute files (*gongdang*) indicate the scale and scope of gifts submitted by Guangdong officials as court native tribute or presentation tax (*kong ga*).[44] The lists comprise imported goods – paintings, clocks – as well as locally made Guangdong crafts. It seems a proportion of *singsongs* – including amber, ivory, coral beads and branches – were given over to skilled local craftsmen to be incorporated into lavish *penjing* miniature landscapes and other locally produced tributes.[45] Whether officials commissioned such items directly or the Hongist securities on their behalf, is unclear. While these high-status gifts were created on behalf of the Guangdong officials, the ultimate recipient was the emperor in Beijing. This adds an interesting stage to the coral network: the incorporation of foreign materials into Chinese handicrafts. As soon as red coral arrived in China, it became enmeshed in a network of tribute focused on the imperial centre. Guangdong officials enclaved coral along with other valued foreign commodities in order to reinforce their own political positions and, in turn, express their gratitude for the imperial favour shown to them.

Although extant lists are incomplete, nevertheless those from the reigns of the Yongzheng (1722–1735) and Qianlong emperors mention coral: an imperial *chaozhou* with eastern pearls and coral beads, coral longevity beads (Figure 3.2 shows the emperor wearing a coral and green jade *chaozhou*, as well as coral beads on his belt), intricate *penjing*, as well as decorative hand mirrors.[46] These were submitted on behalf of the governor-general of Guangxi and Guangdong Provinces (*Tsontuck* or Viceroy), the governor of Guangdong (*Fuyuan*) and the Hoppo (*Hubu*) and his deputy for imperial birthdays and important festivals. For example, in September 1733, governor-general Yang Yongbin sent a tray of coral longevity beads to Yongzheng. In the same year, Hoppo Mao Keming and his deputy, Zheng Wusai, gifted five court necklaces made of coral, *qinan*, amber, *jiashilun* and rose quartz.[47] In 1771, two coral court necklaces were sent by Governor-general Li Shiyao and Governor Debao to the Qianlong emperor in honour of his sixty-first birthday.[48] These records suggest that through the process of being skilfully worked by local artisans, non-native materials, such as coral, amber and ivory were acculturated into high-status Chinese artefacts; gifts fit for an emperor. In other words, whether red coral was enclaved for direct transmission to the treasury, or given for local crafting, the ultimate destination of incoming coral was the emperor as centre of the Chinese world.

It is not possible to be precise about the quantities of imported coral incorporated into gifts since coral was often a component in larger decorative ensembles, such as the *penjing* arrangements for which Guangzhou craftsmen were famed. However, it is clear that imported materials were being used for this purpose. And while the emperor may not have had direct control over the production of such tributes, it may be assumed that the Guangdong officials were eager to please their emperor and that these coralline gifts were calculated to perform several functions. As well as fulfilling annual tribute demands, the quality of gifts indicated the appreciation of the officials' positions to the emperor; they demonstrated the skills of the Guangdong craftsmen, as well as delighting and surprising the court with culturally appropriate novelty. Gifts generally conveyed the wish for the long life and good fortune of the emperor. Thus, layers of cultural agency and economic value were added to red coral through this process of enculturation.

Guangdong officials were well placed to present extravagant gifts to their emperor; they had access both to the raw materials at their point of entry and to the craftsmen capable of creating such luxuries. As yet, we know little about the lapidaries of Guangzhou during the eighteenth century nor the exact dynamic through which imperial gifts were commissioned. Guangzhou became a specialist production centre from the Ming period onwards, known for skilled and varied crafts.[49] Costume historian Beverley Jackson estimates that 'over 250,000 men, women and children were engaged in carving jade, ivory, tortoiseshell and mother-of-pearl; they worked gold, wove silk, and made furniture, porcelain, pottery and lacquerware, as well as the intricate kingfisher [and coral] feather-work for both the domestic market and export trade.'[50]

A nineteenth-century guide, entitled *Walks in the City of Canton* by Rev. John Henry Gray (1823–1890), indicates the division of craftsmanship in the late nineteenth century. From Gray, we learn that Great New Street, *Tai-San-Dai,* was the main street of lapidaries at this time, where shops 'abound with ornaments of jade stone, coral and lapis-lazuli.'[51] Jewelled kingfisher feather – and coral – headdresses and accessories were made by specialist feather-workers in the same street. Ivory and sandalwood carving was a separate craft, carried out by different workers, albeit using similar tools and techniques; their workshops were nearby in First Tin Alley, *Uen-Sek-Hong.*[52]

Domestic Chinese annual tributes and duties were two of the mechanisms through which coral moved to the imperial centre. Now I turn to an international dimension of the transmission of coral to Beijing.

Foreign tribute

The tributary system was a cornerstone of Chinese power. Asian and European nations were similarly expected to pay their respects to the Chinese emperor through gifting. It was the Qing dynasty's abilities to attract and manage regional relations and maintain their position as the primary tributary state within Asia that enabled China to continue as regional powerhouse.

Another route by which red coral entered imperial spheres was via those few foreign diplomatic missions that were permitted to travel to Beijing. At this time, no European trader was permitted to do this. Beijing, the administrative capital and the imperial court of Qing China, was 2,400 kilometres to the northeast. Therefore, once European ambassadors had arrived in Guangzhou, they were still several weeks' journey away from the capital, via the Hangzhou-to-Beijing Grand Canal.

In 1667, the German Jesuit and court astronomer to Emperor Shunzhi (1644–1661), Father John Adams (1592–1666), detailed the tributes presented by a Dutch delegation, led by Pieter van Goyer and Jacob de Keyser in 1655–1657.[53] The Catalogue of the Presents to the Court of China included several coral items:

> The Presents for the EMPEROUR[sic]: . . . Two Pounds of choice Corral; One Branch of polished Corral, weighing one pound and a half [680 grams] . . .
> The Presents for the EMPERESSES Mother: . . . Three Rosares [rosaries] of Corral Beads; One Branch of Corral . . .
> Presents which Pieter van Goyer and Jacob de Keyser made to the EMPEROUR . . . Two Rosares of Corall Beads. [54]

Johannes Nieuhof, a steward to the ambassadors, recorded how the mid-seventeenth-century tribute system worked. Before meeting imperial officials, the delegation was instructed to present a list of gifts for consideration. Once this had been checked over and approved, their gifts were finally accepted. Their quality and quantity were carefully assessed and the success of a mission was judged according to the offerings. In addition there was another form of gifting, known as 'tribute trade'; Zhao reports that the Kangxi emperor was so shocked at the cost of receiving a later Dutch embassy that he amended the previous Dutch tribute trade stipulations.[55]

Despite knowledge of an imperial fondness for curiosities, it is perhaps surprising that General Macartney's well-documented British Embassy to the Qianlong emperor, 1792–1794, omitted coral among its extensive and carefully-selected gifts.[56] The official motive for Macartney's submission was that it would not 'be becoming to offer trifles of momentary curiosity but little use'.[57] Rather:

> His Britannic Majesty has been therefore careful to select only such articles as may denote the progress of science and of the arts in Europe and which may convey some of the information to the exalted mind of his Imperial Majesty, or such others as may be practically useful.[58]

The Qianlong emperor's reply to King George III illustrates the cultural gaps and trade imbalance between the two Empires:

> Our Celestial Empire possesses all things in prolific abundance and lacks no products within its borders. There is therefore no need to import the manufactures of outside barbarians in exchange for our own produce.[59]

Despite an imperial appetite for curiosities such as coral, clocks and silver, Britain was able to offer few goods that the Chinese desired in exchange for their tea, porcelain and silks. This imbalance would eventually play a significant role in the Opium Wars of the nineteenth century.

Imperial workshops

Through presentation gifting or foreign tribute, red coral pieces, beads and branches found their way to the Imperial treasury for use in the Imperial workshops (*zaoban-chu*).[60] Imperial workshops came under the direct control of the emperor, via his household officials; several Qing emperors took a personal interest in their workshops and imperial craftsmen. Evelyn Rawski provides details about the structure of the workshops of this period. The *zaobanchu*, producing regalia, *objets d'art* and religious objects, were located in palaces around Beijing, including Yuanming Yuan, the eighteenth-century imperial Summer Palace. The *zaobanchu* were managed by the Imperial Household Department (*Neiwufu*), in turn controlled by palace eunuchs under the direction of Ministerial Councillors. They in turn, took their orders directly from the emperor himself. Rawski says:

> In 1693, the workshops (*zaobanchu*), supervised by the Imperial Household Department were expanded into fourteen units, each specialising in the production of textiles, metal, glass, enamels, leather, icons, paintings or printed books. At their peak in the Qianlong reign, there were thirty-eight workshops located not only in the Forbidden City but also within the imperial villas.[61]

Some workshops specialised in technologies introduced from Europe, including glass-making and enamelling. Yang reports that around 1680, thirty new workshops were set up including a glass factory, an enamel workshop, with a painting work-shop, a gilding workshop, and an ivory workshop.[62] The workshops attempted to attract the best craftsmen in the empire to Beijing.[63] Goldsmiths and lapidaries worked imported coral and ivory, as well as native bamboo.[64] Nevertheless, it was acknowledged that Guangdong's craftsmen were particularly skilled. It seems that during the early Yongzheng reign at least, the skills to carve coral were not yet as highly developed. One record from the Imperial Jade Workshop in 1760, the sixth year of Yongzheng's reign states:

> Make a few coral belt plaques using the peach-shaped box with dragon as prototype. If the Palace Workshop cannot do it, wait till someone goes to Guangdong and have them done in Guangdong.[65]

The Yongzheng emperor appears to have rationalised the workshops, while his son, Qianlong increased their number again.[66] From the Kangxi period (1661–1722) onwards, *zaobanchu* were located in the Hall of Mental Cultivation (*Yangxindian*) in the Inner Palace of the Forbidden City, close to the Emperor's personal quarters.[67] Qing emperors liked to keep their craftsmen close at hand. In the case of Kangxi, it was 'witnessing the creative process' that he enjoyed most.[68] Perhaps, like con-temporary European monarchs – such as Louis XVI of France (1754–1793) whose hobby was making locks – the Qing emperors enjoyed watching or participating in practical crafts as a distraction from the burdens of empire.[69] Unsurprisingly, given the longstanding Chinese appreciation of jade, records show it was one of the most widely noted precious materials. On the other hand, the most controlled gemstone was *dongzhu* (eastern freshwater pearls) derived from the Manchurian homeland and associated with Qing power; only members of the royal family were permitted these gems.[70] *Shanhu* appears frequently in the 1755 records, almost as frequently as jade.[71] Other gems, such as turquoise, lapis lazuli, ivory and coloured glass were all specified for use in imperial ornaments and regalia, to be set or inlaid into gold and silver settings.

Zaobanchu records also indicate the chain of command and show something of the scale and level of artisanal production within which the working of coral took place. It was an enormous organisation, in need of a number of individuals in bureaucratic or managerial roles. They emphasise that considerable effort went into the dictating the shape, size, and qualities of materials used. The emperor's orders contain specific requests about sizes, quantities, and qualities for the use of red coral. Imperial orders or decrees for work were passed from the Ministerial Councillor to the Eunuchs.[72] Typical orders from 1755 read:

> In this year, on the second lunar month, on the first day, Ministerial Coun-cillor Jibai Shixiu came with twelve spheres. 'It is the Emperor's decree that the coral beads, a turquoise *yaogu* [bottle-gourd shaped] and lapis-lazuli lids [this perhaps refers to cabochons] should be made into a pendant. This must be done with haste.' End of the Emperor's order.

On the twenty-first day of this lunar month, Ministerial Councillor Jibai Shixiu ordered that the twelve spheres fixed onto the *dongzhu* [eastern pearl] must be collected on this day and exchanged along with the turquoise and coral mounted *yaogu* with the gold dragon heads on. The large engraved spheres of coral must be mounted on the belt in order for the piece to be complete. A series of hooks were also given to Eunuch Hu Shijie. End of Record.[73]

Although brief and to the point, such orders give insights into the types of objects being ordered. They also demonstrate that as well as being kept busy making new items, craftsmen were required to carry out repairs or to remodel objects. Expensive materials were evidently reused. There are a range of possible motivations for recycling precious materials such as coral. These include the fact that coral was considered too valuable to waste; as a means of control over materials; as a demonstration by the imperial household of economy measures or of anxiety over supply. Whatever the reasons, the records show that coral was highly valued and recycled.

In addition to the daily needs of the vast imperial household, the production of luxuries was prodigious. Silks, bejewelled items and other gifts were central to China's political system and its network of allegiances at home and abroad.[74] Gifts for nobles, as well as for the diplomatic, regional and international networks kept craftsmen busy through the year. Typical presents, such as honorific wish-giving *ruyi* sceptres and snuff bottles crafted from humble bamboo or precious coral, were produced in their thousands to mark annual festivals, imperial birthdays and diplomatic visits.[75] The tradition of gifting snuff bottles seems to date to around 1724 (Yongzheng's reign). Rawski notes that in 1755, 500 snuff bottles and 3,000 other items were required for the emperor's stay at his summer palace, in Rehe.[76]

The Kangxi and Qianlong emperors took a particularly keen interest in the production of regalia, gifts and other artefacts.[77] Red coral was used and esteemed at the highest level of power and politics in China and its selection for gifting came under direct imperial control, underlining its importance in the court system. *Shanhu* was reserved for imperial use and the emperor played an active role in deciding the forms, quality and application of the coral. As *zaobanchu* records illustrate, there are numerous direct imperial pronouncements where red coral was the material of choice. Imperial patronage and demands for quality materials and craftsmanship were at the very heart of the coral network. In practical terms, this was the end of the coral network, at the same time it was the beginning, the motivation that drove the trade. In other words, the imperial desire and appetite for the consumption of coral and the control over its use provided an impetus for the long-distance trade in coral.

Concepts of preciousness and treasure

It is important to consider why the Chinese preferred rose-red coral, either unworked as whole 'trees', or worked into large, unblemished spherical beads, in other words, why red coral was selected among other valued native and foreign materials for special treatment at the imperial court. Chinese attitudes to colour hierarchies and preciousness are crucial to understanding how coral was used, represented and written about in Qing China. Furthermore, such an exploration allows a reflection on making, as part of a broader cultural enclave of materials for privileged use.

Chinese artefacts are not merely ornamental. Considerable energy and time was invested in decorating the Chinese material world with appropriate patterns, motifs and in particular materials. According to Terese Tse Bartholomew:

> the decoration on a piece of Chinese art serves two functions: it enhances an otherwise plain surface and it usually presents a veiled auspicious meaning. When an object has no surface decoration, its shape may sometimes denote something auspicious.[78]

The desire to surround oneself with 'good omens' and favourable motifs suggests a fear of the opposite. It implies that 'auspicious' decoration will provide apotropaic protection, 'supposedly having the power to avert an evil influence or bad luck'.[79] As we have seen, there was spiritual freighting on the term 'treasure'. Coral was included among the Eight Precious Things.[80] Patricia Bjaaland Welch notes that these 'are drawn from a large pool of primarily secular good luck symbols, although sometimes one or more of the Eight Treasures of Buddhism are included'.[81] Several of these – ivory, rhinoceros horn and red coral – originated from distant lands.[82]

Red coral is essentially metamorphic. In China, it has a long history of association with medicinal, even magical, properties. It is unsurprising therefore that *shanhu* was endowed with the power to attract favourable energies and deflect unfavourable ones. In uncertain circumstances, there is comfort to be obtained by covering oneself in, or surrounding oneself with, protective and positive motifs and materials. One early printed example, now in the British Museum Collection, shows coral in a protective guise in a woodblock print from the Dunhuang Caves, dating from the Five Dynasties (AD 947), an ancient period of warfare. In it, Vaiśhravaṇa, Guardian King of the North, appears with his sister, Shri Deva (on the left) who holds a *penjing* of auspicious objects, including two branches of coral.[83]

Coral was not simply considered protective, serving the purpose of attracting auspiciousness. It was also understood as precious. This too is a complex term. Here, 'precious' or valuable' is used as a translation for *baogui*, and refers to materials valued, both emotionally and financially, in China, rather than in Europe. An eighteenth-century encyclopaedia details 'treasures' or precious minerals, *baozang*, although this text depends on earlier, previously established systems of preciousness.[84] In Chinese, *baoshi* is defined as a 'precious stone', 'gem', 'stone', 'jewel'.[85] From a European point of view this generates something of a contradiction. While Europeans perceived pearls, diamonds and other gems as highly valuable, in China the most precious of stones is jade; whereas diamonds were less prized, known as *zuanshi*, literally 'drillstone'. Further, it should be noted that Chinese gems were rounded into cabochons; cutting and faceting was not an Asian practice. Qing craftsmen were unquestionably able to produce such effects had these been desirable. In other words, the taste for uncut gems was a cultural preference, rather than lack of skill. It is important not to confuse the material forms considered precious in Europe with those considered precious in China. In Europe, red coral and amber were considered as semi-precious, whereas *shanhu* and *hupo* were highly valued in China.

The character *bao* 寶 is at the same time a noun 'treasure' and the adjective 'precious'. It is a popular, though rather complex term. Dubin points out that the character was 'originally the outline of a house enclosing symbols for cowrie shells and jade beads.[86] There is a link between ruling and wearing jade beads. 'Treasure' is applied to a notable person, a valued object or an idea, including the concept of a national treasure. In his speech in 81 BCE, the Lord Grand Secretary referred to corals as *guobao*, 'national treasures'. These objects were the exclusive property of the emperor, kept in his treasuries and subject to his whim. In other words, the emperor and the nation seem to have been synonymous. The term implies that the emperor is the 'guardian' of this 'treasure' and keeps it safe on behalf the people. The possession of foreign rarities, such as red coral, provided status, respect and wealth, both in the eyes of the Chinese and their neighbours.

Red coral possesses physical qualities that were admired and valued in China. Coral's natural form resembles a plant with wood-like graining and branches, yet it appears unnaturally coloured and polishes to a bright glassy lustre. It is both hard, like a stone, yet brittle. It is a product of the mysterious sea realm and associated with paradise and other-worldliness. It is an elusive, liminal and metamorphic substance. Above all, red coral is inherently red; rose-red coral was an indication of good fortune for its wearer. In China the concept of the colour red is a potent, predominantly optimistic hue with longstanding deep-rooted connections to life-blood, power, success, fertility, vitality and longevity. Festivals and celebrations are associated with the colour. Moreover, red was frequently reserved for nobility, therefore further linked with elite status. Red is one of the five elemental colours, *wuxing*, associated with fire, action, the direction of the south and the season of summer. It is linked to the mythical red bird, the phoenix, and thus to the empress, the begetter of imperial dragons. Coral's fire element and *yang* essence of the sun combined well with the *yin* essence of imperial pearls and the moon. Red coral with eastern freshwater pearls was a potent combination on the imperial *chaozhu* of the emperor and his consort.

Conclusion

The coral network – the coral trade between the Mediterranean and Imperial China – was an established phenomenon by the eighteenth century. Archaeological and textual evidence indicates that red coral was considered 'national treasure' in China for at least two thousand years. Significant human effort was invested in the transportation of coral across vast distances. International trade takes place on the basis that items may be conveyed over a distance and sold for a profit or exchanged for desirable commodities. Thus the accrued value of distance results in a financial or cultural benefit for those involved. The early modern Asian trade was fuelled by a European desire for spices and silks; and later for porcelain and tea, however European traders were unable to offer the Chinese many desirable commodities in exchange; coral, amber and ivory were exceptions.

Red coral's eighteenth-century journey began off the coast of North Africa and concluded half a world away in the palaces of the Qing emperors. Along its stages, or nodes, *Corallium rubrum* was transformed both physically and culturally, accruing economic value and potent social agency in its cross-cultural passage from *coralli* to *shanhu*. What began as a hard-to-obtain marine commodity, metamorphosed into a precious, restricted, imperial curiosity. At the simplest level, red coral was a unit of exchange. To those who valued it, red coral was a mysterious, magical, precious substance that amazed and delighted those fortunate enough to possess it. Ancient Chinese ideas about belief, spirituality and the magical and awe-inspiring qualities of red coral affected its powerful agency.

Britain dominated the European trade with China in the eighteenth century, when private trade in *singsongs* grew to account for over half of the Qing Empire's foreign imports. By separating out the stages of this early-modern exchange, we have been able to explore some of the mechanisms through which coral transformed physically and culturally, accruing economic value and potent social agency in its cross-cultural passages from *coralli* to *shanhu*. There were control mechanisms at both ends of the coral network – in London, the EEIC controlled licences and the quantity of private trade permitted, and in China, red coral was the preserve of the emperor; all imports reserved for him. Some were able to manipulate the system to their advantage. Indeed, the fact that coral was restricted may have enhanced its attraction to those who wished to demonstrate their status.

At the same time, the coral market in China was only as large as the imperial appetite. Unlike in India, where the distribution of imported coral was unregulated, except through the mechanism of price, the coral market in China was limited by imperial demand. In China, coral was officially distributed to the nobles and elite through imperial favour. Since the majority of the coral reaching China was gifted to the emperor, or enclaved for his use, the quantities of coral were not required to be immense; supply merely needed to be sufficient and assured; it seems that the regular consignments of coral were adequate for imperial purposes. The quantity of extant early to mid-Qing artefacts incorporating red coral testifies to the fact that coral was arriving in ample quantities.[87]

As coral moved along this network, the terminology associated with coral shifted, as did the ways in which coral's value was quantified and categorised. *Coralli* began its journey as a raw material, a commodity, trade good or licensed item. It became ship cargoes and packed into boxes or chests. Once in China, it was *shanhu* – tribute, gift, imperial curiosity and ultimately national treasure. En route, coral was judged according to its form, quality and weight – by size, by unit – beads, pieces or 'trees', by pecul or by 'goodness'. Shifting linguistic terms reflect the changing attitudes and perception of red coral as it moved.

The distance that red coral travelled and the restrictions placed upon it were significant factors behind the cultural value ascribed to it. In addition to these allures, coral's mysterious natural qualities – its colour, form and marine provenance – allowed for multi-layered and long-standing cultural associations to be projected upon it.

Notes and References

1. My thanks go to Anne Gerritsen, Giorgio Riello and Maxine Berg of the Global History and Culture Centre at the University of Warwick; to Margit Thøfner, John Mitchell and Steven Hooper, Sainsbury Institute for Art, University of East Anglia; to Sun Yue and Liu Yue, Department of Ancient Utensils, Palace Museum, Beijing, Tung-Ho Chen, National Palace Museum, Taipei, and Matthew Owen in Beijing, to Polly Kwong in Hong Kong and Gilly Thomas of Visual Impact Graphics for their support.
2. Paul Van Dyke, *Merchants of Canton and Macao: Politics and Strategies in Eighteenth-Century Chinese Trade* (Hong Kong: Hong Kong University Press, 2011), 224.
3. *Coralli* is the Italian word for coral. In Mandarin, coral is known as *shanhu*.
4. Gedalia Yogev, *Diamonds and Coral Trade Route: Anglo-Dutch Jews and Eighteenth-Century Trade* (Leicester: Holmes & Meier Publications, 1978), 102–109.
5. *Huangchao liqi tushi* 皇朝禮器圖式 (Illustrated Precedents for the Ritual Paraphernalia of the Imperial Court), 1759 (Yangzhou, 2007), 107, printed in 1766 by the *Wuying dian* (Hall of Military Glory), Fourth scroll, *Guanfu* 1. Translated by Matthew Owen.
6. Ibid. Each equinox and solstice was represented by a cardinal colour.
7. Gary Dickinson and Linda Wrigglesworth, *Imperial Wardrobe* (Berkeley: Ten Speed Press, 2000), 98–114.
8. John E. Vollmer, *Ruling from the Dragon Throne: Costume of the Qing Dynasty* (Berkeley: Ten Speed Press, 2002), 81–85.
9. Ibid.
10. *Huangchao*, 200, 1–2, Vollmer, *Ruling from the Dragon Throne,* 97–99.
11. Luther Carrington Goodrich and W.A.C. Adie, *A Short History of the Chinese People* (London: Allen & Unwin, 1969), 41.
12. Igor Kopytoff, 'The Cultural Biography of Things: Commoditization as Process', in *The Social Lives of Things,* ed. Arjun Appadurai (Cambridge: Cambridge University Press, 1986), 73.
13. For example, the *Book of Tang* details the 'Roman' method of harvesting coral in the seventh or eighth century. Liu Xu, *Tang Shu,* K'ai ming edition 221b, 4155c, Chapter cclviii.b, article *Fu lin.*
14. Edward H. Schafer, *The Golden Peaches of Samarkand: A Study of T'ang Exotics* (Berkeley and Los Angeles: University of California Press, 1962). Irene M. Franck and David M. Brownstone, *The Silk Road: A History* (New York: Facts on File, 1986), 107. The provenance and date of the album leaves are uncertain. They are attributed to Lu Lengjia, with faked seals of the Emperors Huizong and Gaozong.
15. Pliny, *Historia Naturalis,* ed. H. Rackham (Cambridge, Mass.: Harvard University Press, 1958–1962), Book 32, Ch. 11 'Coral: Forty-Three Remedies and Observations'.
16. El Kala, Algeria and Tabarka, Tunisia.
17. Jean-Baptiste Tavernier, *Travels in India,* ed. Valentine Ball. Translated from the 1676 edition. (New Delhi: Munshiram Manoharlal, 2000), 104–106. Arguerrel is possibly modern-day Alghero.
18. Leghorn, Northern Italy.
19. The coral harvesting season ran from late spring to early summer.

20. The *Oxford English Dictionary* states: 'A commodity is a raw material or primary agricultural product that can be bought and sold'.
21. Lewis Feuchtwanger, *A Treatise On Gems: In Reference to Their Practical and Scientific Value* (New York: A. Hanford, 1838), 154–158. There were multiple forms and terms for coral, e.g. *Cadentias,* is another mentioned in: British Library, IOR/V/27/46/66, *Letters from Fort St George* ff. 181–182 Madras, 15 September 1761.
22. Feuchtwanger, *A Treatise On Gems,* 154–158.
23. This may be a misspelling of *greggio*, which means raw in Italian.
24. *A Calendar of the Court Minutes of the East India Company, 1677–1679*, ed. Ethel Sainsbury (Oxford: Oxford University Press, 1938), 52–53; IOR 354.5P.
25. Yogev, *Diamonds*, 102–109.
26. In EEIC records, East Indies may refer to South Asia as well as to China. It is therefore difficult to determine the final destination. Nevertheless, some records do specify China, as the following example indicates.
27. British Library, IOR/B/80/73 *Court Book*, April 1764–March 1765, ff. 313. £3,000 is the equivalent of *c.* £150,000 today.
28. Gravesend.
29. Fort Marlborough in Bencoolen (modern Bengkulu), western Sumatra, was another *entrepôt*.
30. Yogev, *Diamonds*, 129.
31. Yogev, *Diamonds*, 81–93.
32. Weng Eang Cheong, *The Hong Merchants of Canton: Chinese Merchants in Sino-Western Trade, 1684–1798* (London: Curzon Press, 1996), 225.
33. Gang Zhao, *The Qing Opening to the Ocean: Chinese Maritime Policies 1684–1757* (Honolulu: University of Hawai'i Press, 2013), 169–186. Gang Zhao offers a new interpretation of the reasons behind this phenomenon.
34. Huangpu, Changzhou Island in the Pearl River.
35. It is possible that the coral was intended for India; nevertheless, it shows the dynamics of the private trade on the EEIC ships.
36. British Library, IOR/L/MAR/B/390S(1) *Hawke: Ledger c.*1765–*c.*1767. A *chop* was a small cargo boat.
37. Hosea Ballou Morse, *The Chronicles of The East India Company Trading to China, 1635–1834,* (Oxford: Clarendon Press, 1929), vol. 5, 30–31.
38. Anthony Farrington, *Trading Places: The East India Company and Asia 1600–1834* (London: British Library, 2002), 120–121; British Library, IOR/10/5, 1761–1769; Volume 5, ff. 61–18 October 1764. A *pecul* was approximately 133 lbs or 60 kgs. Therefore, the cargoes contained the equivalent of over 270 kilograms of coral beads and over 55 kilograms of coral pieces.
39. It should be noted that other *Corallium spp.* of red coral derived from the Pacific and other sources. By the turn of the nineteenth century, Japanese and other Pacific red corals had been discovered and were being exploited in quantity. CoP14.21 2007, 1–22. Japanese coral fishing began in 1804 and expanded to Taiwan and the neighbouring islands from 1868. Ptak suggests that some forms of Japanese coral may have been reaching China at far earlier dates. Yang notes that some corals came from local waters. Nevertheless, before the nineteenth century, it seems that most red coral in China was Mediterranean *Corallium rubrum,* where it was particularly prized for its rose-red colour and longstanding cultural associations. Roderick Ptak, 'Notes on the Word *Shanhu* and Chinese Coral Imports from Maritime Asia *c.*1250–1600,' *Archipel* 39 (1990), 65–80; Yang Boda, *Tributes from Guangdong to the Qing Court* (Beijing: The Palace Museum, and the Art Gallery, The Chinese University of Hong Kong, 1987), 39–67; Cheong, *Hong Merchants,* 111–113, Paul van Dyke, *The Canton Trade: Life and Enterprise on the China Coast, 1700–1845* (Hong Kong: Hong Kong University Press, 2005), 25.
40. Van Dyke, *Merchants of Canton and Macao*, 3. Private trade also refers to independent foreign ships.
41. Van Dyke, *Merchants of Canton and Macao*, 224.

42. Van Dyke, *Merchants of Canton and Macao*, 224.
43. Van Dyke, *Canton Trade,* 25.
44. Cheong, *Hong Merchants*, 225; Yang, *Tributes from Guangdong*, 39–67.
45. Yang, *Tributes from Guangdong*, 39–67.
46. Ibid.
47. Ibid 29th day, 8th month, 11th reign year. Some terms are unidentified.
48. Yang, *Tributes from Guangdong*, 39–67.
49. Ruan Huaduan, *Gems from the South: Traditional Crafts of Guangdong Province* (Hong Kong: University Museum and Art Gallery, the University of Hong Kong, 2002), 30–48.
50. Beverley Jackson, *Kingfisher Blue: Treasures of an Ancient Chinese Art* (Berkeley: Ten Speed Press, 2001), 41–54.
51. John Henry Gray, *Walks in the City of Canton* (Hong Kong: De Souza & Co., 1875), 292.
52. Gray, *Walks in the City*, 292.
53. John Adams, *A Narrative of the Success of an Embassage sent by John Maatzuyker De Badem, General of Batavia unto the Emperour of China & Tartary, The 20th of July 1655* (1667), 14–16.
54. Adams, *A Narrative*, 14–16.
55. Johannes Nieuhof, *An Embassy from the East-India Company of the United Provinces to the Grand Tartar Cham Emperor of China* (London: John Macock, 1673), 114–146.
56. Zhao, *Qing Opening*, 99–115.
57. British Library, IOR/G/12/20 ff.142 and additional items added to the Embassy in Macao.
58. British Library, IOR/G/12/20 ff.142.
59. Mark Elliott, *The Emperor Qianlong: Son of Heaven, Man of the World* (New York and London: Longman, 2009), 134–139.
60. *Zaobanchu* (ZBC) records indicated that precious gems were also purchased in Beijing from Chinese traders.
61. Evelyn Rawski, *The Last Emperors: A Social History of the Qing Imperial Institutions* (Berkeley and London: University of California Press, 1998), 175–181. The dates of the establishment of some of the workshops appear to be uncertain.
62. Yang Boda, 'The Palace Workshops and Imperial Kilns Snuff Bottles of Emperor Qianlong,' *Arts of Asia* 26.5 (1996): 65–77.
63. Additional information about Qing workshops can be gleaned from other scholars who have examined glassware, snuff bottles and ivory carving, etc.
64. Regina Krahl, 'The Kangxi Emperor: Horseman, Man of Letters, Man of Science' in *China: The Three Emperors*, ed. Evelyn Rawski and Jessica Rawson (London: The British Museum, 2005), 208–239.
65. Ming Wilson, '1760: An Important Year in the Production of Chinese Jade', *The Annual Woolf Jade Lecture, The Oriental Ceramic Society* (London: The Oriental Ceramic Society, 2009), 51–60.
66. Yang, *Palace Workshops*, 65–77.
67. Krahl, *Kangxi Emperor*, 213–214.
68. Ibid.
69. Harvey Chisick, *Historical Dictionary of the Enlightenment* (Lanham, MD: Scarecrow Press, 2005), 263–264.
70. Dickinson and Wrigglesworth, *Imperial Wardrobe*, 100.
71. *Qinggong Zaobanchu* (ZBC), Records from the Imperial Workshops 1755, 2005. Translated by Matthew Owen.
72. Two Ministerial Councillors are named: Jibai Shixiu and Ji Jinhui. The three eunuchs named are Hu Shijie, Ling Youfu and Wang Baozhu, with Hu Shijie's name appearing most frequently in the records for 1755–1756. There was also a Deputy Manager who passed orders on. The department appears to have been managed under the department of Qing Affairs. The general manager was Wang Changgui.

73. ZBC records, 516–35.
74. Rawski, *Last Emperors*, 51–55.
75. Rawski, *Last Emperors,* 272–278.
76. Rawski, *Last Emperors*, 175–178.
77. Rawski, *Last Emperors*, 175–178; Krahl, *Kangxi Emperor*, 208–239.
78. Terese Tse Bartholomew, *Hidden Meanings in Chinese Art* (San Francisco: The San Francisco Asian Art Museum, 2006), 16–19.
79. R.E. Allen, *The Concise Oxford Dictionary* (Oxford: Oxford University Press, 1991).
80. Patricia Bjaaland Welch, *Chinese Art: A Guide to the Motifs and Visual Imagery* (Tokyo, Rutland and Singapore: Tuttle, 2008), 228–229.
81. Bjaaland Welch, *Chinese Art*, 228–229. Bjaaland Welch lists the most commonly observed combinations of Precious Things as: a pearl (*baozhu*) for good fortune; a lozenge (*fangsheng*); a stone chime (*qing*); a pair of rhinoceros horn cups (*xijiao*) for health; a metal coin or pair of coins (*jinqian*); ivory tusks (*xiangya*); branching coral (these latter three objects are symbols of wealth and status); a disk-shaped mirror (*jing*) for fidelity; a roll of scrolls (*juanzhou*) for wisdom and culture; and, finally, a *ruyi* sceptre, for honour and longevity.
82. China native elephants and rhinos became extinct in ancient times.
83. *The Printed Image in China: From the 8th to the 21st Centuries*, ed. Clarissa von Spee (London: The British Museum, 2010), 67, No. 7. British Museum: 1919, 0101, 0.245; Ch.xxx.002.
84. Peter Hardie, *China: Hardstones.* Vol. 13 of *The Grove Dictionary of Art*, ed. Jane Turner (Oxford: Oxford University Press, 1996), 88–91; Zhang Ying et al, *Yuanjian leihan,* (The deep mirror of classified knowledge), WSQ edition, 1710.
85. Bjaaland Welch, *Chinese Art*, 244.
86. Lois Sherr Dubin, *The Worldwide History of Beads* (London: Thames and Hudson, 2009), 166.
87. In the late Qing period, Asia-Pacific sources of coral were exploited affecting the quantity and quality of coral available. Scientific testing is required to determine the origins of the various species of *Corallium spp.* in Qing artefacts.

PART II

Objects of global connections

4

BEYOND THE *KUNSTKAMMER*

Brazilian featherwork in early modern Europe[1]

Mariana Françozo

Introduction

The small town of Isselburg, northwest Germany, is home to the imposing Wasserburg-Anholt Schloss, originally a twelfth-century fortress transformed into a castle and belonging since 1649 to the Salm noble family. A visit to the property includes a tour of the many lavishly decorated rooms of the castle, from the library to the art galleries. The *Rittersaal* showcases about seventy portraits of the members of the Bronckhorst-Batenburg and Salm-Salm families, disposed along two 16-metre wide lateral walls. Amid the sober portraits, one image stands out: a young noble lady wears a white satin dress, a pearl necklace and a cape made of red and yellow feathers (Figure 4.1). On her left shoulder, a brooch ties the two extremities of the cape together, so that it is hung in the form of a royal mantle. The red feathers of the cape are combined with a red-feathered headdress. The lady is carrying a spear and poses before a tropical landscape background.

This is a portrait of Princess Sophie of the Palatinate, daughter of Frederick V, Elector Palatine and Elizabeth Stuart. It was painted by Sophie's older sister, Louise Hollandine of the Palatinate. The painting stands out because of the unique costume worn by the sitter. While the depiction of noble ladies dressed up in costumes or as allegorical characters was not uncommon in early modern portraiture, the use of feathered ornaments, combined with the tropical background, renders this portrait exceptional. Why would Sophie of the Palatinate have dressed up like this? In an attempt to answer this question, this chapter focuses on the production, consumption, and transformation of featherworks along the global paths these artefacts travelled in the early modern period.

Feathers and featherwork were part of collections of curiosities in the sixteenth and seventeenth centuries and constitute today one of the highlights of ethnographic museums. In particular, the featherwork produced by Amazonian and coastal Tupi

FIGURE 4.1 *Portrait of Sophie of the Palatinate*, by Louise Hollandine of the Palatinate, undated. Oil on canvas, 104 × 86 cm. Wasserburg-Anholt Castle Collection, Isselburg, Germany. Inv. Nr. 729. © Prince of Salm-Salm, Anholt.

societies in the territory that is present-day Brazil proved to be a valuable possession for early modern collectors and modern ethnographic research alike.[2] Since the mid-twentieth century, anthropologists and historians have been trying to locate and document the importance of Brazilian ethnographic collections in Brazil and in Europe.[3] This effort has so far resulted in a number of beautifully illustrated catalogues and more recently some extraordinary museum exhibitions highlighting the historical importance, ethnographic value and aesthetic quality of featherwork produced by American indigenous peoples, especially those in Brazil.[4] Likewise, the sheer number and variety of feathered materials in contemporary ethnographic museums worldwide provide proof of the value of featherwork as a distinct type of collectible material culture.

Some of the most prized feather capes and ornaments are those that were brought to Europe from colonial Latin America in the early modern period. Three of the most well-known pieces are a sixteenth-century red feather cape ascribed to the Tupinambá indigenous group that is now at the Musée du quai Branly in Paris (Figure 4.2), and the two feather capes kept at the National Museum of Denmark in Copenhagen.[5] The latter museum also holds a valuable collection of about a dozen other feather adornments, all dating from at least the second half of the seventeenth century (or possibly earlier), when they were first described in *kunstkammer* inventories.[6]

Feathers were brought from Latin America to European curiosity cabinets in different formats: as feather ornaments of different types (capes, headdresses, bonnets, bracelets, knee and ankle ornaments), as separate sets of birds' feathers, as part of beautifully elaborated artefacts made of wood, stone or other materials, or as entire birds. To cite but a few examples, the eminent Dutch collector Bernardus Paludanus, doctor at the city of Enkhuizen, listed in a 1617 inventory his ownership of a variety of birds, birds' eggs and a chest with feathers of birds, as well as clothes and ornaments made of birds' feathers.[7] The Bibliothèque de Sainte-Geneviève in Paris owns a rare Amazonian stone axe, part of the cabinet of curiosities of the Sainte-Geneviève Abbey already by the late seventeenth century. The semi-lunar metal blade is fixed on a wooden handle covered in cord, which retains traces of red feathers once vertically attached to the cord.[8] Examples of feathers in cabinets of curiosity of the early modern period are relatively plentiful, especially considering the limitations of research into this perishable kind of material.[9]

This chapter investigates the uses and meanings attached to feathered ornaments in the sixteenth and seventeenth centuries. It will particularly look at the production and usages of feather ornaments in indigenous societies in the coastal area of colonial Brazil and at the later incorporation of such artefacts into European collections. Drawing evidence from written accounts that depict the social and material lives of indigenous peoples in coastal Brazil, this chapter begins by describing the ways in which indigenous societies – and particularly the coastal Tupi – obtained and transformed feathers into elaborate and distinct types of feather ornaments, and how these artefacts were ritually used in specific moments of community life. Secondly, this chapter considers the impact of the colonial encounter in the production of featherwork and proposes that these artefacts exemplify the transformation and reinvention of indigenous material culture in the colonial context. Indeed, once produced and used by native societies all over the Americas, after 1492 featherwork quickly entered the vast networks of material exchange. As such, they became prized possessions for European collectors. The third section of the chapter thus looks into how feathers became part of *kunstkammers* in three different material forms: as featherwork, as loose sets of feathers, and in the form of entire birds.

FIGURE 4.2a Cape. Rio de Janeiro, America, sixteenth century, Tupinambá, (front). Paris, Musée du quai Branly. Feathers, cotton, natural fibres, glass beads. 117 × 108 × 10 cm, 840g. Inv. N: 71.1917.3.83. Restored with the support of Centre des Jeunes Dirigeants de Paris © 2015. Musée du quai Branly. Photo Claude Germain/Scala, Florence.

FIGURE 4.2b Cape. Rio de Janeiro, America, sixteenth century, Tupinambá (back).

Contrary to other objects in early modern European collections, feathers and feath- erwork were mobile items: they were exchanged between collectors, borrowed and lent, worn by models sitting for portraits, used at festivities, and even physically transformed as they changed hands. Therefore, the last two sections of this chapter address the mobility of featherwork. By discussing examples from festivals, pageants, and ballets in early modern Europe, it looks into how feathers and featherwork were used outside of the confined walls of the *kunstkammers* as part of costumes. As such, this chapter argues that feathers and featherwork were essentially mobile in their physical existence – both in their indigenous and European usages. Likewise, they were unstable objects that – because of their values, functions, and meanings – were directly dependent on their ever-shifting physical uses.

The production and circulation of feathers and featherwork in colonial Brazil

The first part of this chain of production and consumption starts in Latin America, where the production and use of feathered artefacts has been an integral part of the lives of indigenous peoples since Pre-Columbian times. Unlike the beautiful pieces of Pre-Columbian Andean featherwork that have been preserved due to the dry climate conditions of the Peruvian coast, the South American lowlands equiva- lents of such materials have perished and thus cannot be found in the archaeologi- cal record.[10] Other types of archaeological finds, however, such as ceramic vessels, stone pendants and axes, and wooden sculptures contain aviary decorations and forms that highlight the importance of birds and feathers to Pre-Columbian Carib- bean and Amazonian societies. Pottery head figurines (*adornos*) from the Santarém ceramic tradition in the Amazon, for example, feature birds such as toucans, parrots and king vultures – some of which contain perforated carbuncles on top of the birds' heads that 'may have served for the insertion of feathers'.[11]

Nonetheless, if the archaeological evidence for the use of feathers by Pre- Columbian societies is scarce, the numerous European chronicles about sixteenth- century Latin America suggest a production and use of feathers and featherwork prior to the arrival of the Europeans that would have continued at least well into the sixteenth century. This is particularly the case for featherwork produced by indigenous peoples in coastal Brazil and Amazonia, evidence for which is pro- vided by a variety of European written sources. The Franciscan André Thevet (1516–1590), for instance, in his 1557 description of trade customs of Amerindians, mentions the existence of an inter-Amerindian trade in feathers. He claims that the Tupi of coastal Brazil received their supply of plumes from the interior of the lands, travelling up to 120 *léguas* (the equivalent to circa 500 kilometres) inland to trade them for other goods. The most appreciated goods, according to Thevet, were the Rhea feathers.[12]

During the first two centuries of the European presence in the Americas, explor- ers carefully observed the skills with which indigenous peoples obtained, collected, and worked the feathers of different species of birds into elaborate ornaments.

French missionary Jean de Léry (1536–1613) noted how the Tupi carefully plucked the feathers out of the birds' bodies three to four times a year in order to make bracelets, headdresses, and other ornaments.[13] Almost one century later, Dutch explorers in Northeastern Brazil would still write about birds and feathers. Zacharias Wagener (1614–1668), a talented amateur artist from Dresden who worked for the Dutch West Indian Company as a kitchen clerk, kept a book of drawings of the animals, plants and curiosities he encountered around Recife. Under the drawing of a parrot, he noted that 'the *brasilianen* know a particular way of hitting them with soft arrows so that they do not get hurt, and can be sold in large quantities for a small price'.[14]

The choice of birds was also an important aspect of the production of featherwork. In his descriptive treatise about the coastal areas of Brazil, Portuguese sugar planter and explorer Gabriel Soares de Sousa (*c.*1540–1591) describes in detail a number of different birds living in those areas and highlights the use that indigenous peoples made of their feathers: the yellow feathers of the *canindé* – the blue-throated macaw (*Ara glaucogularis*) – for instance, were used by the Indians to make feather bonnets, and the long feathers of the macaw's tail, to decorate their clubs; the black feathers of the *uraçu* or harpy eagle (*Harpia harpyjaare*) were placed in the rear end of arrows.[15] André Thevet also mentioned the use of toucan tail feathers, yellow and long, in the decoration of clubs and the manufacture of feather capes and bonnets.[16]

This points to the importance attributed by indigenous peoples to specific colours and shapes of feathers for distinct purposes. Recent ethnohistorical studies have highlighted that the red-coloured feather of the *guará* – the scarlet ibis (*Eudocimus ruber*), for example, was specially praised and therefore used in the making of sumptuous feather headdresses and capes; for the same reason, colour modification processes would have been employed to achieve the desired colour in otherwise white or green feathers. So in the absence of scarlet ibis feathers, the same sumptuous headdresses and capes could also be made with red, artificially coloured chicken or parrot feathers.[17]

In fact, a particular technique of colour modification known as *tapirage* played a significant role in the production of featherwork in the colonial period. *Tapirage* can be defined as the artificial discoloration of feathers in live birds, as opposed to the alteration of colour in feathers that have been already plucked out of the animal.[18] Sixteenth-century accounts about colonial Brazil already identified and described this process for their European readerships. Soares de Sousa explained how the Tupinambá made red and yellow feathers out of white ones: *tapirage* was performed on parrots by plucking out their green feathers and rubbing the blood of a toad on the birds' skin and particularly on the recently opened pores, which would result in the new feathers growing yellow.[19] Feathers were also transformed and dyed after having been taken from the birds. Jean de Léry recounts that the Tupinambá would take white chicken feathers, boil them and dye them with Brazil wood, cut them in very small pieces before gluing them onto their bodies 'so that they are feathered all over'.[20]

The value and the different uses of featherwork did not go unnoticed by European observers. Zacharias Wagener wrote that feathers were appreciated by the most powerful men in the colony of Dutch Brazil.[21] George Marcgraf (1610–1644), the scholar and naturalist known for his part in the making of the book *Historia Naturalis Brasiliae* (1648), also wrote about the Tapuia and their headdresses, describing in detail their making and use: the feather cloak included a hood made of elegant red *Guará* (scarlet ibis) bird plumage, as well as black, green and golden feathers, which – according to him – would protect from the rain.[22]

Most of the early accounts, however, refer mainly to the ritual and performative use of feathers amongst the Tupi societies of coastal Brazil (Figure 4.3). The Tupinambá used feathers and featherwork in the ritual process of killing a captive – one of the most fundamental moments of tribal social life, as war, ritual vengeance and captivity were central elements of Tupinambá cosmology.[23] The warrior chosen to kill the prisoner would have his body painted with the fruit of the *jenipapo* tree (*genipa americana*); on his head he would wear a feather diadem, and on his legs and arms, bracelets and ankle feather ornaments. The club used to kill the captive was likewise decorated with long yellow feathers. In the same manner, when a village head (*principal*) died, his body would be first covered with honey and then adorned with different types of colourful feathers, as well as a feather bonnet, before being interred.[24]

Such precise and carefully ritualized use of feathers and feathered ornaments can only be properly understood in the context of Amerindian cosmologies. Marcy Norton has identified five different ways in which Amerindian societies related to birds and their feathers during the time of European conquest: 'hunting, taming, eating and/or enjoying the songs of wild birds; raising and eating domestic birds; harvesting and trading feathers from which to create art and adornment; mimicking birds in ritual performances; auguring and deifying birds'.[25] The last three forms of engagement are particularly relevant for the purposes of this chapter, for the indigenous production and consumption of featherwork guaranteed the proper continuation of ritual and social life in the villages. Much more than 'mimicking' birds, however, ethnohistorical sources show that indigenous warriors ritually *became* birds by wearing a bird's skin – as represented by a feather cape, bonnet, diadem, or the entire set with ankle and arm ornaments. Jean de Léry noted this transformation while perhaps being unaware of its cosmologic importance: 'with their bodies, arms, and legs all bedecked', the Tupinambá 'seem to be all downy, like pigeons or other birds newly hatched'.[26] In fact, in the Tupinambá ritual sacrifice described above, both the captive and the warrior became birds: the feather ornaments would make the captive a parrot, and the warrior a bird of prey.[27] Thus the use of feathered adornments had the metaphorical function of facilitating the ritual and symbolic transformation of men into birds. Moreover, as Amy Buono suggests, explicit weaving and dying techniques were employed for different featherworking outcomes: 'The textural contrast between the Tupi feathered bonnet and the full-length cape' can be understood to materially signify a (respectively) new-born and an adult bird.[28]

FIGURE 4.3 Tupinambá Dance. In Theodor de Bry, *Dritte Buch Americae, darinn Brasilia durch Johann Staden von Homberg auss Hessen, auss eigener erfahrung in Teutsch beschrieben* (Franckfurt am Main, 1593). Special Collections, University of Amsterdam, OTM: OF 82–9.

Feathers and the colonial encounter: exchange and transformation

While Europeans observed and marvelled at such complex featherwork techniques, indigenous peoples of coastal Brazil quickly realized the value of such objects to European traders and colonizers. Thus the production of featherwork likely increased after 1500, slowly but steadily fuelled by the growing European market for indigenous rarities. Traditional indigenous uses of feathers and featherwork in rituals and village life continued after the advent of European conquest; however, new modes of production (including the intensification of colour modification techniques) may have been one of the consequences of increased demand for the feather ornaments. The feather cape at the Musée du quai Branly is an exceptionally good example: while manufactured according to traditional indigenous techniques and materials, it also includes a rim decorated with blue and white beads. This cape was likely produced after 1500 and scholars have debated whether or not it belonged in the collection of André Thevet.[29] In any case, the use of beads indicates the incorporation of European materials into the fabrication of indigenous artefacts. Likewise, the disruption of pre-Columbian social order and the creation of colonial society made way for new modes of use for such artefacts. For instance, in the *aldeias* – indigenous villages created and controlled by Catholic missionaries – indigenous practices and values would be transformed and adapted into this new colonial setting. As Amy Buono suggests, Jesuits likely encouraged the production of feather ornaments to be used in the conversion and Catholic rituals such as baptism organized by the priests in the *aldeias*.[30]

Therefore, instead of adopting a conservative, one-sided perspective that insists on the complete devastation of indigenous material and cultural forms, I argue that the colonial encounter also stirred the ongoing transformation of indigenous practices – and likewise, in this particular case, the production, exchange, and sale of featherwork. Far from being static entities awaiting the impact of European 'discovery', Latin American – and specifically Amazonian and coastal Brazilian indigenous societies had already been part of ever-changing systems of intergroup dynamics. These dynamics were built upon alliances, warfare, captivity and enemy vengeance, as well as upon commerce and trade. Migration and reformulation of intertribal politics were an essential element of their social life and cosmologies, instigated both by crises and conflicts internal to these societies and by external disruptive factors – of which, of course, the eventual European conquest would be the ultimate driving force. As part of such ongoing transformations, the incorporation of European trade goods played a major role in the creation of colonial (indigenous) societies. European products were 'rapidly assimilated into aboriginal networks of trade and commerce, and Europeans themselves were often seen as trade partners with whom social and political alliances could be made'.[31]

By the mid-sixteenth century feathers and featherwork had thus become an important component in the direct trade between indigenous peoples and Europeans, as well as in acts of diplomacy and in establishing commercial and political alliances. The image of indigenous people in coastal South America selling or exchanging native products and animals with Europeans soon became news – and eventually a recurrent topic – in European maps, books and prints. Surekha Davies has discussed some early examples of such depictions in French maps. One of the earliest examples can be found in the *Vallard Atlas* of 1547, where Tupi men and women are depicted exchanging tamed parrots and monkeys with Europeans.[32] This type of image would soon make its way into other formats of printed matter. In 1562, the French publishers and book illustrators André Breton and François Desprez published what is now known as the first costume book depicting the habits and clothes worn by peoples in different parts of the world: the *Recueil de la diversité des habits*.[33] In that volume, for the first time in a costume book, a Brazilian (indigenous) man is depicted wearing a feather ornament on his back, and the Brazilian woman is described as someone who 'sells monkeys and parrots' to the Europeans (Figure 4.4).[34] The printed representation of such exchanges seems to have corresponded to lived experiences in the other side of the Atlantic. Almost a century after the publication by Desprez, Peter Hansen Hajstrup (1624–1672),

FIGURE 4.4 Images 'La Bresilienne' and 'Le Bresilien', in François Deserps, *Recueil de la diversité des habits, qui sont de présent en usage, tant ès pays d'Europe, Asie, Affrique et isles sauvages, le tout fait après le naturel* (Paris: Imprimerie de Richard Breton, 1564). Special Collections, University of Amsterdam, OTM: OK 68–27.

a Danish soldier working for the Dutch West India Company in Northeast Brazil in the 1640s, reported in his diary how pleased he was when he received 'a beautiful parrot in sign of friendship' from indigenous leader Janduí.[35]

The collecting of featherworks in Europe

While explorers in the New World described the making, use, exchange, and selling of featherwork by the indigenous peoples, on the other side of the Atlantic collectors became rapidly aware of and highly interested in such materials.[36] Soldiers, sailors, and others would take back all sorts of rarities from the New World to be given as gifts or exchanged for money. In 1641, upon his return from Brazil to the Netherlands, Zacharias Wagener took with him a special parcel: arriving in Texel on 20 June that year, he made his way via Haarlem to Leiden and The Hague in order to deliver 'letters, drawings, and parrots' entrusted to him by Count Johan Maurits of Nassau-Siegen (1604–1679), then governor of Dutch Brazil.[37] In fact, much like feathers and featherwork, parrots had also become a prized possession for European collectors and even for a less specialized audience, as they also served as domesticated, home animals. According to Marcy Norton, before 1500 Europeans had already developed long traditions of human–aviary relationships that would provide a frame of reference for the introduction of South American parrots as pets in the sixteenth century.[38] It is thus not uncommon to find birds featuring in collection inventories, and the references to the exchange of parrots between Europeans and Amerindians are abundant, as we have seen.

The early modern European reception of birds, feathers and featherwork involved collectors in both Northern and Southern Europe, and particularly those in the large centres such as Paris, Milan, Florence, Antwerp, Amsterdam, and Copenhagen, among others.[39] Although there is no accurate assessment as to the number of feathered ornaments made in Brazil and sent to Europe,[40] there was undeniably a market for exotic birds, feathers and featherwork especially amongst collectors in Northern Europe. Caspar Schmalkalden, a former employee of the Dutch West and East India companies, upon returning from his travels in South America and Southeast Asia to his hometown Gotha, Germany, became keeper of the *kunstkammer* of the Duke Ernst I of Saxe-Gotha-Altenburg. As such, in 1656 he received detailed written instructions from the Duke to travel to Amsterdam and purchase a number of items for his new collection, including small West-Indian birds, bows and arrows of the 'savages from East and West-Indies', and 'Indian baskets'.[41] As historian Elke Bujok has shown, around 1660 feathered objects ascribed to the Tupinambá 'were offered to the Wolfenbüttel court: a red coat, a yellow hood, a yellow collar and eight bands for arms, legs and hips' for the expensive price of 100 *Reichstaler*.[42]

Little is known in regards to the physical distribution of objects inside *kunstkammers*.[43] The few detailed inventories as well as room descriptions suggest that South and North American feathered ornaments were placed alongside artefacts from Africa and Europe irrespective of geographies of origin. In fact, cabinets of curiosities have been described as a 'mixing of objects' or a spatial experience of an 'aggregate of multiple objects'.[44] This does not imply that *kunstkammers* were unordered spaces or simple accumulations of *exotica*. On the contrary, these collections followed ordering systems germane to the early modern collector's mindset. For instance, objects could be arranged according to the materials they were made of, which would permit the display of crafted feathered adornments next to stuffed birds.[45] Moreover, as this chapter explains, feathers and featherworks could be taken out and returned to the *kunstkammer*, or could likewise be lent out for more dynamic display purposes. Besides the usual form of exhibiting collected artefacts within rooms, collectors also actively used and displayed featherwork outside of the confined spaces of the collection as costume in court festivities such as pageants and masquerades. This shows the possibility of an external continuity of the collection beyond the walls of the *kunstkammer*, as objects in festivities (particularly but not exclusively feathers and featherwork) could be showcased to a wider public.

While being displayed within and beyond *kunstkammers*, featherwork was a powerful and widely recognized representation of South America, and of its indigenous inhabitants in particular.[46] The first visual association of native peoples of coastal Brazil with feathers dates to as early as 1505, in the form of a woodcut portraying a group of Tupinambá men wearing feather skirts and headdresses.[47] Visual representations of the non-European world had already been popularized in the course of the sixteenth century and as such they standardized the repertoire of cultures and peoples of the world for European audiences.[48] In this sense, publications such as Desprez's 1562 costume book and the printing, translating and reprinting of numerous travel accounts on the Americas were instrumental not only in associating South American native peoples with feathers but also in familiarizing early modern Europeans with these visual patterns.[49] As historian Johann Verberckmoes states, 'no dress was more stereotyped than feathers for the Amerindians . . . In the early modern European representations, feathers almost equalled the "Indians" who wore them on their head, arms, and legs'.[50]

Performing feathers in early modern European festivals

In the early modern period, the typical elements of court entertainment were drawn from Classical Antiquity through the performative use of Greek and Roman characters and myths. The gradual incorporation of the Amerindian element in such events was a consequence and a reflection both of the place of the New World in the early modern mindset as well as of the development of specific forms of cultural performances in Europe. The presence of Amerindian characters in European pageants has been compared to that of wild men in medieval and Renaissance festivities, by way of a 'theatrical blending' of these two elements.[51] While this may be a somewhat exaggerated appraisal, there certainly was some degree of continuity in the cultural preconceptions that helped shape the image of Amerindians in early modern Europe. However, the uninterrupted and increasing contacts and encounters that took place in the Americas and were continued on European grounds quickly guaranteed that a selection of objects and cultural elements became attached to the ethnic or geographical identification of non-Europeans in court festivities. A handful of objects signifying otherness and referencing continents such as America and Africa were employed in pageants and festivities: feathers, maraca rattles, baskets, bows and arrows. The types of cultural stereotypes that these events helped to create were relatively persistent. In this process, feathers and featherwork became the quintessential signifiers of America.

This performative construction of ethnic identities started as early as 1493, on the occasion of Christopher Columbus' triumphal entry in Barcelona. Having left Seville for Barcelona in the company of a few indigenous men, probably coming from the island of Hispaniola, Columbus and his entourage presented to King Ferdinand and Queen Isabella a selection of 'things never seen before in Europe' such as charming and colourful green parrots and ornaments made with gold, pearls, and fish bones. According to the description by Bartholomé de Las Casas, not only the monarchs but all members of the court and many inhabitants of the city of Barcelona came to the streets to see 'the Indians and the parrots' and the many objects they carried.[52] The display of gold ornaments undoubtedly aimed at convincing the Catholic monarchs about the opportunity and need for new voyages to the New World. The presentation of parrots together with the Indians, on the other hand, shows a metaphorical association that would prevail in the image of the Amerindian as related to feathers and featherwork.[53]

Columbus' display of Indians and feathers was thus explicitly connected to the context of early discoveries and the immediate need to stimulate and guarantee the financial support for new travels of exploration. In the course of the next two centuries, and particularly during the sixteenth century, the use of feathers and featherwork in public festivities or courtly entertainment responded to localized, dynastic or national political struggles.

One of the most paradigmatic examples is the Royal Entry of Henry II and Catherine de Medici into Rouen in 1550. On that occasion, a group of 250 men dressed as Tupinambá Indians, as well as fifty Tupinambá brought from Brazil, mimicked the life of an indigenous village in Brazil: some men chopped down and traded wood, others were lying in hammocks, another group of men was hunting animals and birds. This re-enactment of a somewhat peaceful village life pointed to the abundance of products that were available for those who would invest in establishing trade with Brazilian peoples. Soon, however, this peaceful scenario would drastically change, as the Tupinambá left their regular occupations to stage a fight between themselves and their enemies, the Tabajaras. This was a political discourse transformed into play, as the Tabajaras were known to be allies of the Portuguese. By defeating the Tabajara – and thus the Portuguese – in Rouen, these 'French Tupinambá' conveyed a message to the French king about the economic and political usefulness of a French-Tupinambá alliance against the Portuguese in the New World that would allow for the exploration of Brazilian riches.

According to Michael Wintroub, not only did this theatrical performance appeal to Henri II and the French court for the political message and economic opportunities it signalled, but also in that the king and the nobility identified with the 'martial spirit' and warrior qualities of the Tupinambá.[54] The very staging of this battle and the organization of the entry, in fact, were closely related to the emergence and establishment of a new elite class in Rouen – a class of merchants and traders interested in doing business in Brazil and eager to convince Henri II of its potential.[55] More tellingly, as pointed out by Surekha Davies, some of the birds and animals used in this event were lent by local traders of Rouen who had been involved in the commerce with Brazil.[56] This is yet another example of the use of collectible items – such as birds and feathers – outside of the confined spaces of *kunstkammers*.

The Royal Entry in Rouen was followed in France by a number of other public and royal festivities, ballets and pageants, where the Amerindian character played an important role.[57] For instance, in 1662 the tournament *Grand Carrousel* was performed as the last festivity held in Paris before Louis XIV moved the court to Versailles. The event was a commemoration of the birth of Louis XIV's son; at a political level, the *Carrousel* aimed at reinforcing the validity of the power of Louis XIV before the French aristocracy. Thousands of people attended and watched the event in the Paris Tuileries gardens. A book was published on the occasion of the tournament depicting the equestrian competition.[58] During the tournament, participants were divided into five quadrilles representing Romans, Persians, Turks, East Indians, and Amerindians, with the king and four of his highest ranking noblemen as the chiefs – the Amerindian king played by Henri II de Lorraine, duke de Guise. The costumes of the Amerindians, specially designed for the occasion, were characterized by the use of feathers.[59] While it is precisely the feathers that made sure the duke would be recognized as an *Amerindian* king, for the purposes of this chapter it is important to note the central place of the indigenous American character, as exemplified both in this event and in the 1550 Royal Entry in Rouen, in the political theatre of early modern France.

Transforming feathers: power and social hierarchy

The use of feathers was therefore an integral element in the characterization of indigenous peoples, both in printed form and in performances. Different formats of public festivities and court entertainment integrated this subject matter in varying degrees and rhythms. The representation of Amerindians was first incorporated into court pageants or royal entries, and only later into the ballet. As Margaret McGowan has aptly shown, the development of costumes for American characters in ballets in France was directly related to the publication of illustrated travel accounts. As such, the gradual development of feathered costumes for balls under Louis XIII made way for a less savage portrayal of Amerindian characters.[60] Elsewhere in Europe, images that circulated in the form of engravings and illustrations to travel books also helped to form a vision of Amerindians that would be replicated in pageants and balls with the use of feathers and featherwork.

Feathers could signify America in a range of modalities. Peter Mason has pointed out how feathers were used in aristocratic contexts where feather diadems were visually associated with royal crowns. As an example, he mentions how Archduke Ferdinand II of Austria used a Pre-Columbian feather headdress as part of the helmet he wore on the occasion of his marriage to Anne Gonzaga in 1582.[61] This example points to the mobility and adaptability of *kunstkammer* or collectible pieces and the constant transformation that these objects could undergo. This same association of feather headdresses with crowns can be illustrated by other festive and exhibiting events elsewhere in Europe.[62]

Such was the case of the Carnival celebrations performed at Stuttgart in 1599 – the tournament *Mannliche und Ritterliche Thurnier und Ringrennen* which featured Frederick I, duke of Württemberg representing Queen America. The event was initiated by a tournament on foot, followed by the parade performing the entrances of Queen America, the Assyrian King Ninus, the Persian King Cyrus, Alexander the Great and Julius Caesar, among others.[63] The prominent place given to Queen America in this parade can be partially explained by the fact that the duke of Württemberg, host of the ceremony, chose to perform as the main character. Two contemporaneous sources described the event: a textual account by M.J. Frischlin, dated 1602, and a series of coloured drawings now belonging to the collection of the Klassik Stiftung Weimar. Both sources were analysed and compared by Elke Bujok, who highlighted the subtle and detailed differences between the two descriptions of the parade: while Frischlin described Queen America wearing a feather crown (*ein Cron auss Federn gmacht*), the Weimar drawings depict a feather-less character, whose body is covered in tattoos, being carried on a litter under a baldachin by four men wearing colourful feather ornaments on their heads and bodies. Two other men walk alongside the litter handling feather fans.[64] In this event, not only was America – as represented by feathers and Amerindians – an integral part of court festivity, it was also given the highest distinction in the hierarchy of peoples and kingdoms displayed during the parade.

In a detailed analysis of the 'Ballet des princes Indiens' that took place in Brussels in 1634, Johan Verberckmoes has suggested that high noblemen dressed up as Amerindians evoked 'the world turned upside down'.[65] At that occasion, the burlesque portrayal of the ruling class as indigenous served to emphasize its status as a dominating group precisely by reversing expected hierarchies. Following the same line of argumentation, as it was part of a Carnival celebration, the Stuttgart parade was the ideal place to invert positions of power. The exhibition of the duke of Württemberg wearing feathered regalia and being carried by loyal feathered (American) subjects served to reaffirm the sovereign status of the duke. Feathers and featherwork could therefore be used to represent aristocratic leadership in public efforts to reinforce the legitimacy of the ruling power – as was the case of the feathered helmet worn by Archduke Ferdinand II. The same effect would also be achieved by inverting the hierarchical order of nations and peoples in carnival parades, such as the Queen America parade in Stuttgart.

At the same time, feathers and featherwork could also function as a mediator or a vehicle to negotiate political positions. In the early modern Dutch Republic, the use of costume in festive occasions, and in fact the very incorporation of masquerades and balls as a central component of court life, were connected to the dynastic struggles of the Dutch and English Royal families. Festivities organized particularly by Elizabeth of Bohemia and her court – living in exile at the Hague since 1620 – included a combination of ballet, music, theatre, and masquerades, featuring allegorical characters as well as characters from Classical Antiquity. Participants were expected to perform in various activities such as dancing, singing, and acting. In fact, masquerades were seen as the successors of the medieval tournaments, as a means for the nobility to display their physical and artistic qualities.[66] The introduction of the Amerindian character and in particular of the use of feathers and featherwork, however, can only be understood in the context of the return of Count Johan Maurits of Nassau-Siegen (1604–1679) to The Hague in 1644, after having served as governor-general of Dutch Brazil for eight years. He is also the central figure behind the portrait of Sophie of the Palatinate wearing a feather cape, presented at the beginning of this chapter.

Next to his activities as a military leader and governor of the Dutch colony, Johan Maurits was an avid collector. During his eight-year tenure in Brazil, he amassed a collection that included specimens of the fauna and flora of Northeastern Brazil as well as artefacts received as gifts from local and distant allies. Feathers, birds and featherworks were an essential part of those acts of gift-giving and entered Johan Maurits' collection as soon as he started establishing political and military alliances with indigenous groups in Brazil.[67] Back in the Dutch Republic, many of the objects in his collection once again circulated within powerful circles of court diplomacy, particularly between Johan Maurits and protestant leaders in Northwestern Europe.

Johan Maurits owned a number of feathered items as part of his collection, which were seen by visitors of his residence, the Mauritshuis.[68] These items did not remain as static objects inside his *kunstkammer*, however, as they were physically removed from the building and actively performed in festive occasions. In 1655, for instance, a ballet was organized in The Hague in which ladies of the courts of Elizabeth of Bohemia and of Amalia von Solms danced in costumes. Mary Stuart I danced the *Ballet de la Carmesse* dressed up 'as an Amazon' – that is, wearing a colourful feathered cloak.[69] This feather cloak belonged initially in the collection of Johan Maurits, for he had been exhibiting his collection to members of the court in The Hague since his arrival to the city in 1644.[70] Moreover, it was in his direct interest to have one of his prized objects displayed with such prominence by a member of the English Royal family, thereby symbolically strengthening his political relationship to the Stuarts and the Oranges.[71] The feather cloak worn by Sophie of the Palatinate (which resembles the portraits of Mary Stuart in subject matter, the sitter's position, and in the way the feather cape is worn as a royal mantle) was likely another example of such political manoeuvring. As I have argued elsewhere, while there is little documentation related to the making of this portrait, Johan Maurits of Nassau was the closest collector to Sophie and her family who owned such a cape, and was eager to establish alliances with the Elector Palatine.[72]

In this same struggle for a position within the powerful dynastic families of the Protestant North, already in 1652 Johan Maurits had organized the celebration of the marriage of William Frederick of Nassau-Dietz to Albertine Agnes of Orange-Nassau at his property in the city of Cleve. On that occasion, members of the court and guests of Johan Maurits re-enacted the battle of Zama between Scipio and Hannibal as part of the festive events. This re-enactment included a ceremonial entry into the city of Cleve, in which 'moors' and 'Tapuia' Amerindians were featured as Carthaginians while still dressed up in ethnically specific costumes: entering the city in two rows of twelve men and tied to each other by chains, these African and Amerindian characters carried respectively baboons and parrots, baskets full of fruit and 'human flesh', and were dressed in loincloth around their waists and feathers on their heads. In this pageant, while the moors and Tapuias were part of Hannibal's army, the feathers helped to underline their ethnic identities as moors and Amerindians rather than as Carthaginians. In opposition to America's eminent place during the Carnival celebrations in Stuttgart in 1599, in this particular event in Cleve Amerindians were given a hierarchical placement below any other group displayed in the parade. Still, their presence served to reinforce Johan Maurits' desired image as a ruler of foreign peoples, in a reference to his governorship in Brazil.

Conclusion

Sourced from the coastal regions of Portuguese America, feathers and featherwork were one of the archetypal examples of the global material culture of the early modern period. A central element in early modern *kunstkammers*, feathers and featherwork arrived in European collections first and foremost as part of global networks of commerce and politics. In this chapter, I have argued that even though these materials travelled distances and were part of a series of trade relations, their meanings were dependent on their collectors and on audiences that saw them – making them global materials with very specific local meanings.

For the indigenous peoples who produced featherwork in coastal Brazil, these objects were primarily related to the ritual ceremonies in which intertribal and spiritual relations would be reinstated via the killing of enemy captives. The symbolic transformation of shamans and captives into birds was an essential component of such ceremonies, materially guaranteed by the wearing of feather artefacts. Soon after the arrival of European colonizers, however, featherwork would acquire yet another set of usages, being one of the key elements in indigenous-European exchanges. As such, the material production of featherwork was also transformed by the incorporation of European materials in their fabrication.

Scholars have maintained that the foreign materials that reached Europe in the early modern period lost their original meanings in their Atlantic or global journeys. Elke Bujok correctly claims that 'objects arrived in Europe completely divorced from their context'.[73] Likewise, Marcy Norton points out that a cultural disconnect took place in the process of exchange and gifting of featherwork: 'overall far more was lost than maintained in the transmission from native America to Europe'.[74] While these claims are to a certain extent correct, they do not seem to consider the very unstable nature of such materials. From an anthropological and historical perspective, neither featherwork nor other material elements of indigenous lives have one singular distinct 'context' or meaning that lasts indefinitely throughout time. Indigenous societies were dynamic prior to and after the advent of European conquest, and as such the cosmological and symbolic uses of material forms underwent constant change. The arrival of the European in 1500 evidently accelerated such transformative processes, and in this new setting featherwork became an element of trade and a vehicle for strategic alliances with colonizers. Once featherworks (as well as loose feathers and birds) reached Europe, they were symbolically incorporated into a realm that wished to represent that very place where they had been collected: America. Furthermore, their presence within *kunstkammers* and their use beyond the walls that held collections as a unit are proof of the mobile and unstable nature of such materials. Mobile, for they travelled distances and were used for different purposes by diverse audiences. Unstable, for their meanings and values were connected to these changing usages.

The early modern period, and particularly the first half of the seventeenth century, witnessed the slow incorporation of the Amerindian character into the vocabulary of court festivities. As the examples from France, Stuttgart, and the Dutch Republic show, the Amerindian became part of a collective, pan-European court imagination that employed the use of feathers and featherwork to signify an individual's – or rather, a festival character's cultural and ethnic belonging to America. At the same time, the political message of each festive event – and hence the place given to the use of feathers and for Amerindians – differed according to context. In the cases of France and the Habsburg Empire, they related to the ongoing reaffirmation of monarchy – as well as to the attempts of the merchant classes to establish a relationship to the crown, as in the case of the Tupinambá village at the Royal Entry in Rouen.[75] In the Dutch Republic, they related to the representation of the successful governorship of Johann Maurits in Brazil and his struggles to achieve a powerful position once back in Europe. The *Ballet de la Carmesse* in 1655 and the marriage of the Oranges in Cleve in 1652 provide compelling examples of the use of collected feathers and featherwork outside *kunstkammers*, thus highlighting their moveable and transformable character. As Dominik Collet has argued, a playful mode of interaction with exotic objects remained possible in aristocratic as well as religious *kunstkammers*.[76] As such, the *kunstkammer* should be seen as a repository of possibilities in cultural representations and comparisons.

Notes and References

1. I would like to thank Anne Gerritsen and Giorgio Riello for their insightful comments and suggestions. An earlier version of this chapter was presented at the conference 'Global Commodities: The Material Culture of Early Modern Connections, 1400–1800,' at the University of Warwick, 2012. I wish to thank the participants of the conference for their feedback, as well as Floris Keehnen for his help with one of the sources.

2. Tupi was the generic name given to all indigenous societies living in the coastal area of Portuguese America during the colonial period. These included the Tupinambá and the Tabajara groups, among others. In contrast, indigenous groups living in the outback (the *sertão*), which only became more involved in colonial society from the seventeenth century onwards, were generally called Tapuia. See John M. Monteiro, 'The Crises and Transformations of Invaded Societies: Coastal Brazil in the Sixteenth Century,' in *The Cambridge History of the Native Peoples of the Americas. Vol. 3, Part 1*, ed. Frank Solomon and Stuart Schwartz (Cambridge: Cambridge University Press, 1999), 973–1023.

3. See, for instance, *Artes Indígenas*, ed. Nelson Aguilar (São Paulo: Associação Brasil 500 Anos Artes Visuais, 2000); *Deutsche am Amazonas. Forscher oder Abenteurer? Expeditionen in Brasilien 1800 bis 1914* (Berlin: LIT Verlag, 2002); Sonia Dorta, 'Coleções Etnográficas: 1650–1955,' in *História dos Índios no Brasil*, ed. Manuela Carneiro da Cunha (São Paulo: Companhia das Letras, 1998), 501–528; Sonia Dorta and Marilia Cury, *A Plumária Indígena Brasileira no Museu de Arqueologia e Etnologia da USP* (São Paulo: Edusp, 2000); *Brésil Indien. Les Arts des Amérindiens du Brésil*, ed. Luiz D.B. Grupioni (Paris: Éditions de la Réunion des Musées Nationaux, 2005); *Índios no Brasil* (Antwerp: Ludion, 2011); Berta Ribeiro and Lucia van Velthem, 'Coleções Etnográficas: documentos materiais para a história e a etnologia', in *História dos Índios no Brasil*, ed. Manuela Carneiro da Cunha (São Paulo: Companhia das Letras, 1998), 103–112.

4. One of the most successful examples is the exhibition 'Beyond Brazil: Tracking Johann Natterer through Space and Time' held at the Museum of Ethnology in Vienna in 2012, which displayed for the first time the collection amassed by the Austrian naturalist Johann Natterer in Brazil between 1817 and 1835. The climax of the exhibition was the display of the numerous feather ornaments dating from 1830 and collected in the Amazon region. See *Beyond Brazil: Johann Natterer and the Ethnographic Collections of the Austrian Expedition to Brazil 1817–1835*, ed. Claudia Augustat (Vienna: Museum für Völkerkunde, 2012).

5. Matters concerning the dating and provenance of such materials are challenging, particularly when it comes to identifying older pieces and trying to trace single object histories back to the early modern period. For the Paris cape, see Alfréd Métraux, 'A propos de deux objects Tupinambá du Musée d'Ethnographie du Trocadéro,' *Bulletin du Musée d'Ethnographie du Trocadéro* 3 (1932): 3–18. For the collection of the National Museum of Denmark, see *Etnografiske genstande i det kongelige danske kunstkammer. Ethnographic objects in the Royal Danish kunstkammer 1650–1800*, ed. B. Dam-Mikkelsen and T. Lundbaek (Copenhagen: Nationalmuseet, 1980). The Museum der Kulturen in Basel, Switzerland, holds another example of a feather cape that is likely to have been made in the colonial period. See Annemarie Seiler-Baldinger, 'Der Federmantel der Tupinambá im Museum für Völkerkunde Basel,' *Atti del XL Congresso Internazionale degli Americanisti, Roma, Genova 3–10 Settembre 1972* (Genova: Tilgher, 1972), vol. 2, 433–438.

6. *Etnografiske genstande,* 30.

7. Paludanus' inventory is housed at the National Library of Denmark, under inventory number Ms. Gl.k.S. 3467, 8. A transcription of some of its items can be found in H.D. Schepelern, 'Naturalienkabinett oder kunstkammer: der Sammler Bernhard Paludanus und sein Katalogmanuskript in der Königlichen Bibliothek in Kopenhagen,' *Nordelbingen: Beiträge zur Kunst und Kulturgeschichte/ Gesellschaft für Schleswig-Holsteinische Geschichte* 50 (1981): 158–182.

8. *Le Cabinet de Curiosités de la Bibliothèque Sainte-Geneviève* (Paris: Bibliothèque Sainte-Geneviève, 1989), 81, object number 121.

9. Christian Feest argues that from the thousands of objects taken from America to Europe until the eighteenth century, fewer than 300 still survive. This is an estimate difficult to ascertain, given that the ongoing research into museum depots and collections may reveal misattributions as well as new findings. See Christian Feest, 'European Collecting of American Indian Artefacts and Art,' *Journal of the History of Collections* 3.1 (1993): 2.

10. Kay L. Candler, 'Ancient Plumage: Featherworking in Precolumbian Peru,' in *The Gift of Birds. Featherwork of Native South American Peoples*, ed. Ruben E. Reina (Philadelphia: University Museum of Anthropology and Archaeology, 1991), 1–15; Esther Pasztory, 'Rare Ancient Featherwork from Peru,' *American Journal of Archaeology* Online Museum Review 112.4 (2008): 1–5.

11. See Arie Boomert, 'Raptorial Birds as Icons of Shamanism in the Prehistoric Caribbean and Amazonia,' in *Patina: Essays Presented to Jay Jordan Butler on the Occasion of his 80th Birthday*, ed. Willy H. Metz, Bernhard L. van Beek and Hannie Steegstra (Groningen: Groningen University, 2001), 109.

12. André Thevet, *Les Singularitez de la France Antarctique* (Paris: Heritiers de Maurice de la Porte, 1557), 90.

13. Jean de Léry, *History of a Voyage to the Land of Brazil, Otherwise Called America* (Berkeley: University of California Press, 1990 [1578]), 88.

14. Zacharias Wagener, *O Thierbuch e a autobiografia de Zacharias Wagener* (Rio de Janeiro: Index, [*c.*1640] 1997), 62.

15. Gabriel Soares de Sousa, *Tratado Descritivo do Brasil em 1587*, ed. Francisco de Varnhagen (Rio de Janeiro: Typographia Universal de Laemmert, 1851), 228.

16. André Thevet, *Les Singularitez*, 91.

17. See Felipe Vander Velden, 'As Galinhas Incontáveis. Tupis, Europeus e Aves Domésticas na Conquista no Brasil,' *Journal de la Société des Américanistes* 98.2 (2012): 116–117; Berta Ribeiro, 'Adornos Plumários,' in *Dicionário do Artesanato Indígena* (São Paulo: Edusp, 1988), 132. For an example of a feather cape made with such artificially coloured parrot and chicken feathers, see Berete Due, 'Artefatos Brasileiros no Kunstkamer Real,' in *Albert Eckhout Volta ao Brasil 1644–2002*, ed. Barbara Berlowickz, Berete Due, Peter Prentz and Espen Waehle (Copenhagen: Nationalmuseet, 2002), 193.

18. Berta Ribeiro, 'Adornos Plumários,' 130. According to Amy Buono, the process of *tapirage* is performed through the external and/or internal application of plant and/or animal-derived substances (such as plant dyes, blood and/or skin secretions from toads and frogs, fats from fish, turtle, chicken or crocodilian eggs, or fat from plants) to particular species of birds (such as the macaw or parrot). See Amy Buono, 'Crafts of Color: Tupi *Tapirage* in Early Colonial Brazil,' in *The Materiality of Color. The Production, Circulation, and Application of Dyes and Pigments, 1400–1800*, ed. Andrea Feeser, Maureen Daly Goggin, and Beth Fowkes Tobin (Farnham: Ashgate, 2012), 235–237. For contemporary Amazonian techniques of obtaining and transforming feathers, see also Ruben E. Reina and Jon F. Pressman, 'Harvesting Feathers,' in *Gift of Birds*, 110–115.

19. Gabriel Soares de Sousa, *Tratado Descritivo*, 312. See also Alfréd Métraux, *La Civilisation Matérielle des Tribus Tupi-Guarani* (Paris: P. Geuthner, 1928), 149.

20. de Léry, *History of a Voyage*, 59.

21. Wagener, *O Thierbuch*, 68.

22. George Marcgraf, *Historia Natural do Brasil* (São Paulo: Imprensa Oficial do Estado, [1648] 1942), 271.

23. Florestan Fernandes, *A Função Social da Guerra na Sociedade Tupinambá* (São Paulo: Pioneira/ Edusp, 1970); Manuela Carneiro da Cunha and Eduardo Viveiros de Castro, 'Vingança e Temporalidade: Os Tupinambá,' *Journal de la Société des Américanistes* 71 (1985): 191–208.

24. Soares de Sousa, *Tratado Descritivo*, 327, 329.

25. Marcy Norton, 'Going to the Birds: Animals as Things and Beings in Early Modernity,' in *Collecting Across Cultures. Material Exchanges in the Early Modern Atlantic World*, ed. Daniela Bleichmar and Peter Mancall (Philadelphia: University of Pennsylvania Press, 2011), 63.

26. de Léry, *History of a Voyage*, 59.

27. Vander Velden, 'As Galinhas Incontáveis,' 117–18. See also Peter T. Furst, 'Crowns of Power: Bird and Feather Symbolism in Amazonian Shamanism,' in *Gift of Birds*, 100–2.

28. Amy Buono, 'Crafts of Color,' 241.

29. See Peter Mason, 'From Presentation to Representation: Americana in Europe,' *Journal of the History of Collections* 6.1 (1994): 1–20. The cape has recently been restored and for conservation reasons is rarely displayed to the public.

30. Amy Buono, 'Crafts of Color,' 242.
31. Robin Wright and Manuela Carneiro da Cunha, 'Destruction, Resistance, and Transformation – Southern, Coastal, and Northern Brazil (1580–1890),' in *Cambridge History of the Native Peoples of the Americas. Vol. 3, Part 2*, 297. See also: Monteiro, 'Crises and Transformations'.
32. Surekha Davies, 'Depictions of Brazilians on French Maps, 1542–1555,' *Historical Journal* 55.2 (2012): 337–339.
33. François Desprez, *Recueil de la diversité des habits qui sont de présent en usage tant ès pays d'Europe, Asie, Afrique et isles sauvages, le tout fait après le naturel* (Paris: Richard Breton, 1562).
34. François Desprez, *The various styles of clothing: A facsimile of the 1562 edition* (Minneapolis: University of Minnesota Press, [1562] 2001), 138–139. See also Ann Rosalind Jones, 'Habits, Holdings, Heterologies: Populations in Print in a 1562 Costume Book,' *Yale French Studies* 110 (2006): 92–121. For a comparison between the *Vallard Atlas* and the Desprez costume book, see Davies, 'Depictions of Brazilians,' 339.
35. Peter Hansen Hajstrup, *Memorial und Jurenal des Peter Hansen Hajstrup (1624–1672)* (Neumünster: Wachholtz Verlag, [1662] 1995), 82.
36. See Christian Feest, 'Mexico and South America in the European Wunderkammer,' in *The Origins of Museums. The Cabinet of Curiosities in Sixteenth- and Seventeenth-Century Europe*, ed. Oliver Impey and Arthur MacGregor (Oxford: Clarendon Press, 1985), 237–244; Christian Feest, 'The Collecting of American Indian Artefacts in Europe, 1493–1750,' in *America in European Consciousness 1493–1750*, ed. Karen O. Kupperman (Chapel Hill: University of North Carolina Press, 1995), 324–360; Isabel Yaya, 'Wonders of America. The Curiosity Cabinet as a Site of Representation and Knowledge,' *Journal of the History of Collections* 20.2 (2008): 173–188. For a detailed analysis of *kunstkammers* as forms of relationship between Europe and the non-European world, see Dominik Collet, *Die Welt in der Stube. Begegnungen mit Aussereuropa in kunstkammern der Frühen Neuzeit* (Göttingen: Vandenhoeck & Ruprecht, 2007).
37. Wagener, *O Thierbuch*, 222.
38. Norton goes on to argue that the types of human–parrot pethood that developed in Europe were direct adaptations of the Amerindian–parrot relationship based on ties of kinship. Norton, 'Going to the Birds,' 77.
39. See Feest, 'Mexico and South America'.
40. A survey conducted in the 1980s by Christian Feest showed that about twenty pieces of featherwork could still be found in European museum collections. Feest, 'Collecting,' 328. As for one specific and very valuable type of feathered ornament – the feather cloak, Amy Buono suggests that there were hundreds of feather cloaks circulating in Europe in the sixteenth and seventeenth centuries, of which today only eleven are still extant in European museums – and none in Brazil. Buono, 'Crafts of Color,' 238, 245.
41. The document was transcribed and reprinted by historian Dominik Collet in *Die Welt in der Stube*, 360.
42. Elke Bujok, 'Ethnographica in Early Modern *kunstkammern* and their Perception,' *Journal of the History of Collections* 21.1 (2009): 10.
43. See Daniela Bleichmar, 'Seeing the World in a Room: Looking at Exotica in Early Modern Collections,' in *Collecting Across Cultures*. See also the special edition of *Journal of the History of Collections* 23.2 (2011) on inventories of early modern collections.
44. Bujok, 'Ethnographica,' 7; Bleichmar, 'Seeing the World,' 30.
45. Feest, 'European Collecting,' 3; Bujok, 'Ethnographica,' 6.
46. See Feest, 'European Collecting,' 4.
47. Mason, 'From Presentation to Representation', 12.
48. Johan Verberckmoes, 'The Imaginative Recreation of Overseas Cultures in Western European Pageants in the Sixteenth to Seventeenth Centuries,' in *Cultural Exchange in Early Modern Europe IV: Forging European Identities, 1400–1700*, ed. Herman Roodenburg (Cambridge: Cambridge University Press, 2007), 375.
49. One of the most influential works in this matter was the collection of travel accounts published by Johann and Theodor De Bry starting in the 1590s. While the De Brys

took the editorial liberty of adding feathers and featherwork to images of natives from Africa and Asia, these images did not affect the popular view that typically linked these materials to South America. For a detailed analysis of the role of the De Bry collection in the development of a pan-European view on foreign peoples, see Michiel van Groesen, *The Representation of the Overseas World in the De Bry Collection of Voyages (1590–1634)* (Leiden: Brill, 2008). For the use of feathers in these representations, see pp. 199–205.

50. Verberckmoes, 'Imaginative Recreation,' 372.
51. August W. Staub and Robert L. Pinson, 'Fabulous Wild Men: American Indians in European Pageants, 1493–1700,' *Theater Survey* 25.1 (1984): 43–44.
52. Bartholomé de Las Casas, *Historia de las Indias* (Caracas: Biblioteca Ayacucho, 1986), vol. 1, 346–347.
53. Parrots had been known in Europe since at least the time of the Roman Empire. In the Middle Ages, they appeared in Christian iconography, although the collecting and use of the birds themselves would only become more common after the fifteenth century. Norton, 'Going to the Birds,' 62.
54. Michael Wintroub, 'Taking Stock at the End of the World: Rites of Distinction and Practices of Collecting in Early Modern Europe,' *Studies in the History and Philosophy of Science* 30.3 (1999): 469. For a detailed analysis of the Rouen entry, and particularly of the French representations of Brazilian peoples therein, see: Michael Wintroub, *A Savage Mirror. Power, Identity, and Knowledge in Early Modern France* (Stanford: Stanford University Press, 2006).
55. See Wintroub, *Savage Mirror*, 36–38.
56. Davies, 'Depictions of Brazilians,' 327.
57. For an overview of the presence of North- and South-American indigenous characters in French ballets, see François Moreau, 'American Aboriginals in Ballets de Cour in Champlain's Time,' in *Champlain: The Birth of French America*, ed. Raymonde Litalien and Denis Vaugeois (Montréal: McGill-Queen's University Press, 2004), 43–49.
58. Charles Perrault, *Courses de Testes et de Bague Faittes Par Le Roy et par Les Princes et Seigneurs de sa Cour En l'Année 1662* (Paris: L'imprimerie Royale, 1670). On the Grand Carrousel, see Natalie Cetre, France Gautier, Iegor Groudiev and Stephanie Groudiev, 'Le Carrousel de 1662,' *Revue de l'Histoire de Versailles et des Yvelines* 86 (2002): 125–162.
59. Staub and Pinson, 'Fabulous Wild Men', 50.
60. Margaret McGowan, *La Danse à la Renaissance. Sources livresques et albums d'images* (Paris: Bibliothèque Nationale de France, 2012), 54.
61. Mason, 'From Presentation to Representation,' 10.
62. See Carina L. Johnson, 'Aztec Regalia and the Reformation of Display,' in *Collecting Across Cultures*, 83–98.
63. A complete textual description of the ceremony has been published in Elke Bujok, *Neue Welten in europäischen Sammlungen. Africana und Americana in kunstkammern bis 1670* (Berlin: Reimer Verlag, 2004), 13–23.
64. Bujok concluded that the textual description by Frischlin is a more accurate, possibly eye-witness account of the festivity, while the Weimar drawings may have been produced later. They contain ample signs of having been used, handled, and modified over the years. Bujok, *Neue Welten*, 149–152.
65. Johann Verberckmoes, 'Brazilian topinanbours and Brussels baroque court ballets (1634),' in *Brasil. Cultures and Economies of Four Continents*, ed. Bart de Brins, Eddy Stols, Johan Verberckmoes (Leuven: Acco, 2001), 65.
66. Simon Groenveld, *De Winterkoning. Balling aan het Haagse hof* (The Hague: Haags Historisch Museum, 2003), 53, 55.
67. See Mariana Françozo, 'Global Connections: Johan Maurits of Nassau-Siegen's Collection of Curiosities,' in *The Legacy of Dutch Brazil*, ed. Michiel van Groesen (New York: Cambridge University Press, 2014), 105–123.
68. See Jacob de Hennin, *De zinrijke gedachten toegepast op de vijf sinnen van 's menschen verstand* (Amsterdam: Jan Claasen ten Hoorn, 1681), 111–121.

69. On the *Ballet de la Carmesse*, see: Nadine Akkerman and P. Sellin, 'Facsimile Edition – A Stuart Masque in Holland: Ballet de la Carmesse de La Haye (1655),' *The Ben Jonson Journal* 11 (2004): 207–258; Nadine Akkerman and P. Sellin, 'A Stuart Masque in Holland: Ballet de la Carmesse de La Haye (1655): Part II,' *The Ben Jonson Journal* 12 (2005): 141–164.

70. See Mariana Françozo, 'Global Connections,' 115–120.

71. Quentin Buvelot has suggested that the cape worn at that ballet was actually manufactured in The Hague after the arrival of Johan Maurits to the city in 1644. He claims feathers of Johan Maurits' collection were used to make the cape. Quentin Buvelot, 'Een bijzonder portret van Mary Stuart door Adriaen Hanneman in het Mauritshuis,' in *Face Book: Studies on Dutch and Flemish Portraiture of the 16th–18th Centuries. Liber Amicorum Presented to Rudolf E. O. Ekkart*, ed. Edwin Buijsen, Charles Dumas, and Volker Manuth (Leiden: Primavera Pers, 2012), 373–380. Mary Stuart I was depicted wearing the feather cape by Adriaen Hanneman in *Posthumous portrait of Mary I Stuart with a servant (ca.1664)*. The painting is today property of the National Portrait Gallery Mauritshuis. For an analysis of this and other portraits depicting the use of featherwork by members of the European nobility, see Mariana Françozo, 'Dressed Like an Amazon. The Transatlantic Trajectory of a Red Feather Coat,' in *Museums and Biographies: Stories, Objects, Identities*, ed. Kate Hill (London: Boydell and Brewer, 2012), 187–199.

72. Françozo, 'Dressed Like an Amazon'.

73. Bujok, 'Ethnographica', 2.

74. Norton, 'Going to the Birds,' 71.

75. Montaigne's essay *Des Cannibales* (1580) provides another example from the textual canon where monarchic power is precisely contested via the metaphorical comparison with Tupinambá Indians.

76. Dominik Collet, 'Kunst- und Wunderkammern,' in *Europäische Erinnerungsorte 3: Europa und die Welt*, ed. Pim den Boer, Heinz Duchhardt, Georg Kreis and Wolfgang Schmale (München: Oldenbourg Wissenschaftsverlag, 2012), 163.

5

THE EMPIRE IN THE DUKE'S PALACE

Global material culture in sixteenth-century Portugal

Nuno Senos

The 5th duke of Bragança and his inventory

From the death of his father in 1532, to his own demise in 1563, Teodósio I led the wealthiest, most prominent and powerful family of the Portuguese nobility as the 5th Duke of Bragança (Figure 5.1).[1] He married twice, first to Isabel, who bore him his first son and heir, John, and later to Beatrice with whom he had two more children, James and Isabel. Thus when he died, survived by four heirs, his estate had to be divided in unequal parts which were very difficult to determine, a delicate and difficult task that, we know now, was never really completed.[2]

In order to solve this problem, an extraordinary inventory was made listing the contents of the family's main palace, in Vila Viçosa, in the southeast of Portugal (Figure 5.2).[3] Its making involved almost thirty men and women of various professional specialties, some recruited from the service of the ducal house, others brought all the way from Lisbon, and it took them the better part of four years to put together over 650 folios (1,300-plus pages), collecting 6,000-plus entries, several of which are very detailed and encompass many objects. It is the largest inventory to have survived from sixteenth-century Portugal and one of the largest of the same period in Europe. It lists everything that could be found inside the ducal palace at the time of the duke's death,[4] from the duchess's dresses to the duke's cufflinks, from the pots and pans in the kitchen to the eucharistic vessels in the chapel, from the shields and daggers kept in the duke's armory to the silver and gold objects he displayed at his table.

Given the exceptional wealth of information it contains, this inventory can be approached from many angles and its data can be used for the analysis of many aspects of the material, social, cultural and even political life in early modern Portugal.[5] In this chapter I will focus on the entries that reflect the duke's interest and involvement in the maritime voyages that the Portuguese had been engaged in

FIGURE 5.1 Portrait of Duke D. Teodósio I of Bragança, print, *c*.1755, Fundação da casa de Bragança. Reproduced with permission of Museu-Biblioteca da Casa de Bragança.

FIGURE 5.2 Ducal Palace of Vila Viçosa. Photo by the author.

since the early fifteenth century. In order to better contextualize this topic, one must keep in mind that by 1563, when the duke died, the Portuguese had been travelling the world – and conquering parts of it – already for a century-and-a-half. They had established several strongholds and sometimes entire cities in Morocco, the Gulf of Guinea, the Island of Mozambique, the western coast of India, Malacca, China, Japan and even Brazil. In the process of establishing their military, religious and commercial presence, sailors, merchants, priests and crown officials had developed sophisticated, transcontinental trading practices that involved all sorts of global commodities, including, but not limited to, works of art.[6]

At the commercial centre of this global trade network and articulating the overseas territories with the European markets stood Lisbon. Duke Teodósio, who, of course, owned a palace and had several agents in the city, had privileged access to these many overseas products. Furthermore, his family had various links to the empire. His father, for instance, had partially financed and personally led the army that conquered Azemmour, in Morocco, in 1513, a feat that was celebrated throughout the ducal palace in various ways including a fresco cycle that decorated its grand staircase. Also, his brother, Constantino, was viceroy of India between 1558 and 1561.[7] Thus, with privileged access to the yearly fleet's cargoes, family connections to the empire, and a virtually unlimited power of acquisition, one could only expect the duke to have a house filled with products coming from all over the world, mirroring the full extent of his connections to the vast globe including a collection of exotic objects.

Indeed, the inventory does not fail this expectation and in it we can find all sorts of products coming from the four corners of the world. The identification and analysis of the pertinent entries, however, raises a number of issues that must be addressed. The selected entries then must be placed in the context of the whole inventory in order to ascertain the relative importance of each item in relation to the other products the duke acquired. I shall also analyse the available information on the way these objects were organized and used inside the palace. It should be explained that this inventory is not organized room-by-room. Instead, each official working in the ducal household was in charge of listing the objects under his/her care regardless of the room in which they happened to be. This raises issues that will also be mentioned. Finally, I will comment on other ways in which the duke's interest for the nascent global world materialized as portrayed by his inventory.

Problems of interpretation

Because of its immense value, one of these objects immediately stands out from the other thousands: a pearl necklace which, priced at 2,184,000 *reis*, is the most expensive item in the inventory by far.[8] The geographic origin of these pearls poses an interesting problem since, as is often the case throughout the inventory, it is not stated. There are several cases, however, in which the origin of objects, though not explicit, can be determined with a fair amount of certainty. From the sixteenth century onwards, thanks to the voyages of Portuguese and Spaniards, most pearls (as well as other precious stones such as emeralds and rubies) reaching the European markets came either from Asia or from the Caribbean. It is therefore safe to assume that the duke's most precious pearls came from Asia, where the Portuguese had conquered Hormuz (1515), the most important trading port for this commodity.

Perhaps an even stronger case can be made for a flask described as being covered in mother-of-pearl.[9] While the inventory fails to state its origin, it is safe to assume that the object in question is an example of the production of the Gulf of Gujarat, in Northwest India, from where originated objects such as caskets, jugs or dishes covered in finely cut mother-of-pearl scales attached to a wooden (often teak) core by means of small nails sometimes made of silver (Figure 5.3).[10] Such objects were much appreciated in Europe and, in time, examples could be found in all major collections.[11]

Several objects made of crystal are also mentioned. Again, the origin of most has not been recorded but a fork and a spoon made of rock crystal and decorated with rubies set in gold can only have come from Ceylon (Sri Lanka) which abounded in rock crystal and rubies and which specialized in the production of such cutlery,

FIGURE 5.3 Mother-of-pearl casket, Gujarat, India. Teak covered with mother-of-pearl, and brass mounts inlaid with quartz (H: 25 cm; L: 33.5 cm; W: 20 cm) © Jorge Welsh Oriental Porcelain & Works of Art, Lisbon/London.

most of which seems to have been appreciated for its refinement rather than actually used at the table.[12]

Finally, as far as geography is concerned, it should also be mentioned that the terms 'China' and 'India' are used to cover a very broad spatial spectrum. For instance, a casket covered in black lacquer with golden decoration, silver hinges and a silver lock, while listed as coming from China, is probably rather Japanese.[13] Likewise, the large ceramic vessels listed in entry 458 are described as coming from India and are called 'martabãs'. This name, however, which was common in sixteenth-century Portugal, comes from the port in which these vessels were bought, which is in Burma (Myanmar) not in India. It is therefore interesting (though not entirely surprising at this early date) to notice that this inventory is very specific when using European geographic references (such as Milan or Medina del Campo) but much more vague when it comes to Asia. In general, it can be said that everything from the Cape of Good Hope to Melaka is referred to as India while China means everything East of Malacca including Japan.

Some of the terminology used in the inventory also poses problems of a different nature. Words such as 'coco' should simply mean 'coconut', a well known exotic fruit, which lent itself to fine carving and precious mountings, and that was much appreciated for its rareness. The duke had five of them, two of which received silver fixings considerably increasing their value. One of them is listed as from the Maldives and its value (6,000 *reis*) is much higher than that of the other ones; three of them were valued a little over 80 *reis* each, indicating they had not yet been transformed into works of art and that they were not precious *cocos-de-mer* but rather plain, North African coconuts.[14] The meaning of the word becomes less clear however when one finds entries listing 'brass coconuts' ('coco de latão', two of them priced at 75 *reis* each), an expression whose meaning remains elusive.[15]

'Porcelain/porcelana' is probably the best example of a term that is used in a wide sense. There are 42 entries that use the word porcelain, corresponding at least to 356 objects.[16] In some cases, the word is used to describe that which we call porcelain today. However, expressions such as 'silver porcelain' ('porcelana de prata'), used to describe two objects,[17] make it clear that the word is not always used in the inventory with the stricter meaning that it has today. Moreover, the term is sometimes used as a type itself: for instance, 'six small porcelains.'[18] Such cases indicate that the term can be used to signify any form of glazed ceramic (as opposed to non-glazed objects, usually listed as being 'made of clay' / 'de barro'[19]) rather than strictly Chinese porcelain proper.

Art and empire: works of art

When considering the duke's acquisitions, it is important to keep in mind that he did not buy exclusively from extra-European locations. His foreign commodities actually encompassed several items from European origin. There are about 410 entries in which the foreign origin of the objects is explicitly indicated, totalling over 3,700 objects (including several weapons and precious stones in large quantities).

These must include at least some of the many listed slaves, who are treated by the inventory as commodities and as such assigned a value. Some show up under a subtitle of their own but not all, and while the origin of most is not indicated, 45 of them are described as 'black', 'Indian' or 'Moorish', which shows their non-European extraction. This brings us to a total of about 440 entries and 3,770 'objects' whose geographic origin can be securely established, amounting to a staggering three million *reis*. The quantity of objects coming from extra-European origins is smaller but nevertheless impressive: over 400 items, totalling an investment a little under two and a half million *reis*.[20]

The distribution of the types of objects that the duke acquired in Europe is informative. In France he bought mostly jewellery and illuminated books; in Germany, furniture and some war and hunting gear; in Flanders, some furniture (mostly involving metal such as metal-reinforced caskets), some weaponry and some musical instruments[21]; and in Italy, silks from Florence, jewellery from Milan, and ceramics (probably majolica) from Pisa and Venice. Finally, by virtue of physical proximity, Spain was the natural source of many of the duke's acquisitions belonging to all sorts of categories. It is interesting to highlight several references to the fair of Medina del Campo where the duke bought all sorts of textiles (from tapestries to clothing and cloth by the yard) as well as Biscay, perhaps the duke's most important foreign market for weaponry.

The list of objects of extra-European origin is more interesting but also much more complex to analyse. Apart from sugar from the plantations of the island of São Tomé, used to make quince jam,[22] only slaves stem from Africa. The list of slaves identified as either black ('preto') or Moorish ('mourisco', meaning from Northern Africa) is interesting and even impressive for two main reasons. First, many of these slaves are skilled workers (including, for instance, eleven musicians, as well as a female slave specializing in the making of preserves and another one in the service of the apothecary)[23] and not simply involved in the performance of hard tasks that demand physical force. And second, perhaps most surprisingly, they were extremely expensive. The cheapest ones, generally non-specialized, were worth 4,000 *reis* (almost two months' worth of the salary of a skilled worker) but a slave's price could be much higher. The top, most valuable positions are all occupied by musicians, with seven of these worth between 40,000 and 60,000 *reis* each. The most expensive one, who must have been a particularly gifted artist, was valued at 100,000 *reis*, which puts him in a category of his own as far as slaves are concerned, and ranks him within the top 100 most expensive items in the whole inventory.[24] The total worth of the duke's African slaves amounts to a staggering million *reis*. In the context of the duke's extra-European possessions, slaves, especially African ones were therefore not only among the most expensive items but they also represent the category in which the duke was willing to spend the most.

As far as African commodities are concerned one more note should be added. In the early stages of the Portuguese presence in the Gulf of Guinea (from the last quarter of the fifteenth century), the Portuguese acquired a number of fascinating objects made of ivory by local artists from Sierra Leone and the Congo.[25] From the latter also came objects such as hats and rugs made of raffia. It is not impossible that the duke possessed some of these objects but the inventory does not allow for the positive identification of any of them.[26]

Likewise, Brazil was not a source of preference for the duke's consumption habits. There are seven emeralds identified as from Brazil but their value (200 *reis* each) rather indicates that they were not emeralds at all but more likely tourmalines, a much cheaper semi-precious stone. Unlike Africa, whose ivory objects could be found in several early modern princely households, Brazilian objects never seem to have raised the curiosity of Portuguese buyers. In fact, it does not seem that whatever material culture did exist in Brazil was ever perceived as collectable by the Portuguese.[27]

A few objects coming from the Spanish New World should be mentioned. There are three entries that explicitly refer to the Caribbean. One of them is a piece of jewelry incorporating a pearl of said origin.[28] Then there is also a painted cloth ('pano pintado'), which is especially interesting because it is described as being so old that it has lost all the painting and is therefore worthless.[29] This means that objects from the Spanish empire (not so frequent in Portuguese inventories of this early period) had raised some curiosity in Portugal at an early date. Finally, and perhaps most interestingly, the duke also had a *plumaria* retable representing Saint John (which one, we are not told), one of the first such works of art recorded in Portugal but valued at a disappointingly low 300 *reis*.[30] While the duke was interested in the events and developments relating to the Spanish empire, as we shall see further ahead, such interest did not manifest itself in the form of works of art.

Thus the vast majority of the duke's extra-European acquisitions came from Asia, identified by the terms Ceylon, China, India, Persia and 'Xio' (Turkey, or rather the Ottoman empire). Of these, the smallest group came from Ceylon and its entries are relatively unproblematic since they all refer to objects that include rubies in them, this island being the most important source of such precious stones at the time. In fact, the duke had over 200 buttons that were made in Portugal using Ceylonese rubies.[31] The most interesting objects from Ceylon are perhaps the two spoons and a fork made of rock crystal and decorated with rubies set in gold, a type that could be found in various other European noble households though mostly at a later date.[32]

China is the declared origin of about fifteen objects, excluding all the porcelain entries, none of which is explicitly identified as coming from that country. As mentioned above, the word China seems to be used to mean at least China and Japan. For instance, four writing cabinets are listed, two of which are lacquered in black with golden decorations and have silver hinges and locks. This description indicates Japanese rather than Chinese objects, a sense that is reinforced by their price, almost ten times more than the other two cabinets also labelled as Chinese but whose description does not indicate a different origin.[33] The list of Chinese items further includes an old and broken chair and a few textile items, mostly made of silk.

There are, however, about 350 objects made of porcelain that must have come from China (Figures 5.4 a and b). A group of porcelains is specifically identified as

FIGURE 5.4a Saucer dish (front) with the armillary sphere of King Manuel I and the 'IHS' Monogram (front and back), China, Ming dynasty, Zhengde period (1506–1521). Porcelain decorated in underglaze cobalt blue (D 30.5 cm), © Jorge Welsh Oriental Porcelain & Works of Art, Lisbon/London.

FIGURE 5.4b Saucer dish (back).

having been brought from India by the duke's brother, the viceroy, as a gift to his sister-in-law.[34] These must correspond to the strict sense that we give to the word porcelain today. The viceroy's porcelain gift to the duchess is worth some attention. It is listed in nine entries of the inventory, which correspond to 100 objects.[35] These include dishes, bottles, jars, and bowls ('*escudelas*', bowls with handles) always in pairs or in larger quantities, the largest being a group of thirty bowls, suggesting that porcelain was usually bought in large quantities. Individual porcelain items were less common and more expensive: a bottle and two jars, valued each at 500 *reis*, are the most valuable items on the list[36] while the cheapest objects, a set of eighteen bowls, were not worth more than a total of 300 *reis*, or 17 *reis* a piece. The whole porcelain gift itself amounted to a far from impressive 11,520 *reis*.

Beyond the viceroy's gift, many other porcelain objects made it to the ducal household. A few (26 objects) were used in the duke's service but the vast majority belonged to the duchess (324). Together with several other objects (over one thousand), they were kept in a special part of the duchess's wardrobe called the 'house of glass and porcelain' ('*casinha dos vidros e das porcelanas*'), where one could find all sorts of jars, dishes, cups, bowls, and bottles made of porcelain, ceramics, glass, crystal and alabaster.[37] The available sources are mute as to the way in which these objects were kept in such space and there is no indication that they were displayed in any way. One must therefore be careful to consider this 'house' as a proto-form of the later, well-known porcelain cabinets. Nevertheless, the fact that these objects were kept in a special room which was part of the duchess's personal lodgings indicates the special position they held within the hierarchy of the palace's contents. It is also worth mentioning that the house of glass and porcelain was a specifically gendered palatial space. Besides the duchess, her daughter-in-law seems to have been starting one for herself, at the time only with six objects, including two expensive bowls (900 *reis* each) described as 'very large'.[38] The men of the house, the dead duke and his son, had small armouries in their wardrobes instead, duplicating the larger, general armoury of the palace.

From Persia and Turkey, the duke acquired almost exclusively carpets. A total of 73 of his impressive set of carpets came from these sources.[39] The most expensive item the duke bought from Turkey was, perhaps not surprisingly, a slave who does not seem to have possessed any particular skill (he worked in the stables) but who took his master's name, Teodósio.[40] All other objects from that country are carpets with values varying, according to size, material, and pattern, between 200 and 28,000 *reis*. Persian carpets were fewer in number (18 against 55 Turkish) but more expensive, their values ranging from 2,800 to 50,000 *reis*. The duke spent a rather impressive amount in these carpets (over half-a-million *reis*) all of which were assigned to be used in his own quarters in the palace with the exception of a Turkish one used in the chapel and a Persian one used in the duchess's lodgings.[41]

The last group of extra-European goods the duke possessed came from India and it ranged from textiles to slaves to jewelry. The duke's Indian textiles include expensive carpets (the most precious of which was a gift from the viceroy[42]), bed-covers ('*colchas*'[43]), curtains,[44] various items of clothing,[45] and even a tent. There were also armoury-related items such as a gunpowder flask made of horn, an inexpensive item that the duke must have cherished since he kept it in his private armoury, in his wardrobe.[46] One of the few jewels identified as coming from India stands out for its price, an emerald ring worth 80,000 *reis*.[47] Finally, there were eight slaves from India, including one who helped in the palace's looms, an embroiderer, and a silk weaver.[48] The ducal household was clearly interested in India's textile-related technology.

Numerous (107 objects) and valuable (over half-a-million *reis*), the group of the duke's Indian objects seems to indicate that India's presence could be felt all over the palace, from the bedchambers where the '*colchas*' adorned the beds, to the chapel where Indian textiles were used in eucharistic vestments, to the armoury, and the palace's workshops. However, one has to wonder how it was that all these foreign and rare items were arranged inside the palace, how it was that they presented themselves to those who lived there and those who visited.

In search of a *wunderkammer*

It is relatively easy to imagine (and document) how some of the many objects referred to above were used, the Turkish and Persian carpets being the most obvious. No description of any event that took place in the ducal palace failed to mention their usage in the various rooms, from the most accessible to the most secluded.[49] It can also be safely assumed that all the curtains and bed linens, all the arms and armoury-related objects, the furniture and the jewellery, and even the fabrics acquired by the yard easily found their way into the many usages they all had in a palace and in a palatial life in constant need of new fixings for the many rooms and new cloths for the various ceremonial and quotidian occasions.

However, the abundant available literature on early modern collecting also suggests that some of these objects – belonging to categories such as *exotica*, *naturalia* or *artificialia*, all present in the inventory – could have been gathered in a special room or set of rooms in which they are offered for display, fruition and/or study following the model of the Central European *wunderkammer* or the Italian *studiolo*.[50] Given everything that has been said so far, one could only expect to find one such similar setting in the Bragança ducal palace.

Several objects have been mentioned that one could expect to find in such a space, such as jugs covered in mother-of-pearl, forks made of rock crystal decorated with rubies, coconuts mounted on silver or lacquered cabinets and caskets. Various other references can be added to this list such as several entries mentioning unicorn horns including a small gold chain from which hung a piece of such substance that the duke wore around his wrist at all times for protection.[51] In the same category falls a bezoar stone, a material also known for its medical prowess.[52] And even materials such as rhinoceros horns (in carved form),[53] tortoiseshell (covering a flask),[54] and coral can be found in the inventory, the latter either as part of objects or simply in the raw form of stems, possibly indicating the interest of the naturalist rather than that of the sumptuary consumer (Figure 5.5).[55]

FIGURE 5.5 Gujarati tortoiseshell casket, Gujarat, India. Tortoiseshell with silver mounts (H 10.5 cm; L 19.9; W 9.5 cm), © Jorge Welsh Oriental Porcelain & Works of Art, Lisbon/London.

Therefore, objects fitting the notion of a *wunderkammer* did exist. But were they organized in such a manner? What was their status within the hierarchy of the contents of the ducal palace? Were they considered *exotic* at all? Such questions cannot be answered by the inventory alone. Information from other (admittedly not very abundant) available sources such as chronicles and descriptions of events (mostly special occasions such as weddings) must be called upon as well.[56]

Taking all into consideration, there seems to be no evidence of there being any kind of *wunderkammer* in the duke's palace. In fact, there is no evidence that the objects mentioned formed a collection at all, i.e., a set of objects systematically acquired and gathered with some discernible criteria and goal. In the inventory, bezoars and unicorns are listed next to reliquaries and crucifixes and seem to have been equally used as propitiatory devices even if of a less than orthodox nature. Chinese porcelain, lacquered cabinets, and *plumaria* paintings were kept together with all sorts of other vessels, furniture and religious utensils. They are not described in a separate list, the vocabulary used to describe them is not in any way different than that used for any other type of objects, and their value does not distinguish them from the others. If anything, the hard data provided by the inventory points in the opposite direction: there are only 33 entries that include exotica (in the strictest sense), totaling 54 objects worth a little over 90,000 *reis*, which ultimately means that the duke was willing to invest more money in a single skilled musician than in the whole of his exotica.

Given the fact that the inventory is not organized according to space (proceeding room-by-room) but rather to service (with each official working in the palace listing the objects under his/her care regardless of the space in which they were kept or used), it is particularly difficult to analyze the items' spatial distribution. Nevertheless, the entries regarding foreign objects that fit the notion of a *wunderkammer* are spread between different officials who do not even all work for the same person (some working for the duke, others for the duchess, and others still for their son and daughter-in-law). This being the case, while not explaining where each item could be found, the inventory clearly indicates that these objects were not all kept together.

Descriptions of ceremonies taking place in the palace (as in any other Portuguese palace of the same period for that matter) are almost entirely mute on the usage of foreign items in the context of the household. It is rather by omission that conclusions may be reached. When describing a banquet, for instance, it is the tapestries hanging on the walls and the silver and gold pieces displayed and/or used that get all the attention and praise. No reference is ever made to an Afro-Portuguese ivory saltcellar, a Gujarati mother-of-pearl jug or even Chinese porcelain being used at the table. This does not necessarily mean that they were not used during meals or otherwise displayed in the palace. But in the context of this palace, they seem to have lost their exoticness. Once a coconut from the Indian Ocean, for instance, was mounted in silver and became a precious work of art, it entered the regular decorative discourse of the palace and became an object to be displayed next to German silver candle holders, on top of a Portuguese table, against the background of a set of Flemish tapestries that tell the story of Alexander. In this ducal palace, and probably in sixteenth-century Portugal at large, coconuts did not join other exotic objects in a special room where a three-dimensional catalogue of the world was assembled. On the contrary, it became part of the normality of what was probably the dominant decorative discourse among Portuguese noble families. The Central European model of the *wunderkammer* cannot be found in this palace but more importantly it clouds our understanding of what was in fact there.

The duke's prized possessions, those that ceremonial descriptions unfailingly mention and for which he paid the most are tapestries (mostly from Flanders), jewelry (which certainly included precious stones coming from far off origins), and silver and gold objects, most of which were unquestionably European. Rock crystal and tortoiseshell objects made in the Asian markets entered their global lives on board Portuguese ships making it all the way to Lisbon. Many continued their global journey towards other European ports and some found their way into special settings that highlighted their *globalness*. In Vila Viçosa, however, they became part of the palace's normality and seem to have settled in everyday life just like all their European counterparts. Even in the context of the 'house of glass and porcelain', objects made of china, a novel material, shared their space with others made of alabaster, glass and crystal, coming from much closer, European workshops. In this palace, foreign objects from far-off origins found themselves at home and thus ceased to be exotic.[57]

The duke's things and the global lives of empires

Having argued against the understanding of the ducal extra-European objects as symptoms of a fascination for the exotic and rather for their integration in a general sense of normality, something must be said about the duke's interest in the nascent Iberian empires. The many objects that he acquired from the various parts of the world and the considerable amount of resources he was willing to assign to their acquisition did not get organized in a proto-museum-like space. Nevertheless they do show that Teodósio was not only very much aware of the various Portuguese and even Spanish possessions throughout the world but also of their material potential. His interest in the vast expanses that Iberia was discovering and exploring outside of its historical boundaries did not manifest itself in the form of the organization of an encyclopedic collection but in a rather different and perhaps less expected way.

Once more, the inventory tells us something on this issue. One of the few groups of objects that can be securely placed in a specific palatial space is that of the items that could be found in the ducal office ('*despacho*').[58] This list, which does not include a single exotic item, makes it clear that this was not a *wunderkammer* or a *studiolo*. In fact, the duke's office was, as the name indicates, a working space. For decoration, a couple of paintings could be found, a portrait of the duke him- self and a *Flight from Egypt*, the former valued at 1,200 *reis* and the latter at a more substantial 7,000 *reis*. Beyond the latter painting, religion also made its presence felt in the somewhat less dignified form of a gesso relief depicting the *Descent from the Cross*, which was broken and almost worthless. A few more items, such as a couple of horse riding fixings and an old banner, may have had some form of sentimental value. Two more very curious entries reflect the duke's interest in technology, which is also discernible in other parts of the inventory and has been mentioned before: an iron used to make glass and a cabinet-making tool. Finally, and most significantly, a series of other objects could be found that related to map-making and reading, including a map itself, a couple of astrolabes, a compass, and navigation needles. Some of these are described as being old, rusty and broken, and none of them exceeds the limited worth of 400 *reis*. This means that they were not in the study for the duke to show to his guests, trumpeting his command of the world or even of a developing science. They were there to be used in everyday life.

The duke's interest in cartography, geography and navigation is further attested, for instance, by a group of over twenty maps that include *mapamundi* as well as maps of Europe, Africa, the Iberian Peninsula, France, England, and India. These maps were accompanied by other cartographic devices such as several nautical charts and three globes,[59] as well as a series of instruments that relate to the world of sailing and map making such as compasses, astrolabes and quadrants. These entries lead us to others that reveal an active interest in sailing and the sea, as well as in geography and the constant novelties about the empires, particularly visible in the duke's extraordinary library[60] where one could find books on sailing proper, such as Pedro de Medina's *The Art of Navigation*, classical geographers and cosmographers such as Strabo and Ptolemy, many works of geographic description, ranging from Marco Polo to more modern travel accounts, many chronicles on the history of the Portuguese empire, including all the most relevant ones, and even some books on the Spanish empire.

These items may not belong to the category that one would perhaps most expect – that of exotica. However, they belong to the realm of the most global of commodities, that which travelled the easiest and the most: knowledge. Thus it becomes clear that the duke was not invested in amassing a museum of extra-European objects but that, on the contrary, his interest in empire was of a rather different though nonetheless scientific nature. In the globalized world of the sixteenth century, the duke of Bragança had access to the world in a way that no one did a century earlier. His interest in it translated in the acquisition of several global commodities, which gain full meaning in a context that includes the transfer of technological and scientific knowledge, one that also takes into account the immense curiosity that many Europeans developed for the wider world that their fellow men were discovering, depicting and describing every day.

Notes and References

1. This essay is part of a research project entitled 'All His Worldly Possessions: The Estate of the 5th Duke of Bragança, D. Teodósio I', hosted by the Centro de História de Além-Mar, Faculdade das Ciências Sociais e Humanas, Universidade Nova de Lisboa / Universidade dos Açores, in collaboration with the Fundação da Casa de Bragança, and financed by the Fundação para a Ciência e Tecnologia (PTDC/EAT-HAT/098461/2008). I am much indebted to Anne Gerritsen for her editorial suggestions.
2. Duke Teodósio has not yet been the object of a biographic study. See *De Todas as Partes do Mundo. O Património do 5th Duque de Bragança, D. Teodósio I*, ed. Jessica Hallett and Nuno Senos (Lisboa: Tinta da China, forthcoming) for a systematic study of this historical figure. For detailed information on the ducal family see Mafalda Soares da Cunha, *Linhagem, Parentesco e Poder: a Casa de Bragança (1384–1483)* (Lisbon: Fundação da Casa de Bragança, 1990).
3. A full transcription of the inventory with numbered entries is available at www.cham. fcsh.unl.pt. For the purposes of this article I shall use this numbering for all *Inventory* references.
4. The sale or offer of objects that took place during the time it took for the inventory to be completed was recorded.
5. The bibliography that explores inventories is vast. For full publication of the primary sources and the attending studies see, for instance *The Inventory of King Henry VIII*, ed. David Starkey (London: Harvey Miller Publishers for the Society of Antiquaries of London, 1998–2012); and *Los Inventarios de Carlos V y la Familia Imperial*, ed. Fernando Checa (Madrid: Fernando Villaverde Ediciones, 2010). See also *The Possessions of a Cardinal: Politics, Piety and Art, 1450–1700*, ed. Mary Hollingsworth and Carol M. Richardson (University Park: The Pennsylvania State University Press, 2010); Jessica Keating and Lia Markey, 'Introduction: Captured Objects: Inventories of Early Modern Collections,' *Journal of the History of Collections* 23.2 (2011): 209–213; or Giorgio Riello, '"Things Seen and Unseen": The Material Culture of Early Modern Inventories and Their Representation

of Domestic Interiors,' in *Early Modern Things: Objects and Their Histories, 1500–1800*, ed. Paula Findlen (London: Routledge, 2013), 125–150. The project 'The Possessions of the Portuguese Merchant-Banker Emmanuel Ximenez (1564–1632) in Antwerp' and its website (http://ximenez.unibe.ch/project/) should also be mentioned.

6. The bibliography on the history of the Portuguese overseas presence is immense. For a fairly recent survey in English, which includes a chapter on the arts by Luís Moura Sobral, see: *Portuguese Oceanic Expansion, 1400–1800*, ed. Francisco Bethencourt and Diogo Ramada Curto (Cambridge: Cambridge University Press, 2007).

7. A chapter on Constantino, by Alexandra Pelúcia, is included in Hallett and Senos (forthcoming).

8. *Inventory*, 1042, described as a string of thick pearls. The second most expensive item, valued at 1,350,000 *reis*, is a set of 10 tapestries especially commissioned (most likely in Flanders) to celebrate Nun'Álvares, the founder of the family. As far as values are concerned, it is helpful to keep in mind that in 1564, a skilled labourer in Lisbon, such as a carpenter or stone carver, earned on average 100 *reis* per day (*c.* 25,000 *reis* per year) while an unskilled one earned around half as much. Project member Leonor Freire Costa established these values for the project.

9. *Inventory*, 2305.

10. Since none of the duke's objects are traceable today, the images in this article are illustrations of the types of objects that are mentioned in the inventory, not attempts at identifying the specific objects themselves.

11. See *Encompassing the Globe. Portugal and the World in the Sixteenth and Seventeenth Centuries*, exh. cat. (Washington DC: The Sackler Gallery, 2007) for examples and a collection of essays on the arts and the Portuguese world.

12. *Inventory*, 147.

13. *Inventory*, 991.

14. *Inventory*, 380 (three coconuts, no origin listed, totalling 250 *reis*), 1364 (one coconut, no origin listed, silver details, 1,000 *reis*), and 2005 (one coconut from the Maldives with a silver foot; the coconut is worth 6,000 *reis* and the object totals 18,000 *reis*, over half the yearly salary of a carpenter).

15. *Inventory*, 401.

16. Some entries use expressions such as 'some', 'several', 'a few', or 'many'. In these cases, it is impossible to determine the precise quantity of objects they total.

17. *Inventory*, 198 and 215.

18. As, for example, *Inventory* 649 ('dezoito porcelaninhas pequeninas') or 2363 ('outo persolaninhas pequenas').

19. For instance, *Inventory*, 2367.

20. The discussion that follows is solely based on entries that explicitly indicate the origin of the objects or on items (such as the slaves) whose extra-European origin raises no questions. As such, items such as the expensive pearl necklace mentioned above, whose pearls were probably Asian but whose origin is not explicitly mentioned, are not taken into consideration.

21. I am not including here the immense commission of tiles the duke made from Antwerp: *From Flanders. The Azulejos Commissioned by D. Teodósio I, 5th Duke of Braganza (c.1510–1563)*, exh. cat. (Lisbon: Museu Nacional do Azulejo, 2012).

22. *Inventory*, 676.

23. *Inventory*, 5671–5681, 5694 and 5696, respectively.

24. *Inventory*, 5676 for the slave, worth as much as, for instance, *Inventory* 1037, a cross with five diamonds and a pearl, in other words, the equivalent of four years' salary of a skilled worker.

25. On these so-called Afro-Portuguese ivories see, for instance, William B. Fagg, *Afro-Portuguese Ivories*, exh. cat. (London: Batchworth Press, 1959), and Ezio Bassani and William B. Fagg, *Africa and the Renaissance: Art in Ivory*, exh. cat. (New York: The Center for African Art, 1988). While these authors have included the Kingdom of Benin in the list of origins for these ivories, more recently Peter Mark, 'Towards a Reassessment

of the Dating and the Geographical Origins of the Luso-African Ivories, Fifteenth to Seventeenth Centuries,' *History in Africa* 34 (2007): 189–211, has convincingly contested this view.

26. *Inventory*, 1774 contains 3 rugs ('*esteiras*') from India, which could actually be African, the word '*esteira*' applying to rugs made of natural fibres and there being no such known examples from India. These were worth 100 *reis* a piece. Of the entries containing ivory, only *Inventory*, 1572, two pieces of an ivory tusk, is probably African; all the others could come just as easily from Asia or even from Europe.

27. To my knowledge, the absence of Brazilian objects in Portuguese households has never been the object of reflection. For the arts of Brazil in the early period of colonization see Nuno Senos, 'The Arts of Brazil Before the Golden Age,' in *Encompassing the Globe. Portugal and the World in the Sixteenth and Seventeen Centuries*, exh. cat. (Washington, DC: The Sackler Gallery, 2007), *Essays*: 131–37.

28. *Inventory*, 38, worth 4,000 *reis*.

29. *Inventory*, 1768.

30. *Inventory*, 1652.

31. *Inventory*, 1254 and 1255.

32. *Inventory*, 147 and 1220.

33. *Inventory*, 95 (which, though broken, was still worth 8,000 *reis*), 991 (13,000 *reis*), 1637 (1,500 *reis*), and 2379 (250 *reis*).

34. This list has its own subtitle and spans entries 650 to 658.

35. This excludes, for instance, an Indian female slave that was part of the gift and was listed in a different part of the inventory (*Inventory*, 767).

36. *Inventory*, 652.

37. For a more detailed analysis of the organization of this space see *De todas as partes do mundo*.

38. *Inventory*, 1970.

39. On the duke's carpets see: *The Oriental Carpet in Portugal, Carpets and Paintings, 15th to 18th Centuries*, exh. cat., ed. Jessica Hallett and Teresa Pacheco Pereira (Lisbon: Museu Nacional de Arte Antiga/Instituto dos Museus e da Conservação, 2007).

40. *Inventory*, 5689 (40,000 *reis*).

41. *Inventory*, 2935 for the most expensive Turkish carpet, 3344 for its Persian counterpart, 2551 for the one used in the chapel, 970 for the one used by the duchess.

42. *Inventory*, 2944, worth 40,000 *reis*.

43. For instance *Inventory*, 3197 and 3314.

44. *Inventory*, 2833 for an expensive example (22,000 *reis*).

45. *Inventory*, 1996 for an expensive shirt (3,000 *reis*) and *Inventory*, 2231 for a hat.

46. *Inventory*, 1869.

47. *Inventory*, 62.

48. *Inventory*, 5655, 5660, and 5682 respectively.

49. See, for instance, the description of the wedding festivities that took place in the palace in 1537, 'Festas, e apercebimentos . . . ,' in *Memórias da Casa de Bragança . . .* (mss.), Biblioteca Nacional de Portugal (BNP), Reservados cod. 1544, fl s. 105v–139. A full transcription of the document is available at www.cham.fcsh.unl.pt.

50. The literature on this topic is infinite, including a periodical, the *Journal of the History of Collections*, published since 1989. Julius von Schlosser, *Die Kunst- und Wunderkammern der Späterenaissance* (Leipzig: Verlag von Klinkhardt & Biermann, 1908) is unanimously considered seminal. Its proposals were only much later picked up in a systematic way from *The Origins of Museums: The Cabinet of Curiosities in Sixteenth and Seventeenth-Century Europe*, ed. Oliver Impey and Arthur MacGregor (Oxford: Clarendon Press, 1985) onwards. Recent studies on the topic included (but are by no means limited to) Hollingsworth and Richardson, 2010; *Collecting Across Cultures. Material Exchanges in the Early Modern Atlantic World*, ed. Daniela Bleichmar and Peter Mancall (Philadelphia: Pennsylvania University Press, 2011); and Findley, 2013. The recent publication of the

English translation of Samuel Quiccheberg's *Inscriptiones*, by Mark Meadow who also wrote the important introduction (Los Angeles: The Getty Research Institute, 2013) is a most welcome addition to the available primary sources.

51. *Inventory*, 1044.
52. *Inventory*, 1183.
53. *Inventory*, 2212.
54. *Inventory*, 2304.
55. *Inventory*, 2224.
56. Besides the above-mentioned wedding description, which is the most important narrative source for this period, see for instance Alexandre Herculano, 'Viagem a Portugal do Cardeal Alexandrino,' *Panorama* 1.5 (1841), 309–312, 338–339 and 409–411, and 2.1 (1842) 211–212, 346–347; António de Oliveira de Cadornega, *Descrição de Vila Viçosa* (Lisbon: INCM, 1982); Magalotti, *Viaje de Cosme de Médicis por España y Portugal (1668–1669)* (Madrid: Sucesores de Rivadeneyra, 1933).
57. See Peter Mason, *Infelicities: Representations of the Exotic* (Baltimore and London: Johns Hopkins University Press, 1998).
58. The term '*despachar*' means 'to work', which is why I do not think that '*despacho*' should be translated as 'study' but rather as 'office'. The ordinances of Duke Teodósio (published in António Caetano de Sousa, *Provas da História Genealógica da Casa Real Portuguesa* (Lisbon: Officina Regia, 1739–1748), vol. 5, 235–252) explain that this was the room in which the duke signed official papers and generally took care of the business of running his interest and estate. The bulk of its content can be found under its own specific heading in *Inventory*, 2385–2403. A few more scattered objects can be found throughout the inventory such as in entries 1656 or 1692.
59. Most of these were kept in the library. See, for instance, *Inventory*, 3532 (mapamundi), 4401 (Europe), 3539 (globe), and 1920 (nautical chart).
60. Encompassing over 1,600 entries, mostly found under *Inventory*, 3518–5130 (studied by Project member Ana Isabel Buescu).

6

DISHES, COINS AND PIPES

The epistemological and emotional power of VOC material culture in Australia

Susan Broomhall

Somewhere around 25 October 1616, the crew of the Dutch East India Company vessel *Eendracht* spied an unfamiliar stretch of coastline. Quickly surveying the area, skipper Dirck Hartogh called upon the cook to flatten a large pewter plate and be ready to engrave it with the message he dictated. This is what it read:

> 1616, on the 25th of October is here arrived the ship de Eendracht of Amsterdam; the upper-merchant Gillis Miebais, from Luick; skipper Dirck Hatichs, from Amsterdam; on the 27th do. set sail again for Bantam; the under-merchant Jan [Stins]; the upper-steersman Pieter [Doekes from Bil]. Anno 1616.[1]

The plate was nailed to a post on the northern edge of what is now Dirk Hartog Island (Figure 6.1). There it remained until 1697 when fellow Company captain Willem de Vlamingh found it lying in the sand at the foot of the then rotting pole, and brought it to the Netherlands where it could be added as early evidence of the Company's mastery over the known globe. Vlamingh replaced it with his own version, also a large pewter plate, replicating Hartogh's words in a kind of homage to his forebear and adding his own name and dates to the history of Dutch East India Company claims over the South Lands.[2]

In this way, two plates on which dinner might well have been served the previous night, became embedded in deeply emotional colonising politics regarding Australia. Objects – from trinkets and toys to precious metal and textiles – had always formed part of the Dutch East India Company's (VOC) strategies of encounter with the South Lands in this period. But many more became part of it, through such unexpected uses as did Hartogh's plate or through shipwrecks that brought coins, glassware, jugs, plates, pipes, and even a consignment of shoes, to the Western Australian coast. This chapter explores how such European objects have been crucial

FIGURE 6.1 Dirck Hartogh dish, *c.*1600–1616. Pewter. Dimensions: d 36.5cm × h 70cm × w 50cm × t 4cm. Rijksmuseum, Amsterdam NG-NM-825. On his way to Asia, the Dutch East India Company captain, Dirck Hartogh, reached the west coast of a land previously unseen by the Company. This is the oldest European object found in Australia.

to, and embedded in, power relations, expressed in social and emotional forms and practices, between Europeans and indigenous peoples in what is now Australia.

In doing so, I am interested in how these objects articulate varied emotions through their materiality, location and assemblage in changing historical and socio-cultural contexts. My analysis connects to recent work on material culture stemming from archaeological, anthropological, and philosophical fields, in particular that which explores the role of objects as agents. This recognises the power of objects, what Jane Bennett describes as 'the curious ability of inanimate things to animate, to act, to produce effects dramatic and subtle.'[3] Objects are no longer seen solely as representations of social relations, but also able to create these as they act on peoples and operate in relation to them.[4] Sociologist Sara Ahmed and archaeologists

Oliver T.J. Harris and Tim Flohr Sørensen have both usefully conceptualised emotions as social and cultural entities generated through relationships between people and things.[5] I argue that VOC objects can be seen to operate in such ways; that is, making and shaping indigenous and European peoples, their knowledge, and their emotional relationships to each other and to yet other things in profound ways since their arrival on the Australian continent some four hundred years ago.

The power of VOC material culture was produced through encounters between peoples that created forms of exchange. These do not necessarily imply equality in what was transferred or to whom, but opportunities through which ideas, feelings, and objects, our focus here, passed between and were created by individuals.[6] Furthermore, objects and people not only operate in relation to each other, but also in particular spaces and in specific historical contexts that themselves construct certain emotional patterns and practices.[7] Conceptually and physically, encounters on the Australian continent took place in environments of power which were asymmetrical, familiar to indigenous peoples, but profoundly foreign to Europeans from the time of the VOC onwards.[8] Yet these encounters have been also rendered different to local peoples by the presence of European vessels, objects and bodies in them, over the past four hundred years, and these same elements gave some sense of familiarity and security to non-indigenous arrivals whether permanent or temporary.[9] I argue that VOC material culture has both signalled and created power, claiming to define the boundaries of social communities, to create identities, feelings, forms of knowledge, a sense of belonging and place, whilst displacing others.

In the following sections, three specific moments of exchange are examined, through documentation produced by the Company, colonial and modern state governments. These are not only important sources but also significant sites for the production and practices of power surrounding material objects. These texts must therefore be understood within the context of their own social and power dynamics, forms of appropriate speech, and as gender, racial, confessional, ethnic and other ideologies operated and were reflected in ritualised textual and organisational performances.

Pride, plates and possession: colonising the South Lands

A widespread scholarly view is that the interactions of the VOC with the South Lands were informed by interests in trade, rather than settlement or conversion.[10] As Eric Ketelaar has stated, the 'Dutch were traders, not colonisers, at least not in the seventeenth and eighteenth century'.[11] While this may have been largely true of the outcome of their actions, at least in relation to the Australian continent, a closer look at the archives, practices and artefacts that remain from successive encounters with the region suggests a more complex understanding of VOC ambitions in the region. They reveal clearly the colonising intentions of the Company, and the importance of material culture in new spaces and exchanges in making these claims for emotional, social, cultural and epistemological power; that is, the power to make and have recognised knowledge about objects, lands and peoples.

In the first half of the seventeenth century, Governors-General in the Asian region issued successive instructions for exploratory expeditions to the South Lands to claim lands and resources that crews encountered, and subordinate local peoples in trading partnerships. Yet, after 1645, the VOC's central governing body, the Heeren XVII in Amsterdam, reoriented the company's objectives to focus on known trading prospects and repressed any more explicit aim of territorial claims.[12] By this point, though, the South Lands had been marked by VOC presence and these encounters documented, such that it could also be argued that no further work was required to establish Dutch claims. By the mid-seventeenth century, upon European maps the Australian land mass held the name Nova Hollandia by which it would be known until (indeed, the western side, after) British claims and then settlement of the colony of New South Wales in the late eighteenth century.

Possession formed a leitmotif of the Company's purpose in the region from the time of the first exploratory voyage. Thus the instructions prepared by the Council in Batavia for the yachts *Haringh* and *Hasewint* in 29 September 1622 (a voyage which did not eventuate) expected commanders in:

> all which places, lands and islands. . . . [to] take formal possession, and in sign thereof, besides, erect a stone column in such places as shall be taken possession of the said column recording in bold, legible characters the year, the month, the day of the week and the date, the persons by whom and the hour of the day when such possession has been taken on behalf of the States-General above mentioned.[13]

Texts constituted vital proof of these 'rights', signifying the new control that the VOC held over local peoples. Crews were to:

> endeavour to enter into friendly relations and make covenants with all such kings and nations as you shall happen to fall in with, and try to prevail upon them to place themselves under the protection of the States of the United Netherlands, of which covenants and alliances you will likewise cause proper documents to be drawn up and signed.[14]

In order to achieve this, commanders would need to observe the landscapes they encountered and the local inhabitants within them. In particular, Company men were to make assessments about the nature of indigenous people, and their organisational and leadership structures, by the ways they engaged with materials and spaces. Crews were instructed to:

> go ashore in various places and diligently examine the coast in order to ascertain whether or not it is inhabited, the nature of the land and the people, their towns and inhabited villages, the divisions of their kingdoms, their religion and policy, their wars, their rivers, the shape of their vessels, their fisheries, commodities and manufactures.[15]

The VOC had a motivation to explore the South Lands to locate products that could be brought into its global trading networks. What might local peoples have, what might they want, and what would they be willing to trade for it? Thus, the instructions required the commanders 'specially to inquire what minerals, such as gold, silver, tin, iron, lead and copper, what precious stones, pearls, vegetables, animals and fruits, these lands yield and produce'.[16] The South Lands had long been fabled to be replete with gold and peopled with giants. Successive VOC instructions required crews to look out for gold: 'certain parts of this South-land are likely to yield gold, a point into which you will inquire as carefully as possible.'[17]

Such were the Company's high hopes and ambitions for the South Lands. However, the realities of the spaces and objects that the VOC crews observed evidently provoked quite different emotional responses. The journals of Jan Carstenszoon, captain of the *Arnhem*, travelling with the *Pera*, skippered by Willem Joosten van Colster, in 1623 on an exploratory voyage for the Company around the northwest of the Australian continent, expressed disappointment at the material culture he could observe worn and used by local peoples. There was little to be discovered about their material possessions, wants and needs by their bodies: Carstenszoon reported that they 'go about stark naked, carrying their privities in a small conch-shell, tied to the body with a bit of string'.[18] He had little success in fulfilling the Company's requests for information about their goods, leaving pieces of iron and string beads to entice the Southlanders to trade but finding generally that they 'seemed quite indifferent to these things'.[19] In making his assessment about the poor trading potential of the region through his encounters with peoples, objects and the environments in which they lived, Carstenszoon concluded that the 'savages' had little interest in his 'pieces of iron, strings of beads and pieces of cloth'.[20] He did however dutifully record in his log at his turning point on the exploratory mission that he had:

> in default of stone caused a wooden tablet to be nailed to a tree, the said tablet having the following words carved into it: 'Anno 1623 den 24n April sijn hier aen gecomen twee jachten wegen de Hooge Mogende Heeren Staten Genl'.[21]

This was a rather more vague claim to possession than that instructed by the Governors, noting the date of their passage but not the individual names of these 'first' explorers. This seemingly half-hearted claim to what appeared to be undesirable lands was reflected even in the poor choice of material available for its record. A wooden tablet could easily rot in the marshy surrounds pinned to a tree about which little detail of location was recorded. It was a first claim that surely lacked the grandeur, dignity and permanence imagined by the Governors. Nonetheless, it reflected key thinking by the Company that would have important ramifications for its later interactions. Carstenszoon had already assessed the local people as 'savages' who had little interest in, and often undisguised hostility towards, these new-comers and their goods. These were not, it seems, people with whom the Company would be required to negotiate a treaty of submission, nor to offer the benefits of its 'protection'; they were instead to be rendered invisible and unasked about the possession of their lands.

Reports back to Batavia from successive crews following Carstenszoon were primed by knowledge of his experiences in the South Lands that were reflected in subsequent instructions from the Governors. Those issued to Abel Tasman in 1644, for example, warned him to take care, since previous voyages had 'ascertained that vast regions were for the greater part uncultivated, and certain parts inhabited by savage, cruel, black barbarians'.[22] The Company's assessments that the lands were unworked and their peoples not formed into coherent societies (at least in the VOC's view) enabled them to confirm their instructions that crews take possession of:

> all continents and islands, which you shall discover, touch at and set foot on, . . . the which in uninhabited regions or in such countries as have no sovereign, may be done by erecting a memorial-stone or by planting our Prince-flag in sign of actual occupation, seeing that such lands justly belong to the discoverer and first occupier.[23]

However, should new areas be found populated by people of recognisably 'civilised' origins, VOC material culture could come in to play in a European understanding of friendship and subordination:

> in populated regions or in such as have undoubted lords, the consent of the people or the king will be required before you can enter into possession of them, the which you should try to obtain by friendly persuasion and by presenting them with some small tree planted in a little earth, by erecting some stone structure in conjunction with the people, or by setting up the Prince-flag in commemoration of their voluntary assent or submission.[24]

As it had for the proposed voyage of the *Haringh* and *Hasewint*, the texts were key to reinforcing the meaning of these objects, objects whose power clearly functioned in partnership with, and in relationship to, each other. Tasman was told to 'carefully note in your Journal, mentioning by name such persons as have been present at them, that such record may in future be of service to our republic'.[25] Thus texts were again required to document the placement, practice and enactment of VOC objects on the continent's shores.

Tasman duly followed his instructions. He recorded in his logs that as they skirted the east coast of what is now Tasmania, landing at North Bay, on 3 December 1642:

> we carried with us a pole with the Company's mark carved into it, and a Prince-flag to be set up there, that those who shall come after us may become aware that we have been here, and have taken possession of the said land as our lawful property.[26]

This assumed that all could 'read' this information from the flag, albeit not as permanent a marker as could have been hoped. However, the surf was so rough that Tasman:

> ordered the carpenter to swim to the shore alone with the pole and the flag, and kept by the wind with our pinnace; we made him plant the said pole with the flag at top into the earth, about the centre of the bay near four tall trees easily recognisable and standing in the form of a crescent, exactly before the one standing lowest.[27]

These trees provided the spatial and material link to the flag that his crew had 'planted' in the Australian earth. Yet these transient markers were imperfect evidence of Company achievement. The reality of affixing Company objects to and in the Australian continent did not prove as simple or easy as the Governors had imagined. Neither Carstenszoon nor Tasman found ready access to permanent materials such as the stone plaques and hospitable environments for their secure placement imagined in the instructions. Each sufficed with materials at his disposal, just as had Hartogh in 1616 with a dinner plate attached to a wooden pole on the desolate island that bears his name. In each case, the claim was ultimately rendered permanent for the Company not only through the material culture at the site, but through the VOC texts which recorded, visualised and circulated these claims through their archives.

This weakness to the power of VOC material culture to make meaning in the South Lands was implicitly recognised in the continued attempts to secure a more definitive claim. In making the case to the *Heeren* in the Republic for a further voyage to the region in 1644, the Batavian Councillors summarised Tasman's first expedition as 'having only met with naked, beach-roving wretches, destitute of rice, and not possessed of any fruits worth mentioning', summations that reinforced and justified the VOC's possessive attention to this territory.[28] For his subsequent voyage, the need for Tasman's artefactual record to document VOC superiority and prior claim against other European powers in the region was paramount and explicit in his instructions. So that 'the fruits of the pains and expense bestowed on this undertaking may not eventually be taken from us by other European nations', Tasman was to claim any lands:

> as have only barbarian inhabitants or none at all . . . recording in what year and season each separate land has by you been reached and taken possession of, and declaring at the same time your fixed intention to send a body of men thither from here by the first opportunity, and thus duly secure to ourselves this property by founding a permanent colony there.[29]

Thus, objects, however ordinary they were aboard vessels, took on in these contexts the name and purpose of the Company, invested with possessive meaning about the lands and peoples which they were placed on and near. The VOC Governors assumed these signed objects would be universally understandable to all peoples, although it seems likely that their main probable readership was intended to be other Europeans. These objects employed by the VOC to claim and possess the Australian lands and people reflected hopes about its potential for resources and a colony, their fears of likely competition, perhaps especially the Portuguese with whom so much of the Indian Ocean trade and positioning was in dispute, and pride in their capacity to achieve the first real access to this still vastly unknown land and people among Europeans.

Evidence from seventeenth-century VOC records suggests that the material artefacts that took on these powerful roles for the Company were often quite ordinary in other circumstances. In these contexts, however, they became invested with new meanings, which shifted from indifference to significance. These objects accrued this position in part because of how and where they were placed. Additionally, though, VOC material culture gained these powers through texts that made them important, by documenting, reinforcing and remembering these objects in their new spaces, in some cases, well beyond their existence in physical form. A wide range of documents, from ships' logs and journals, to petitions and summative reports among personnel in Company outposts as well as to the *Heeren* in Amsterdam made, visualised and materialised these claims. Moreover, these textualised, emplaced objects functioned as claims to spaces because the spaces themselves were viewed as accessible to European ownership, an interpretation made in part through principles about the rights of 'barbarians' and 'undoubted lords' to lands as defined by these same VOC texts and made through Company observations of the use of material culture and spaces by local peoples.[30] The complexities of indigenous knowledge and emotions about the Company arrivals had no place or purpose in such VOC texts. Material culture, that is, shipboard objects, spaces and texts, operated together to afford epistemological and emotional power to certain VOC artefacts, placed on the Australian continent, and documented in Company records. Their legacy would be profound.

Company, coins and colonisers: exploiting indigenous knowledge and emotions

VOC material culture would take on new power in the British colonial era. In 1829, the Swan River Colony was settled by the British Government on the western coast of the Australian continent, operating around the location of present-day Perth.[31] Historical and anthropological scholars have demonstrated how colonial, settler and missionary ideologies and practices embedded local peoples and spaces in new power relations through objects at this period.[32] This section, however, examines the trajectory of VOC material culture in the colonial era. The apparent 'discovery' of Company objects, artefacts that had been known to local peoples and were revealed through indigenous contacts, just a few years after the colonists arrived, created opportunities to form alternative social alignments, to forge new allegiances and gave rise to new power to make knowledge for both indigenous and European peoples.

In July 1834 a curious story began to circulate in the nascent British settlement. *The Perth Gazette* reported that a group of indigenous people had arrived at Guild-ford, announcing that men from the Weel group had told them that:

> a ship was wrecked ('boat broke') on the coast to the northward, about 30 (native) day's walk from the Swan – that there was white money plenty lying on the beach for several yards, as thick as seed vessels under a red gum tree. They represented that the wreck had been seen six moons ago.[33]

These objects had not been disturbed and thus there was no physical evidence for colonists to confirm this information. However, the men had elaborated further to local people that:

> there were several white men, represented to be of very large stature, ladies, and 'plenty piccaninni' – that they were living in houses made of canvas and wood . . . – that there are five such houses, two large and three small . . . that the white men gave the Weel men some gentlemen's (white) biscuit and the latter gave in return spears, shields etc.[34]

These accounts suggested the shipwreck of a sizeable vessel, leaving European men, women and children stranded in a remote location. The need for a swift response was, as *The Perth Gazette* opined, 'influenced by feelings of humanity, which the scenes of distress have pictured to their minds'.[35] The colony reacted promptly to the imagined fate of these victims of the treacherous Australian coast, dispatching two vessels, the *Monkey* and *Fanny*, within a fortnight of the news, to scour the coastline where they believed the vessel was wrecked.[36]

At the same time, one settler, George Fletcher Moore, who had learned a little of the local Noongar language, sought out a man understood to be a leader among his people.[37] Moore explained to him what was at stake for the Europeans in deeply emotional terms, 'in his language and manners as well as I could use them':

> White man's friends are sitting on the ground sorrowing, at a distance – the ship which has walked with them over the sea now lies dead, broken on the rocks, white men here are sorrowful – white men here will give a paper-talk to black man, – black man will give that paper-talk to white men at a distance, who will see it and rejoice.[38]

Assumptions about Aboriginal feelings were also crucial to Moore's request though. The colony had been fraught with violence from its inception, escalating through the 1830s from harsh British punishment for acts of Aboriginal 'stealing' and Aboriginal payback killings, to large-scale confrontations and massacre of the local Aboriginal peoples. This man was a suspect in the murder of a British soldier earlier that year, a crime for which his son already languished in jail for his suspected part.[39] Moore suggested that if he took a letter to the shipwreck survivors, both might be pardoned: 'white men at a distance will give another paper-talk to black men, who will give it to white men here, and the Governor will then say to [the man's son], "walk away, friend"'.[40] In the narrative he constructed for *The Perth Gazette* about his intervention, Moore opined: 'The mention of [his son's] name raised the feelings of the father.'[41] He hinted further at the man's desire to align himself with the colonists, recounting how the man confirmed if he were to deliver the letter, would 'white man here presently be friend?'[42]

This gave the man strong motivation to accept the mission and achieve it successfully, but 22 days later, he returned, having not ascertained any further news or remains of a European ship or people.[43] He had travelled to the geographic and cultural boundaries of his country and then sought information across the networks of those in neighbouring areas. He confirmed that 'they all tell him there is "money plenty" on the shore just where the waves beat on the beach; that the pieces of money lie on the top of one another, and he indicates that they cover a good space of ground.'[44] However, he had not physically travelled to the site and could produce no material support for these claims, being culturally prohibited from accessing the site directly at this time of the year (although he had expressed 'a determination to go in the same direction when the "egg" season commences . . . [when he would] be able to reach the spot where the money is represented to be lying'[45]). As a result, the 'proscribed native' was made to wait a further month while the governor and newspaper of Perth debated publicly whether he had sufficiently honoured his agreement to warrant a pardon: 'It is difficult to determine what credit may be given to [his] statement, – and whether he actually went the distance he represents.'[46] On 6 September, it was announced: both 'the Outlaw' and his son would be pardoned.[47] The colonists' vessel equally returned having been no more successful in locating survivors. Indigenous information about what appeared to represent European artefacts had instigated strong feelings among the colonists, but it was an uncertain form of truth for them. None of the Aboriginal men had produced physical evidence by which their knowledge might be tested satisfactorily in European terms. The 'texts' of their oral narratives did not verify and create claims that were accepted by the colonists.

Aboriginal engagement with early European materials would have profound consequences for local relations with the new colonial forces at the Swan River Colony. It is now thought that the material artefacts reported in this exchange were likely to have been those from a VOC vessel, which had, potentially more than a hundred years earlier, been wrecked upon the coast. Indigenous memories had passed through the information pathways of song lines and boundaries of countries, described in a temporality that was not shared by the colonists. These accounts may in fact offer some evidence of what occurred to one of the known VOC crews to be wrecked on the western coastline and may suggest how its survivors interacted with local populations, trading biscuits for weapons, in an exchange to ensure their survival.[48] For a local man and his son surviving in the colonial era, however, encounter even with the talk of early European material culture was to have life and death consequences. His investment in the reality of European coins would, in the end, spare not only his own life but that of his son. On such terms, it would be little wonder that other indigenous peoples might have made the choice to keep the knowledge that they had of European discoveries to themselves.

Reports of material culture of European ships such as coins and sail cloth, as well as of European peoples, provoked strong emotional responses in the British colonists themselves struggling in the profoundly remote and unfamiliar climate of the Swan River Colony. Feelings about the meaning of such finds, imagining the distress of abandoned Europeans in this harsh land, inspired the colonists to action. European material culture in these sites took on new power and meaning – not the financial worth of the coins but what they might say about their lack of value in these inhospitable climes of the Australian continent. At the same time, VOC objects, or the idea of them, locked local peoples into new power relations with the British colonial community. These objects offered Aboriginal people an opportunity to forge new connections with the colonists, providing services, skills and knowledge of the local environment that were essential to the European population. Their 'location' thus offered an access point to recognition of the need for indigenous knowledge, as trackers, and as conduits to social networks of power to secure information that colonisers desired. Aboriginal peoples were active agents in this colonial encounter created by the (at least potential) collision of European material culture and the Australian continent, securing benefits for themselves as individuals, families and local groups.[49]

Old objects, new knowledge, mixed emotions

VOC artefacts still have deeply divided emotional and epistemological power for populations in Australia as well as overseas, as they continue to form part of uneven power relations between their land of origin and their placement on the Australian continent. This section explores these meanings for both Aboriginal and non-Aboriginal communities today.

VOC artefacts in Australia remain the legal property of the Dutch Government. However, an agreement negotiated between Australia and the Netherlands in 1972 sees Australia bear the costs of recovery, conservation, storage and display of VOC objects while sending a representative collection of artefacts to The Netherlands. Artefacts that have been found on the coast are those of everyday shipboard life, cargo and even ballast, and include glassware, dishes, pipes, coins, elephant tusks, textiles, breech block, bottles, navigational instruments, and musket balls. Awe and wonder at material cultural remains that have withstood the harsh conditions of the rough seas and exposed landscapes are a cornerstone of the current museological presentation. Perhaps the most spectacular remaining artefact is the monumental sandstone gate, carried as ballast upon the VOC *Batavia*, destined to be the grand entrance to the city of Batavia. Recovered from the ocean off the coast, this was meticulously reconstructed and now stands in the Western Australian Museum's regional collection at Geraldton on the mid-western coast of Australia, close to its underwater resting place. Indeed, so important is this iconic object understood to be (although never intended for the Australian continent) that a replica is also displayed in the Museum's flagship Shipwreck Gallery, in the port city of Fremantle, Western Australia, a double colonial reconstruction by VOC objects.

The 400th anniversary of Dirck Hartogh's arrival in Australia in 2016 is expected to generate celebrations, suggesting it remains meaningful to contemporary Australia's understanding of its identity and history. Its significance reflects the presentation of VOC material culture in the Western Australian Museum's collections displayed at Fremantle and Geraldton where Company objects offer evidence of an interest and claim to the Australian land prior to the French or British. This narrative has some roots in the parochial political perception of the oft-forgotten western third of Australia (whereas the foundational commemorative dates of British settlement (1788) are all centred upon east coast sites). Both narratives continue to vest value in European connections to the continent. In 1994, a Select Committee of the Western Australian Legislative Assembly was convened to determine the primary and secondary discoverers of the *Tryall*, and four shipwrecked VOC vessels, *Batavia, Vergulde Draeck, Zuytdorp* and *Zeewyk*. In its conclusions, the report stated that further research should be conducted on the possibility of contact between local peoples and VOC crews, justifying this attention on the basis that:

> generations of Australian schoolchildren have been taught that Australia was settled by the British at Port Jackson in 1788. Evidence put before the Committee and reading material made available to our members strongly suggests that, in fact, a significant European presence could have been in Western Australia at least 76 years earlier. If these theories are proved to be true, they would undoubtedly challenge conventional notions of early British settlement.[50]

The relationship of Aboriginal peoples to these objects is less straightforward however. The Select Committee's decisions had deep economic and political significance.[51] It recommended that all primary discoverers of the shipwrecks should each receive ex-gratia payments of up to AU$25,000 and secondary discoverers up to AU$5,000.[52] The report recapitulated a series of indigenous oral histories that suggested knowledge of both Dutch survivors and the shipwreck site but stated that the non-Aboriginal claimant, Tom Pepper:

> does not seem to have known about these traditions in April 1927 when . . . he came to the Zuytdorp Cliffs and found coins and other relics from the *Zuytdorp*. There is considerable weight of testimony as to Pepper's integrity and honesty. . . . Undoubtedly he was the first to **report** the discovery of the relics near the site to the responsible authorities, and thus to identify the locality of an historic wreck, although without discovering the wreck itself.[53]

The Committee acknowledged though that 'around the same time, according to the widely supported testimony of family members, Tom Pepper's sister-in-law', an indigenous woman, 'had discovered a number of artefacts from the *Zuytdorp* in the same locality.' They concluded that it was 'impossible to demonstrate that she was on the site ahead of Tom Pepper . . . On the other hand, she may already have been aware of surviving Aboriginal traditions. It is understandable that she did not make a public report of her finds, given the constraints affecting the Aboriginal population at that time, but she initiated an important oral tradition'.[54] The Committee thus ranked her as a 'secondary discoverer' of *Zuytdorp* relics but not the wreck itself.

Finally, the Committee concluded that geologist Dr Phillip Playford, who has written extensively on his part in the *Zuytdorp* discovery,[55] was also a primary discoverer because 'stimulated by meeting Tom Pepper at Tamala in 1954 . . . [he] undertook the detailed historical research which led to the positive identification and pinpointing of the *Zuytdorp* wrecksite'.[56] Thus, two non-Aboriginal men were awarded substantial payments that were not given to the indigenous woman who, the report acknowledged, had found relics at the same time.[57] What differed then between their actions was that she had not alerted government authorities to her knowledge of VOC material culture. Non-Aboriginal authorities were once more deriving power and meaning from their assessment of how Aboriginal people interacted and used material culture. Moreover, although there has been a considerable shift since the landmark High Court decision, *Mabo* v *Queensland* (1992), that saw the recognition of native title in Australia, this judgement appears to reflect the Australian legal system's struggle to accommodate Aboriginal oral testimony alongside European forms of textual claims. The Committee's decision remains a source of considerable contention in the region. At the 2012 Zest Festival (a celebration of the three-hundredth anniversary of the *Zuytdorp* shipwreck in the area of the present-day town of Kalbarri[58]), the grand-children of the Aboriginal 'secondary discoverer' interjected loudly in a lecture in which Playford recounted his history of the find, insisting on the primary role of their ancestor. Indigenous knowledge of early European objects has remained for some a bitter experience.

In contemporary Australia, VOC material culture continues to hold cultural and political valence and epistemological power. Within the wider non-Aboriginal community of Western Australia, its presence offers a provocative opportunity to assert an alternative, western coast narrative of early European contact. The history of European interaction, if not 'successful' settlement, starts in 1606, not 1788. Moreover, in the hands of those who can assert their knowledge in European modes of documentation, these artefacts have provided both recognition and financial reward.

Futures

Evidently, VOC material culture has long been embedded in colonial social and power relations. But these objects are more than signs of these relations, they have also been agents in these processes and continue to elicit and generate strong emotional reactions and forms of knowledge today for a wide variety of communities. These objects have defined claims, displaced others, created European alignments and excluded Aboriginal peoples from access, rights and emotional connections to their own lands. These alignments and exclusions are expressed in practices of power that have been emotional, social and epistemological, and they have been achieved through material objects. The emotions, knowledges, and social alliances that such artefacts have produced have shifted over time, in the context of differing historical and socio-cultural settings, in response to their varied assemblages, changing material form and shifting use and constructions. However, it is noticeable that in almost every context to date, colonising powers have held the upper hand to determine the meaning and outcome of these emotion–object exchanges, perpetuating the dispossession of Aboriginal people.[59] However, both the presence of VOC objects, and knowledge of their location, coupled with oral history traditions of contact in the region, may yet have implications for an ongoing Nhanda native title claim over the region.[60] These objects and their presence on the Australian continent will thus continue to create both affect and effect into the future.

Notes and References

1. Eric Ketelaar, 'Exploration of the Archived World: From De Vlamingh's Plate to Digital Realities,' *Archives and Manuscripts* 36.2 (2008): 28, f. 4.
2. I apply the term South Lands to a broad region containing the islands of New Guinea, Australia, New Zealand, Tonga, Fiji, Indonesia and the Solomons, explored in VOC voyages, as a conceptual and geographical entity in the Company's view, a region forged through imagination and encounter, following ideas developed first in G. Dening, *Islands and Beaches: Discourse on a Silent Land, Marquesas 1774–1880* (Melbourne: Melbourne University Press, 1980).
3. Jane Bennett, *Vibrant Matter: A Political Ecology of Things* (Durham: Duke University Press, 2010), 6.
4. See Daniel Miller, 'Materiality: An Introduction,' in *Materiality*, ed. Miller (Durham: Duke University Press, 2005), 19.
5. Sara Ahmed, *The Cultural Politics of Emotion* (New York: Routledge, 2004), 8; Oliver J.T. Harris and Tim Flohr Sørensen, 'Rethinking Emotion and Material Culture,' *Archaeological Dialogues* 17.2 (2010), 153.
6. *Oceanic Encounters: Exchange, Desire, Violence,* ed. Margaret Jolly, Serge Tcherkézoff, Darrell Tryon (Canberra: ANU EPress, 2009); and *Exchanges: Cross-cultural Encounters in Australia and the Pacific,* ed. Ross Gibson (Sydney: Historic House Trust of New South Wales, 1996).
7. Benno Gammerl, 'Emotional Styles – Concepts and Challenges,' *Rethinking History: The Journal of Theory and Practice* 16.2 (2012): 161–175; Andreas Reckwitz, 'Affective Spaces: A Praxeological Outlook,' *Rethinking History* 16.2 (2012): 241–258; *Spaces for Feeling: Emotions and Sociabilities in Britain, 1650–1850,* ed. Susan Broomhall (London: Routledge, 2015).
8. On the conceptualisation of contact zones, see Mary Louise Pratt, *Imperial Eyes: Travel Writing and Transculturation* (London: Routledge, 1992); Greg Dening, *Islands and Beaches: Discourse on a Silent Land, Marquesas, 1774–1880* (Melbourne: Melbourne University Press, 1980); Dening, 'Voices from the Beach,' in *Exchanges,* 163–184; Jolly, 'Beyond the Beach? Re-articulating the Limen in Oceanic Pasts, Presents, and Futures,' in *Changing Contexts, Shifting Meanings: Transformations of Cultural Traditions in Oceania,* ed. Elfriede Hermann (Honolulu: University of Hawaii Press, 2011), 56.

9. A number of detailed studies examine indigenous perceptions of these and other exchanges with Europeans during this period, including Sylvia J. Hallam, 'A View from the Other Side of the Western Frontier: Or "I Met a Man who Wasn't There . . .",' *Aboriginal History* 7.2 (1983): 134–156; J.S. Kartnin and Peter Sutton, 'Dutchmen at Cape Keerweer: Wik-Ngatharra Story,' in *This is What Happened: Historical Narratives by Aborigines*, ed. Luise Hercus and Peter Sutton (Canberra: Australian Institute of Aboriginal Studies, 1986), 82–107; *Strangers on the Shore: Early Coastal Contacts with Australia,* ed. Peter Veth, Peter Sutton and Margo Neale (Canberra: NMA Press, 2008); Maria Nugent, *Captain Cook Was Here* (Melbourne: Cambridge University Press, 2009); Shino Konishi, *The Aboriginal Male in the Enlightenment World* (London: Pickering and Chatto, 2012); Michael Davis, 'Encountering Aboriginal knowledge: Explorer Narratives on North-east Queensland, 1770 to 1820,' *Aboriginal History* 37 (2013): 29–50.

10. Günter Schilder, *Australia Unveiled: The Share of the Dutch Navigators in the Discovery of Australia* (Amsterdam: Theatrum Orbis Terrarum, 1976); J. Peter Sigmond and L.H. Zuiderbaan, *Dutch Discoveries of Australia: Shipwrecks, Treasures and Early Voyages off the West Coast* (Adelaide: Rigby, 1979); Günter Schilder, 'New Holland: The Dutch Discoveries,' in *Terra Australis to Australia*, ed. Glyndwr Williams and Alan Frost (Melbourne: Oxford University Press, 1988), 83–115; Robert Clancy, *The Mapping of Terra Australis* (Sydney: Universal Press, 1995).

11. Ketelaar, 'Exploration,' 20. See also Sigmond and Zuiderbaan, *Dutch Discoveries of Australia*, 136; Bruce Donaldson, 'The Dutch Contribution to the European Discovery of Australia,' in *The Dutch Down Under, 1606–2006*, ed. Nonja Peters (Crawley: University of Western Australia Press, 2006), 23.

12. *The Part Borne by the Dutch in the Discovery of Australia 1606–1765*, ed. J.E. Heere and trans. C. Stoffel (London: Luzac, 1899), xiv.

13. Instructions, 29 September 1622, in *The Part Borne by the Dutch*, 20.

14. *The Part Borne by the Dutch*, 20

15. *The Part Borne by the Dutch*, 19.

16. *The Part Borne by the Dutch*, 19.

17. *The Part Borne by the Dutch*, 20.

18. Journal of Jan Carstenszoon, 1623, in *The Part Borne by the Dutch*, 29.

19. *The Part Borne by the Dutch*, 29

20. *The Part Borne by the Dutch*, 41.

21. *The Part Borne by the Dutch*, 38.

22. Instructions, 29 January 1644, in *Abel Janszoon Tasman's Journal: of his Discovery of Van Diemens Land and New Zealand in 1642*, ed. and trans. J.E. Heeres and C.H. Cootes (Amsterdam: Frederik Muller and Co, 1898; repr. Los Angeles: N.A. Kovach, 1965), 147.

23. Instructions, 13 August 1642 in *Abel Janszoon Tasman's Journal*, 136.

24. *Abel Janszoon Tasman's Journal*, 136.

25. *Abel Janszoon Tasman's Journal*, 136.

26. *Abel Janszoon Tasman's Journal*, 15.

27. *Abel Janszoon Tasman's Journal*, 15–6.

28. Letter from the Councillors, December 23, 1644, in *Abel Janszoon Tasman's Journal*, 156.

29. Instructions, 29 January 1644, in *Abel Janszoon Tasman's Journal*, 152.

30. Although it was not articulated in these terms, this VOC practice would seem to have resonances with the later *terra nullius* principle that governed eighteenth-century British claims to the Australian continent. See David Day, *Claiming a Continent: A New History of Australia* (Sydney: Harper Collins, 1997); Henry Reynolds, *Dispossession: Black Australians and White Invaders* (St Leonards: Allen & Unwin, 1989); Stuart Banner, 'Why Terra Nullius? Anthropology and Property Law in Early Australia,' *Law and History Review* 23.1 (2005): 95–131; Larissa Behrendt, 'The Doctrine of Discovery in Australia,' and 'Asserting the Doctrine of Discovery in Australia,' in *Discovering Indigenous Lands: The Doctrine of Discovery in the English Colonies* (Oxford: Oxford University Press, 2010), 171–86, 187–206.

31. On early Western Australian and colonial history, see F.K. Crowley and B.K. de Garis, *A Short History of Western Australia* (Melbourne: Macmillan, 2nd ed. 1969); *A New History of Western Australia*, ed. C.T. Stannage (Nedlands: University of Western Australia Press, 1981); Bob Reece and C.T. Stannage, *European–Aboriginal Relations in Western Australian History* (Nedlands: Studies in Western Australian History, 1984); Jane Davis, *Longing or Belonging? Responses to a 'New' Land in Southern Western Australia, 1829–1907* (PhD Thesis, University of Western Australia, 2008); Shino Konishi and Maria Nugent, 'Newcomers, *c.*1600–1800' and Grace Karskens, 'The Early Colonial Presence, 1788–1822,' in *The Cambridge History of Australia*, ed. Alison Bashford and Stuart Macintyre. *Vol. 1: Indigenous and Colonial Australia* (Cambridge: Cambridge University Press, 2013), 43–67, 91–120.

32. See Broomhall, 'Emotional Encounters: Indigenous Peoples in the Dutch East India Company's Interactions with the South Lands,' *Australian Historical Studies* 45.3 (2014): 350–367. See also: *Object Lessons: Archaeology and Heritage in Australia*, ed. Jane Lydon and Tracy Ireland (Melbourne: Australian Scholarly Publishing, 2005); Bruce Buchan, 'Traffick of Empire: Trade, Treaty and Terra Nullius in Australia and North America,' *History Compass* 5.2 (2007): 396–405; Tiffany Shellam, *Shaking Hands on the Fringe: Negotiating the Aboriginal World at King George's Sound* (Nedlands: University of Western Australia Press, 2009); *Missionaries, Indigenous Peoples and Cultural Exchange*, ed. Andrew May and Patricia Grimshaw (Brighton: Sussex Academic Press, 2010); *Making Settler Colonial Space: Perspectives on Race, Place and Identity*, ed. Penny Edmonds and Tracey Banivanua Mar (London: Palgrave Macmillan, 2010); Shellam, 'Tropes of Friendship, Undercurrents of Fear: Alternative Emotions on the "Friendly Frontier",' *Westerly* 57.2 (2012): 16–31.

33. *The Perth Gazette, and Western Australian Journal*, 12 July 1834, 318.

34. *Perth Gazette*, 318.

35. *Perth Gazette*, 318.

36. *Perth Gazette*, 19 July 1834, 322.

37. Traditional Aboriginal protocol withholds the name and image of deceased individuals. On Moore, see: *The Millendon Memoirs: George Fletcher Moore's Western Australian Diaries and Letters, 1830–1841*, ed. J.M.R. Cameron (Carlisle: Hesperian Press, 2006).

38. *Perth Gazette*, 12 July 1834, 318.

39. *Perth Gazette*, 10 May 1834, 282.

40. *Perth Gazette*, 12 July 1834, 318

41. *Perth Gazette*, 318.

42. *Perth Gazette*, 19 July 1834, 322.

43. *Perth Gazette*, 9 August 1834, 334.

44. *Perth Gazette*, 334.

45. *Perth Gazette*, 334.

46. *Perth Gazette*, 334.

47. *Perth Gazette*, 6 September 1834, 351.

48. On this topic, see Rupert Gerritsen, 'The Evidence for Cohabitation between Indigenous Australians and Marooned Dutch Mariners and VOC Passengers,' in *Dutch Down Under*, 38–55.

49. I am adapting the phrase of Shino Konishi, who, together with Bronwyn Douglas, reminds us that 'indigenous peoples were not passive victims, but also participating members in these exchanges.' Konishi, *The Aboriginal Male*, 19. Douglas, 'In the Event: Indigenous Countersigns and the Ethnohistory of Voyaging,' in *Oceanic Encounters*, 193.

50. *Select Committee on Ancient Shipwrecks Report, Presented by Hon. P.G. Pendal, MLA*, (Legislative Assembly, Western Australia, 17 August 1994), 22.

51. Nonja Peters, 'Too Late to set the Wreckord Straight?' in *Dutch Down Under*, 34–37, briefly outlines the payments and competing knowledge claims.

52. *Select Committee*, i.

53. *Select Committee*, 14. Bolded text in the original.

54. *Select Committee*, 17. She was recommended for a posthumous Parliamentary Medal of Honour, 9.

55. Phillip Playford, *A Carpet of Silver: The Wreck of the Zuytdorp* (Nedlands: University of Western Australia Press, 1996).
56. *Select Committee*, 18.
57. *Select Committee*, 19.
58. See *Still Life/Our Life: Emotions across Time, Art and Place. The Zest Festival, June 2012*, ed. Susan Broomhall and Rebecca Millar (Crawey: Australian Research Council Centre for the History of Emotions, 2012).
59. As described by Edmonds and Banivanua Mar, 'Introduction,' *Making Settler Colonial Space*, 4.
60. http://www.nntt.gov.au/Applications-And-Determinations/Search-Applications/Pages/Application.aspx?tribunal_file_no=WC00/13

7

ENCOUNTERS AROUND THE MATERIAL OBJECT

French and Indian consumers in eighteenth-century Pondicherry[1]

Kévin Le Doudic

Pondicherry, located in South India on the Coromandel Coast, was the main trading post of the French East India Company in the Indian Ocean in the eighteenth century. The city was a commercial hub through which a vast array of merchandise and consumer goods from India, Europe and the Far East circulated. This exceptional variety was equalled by the diverse social, professional and ethnic origins of consumers and merchants passing through or residing in Pondicherry: among them were Europeans (both born in Europe and in Asia), and Indians of all backgrounds. These two distinct groups – Europeans and Indians – lived together in this small enclave on the Coromandel Coast and found themselves consuming the same products. Material objects served as interface in the creation of ties between these two groups. While objects facilitated encounters between these groups, individuals did not necessarily purchase and consume these objects for the same reasons or in the same ways. The consumer's background influenced the form and nature of these encounters.

The encounters that took place between the Indian population and the French in the eighteenth century require us to consider the specific role played by artefacts. It is important to keep in mind that people are at the core of consumer processes and that material objects are merely evidence of a person's choices or reactions to a variety of factors and forces. In the case of the French in India, the person in question is someone catapulted into an unfamiliar environment, interacting with people from different cultural backgrounds. The artefacts that are part of such encounters have to be analysed from a multidisciplinary perspective that includes history, art history, sociology, ethnology, and even philosophy in order to better understand a person's relationship to the natural, social and cultural environment. An object is above all the product of a group of individuals living in a specific context. The study of objects divorced from their wider context would produce an analysis of aesthetics, which is important in its own right, but not the same as a material culture approach.[2]

Although the history of the French presence in Asia in the early modern era is now well known, it is primarily understood from a political and economic perspective.[3] New research on Asia, with a particular focus on encounters between Europeans and Asians, has emerged over the past few years. This research includes a number of unpublished works developed through innovative approaches to archives and material sources.[4] For example, new perspectives have been opened by the study of documents produced by French notaries in Pondicherry.[5] Notarial archives make it possible to look at daily life in this trading port through the prism of material culture. The encounters that took place between Europeans and Indians can therefore be studied through the analysis of inventories of property after death, auction reports, property transactions, seizure of property reports, and commercial contracts. The information they provide can then be used to match what was described in the notarial deeds with what remains of the architectural and material heritage.

The main aim of this chapter is to explore how the encounters between Europeans and Indians can be studied through the process of exchange, and more generally through the consumption of objects in a specific context. To what extent did these two cultural groups consume the same products? Did consumer behaviour differ according to category of objects, and if so, how can this help clarify the question of encounters between Europeans and Indians around the object? After considering the demographic and social structure of Pondicherry, this chapter will examine three types of encounters that shaped material life in the city: what I define as an 'unavoidable encounter' shaped by the very presence of a small but significant European community; the 'commercial encounter' that was at the very heart of a French presence in the Indian Ocean; and a 'cultural encounter', one expression of which can be traced in material goods. The essay concludes by evaluating the methodological approach adopted here.

Limited land: fostering encounters between two cultures

Pondicherry was originally a single territory of approximately 6,900 hectares, granted to the French in 1672 by local princes. Over the course of various negotiations, adjacent small villages such as Villenour and Bahour were also added. This French trading port did not significantly differ from its English or Dutch counterparts in India. On the contrary, the French followed in the footsteps of the English and Dutch trading companies established in 1600 and 1602 respectively. Both had in turn been inspired by the Portuguese, who had founded their *Estado da India* at the beginning of the sixteenth century. Pondicherry was organised and operated in the same way as other European trading ports in India and other parts of Asia, such as the Dutch trading port of Batavia. The objectives of the European traders were largely the same: to nurture and facilitate trade by all possible means. Both human and logistical networks relied on the same underlying structures. Only long-term objectives varied. France sought to develop an empire of trading ports in India but, unlike Britain, had no aspirations to create anything resembling a colonial empire.

The successive governors of French trading ports in India did not cultivate a desire for territorial expansion.

Pondicherry was peculiar in that a canal divided the city into two distinct areas (Map 7.1).[6] To the west, various Indian communities inhabited the *Ville Noire* (Black Town), dividing this area further into distinct neighbourhoods. To the east, along the coast, the European population inhabited the *Ville Blanche* (White Town). Nevertheless, the study of property ownership throughout the eighteenth century demonstrates that space was not so categorically divided according to community of origin. Probate inventories and property sales show that many of the French passing through India for a few months at a time rented rooms from Indians in the *Ville Noire*.[7] By 1719 an Indian community of merchants and traders had settled in the northern part of the *Ville Blanche*.[8] Mobility – perhaps even social mixing between Europeans and Indians – was therefore present in certain places and at certain periods within Pondicherry.

Pondicherry was a crossroads of different communities both from the subcontinent and from other parts of Asia and Europe. Some of them were permanent residents, though a substantial share of the population was rather mobile. This explains why the estimation of Pondicherry's population is a delicate matter.[9] The trading port hosted up to 2,000 French nationals out of a total population of possibly 120,000 people.[10] In spite of this relatively low number, the French left many traces

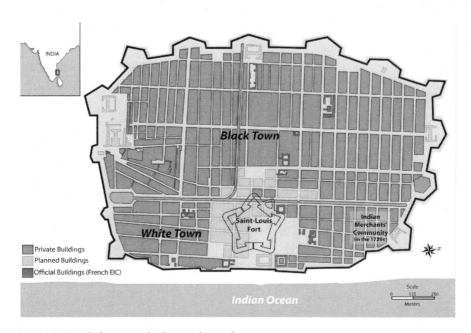

MAP 7.1 Pondicherry in the late eighteenth century.
Source: Re-interpretation from *Pondichéry, plan de la ville et des fortifications 1774*, watercolour quill drawing on paper, scale of 1/1000ᵉ, Archives Nationales d'Outre-Mer, Dépôt des Fortifications des Colonies (FR ANOM 26DFC483D) © Concept: K. Le Doudic / Design: Y. Denécé & K. Le Doudic, 2014.

in the archives and even in the physionomy of the *Ville Blanche*. Unfortunately, this cultural heritage is still inadequately protected, and architectural testaments to the French presence continue to disappear, in spite of the efforts of heritage protection agencies.

If the study of Pondicherry from a demographic perspective is difficult due to a lack of sources, it is perhaps more suitable to study the city in terms of its flux of people and goods. Like other European factories (i.e. trading ports belonging to European nations) in India, Pondicherry was characterised by a dual movement: of goods and merchandise between Europe and Asia and within Asia; and of people involved in ensuring the functioning of both trade and government. This intense flow of people arose from a number of factors: a highly mobile indigenous population; the patterns of arrival and departure of the East India Company's ships to and from Europe as well as those bound for Indian trade in Asia; the movement of ship travellers and passengers; and the circulation of administrative and commercial personnel between the trading posts of Asia. Pondicherry was a corridor through which a multitude of persons of very different backgrounds transited, but most of these found themselves united around a common goal: to trade, or at least serve commercial activities. Some of those who used the Pondicherry 'corridor' as a stopover stayed for some time in the trading port. The majority of such individuals consisted of the numerous sailors who travelled on board the Company's ships that sailed between Lorient and the Indian Ocean. It is reasonable to suggest that 35,000 to 40,000 people set sail from France and passed through Pondicherry in the fifty years between 1720 and 1769.[11] The movements of local and European populations within the Indian Ocean region must also be added to this figure in order to fully grasp the dynamism of Pondicherry in the eighteenth century.

An unavoidable encounter: adapting to one's environment

Any study of material culture and consumption in eighteenth-century Pondicherry needs to consider the issue of supplies and their origin. India could not supply all of the products the French needed. Although the subcontinent was the primary supplier of textiles for daily use, which were also exported to Europe, it only provided a small variety of foodstuffs and construction materials. The French therefore had to import a variety of products. From Europe, for instance, they imported alcohol and metals for minting. A wide array of small objects completed the outgoing European cargo: small furniture, weapons, jewellery, books, and, seafarers' *pacotille*.[12] However these two supply networks were still insufficient. The French naturally relied on the trade of various goods within India, which was highly developed through private commerce, in order to feed the Pondicherry market with products from a wide geographic area, ranging from the East of India, to Ceylon and Japan, the South of India, the Maldives, Mascarene islands and Madagascar, the West of India, as well as Mocha to Turkey. Some of the products imported from this wide geographic area were at times re-exported to Europe, mostly porcelain and textiles from China and certain small manufactured objects such as fans, cabaret tables, and writing desks. Other products were intended specifically for consumption in India: from China came jam and sugar; from Japan wine; from the Philippines raw materials and other supplies such as wood, copper, tombac (a metal alloy), gold, and ivory; and from Java sugar and local alcohol.[13]

These commercial networks determined which merchandise and products were available to the French residing in India. In-depth knowledge of these networks makes it possible to distinguish two types of consumption: a 'voluntary consumption', when products were available in sufficient number and variety; and inversely, an 'imposed consumption' dictated by necessity when there was a lack of products available, or at least a scarcity of certain goods.

Research for the period 1700–1778 shows that the French were constantly striving to recreate their European-style daily life.[14] This was particularly true for architecture and the furniture used in European homes. In terms of architecture, the French favoured a very particular style for the layout and construction of their homes in the *Ville Blanche*. Neoclassic architectural forms with white plastered pillars and spacious porticos proliferated. However, the availability of materials and the climatic conditions forced the French to use teak for doors and windows, and to reorganise the layout of their homes. They consequently adopted a new living space, inspired by traditional Indian architecture: the veranda (Figure 7.1). This roofed gallery was sheltered from the sun but made it possible to take advantage of a breeze, and performed the same role as it did for the Indians: it provided a meeting place where people could talk and rest.

Sometimes unexpected forms resulted from these cultural encounters: hybrid furniture is one of the best examples (Figure 7.2). The term hybrid furniture refers to a type of furniture made from locally sourced materials (teak, ebony and rosewood for the most part), but designed according to French style. Most carefully tended French domestic interiors were predominantly furnished with stylistically coherent ensembles. This was particularly the case of reception rooms such as the salon and dining room. Louis XV or Regency styles dominated throughout the eighteenth century, although the Louis XVI style made an appearance towards the end of the 1770s. Chairs, armchairs and, of course sofas and settees – the most practical pieces of furniture – were often in French style. Seats and backs were for the most part fashioned from cane, as cane surfaces were significantly more comfortable in the high temperatures of the Coromandel Coast. Upholstering fabrics, however, adorned the most opulent furniture. Damask was the fabric of choice.

At first glance, such furniture could perfectly embody the encounter between Asia and Europe. Although it truly bears witness to a European past in India, it is first and foremost shaped by the availability of materials in the trading ports, and the desire to recreate a Western lifestyle on Asian soil. It was on the whole not feasible to have wood shipped from Europe, and even if it had been feasible, European wood would still not have been suited to the South India climate. Besides, carpentry, joinery and cabinetmaking workshops operated by both French and Indians

FIGURE 7.1 Veranda of the Lagrenée de Mézières hotel, last third of the eighteenth century. This building is located in rue Romain Rolland in Pondicherry. Photo © Kévin Le Doudic, February 2014.

had developed in Pondicherry, thus making it possible to create replicas of western furniture. In this context, this type of furniture, which was very widespread in the eighteenth century, reflects cultural inertia rather than any active search for distinctive forms, styles and materials. Certain pieces also betray a certain lack of understanding on the part of Indian artisans manufacturing French furniture from Western designs in their Pondicherry workshops. For example, on the edge of the arms of certain teak settees, there are three to four aligned half-spheres carved in the wood. This is evidence of the lack of knowledge of western techniques and styles,

FIGURE 7.2 Louis XVI style settee, late eighteenth–early nineteenth century. Teak (?), gilding and textile. Museum of Pondicherry, India. Photo © Kévin Le Doudic, 2007.

as the little domes are in fact the heads of upholstery nails. In the original design, these nails held the fabric on the arms in place. However these nails naturally became obsolete on a wood and cane replica without upholstery.

The French also took advantage of the great variety of Indian textiles to clothe themselves in light clothes better suited to the local climate, but tailored in a European style. Indian fabrics were taken to Pondicherry tailors, who fashioned a variety of clothes suited to European tastes for negligible sums.[15] Inventories of property after death are replete with references to clothing in styles popular with their mainland Europe compatriots. In the inventory of property after death of Pierre Le Gardeur de Repentigny, a former infantry colonel who was a major general of troops of India and former King's commander in Mahé, the notary lists the following among his possessions (Figure 7.3):

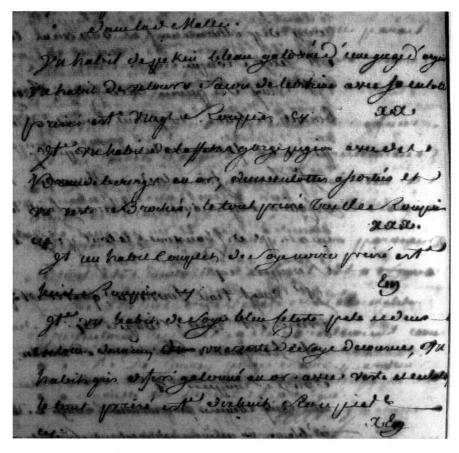

FIGURE 7.3 Excerpt from Pierre Le Gardeur de Repentigny's probate inventory, 1776. ANF, ANOM, FT, EFI, DPPC, Fonds Inde, P099, 30 May 1776. Photo © Kévin Le Doudic, August 2008.

In a trunk
A coat of blue Pekin fabric trimmed with silver gauze
A coat of lutestring type velvet and matching breeches
Estimated value of twenty Rupees cy XX
A coat fashioned from dove shot taffetas with
Gold toggle clasps, two matching breeches and an
Embroidered waistcoat, with an estimated value of thirty rupees
cy XXX
It. A coat of black silk, estimated value at
Eight Rupees cy VIII
It. A pale sky blue silk coat and two
matching breeches, an unsewn waistcoat of silk, a

Grey coat . . . with golden tassels with waistcoat and breeches
With a total estimated value of eighteen Rupees

Clothing articles, as well as the materials and techniques used – particularly toggle clasps which could be used on military uniforms as well as on civilian clothes – perfectly illustrate French style of dress in Pondicherry in the eighteenth century, at least for the affluent. These descriptions equally correspond to the fashions worn in France at the same period.[16] The French used textiles available in India. Nevertheless, this was not a particularly difficult constraint as these fabrics were highly sought after in Europe and were very much prized by 'expatriate' consumers in India. However the majority of the population had access to these textiles. How then could the elites ensure that they distinguished themselves from the lower classes? They simply decorated their dress with accessories and materials from France, which were prohibitively expensive and therefore inaccessible to the lower classes. Pondicherry's leading figures accessorised their shirts, waistcoats and coats with imported haberdashery: ribbons, Le Havre lace, or gold and silver coat buttons. These are all examples of the non-commercial encounter between Indians and Europeans in which European material culture was both culturally preserved and adapted to new circumstances.

The commercial encounter: the reason behind the French presence in India

The French and Indians were most frequently brought into contact with each other as a result of commercial activities. This was the primary purpose for the European presence in India: to ensure the supply of Asian products to Europe. In this regard, Europeans relied on a commercial network that had been developed over centuries by Indian and Asian merchants who played an intermediary role between local producers and private buyers, or buyers acting on behalf of the East India Company. The key figure in these networks was the Company broker, also called *dubash*. Brokers were Indian merchants-in-chief in European trading ports. One of the most famous was Ananda Ranga Pillai, who was at the service of the French governors of Pondicherry. He was an interpreter, diplomat and above all a commercial intermediary. He is well known for his *Private Diary*, which he kept between 1736 and 1761. This diary is an exceptional source of information on daily life in mid-eighteenth-century Pondicherry, the social relationships between the different European and Asian communities as well as their commercial and diplomatic activities.[17]

The exact organisation of French supply networks of Indian products is not easy to trace; business agreements signed between French purchasers and Indian artisans are rare. Only one such agreement has survived in the French notarial documents of Pondicherry.[18] The agreement names each Indian merchant, and specifies that they were jointly liable for fulfilling the terms of the agreement with the French.

In the event that one merchant failed to fulfil his obligations, all of the Indians would have been held liable. The date and location of delivery (the Pondicherry fort) are both specified, and there is a detailed inventory of products ordered. The agreement was for the delivery of several types of cloth: guinea, chavonis, betille, organdies, Tranquebar and Pondicherry handkerchiefs, Cuddalore baize, and Palia-cate gingham, for which the precise dimensions and quality were detailed, as was the price of purchase. This last item is important: up until recently, it has been difficult to determine the purchase cost of merchandise in India, and therefore to calculate the profit that trade with Asia brought to the East India companies and private merchants. The discovery of this data has not however resolved the prob-lem: the merchandise was purchased in local currencies such as pagodas, rupees and fanons. A further problem therefore arises from the exchange rate between Indian and European currencies. Historians have until recently assumed that the exchange rate remained the same throughout the eighteenth century. However, the notarial archives of Pondicherry prove the contrary: there were large currency fluctuations, depending on the political upheavals and numerous wars that punctuated the early modern period.[19]

Merchandise was at the heart of the relationship between the Europeans and Indians. Both parties met regularly at the auctions held after a death or property seizure. Here they could purchase goods for resale, or products for personal con-sumption. Moreover, commercial contracts bear witness to business partnerships being concluded when ships were fitted out for internal Asian trade. Several con-tracts drafted in French, Tamil, Portuguese and Arabic show evidence of this. In some cases, the boats belonged to Indians who hired out their services to Europeans in order to set sail for Mocha, Manila or Aceh. These same ships were in fact often repurchased from the East India Company. Commercial activities were continued in the trading port especially around Pondicherry's Grand Bazaar, also known as the Saint Lawrence Bazaar. The Bazaar had many shops where people could acquire commodities for everyday use or trade. Although these shops were managed by Indians, sometimes their owners were French, as in the case of Charles de Flacourt who, in 1720, owned 65 shops in this market.[20]

The cultural encounter: a willing openness to the other

Encounters were not only imposed or commercially induced. A real willingness to open up towards the other can be sensed both on the part of Europeans and Indians. Well-to-do Indians, for instance, took part in auctions in which they could acquire goods that had belonged to the French or other Europeans. They showed a real interest in French products for personal use as confirmed by post-mortem inventories. Indians bought clothes tailored in the European style, such as waistcoats, shirts, breeches and even tights. They completed this western pano-ply with accessories, such as shoe buckles and walking canes. This willingness to imitate the French was combined with an interest in western culture and habits:

they bought European china, collected French weapons, and were interested in literature, as can be seen by the purchase of French books. Mirrors were acquired for use in their homes. This interest on the part of Indians in European goods is apparent in the consuming habits of Ananda Ranga Pillai, that one might say were influenced by European taste. His home reflected this: although the ground floor followed Tamil layout and architecture, the first floor was fashioned in pure neoclassical style, complete with ionic columns and wrought iron balustrade. Ananda Ranga Pillai remains an exceptional example, but provides us with a fascinating insight into the range of possibilities the exchange of goods and lifestyles afforded.[21]

There is no comparable example among the French: they seemed to have become viscerally attached to preserving their European identity. From the moment they settled in Pondicherry in the last quarter of the seventeenth century,

FIGURE 7.4 Pair of statuettes of parrots perched on rocks. China, Jingdezhen (?), Kangxi period (1662–1722), Porcelain, overglaze polychrome enamels; H: 20.5cm. Purchased with the help of the FRAM, Inv. 2012.7.1 and 2. Photo © D. Goupy. East India Company's Museum, City of Lorient, France.

the French relentlessly sought to replicate the environment that they had left behind in France, an attitude that would become the hallmark of belonging to the French community in India. It was considered essential to live in a neoclassical house in the *Ville Blanche*, furnished with Louis XV style furniture, and to dress according to French fashion. The only Indian products they possessed were those imposed as a result of supply constraints. However, as generations of French succeeded one another in Pondicherry, a new interest developed. By the middle of the eighteenth century, Asia was making its way into European interiors: not only in the form of products for everyday consumption, but as decorative elements and art objects.[22] Although some Europeans owned large collections of oriental artefacts, such as Moorish weapons, most were satisfied with a few Chinese bronze lions or glazed terracotta figurines representing animals or women (Figure 7.4).

Statuettes of parrots, or of birds in general, had pride of place in French interiors both in India and in France. Although they were not sold at the East India Company's official sales, many made their way into collections in France. This was probably thanks to the private trade as such objects were brought back from India by sailors and ship passengers. These statuettes were found in porcelain collections, as well as on top of mantelpieces and doorframes. Parrots perched on rocks were commonplace, with minor variations as to the rock, which could be hollow or solid.[23] Hanging decorations were also of particular interest: engravings depicting scenes of everyday life in India or China hung alongside oil paintings featuring European landscapes. This interest in Asian art was combined with a growing interest in learning about Oriental peoples, as is reflected in library inventories. The increasing Asian presence in French interiors was striking evidence of a growing taste for exoticism and curiosity for oriental objects, rather than of the 'Indianisation' of European society in India. The private sphere remained impervious to Asian influences. This was particularly the case of education and religion, though material objects to be found in museum collections may raise a number of questions.

The torch-bearing angel in Figure 7.5 is evidence – at least in form – of a religious syncretism that emerged in India. The subject is of Christian origin and was certainly used for worship. Nevertheless, this angel's posture is definitely Indian and draws on traditional Dravidian statuary, characterised by the swaying hip. The plant garland, hairstyle and head ornaments accentuate the Asian inspiration of the statue. This religious syncretism must nevertheless be understood in context. The material openness of western religions was not necessarily an openness to the foundations of belief, nor even to worship practices. Church worship in Pondicherry closely followed the rituals and practices adopted by the Church in France. People and objects had precisely designated roles in ecclesiastical ceremonies. We have examples of Christian liturgical artefacts produced in Asia that adopt local stylistic references.[24] While this evolution may be taken as a sign of openness to Asian cultures and an interest in local techniques, the evangelical objectives of missionary priests officiating in Asia remained religious conversion.[25]

FIGURE 7.5 Torch-bearing angel, Coromandel Coast, India, *c.*1680–1700. Sculpted teak, gilded and polychrome overlay. © Museum of Decorative Arts of the Indian Ocean, Saint-Louis, Réunion Island (France), Inv. OA.1999.1113.

Methodology

In order to address the question of encounters, a particular methodological approach has been used. It is based on three stages: defining the origin of the products in question; followed by the way in which they are consumed; and finally identifying the types of encounters to which they refer. Objects in circulation in Pondicherry in the eighteenth century could have three possible origins: 'European', that is, coming from Europe; 'Indian', or more widely Asian; and finally, 'mixed', that is, a combination of European styles and Indian materials.[26] The second stage consists in identifying the way in which these objects were consumed. It could be 'unilateral': Indian objects exclusively consumed by Europeans; and inversely European products consumed exclusively by Indians. Consumption could also be 'bilateral', including Indian objects consumed both by Indians and Europeans, and European products consumed both by Europeans and Indians.

The data available allows us to produce an overview synthesising French and Indian consumption in Pondicherry and organised according to category and origin of goods (Figure 7.6). Six categories of goods consumed in Pondicherry by both Indian and French were selected: clothing and apparel, luxury accessories, furniture and furnishings, foodstuffs, non-essential decorative, artistic and cultural items, and finally, items used for educational, or religious or spiritual purposes. Hatching helps

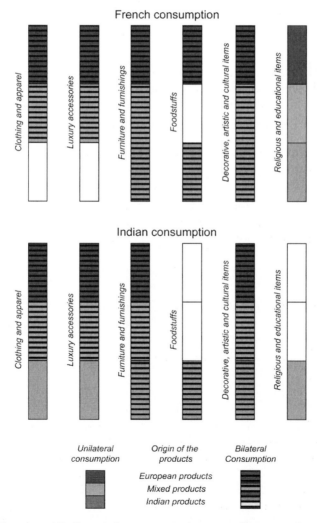

FIGURE 7.6 French and Indian product consumption, according to product origin.
© Concept & Design: Y. Denécé and Kévin Le Doudic, 2014.

clarify and make it possible to quickly identify the goods owned by both cultural groups, i.e., which commodities are the object of bilateral consumption.

The most obvious finding is that overall, the French and Indians consumed the same products, with the exception of objects from the religious and educational domains which remained impervious to sharing and encounters. Although a certain form of syncretism could occasionally arise, it did so in form but never in substance, as has been previously demonstrated. On the other hand, two categories were shared in full by both cultural groups, both of which were essential to the home environment: furniture and furnishings, as well as decorative, artistic and cultural items. French and Indians therefore owned objects from these two categories and originating from their own culture, the culture of the other group, and from a combination thereof. Collections therefore include European as well as Indian weapons, Chinese prints and French oil paintings, glazed terracotta Asian statues and neoclassical Western style mirrors in gilded teak.

Encounters in the two remaining categories were less apparent. In terms of clothing and luxury accessories,[27] Indians owned products of all origins in contrast to the French who excluded Asian products. This was due to the fact that some Indians sought to identify with the Westerners inhabiting the trading post with whom they were in contact for commercial purposes. For the French, the mechanism was completely different: clothing was essential to social distinction and identification with the norms and values of French society. It was impossible to dress in Indian style. Finally, Indians displayed an attachment to traditional foodstuffs, and exclusively consumed Asian products. The French used Indian foodstuffs, but only as a result of what was locally available. They naturally had to feed themselves using local produce, but they did so in accordance with French culinary tradition in terms of the composition and organisation of meals.[28]

Conclusion

By studying French and Indian consumption in Pondicherry in the eighteenth century, it is possible to tackle the question of encounters between these two cultural groups. Material artefacts were indeed interfaces for encounters, as most were consumed by all people inhabiting the trading port, though with notable differences. They reveal the variety of ways in which Europeans and Indians interacted within the confined space of the port city. I have here tried to show how such 'encounters' and interactions took different forms ranging from purely commercial to cultural ones. I have used surviving artefacts, travel accounts and various testimonies of contemporaries to contextualise these social and cultural interactions, revealing the encounters around the material object in eighteenth-century Pondicherry.

Notes and References

1. This chapter is a reworking of a paper originally delivered at the international conference 'Global Commodities: The Material Culture of Early Modern Connections 1400–1800,' held at the University of Warwick's Global History and Culture Centre on

12–14 December 2012. My participation was made possible thanks to the financial support of the Economic History Society and my research laboratory at the University of South Brittany in Lorient (Univ. Bretagne-Sud, UMR 6258, CERHIO, F56100 Lorient, France), for which I am truly grateful. I would also like to thank Anne Gerritsen and Giorgio Riello for their invitation to this conference. I am also grateful to the Musée de la Compagnie des Indes (Museum of the French East India Company) at Lorient (France) and the Musée des arts décoratifs de l'océan Indien (Museum of Decorative Arts of the Indian Ocean) in Réunion Island (France) for allowing me to reproduce works in their collections. My thanks also to graphic and video designer Youenn Denécé (Quimper, France), for his help in creating the diagram and map.

2. Museum curators provide valuable contributions to our understanding of the history of material culture. An aesthetic analysis of the object, including the materials and techniques used, complement archival research, filling the voids left by written sources. At the international conference on neoclassicism in the European colonies organised by the Museum of Decorative Arts of the Indian Ocean in Réunion Island (France), 15–17 December 2011, this synergy between historians' and art historians' contributions to the field was clear. See Thierry-Nicolas Tchakaloff, ed., *Neoclassicism in the European Colonies of the 18th and 19th Centuries* (Saint-Denis de La Réunion: Museum of Decorative Arts of the Indian Ocean, 2013). The full English text is available at: http://madoi.re/evenements/actes-neoclassicisme/.

3. Key texts surveying the history of the French East India Company are: Philippe Haudrère, *La Compagnie française des Indes au XVIIIᵉ siècle, 1719–1795* (Paris: Librairie de l'Inde, 1989) for the eighteenth century; Marie Ménard-Jacob, 'Les jours et les hommes de la première Compagnie des Indes royale des Indes orientales (1664–1704)' (PhD thesis under the supervision of Professor Gérard Le Bouëdec, Lorient: University of South-Brittany, 2012) for the seventeenth century. Since the start of the twentieth century, there have been several biographical works on notable persons of India. The main biographical authors include Yvonne Robert Gaebelé, Edmond Gaudart, Marguerite V. Labernadie, and Alfred Martineau.

4. This research on encounters around the object between French and Indians in Pondicherry was inspired by Romain Bertrand's work, in particular: Romain Bertrand, *L'Histoire à parts égales: récit d'une rencontre Orient–Occident (XVIᵉ–XVIIᵉ siècles)* (Paris: Seuil, 2011). It is a continuation of my doctoral thesis work: Kévin Le Doudic, 'L'Inde vécue. De l'objet à la société: les Français à Pondichéry, 1700–1778' (PhD thesis under the supervision of Professor Gérard Le Bouëdec, Lorient: University of South-Brittany, 2015).

5. The French notarial archives of Pondicherry can be consulted at the Archives Nationales d'Outre-Mer (ANOM) in Aix-en-Provence (France), under 'Fonds Territoriaux' (FT); 'Établissements français de l'Inde' (EFI); 'Dépôt des Papiers Publics des Colonies' (DPPC) (1699–1814); series P: 'Notarial archives of Pondicherry' (1699–1814), esp. P001 (1699–1700) to P102 (1778). Of the 102 collections of official documents and registers, 502 deeds form the main corpus.

6. On the history and evolution of Pondicherry, see: Jean Deloche, 'Du village indien au comptoir de la Compagnie des Indes. Pondichéry (1673–1824),' in *Le goût de l'Inde*, ed. Gérard Le Bouëdec and Brigitte Nicolas (Rennes/Lorient: Presses Universitaires de Rennes/Musée de la Compagnie des Indes de la Ville de Lorient, 2008), 116–125, as well as: Jean Deloche, *Le vieux Pondichéry, 1673–1824, revisité d'après les plans anciens* (Pondicherry: Institut Français de Pondichéry/École Française d'Extrême-Orient, 2005).

7. For example, the infantry captain Vibesa rented a room in the *Ville Noire* from an Indian named Eterasse. 'Inventaire des biens de feu Vibesa,' ANOM, FT, EFI, DPPC, fonds Inde, P076 f 069, 10 April 1752.

8. Candapa Chetty owned a house in the northern part of the *Ville Blanche*: 'Inventaire des biens de Candapa Chetty,' ANOM, FT, EFI, DPPC, fonds Inde, P015 f 113, 21 August 1719; 'Vente des biens de Candapa Chetty,' ANOM, FT, EFI, DPPC, fonds Inde, P201 f 113, 30 December 1719. Moutouranga Chetty owned two homes in the same area: 'Vente des biens de Moutouranga Chetty,' ANOM, FT, EFI, DPPC, fonds Inde, P015 f 069, 4 May 1719; 'Inventaire des biens de Moutouranga Chetty,' ANOM, FT,

EFI, DPPC, fonds Inde, P015 f 053, 5 May 1719), as did Nallesamby: 'Inventaire des biens de Nallesamby,' ANOM, FT, EFI, DPPC, fonds Inde, P015 f 107, 21 August 1719.

9. A meticulous study on the official records of Pondicherry, cross-referenced with the crew lists from the French East India Company's ships – to identify all passengers – and with the notarial archives of Pondicherry would make it possible to obtain a relatively reliable assessment of the number of French who passed through the trading post in the eighteenth century. Unfortunately, the sheer volume of work that such an analysis would require has to date dissuaded researchers from carrying out such a study. An approximation of the French and Indian population in Pondicherry can nevertheless be identified by cross-referencing information provided in previous works; contemporary testimonies from published sources; and data from archival resources.

   For previous works on the subject, please see: Jacques Weber, 'La mosaïque Pondichérienne,' in *Pondichéry, 1674–1761. L'échec d'un rêve d'empire*, ed. Rose Vincent (Paris: Les Éditions Autrement, 1993), 144; David Annoussamy, *L'intermède français en Inde. Secousses politiques et mutations juridiques* (Pondicherry: L'Harmattan /Institut Français de Pondichéry, 2005); Maurice Maindron, *Dans l'Inde du Sud. Le Coromandel* (Paris: Alfonse Lemerre Éditeur, 1907), 127; Achile Bédier and Jean Cordier, *Statistiques de Pondichéry (1822–1824), texte établi, indexé et présenté par Jean Deloche* (Pondicherry: Publication by the Institut Français d'Indologie, 1988); as well as the synthesis in Kévin Le Doudic 'Les Français à Pondichéry au XVIIIᵉ siècle. Une société redessinée par sa culture matérielle,' in *L'Asie, la mer, le monde. Au temps des Compagnies des Indes*, Gérard Le Bouëdec ed. (Rennes: Presses Universitaires de Rennes, 2014), 177–198. For contemporary testimonies contained in published sources, please see: Claude Marie Guyon, *Histoire des Indes orientales anciennes et modernes*, volume 3 (Paris: P.N. Plotin imprimeur libraire, 1744), 247 and 253; Ernest Lennel de La Farelle, *Deux officiers français au XVIIIᵉ siècle. Mémoires et correspondance du chevalier et du général de La Farelle* (Paris: Berger-Levrault, 1896); Guillaume Hyacinthe Joseph Jean Baptiste Le Gentil de La Galaisière, *Voyage dans les mers de l'Inde, fait par ordre du Roi à l'occasion du passage de Vénus sur le disque du soleil, le 6 juin 1761 et le 3 du même mois 1769, par M. Le Gentil de l'Académie Royale des Sciences*, 2 volumes (Paris: Imprimerie Royale, 1779).

   For archive resources, please see a document that until recently has been relatively neglected and that is a great help in estimating Pondicherry's population: 'Recensement de la population de Pondichéry en 1769,' National Archives (Paris-France), Fonds des colonies, series C^2: 'Inde et Compagnie des Indes,' $C^2$210 f 334.

10. Main demographic data can be summarised as follows: 1705: 400 Europeans for a total population of 30,000 in the trading post; 1740: 1,200 French for a total population of 120,000; 1761: 2,000 French for a total population of 23,000; in 1769: 971 French for a total population of 27,473.

11. This figure has been derived from the data analysis of crew lists preserved at the Service Historique de la Défense, département Marine du port de Lorient (France) (Defence Historical Service, Marine department of the port of Lorient, France), and the works of: René Estienne, *Les armements au long cours de la deuxième Compagnie des Indes (1717–1773). Tableaux tirés des sous-séries 1P et 2P* (Vincennes: Defence Historical Service, 1995), 133; and Philippe Haudrère, *La Compagnie française des Indes orientales au XVIIIᵉ siècle, 1719–1795* (Paris: Librairie de l'Inde, 1989), 599, 850, 894.

12. For a detailed study of the essential role played by *pacotille* (low value goods used for exchange), see: Eugénie Margoline-Plot, 'Les pacotilles d'indiennes, la boutique et la mer. Organisation, structures et logiques d'une économie parallèle en Bretagne au XVIIIᵉ siècle' (PhD Thesis under the direction of Professor Gérard Le Bouëdec, Lorient, University of South-Brittany, 2012).

13. For more information on the supply of goods to Pondicherry, and to French trading ports in India in general, particularly in terms of Far-eastern commodities, see Kévin Le Doudic, '"Exotic" Goods? Far-Eastern Commodities for the French Market in India in the Eighteenth Century,' in *Goods from the East*, ed. Maxine Berg, Felicia Gottmann, Hanna Hodacs, and Chris Nierstrasz (Basingstoke: Palgrave/Macmillan, 2015), pp. 216–228.

14. This characteristic is not specific to the French of Pondicherry, or other French trading ports. See: Jean Deloche, *Old Mahe (1721–1817) According to Eighteenth-Century French Plans* (Pondicherry: Institut Français de Pondichéry / École Française d'Extrême-Orient, 2013). Europeans in general pursued the same objectives regardless of the country in which they settled. This same trend is noted in different trading ports throughout India. The English, for instance, sought to obtain furniture and architectural replicas that reflected those used in England. See Amin Jaffer's work on furniture, in particular: Amin Jaffer, *Furniture from British India and Ceylon. A Catalogue of the Collection in the Victoria and Albert Museum and the Peabody Essex Museum* (London: Victoria and Albert Museum, 2001). Recent material culture research on the Dutch in Batavia shows a similar dynamic. See Michael North's research, in particular: Michael North, ed., *Artistic and Cultural Exchanges Between Europe and Asia, 1400–1900: Rethinking Markets, Workshops and Collections* (Surrey / Burlington: Ashgate, 2010). From the start of European settlement in India with the arrival of the Portuguese, settlers developed a taste to surround themselves with references from their country of origin. This is clearly demonstrated in Alexandra Curvelo's work on Goa: Alexandra Curvelo, 'Quelques notes sur la culture matérielle Portuguaise en Inde au cours des XVIe et XVIIe siècles,' in *L'Asie, la mer, le monde. Au temps de la Compagnie des Indes*, 199–212. Raphael Moreira reaches the same conclusions in relation to Brazil. Raphael Moreira, 'Néoclassicisme colonial: Saint-Louis du aragnan au Brésil et Goa en Inde, deux capitales portugaises des XVIIIe et XIXe siècles,' in *Le néoclassicisme dans les colonies européennes, XVIIIe–XIXe siècles*, 194–211. North America witnessed the same phenomenon, which always included a certain adaptation to local tastes. See Katherine Hall, 'Le goût néoclassique en Louisiane entre 1780 et 1840,' and David Barquist, 'Interprétations Nord-américaines du néoclassicisme britannique à la fin du XVIIIe siècle et au début du XIXe siècle,' both in *Le néoclassicisme dans les colonies européennes, XVIIIe–XIXe siècles*), 256–78. The former French colonies that have since become the French departments of Guyana (South America) and Réunion Island (Indian Ocean) both have a significant architectural heritage that reflects this determination to obtain and create references to Europe. Céline Frémaux, 'Le néoclassicisme comme élément fédérateur dans les colonies européennes XVIIIe–XIXe siècles. Déclinaisons de l'architecture néoclassique en Guyane: des constructions coloniales aux maisons créoles,' in *Le néoclassicisme dans les colonies européennes, XVIIIe–XIXe siècles*, 104–22; Bernard Leveneur, *Petites histoires de l'architecture réunionnaise. De la Compagnie des Indes aux années 1960* (Sainte Clothilde de La Réunion: Éditions du 4 épices, 2007). Réunion Island is particularly interesting as it allows us to identify a real circulation of specific fashions within the Indian Ocean region. Pondicherry's architectural models were transferred to Bourbon Island (Réunion Island's former name) but only in the form of 'screen façades,' incorporated onto old houses.

15. Inventories of property after death provide several indications of the cost of having clothes made by Indian tailors. Mathurin Garnier's for example specifies the following: tailoring one coat: 6 fanons, one shirt: 1 fanon, one waistcoat: 2 fanons, one pair of breeches: 1 fanon (source: *Mémoire de ce que Mathurin Garnier doit, à son retour des Maldives, à Le Basque*, ANOM, FT, EFI, DPPC, fonds Inde, P023 f 617, 1st July 1721).

16. Daniel Roche, *La culture des apparences. Une histoire du vêtement XVIIe–XVIIIe siècle* (Paris: Librairie Arthème Fayard, 1989).

17. Ananda Ranga Pillai's journal is translated into English: John Frederick Price, *The Private Diary of Ananda Ranga Pillai. 1736–1760*, vols 1 to 3 (Madras: 1904–1928); Henry Dodwell, *The Private Diary of Ananda Ranga Pillai. 1736–1760*, vol. 4 to 12 (Madras: 1904–1928). A selection of the most important passages was published and analysed in French: Pierre Bourdat, *Les grandes pages du 'Journal d'Ananda Ranga Pillai,' courtier de la Compagnie des Indes auprès des gouverneurs de Pondichéry (1736–1760)*, preface by Jean Deloche (Paris: L'Harmattan, 2003).

18. 'Contrat de la Compagnie avec les anciens marchands du 21 avril 1738. Envoyé copie en Europe le 10 février 1739 à la Compagnie par La Reine,' ANOM, FT, EFI, DPPC, fonds Inde, P054 f 118, 21 April 1738.

19. Philippe Haudrère provides an exchange rate of 8 *livres tournois, L.T.* (Tournois pounds) 2 *sols* and 5 *deniers* for 1 pagoda throughout the eighteenth century: Philippe Haudrère, *La Compagnie française des Indes au XVIIIᵉ siècle, 1719–1795* (Paris: Librairie de l'Inde, 1989), 829. However, the French notarial documents of Pondicherry indicate the following exchanges rates: 1 pagoda is worth 5.5 L.T. from 1700–1709; 5.1 L.T. from 1710–1729; 5.5 L.T. again from 1740–1749; and finally 8.55 L.T. in 1778.
20. 'Inventaire et vente des biens de feu Charles de Flacourt,' ANOM, FT, EFI, DPPC, fonds Inde, P017 f 277, 19 October 1720; 'Vente des marchandises du Bengale de feu Charles de Flacourt,' ANOM, FT, EFI, DPPC, fonds Inde, P017 f 248, 2 March 1721; Compte de feu Charles de Flacourt fait à Chandernagor, ANOM, FT, EFI, DPPC, fonds Inde, P017 f 249, 26 December 1720.
21. Ananda Ranga Pillai's interest in French culture could sometimes reach a high degree of admiration (particularly for J.F. Dupleix, the governor of Pondicherry) which is often palpable in his *Private Diary*. For more information on his home, see: Jean Deloche, *Pondicherry Past and Present* (Pondicherry: Institut Français de Pondichéry and École Française d'Extrême-Orient, 2007), CDROM.
22. Valérie Bérinstain, Claude Sandjivy and Thierry-Nicolas Tchakaloff, 'Naissance d'un style,' in *Pondichéry 1674–1761. L'échec d'un rêve d'empire*, ed. Rose Vincent (Paris: Les Éditions Autrement, 1993), 164–182. Also see Amin Jaffer's works cited above.
23. Brigitte Nicolas, *Au bonheur des Indes Orientales, Musée de la Compagnie des Indes* (Lorient: Palantines, 2014), 108–109.
24. Gauvin Alexander Bailey, 'Religious Encounters: Christianity in Asia,' in *Encounters. The Meeting of Asia and Europe, 1500–1800*, ed. Anna Jackson and Amin Jaffer (London: V&A Publications, 2004), 102–123.
25. Jean-Pierre Duteil, 'Les missionnaires catholiques en Inde au XVIIIe siècle,' in *Le Goût de l'Inde*, 96–105; Évelyne Hiet-Guihur, *Le voyage dans la formation des missionnaires de la Société des Missions Étrangères, 1660–1791* (Unpublished PhD thesis, Université de Bretagne-Sud, 2011).
26. To date, sources have not yet identified mixed objects combining Indian style with European materials.
27. Luxury accessories are objects that accessorise an outfit and which confer a heightened social distinction on the wearer: jewellery, shoe buckles, walking canes, etc. These are completed by various means of transportation such as sedan chairs, palanquins and carriages.
28. Menus or recipes from eighteenth-century Pondicherry are rare. Only one author provides a description of a sumptuous meal served for Dupleix, governor of the trading post, in 1759:

> 'First service: a broth and two soups garnished with chicken and truffles; a pigeon pie garnished with artichoke heart and ham; capon in cream sauce; a large chicken with ham, olives and artichoke heart; a dish of chicken with [bapily]; duck with capers, anchovies, ham and artichoke heart; grilled lamb chops, grilled beef tripe; a platter of small patés. Second service: roast turkey; roast capon [baldé]; roast duck; almond pie; iced cabbage; artichoke hearts; a duck stew; two salads; eggs for the salads. Dessert: Plate of ripe mango; pomegranate and guava; fourteen biscuits, two plates of macaroons, two plates of white pralines, four dishes of jam'.

> In Marguerite V. Labernadie, *Le vieux Pondichéry, 1674–1815. Histoire d'une ville coloniale française* (Pondicherry and Paris: Imprimerie Moder andurmi E. Leroux, 1936), 270.

PART III

Objects of global consumption

8

CUSTOMS AND CONSUMPTION

Russia's global tobacco habits in the seventeenth and eighteenth centuries

Matthew P. Romaniello

Russia's historical relationship with tobacco is unlike any other country in the world, with Muscovy's tsars enforcing the longest ban on tobacco imports ever attempted. Following Peter the Great's (r. 1692–1725) legalization of tobacco imports at the end of the seventeenth century, the tobacco trade flourished in the eighteenth century.[1] Though the Petrine court enjoyed smoking pipe tobacco elite consumers in eighteenth-century Russia preferred snuff, aping elites throughout Western Europe. By the nineteenth century, smoking joined snuff as a popular habit and, by the end of that century, the machine-rolled cigarette marked mass consumption throughout the Empire as much as any part of the world.

The two-century transformation of Russia from a country without tobacco to one of the world's great consumers has dominated recent historiographical interest in Russia's tobacco history.[2] However, this trend has overwhelmed the counter-narratives of tobacco's adoption and consumption throughout the empire. Though the ban was in place, tobacco was smuggled into European Russia to meet the demands of a developing market and it was legally imported into Russia's Asian possessions, becoming a part of Siberian trade with Bukhara, India, Iran, and China. By the eighteenth century, Russia's reliance upon tobacco in Siberia for its ability to facilitate the fur trade with the indigenous population led to tobacco's introduction to Kamchatka, Russia's far eastern peninsula in the north Pacific, where smoking quickly became a habit among the Chukchis and Itelmen. Despite the government's support for the longest ban on tobacco sales in world history, tobacco became a widespread commodity there as much as any other region of the globe.

Considering the conflicting narratives of tobacco's history in Russia, understanding its adoption and consumption by varied groups defies easy classification. Commodities studies offer a variety of analytical models to resolve this issue, particularly the idea of a 'commodity network', in which the 'connections between actors are seen as complex webs of interdependence' rather than as a linear set of links.[3] Furthermore, studying different regions in Russia reveals the process of 'localization' by unpacking the articulation of consumption habits as different ethno-linguistic groups refashioned the product within their own cultural contexts.[4] Uncovering tobacco's hidden history across Russia manifests the empire's position at the crossroads of multiple international networks, where different cultural adoptions reinforced regional variations among the diverse populations of the empire. A single commodity, tobacco, did not unify the empire with a common habit, rather it demonstrates the multivalent nature of the diverse cultures within the borders of the world's largest empire, spanning from the Baltic Sea in Europe to the shores of North America.

Prohibiting tobacco

One of the earliest appearances of tobacco in Muscovy was in 1609, when the pipe-smoking English envoy posted in Iaroslavl' started 'a great conflagration that caused much damage', according to one eyewitness.[5] By the 1620s, further tobacco incidents warned the tsar of its increasing danger. In February 1627, the governor of Tobol'sk petitioned Tsar Mikhail Fedorovich with a request to resolve the problem of the accumulating debts of military servitors in Siberia, incurred from their tobacco habits. The tsar's solution to this problem was a comprehensive blockade against the tobacco trade. He decreed that no one would be allowed inside a Russian or Siberian city with tobacco, and that no merchant could be allowed to sell tobacco to a military servitor anywhere. Furthermore, any merchant caught with tobacco should be 'exiled' from Russian lands, physically removing the tobacco and any potential of it being purchased within Muscovy's borders.[6] The formal prohibition against tobacco was only the opening salvo in a long campaign to curtail tobacco sales and use. By 1633–1634, the tsar extended his ban on tobacco to all cities in Muscovy, 'on pain of the death penalty'.[7]

Unlike in European Russia, there was no formal ban on the tobacco trade in Siberia, though its sale was forbidden within town walls. Without question, the state's only concern was preventing its own soldiers from acquiring debt from tobacco's cost; otherwise, the trade in tobacco continued largely unregulated throughout the seventeenth century.[8] Instructions to the governor of Bratsk from 1642, for example, warned that 'Anyone who illegally plays cards for money or for grain or tobacco, and in so doing causes some offense or injury to natives, is to be mercilessly whipped for his misconduct'.[9] By 1646, a de facto monopoly on the tobacco trade was established when Ivan Eremeev, Ivan Tret'iakov, and their colleagues received permission to sell tobacco throughout Siberia. According to the grant, they could sell to other traders, Muslim Tatars, musketeers, and other men in military service, but 'no one may smoke inside Siberia's towns or hold on to tobacco to sell it.'[10]

In Siberia the tobacco trade flourished even with the limited control over the trade the state imposed. In particular, the habit seemed to have spread among the local indigenous populations. In 1657, the state treasury gave three and a half puds of tobacco (543 lbs.) to a Bukharan trader, Seitkul Ablin, as a gift for the Kalmyks as

FIGURE 8.1 Johann Gottlieb Georgi, *Russia: Or, A Compleat Historical Account of All the Nations which Compose that Empire* (London: J. Nicholas and T. Cadell, 1783), vol. 4, plate 14, courtesy of the Rubenstein Rare Book & Manuscript Library at Duke University.

part of his embassy to China, to ease his transit through Kalmyk territory.[11] In fact, the Kalmyks seemed entranced by tobacco, as it became one of the most common goods exchanged between Russian merchants and the nomads. As one visitor to Siberia wrote in the late seventeenth century, 'The Muscovites bring all kinds of goods with them and in exchange the Kalmyks offer livestock and draft animals, their sweetmeats, and Chinese tobacco' (Figure 8.1).[12]

The combination of unrestricted tobacco sales to the indigenous community and the product's general popularity led to widespread tobacco use throughout Siberia, even if the method of smoking was unusual by European standards. In 1680, a Catholic missionary living in Tobol'sk, Iurii Krizhanich, described the following scene, in which the Bukharans:

> bring in Chinese tobacco, too, cut so fine it is like human hair. It is so fine, in fact, that at first many people do not believe it really is tobacco; but Russian merchants maintain they have seen with their own eyes how the Chinese cut tobacco leaves like this. The tobacco is available in a dark color, or a light shade, or green. The dark tobacco has a very pleasant aroma and produces a greater headiness than the other varieties, so persons who have weak heads should avoid using it. They say that this tobacco is cured in a sugar solution.

> The Chinese and Russians who use it revel in the smoke. They fall into a swoon and are subject to convulsions, and some even breathe their last.[13]

While the Chinese did regularly treat their tobacco with sweeteners, this preparation would not cause seizures. Convulsions, however, were not uncommon among Middle Eastern preparations where the tobacco had been cut with henbane to increase its hallucinogenic effects.[14] One of the Siberian groups directly north of the Bukharans, the Ostiaks, also adopted this Middle Eastern habit, revealing the northern extent of this trade route. One of the first to witness the Ostiaks using a water-pipe was Peter the Great's ambassador to China in 1692–1693, Evert Ysbrant Ides:

> To smoke Tobacco (to which all both Men and Women are very much addicted) instead of Pipes they use a Stone Kettle, in which they stick a Pipe made for that purpose, and at two or three drawings after they have taken some Water in their Mouths, can suck out a whole Pipe; and they swallow the Smoak, after which they fall down and lye insensible, like dead Men with distorted Eyes, both Hands and Feet Trembling for about half an Hour. They foam at the Mouth, so that they fall into a sort of Epilepsie: and we could not observe where the Smoak vented it self, and in this manner several of them are lost.[15]

While the physical reaction resembles Krizhanich's earlier description, Ides's was clearly describing a water-pipe, though he was unfamiliar with its use. The combination of the strong physical reaction suggesting henbane, or tobacco mixed with henbane, and the water-pipe, indicates the Ostiaks had adopted the consumption habits of the Middle East, which were unlike the pipe-smoking practices of Europe or China.[16]

Unlike the Ostiaks of western Siberia, indigenous Siberians in the east were more likely to purchase tobacco exported from China for pipe smoking. Following the Treaty of Nerchinsk (1689), Chinese records demonstrate that Russian traders purchased 'ball' tobacco in China, which was tobacco rolled and bound together with some type of sweetener.[17] Ides also observed large-scale tobacco plantations along China's Russian border, indicating at the least the ease of carrying tobacco across the border.[18] Siberia appears divided into two regional networks, with eastern Siberia supplied by China and its tobacco plantations and western Siberia connected by Bukharan traders to the plantations of Iran and India. Eastern and Western Siberia, therefore, were divided by both trade routes and consumption habits, as water-pipe tobacco preparations would not have been suitable for pipe-smoking and vice versa, limiting the potential exports of these tobacco products to certain regions within the Russian Empire.

Meanwhile, despite the comprehensive ban in European Russia, its market also seemed to be expanding throughout the seventeenth century. West Europeans, in particularly the English and Dutch, smuggled tobacco into European Russia throughout the century, partially in pursuit of potential trade and partially for their own use.[19] While there are no official accounts of the death penalty being enforced as threatened by the 1633/4 ban, accounts of public torture of Russian tobacco merchants do exist. Adam Olearius, a secretary in the embassy of the Duke of Holstein, observed eight men and one woman being beaten with a knout as punishment for selling tobacco and vodka on 24 September 1634.[20] In a largely illiterate society, the exhibition of the state's penalties imposed on tobacco was more effective than just the written word. It is hard to imagine that anyone in Muscovy was unaware of the serious consequences for selling tobacco. Yet Olearius suggested it did little to dissuade interest in the product, commenting that 'the Russians also greatly love tobacco . . . The poor man gave his kopek as readily for tobacco as bread'.[21]

Perhaps encouraged by its popularity, English and Dutch merchants regularly smuggled leaf into Russia, risking the consequences of breaking the ban. In 1634, Phillip Coffy was arrested and imprisoned after tobacco was discovered among his possessions. King Charles I entreated Tsar Mikhail Fedorovich to free Coffy, who was 'altogether ignorant and innocent' of the charges, adding this request to another complaint against the persistent searches of all English merchants in Arkhangel'sk.[22] However, just two years later the king once again called for an Englishman's freedom, this time for John Cartwright, who also had been arrested for smuggling tobacco.[23] Some of the smuggled tobacco may have been for personal use. In December 1663, the local townsmen from the northern city of Kholmogory protested the scandalous actions of the Dutch merchant Michael Meier. Whenever he received other foreigners traveling from Arkhangel'sk, 'they drank and smoked tobacco, and played many games'. During Lent, Meier consumed enough 'tobacco, meat, and fermented milk' that 'a great stench' emanated from his house strong enough to be smelled in church.[24] Smuggling continued with sufficient regularity that the English envoy to Muscovy had a form letter on hand to petition the tsar for a smuggler's freedom, known as 'Wryting Instituted [Several pretended Reasons, etc.] Marked No. A'.[25]

Foreign merchants believed successful smuggling proved there was a demand for tobacco, leading to persistent efforts to convince the Russian government to overturn its prohibition. The tsar received repeated complaints from English merchants beginning in the 1630s about illegal searches for tobacco in Arkhangelsk and Vologda. By 1639, the complaints had become so numerous that the tsar questioned officials in Vologda about their invasive searches, warning them to halt their actions for fear of limiting foreign trade.[26] Of course, this instruction was not a command to stop forcing merchants to declare all of their trade goods upon entry into any Muscovite city for tax purposes, just to be more judicious in their tobacco accusations.

Creating Russian habits

Smuggling may have brought tobacco to European Russia, but the legal division of the empire remained, with the tobacco ban in force in Moscow while Siberia continued to have its trade with China. This situation would only change during

the reign of Peter the Great (1692–1725), when he overturned the ban. This decision was less an endorsement of smoking and far more an economic one, as the tsar
needed to raise funds for his planned Grand Embassy to Western Europe in 1696,
and allowing sales of the previously banned commodity created new revenue for
his government. There was no repeal of the prohibition announced when the tsar
granted one of his merchants, Martin Bogdanov, a contract to sell tobacco in Russia
for one year beginning on 1 December 1696. This first contract had an important
caveat, as the mechanism for Bogdanov to acquire any tobacco to sell was left to
his own devising, but the contract required him to pay the government the taxes
for his theoretical sales immediately. In a note accompanying the contract, the tsar
suggested that since foreign merchants smuggled tobacco into Russia, legalizing its
sale would not only provide his coffers a one-time payment for the privilege but
also guaranteed an increase in tax revenues from ongoing sales.[27]

Peter's note was the first sign that Bogdanov's contract was not just a temporary
solution to his revenue shortfall, but rather a plan to legalize tobacco permanently.
In the same year as Bogdanov's contract, Peter changed tobacco policies in the
entrepôt of Astrakhan on the Caspian Sea, which was the entry point for all merchants from across 'Asia'. In Peter's instruction to the governor of Astrakhan, tobacco
would be confiscated from foreign merchants upon their arrival in Astrakhan, but
returned to them upon their departure; individual merchants could carry approximately eighteen pounds for their personal use into the city.[28] The next year, the
tobacco situation continued to improve. A foreign merchant, Thomas Fathonreckt,
was given a one-year contract to import tobacco into European Russia, which was
the first time imports into the territory had been allowed since 1649. Based on
these changes, English merchants knew the time was right to seek the overturn of
the tobacco ban, arguing in London that 'The extent of those Territories, the number of the people, and their passionate love of Tobacco, being such, that a free use of
it there, and liberty to import it, would be of very great advantage'.[29]

The very next year, in 1698, English tobacco merchants had their long-held
hopes fulfilled, as Peter the Great signed a multi-year contract with King William
III, to allow a company of English merchants to import a high volume of tobacco
into European Russia.[30] The new 'Tobacco Company' was required to import 3,000
hogsheads of tobacco (3 million pounds; 1 hogshead = 1,000 pounds) in the first
year (1699), and 5,000 hogsheads in the second. After the second year, the contract
was renewable annually for another 5,000 hogsheads, for up to seven years. Under
the terms of the contract, tobacco could be sold anywhere in the kingdom (a later
point of contention), and the tsar agreed to ban all other tobacco imports, which was
hardly a concession as no other supply of tobacco was legally allowed into Muscovy.
The tsar agreed that Ukrainian-grown tobacco would not enter Russia to preserve
the English monopoly for European Russia.[31] While the expansion from zero legal
imports in 1696 to 3 million pounds of leaf imported only three years later was an
optimistic assessment of the market, English estimates of tobacco imports in the
other 'northern' states indicate this number was within the consumption level of
Russia's neighbours. Denmark and Norway imported approximately 2.5 million

pounds per year, and Sweden imported 4 million.[32] With a larger population than either, the figure for Russia was not unreasonable, but the transition from no legal consumption to a comparable level to Russia's neighbours with an established habit was ambitious. English records indicate the steady decline of their own tobacco smuggling with the advent of the legal tobacco monopolies, but, in 1695, the year before Bogdanov's contract, the English only sold about 4,300 pounds of tobacco in Arkhangelsk, far less than the three million pounds they exported just three years later.[33]

The sudden arrival of a high volume of tobacco would have been shocking to a Russian of that era, following the abrupt reversal of the long prohibition. It is not surprising, therefore, that smoking tobacco was included among the dangerous innovations of the new court in an early eighteenth century woodcut (Figure 8.2). Here we see two elite men at home, depicted in Western clothing with clean-shaven faces. They have chosen to spend an evening painting, gambling, and smoking, which were new pastimes introduced in the Petrine court. While the elites in the foreground seem at ease with their new hobbies, the servants in the background have been corrupted

FIGURE 8.2 'Paramoshka at Savoska's House'. Woodcut, second quarter of the eighteenth century. From V.S. Bakhtin, *Russkii lubok, XVII–XIX vv.* (Moscow: Gosudarstvennoe izdatel'stvo izobrazitel'nogo iskusstva, 1962), plate 20.

by the exposure to these foreign habits. Elite Russians might have adopted the Western customs to stay in fashion, but this woodcut indicates that smoking, along with the other new practices of the court, was not popular.

It is safe to conclude that the diffusion of the tobacco habit during Peter's lifetime was slow at best. With the combination of a decades-long ban on the product and smoking's association with the new, and unpopular court culture, the potential audience for tobacco in 1700 was limited.[34] Despite the English estimates of what the Russian market could bear, sales were definitely sluggish, leaving the English Tobacco Company with most of the leaf imported in the first two years of the contract unsold almost a decade later.

Adding to the social and cultural challenges, the Tobacco Company had imported Virginian leaf tobacco, which had been diminishing in popularity throughout the Baltic region. English merchants operating in the Baltic reported to the Board of Trade and Plantations that 'the hot and dry Tast' of Virginian leaf was not 'agreeable to the Northern Palate'. As a result, the Dutch had recently dominated the market by producing two different tobacco products. They had found success by mixing Baltic-grown tobacco in equal proportion with the stalks of Virginian tobacco, flattened and cut to produce a milder tobacco blend. This mix could then either be sold as cut tobacco for smoking, or wrapped in a large Virginian leaf and marketed as rolled tobacco. Not only was the taste more appealing but also, in the words of the Board of Trade, 'its Cheapness recommends it to those Markets'.[35] Attempting to sell more expensive Virginian leaf, and not offering the products that had produced the Dutch successes in the Baltic, the Tobacco Company was destined to struggle in the Russian market, even if tobacco had been popular, as it was neither mild nor cheap. Furthermore, with established tobacco markets in the Swedish port cities of Riga and Tallinn, which themselves would soon be Russian cities, the English difficulties in navigating the Russian market were only increasing.

This is not to imply that the Tobacco Company was unaware that they had failed to crack the market. In the spring of 1705 (seven years after first arriving), the London-based contractors dispatched two tradesmen to Moscow with the necessary tools and products to manufacture cut and rolled tobacco from their supplies of Virginian leaf. Possibly because the new product was not immediately associated with the century-long ban on leaf tobacco, or because it better suited Russian palates, the new rolled tobacco started to sell almost immediately, according to the Company's early reports.[36]

Success in Moscow's marketplace, however, also sparked some fears in London about the potential loss of a 'secret' English technology, if the English master tradesmen trained their local labour force in their specialist techniques. In 1705, the year the new tobacco factory was established in Moscow, the newly-arrived English Consul, Charles Whitworth, was ordered to destroy the tobacco factory and all its contents, and immediately remove the tradesmen from Russia. Ironically, Whitworth arrived in Moscow with instructions to do everything possible to resolve the tobacco contract and assist the merchants, but within a few months his task was to remove the only successful part of the English trade. Whitworth would prove far more successful in destroying the factory than he would be in selling the remaining Virginian leaf. As soon as he received his instructions from London in July 1705, Whitworth had accomplished his assignment, which resulted in his remaining in Moscow for another three years while he sought a resolution to selling the remaining loose-leaf tobacco.[37]

Though the destruction of the factory was unfortunate for tobacco sales, Whitworth's description of the factory provides remarkable detail about the method of finishing tobacco that had become popular. The key to the operation seemed to be the addition of a special 'liquor' to flavour and colour the tobacco to adjust its taste. When Whitworth and his assistants destroyed the factory, they burned five 'parcells of Ingredients' to make the liquor, which was stored in barrels. The factory was highly mechanized, with 'three engines set up for cutting Tobacco, and . . . the plates & Cranes for two more.' After being cut, the tobacco was flavoured with the liquor, the excess of which was allowed to drain through a sieve, and then the seasoned cut leaf was put into 'several large engines for preparing the Tobacco into form.' There were several wooden tables throughout the factory for sorting the leaf, and the machines themselves were made out of iron, with copper wheels.[38] Considering that all of the equipment was imported from England, the factory was a substantial investment into developing Moscow's tobacco market.

The Foreign Secretary, the Board of Trade and Plantations, and Whitworth all believed the destruction of the factory to be necessary to protect English interests from the potential of a trained Russian workforce utilizing the machinery to prepare Ukrainian tobacco as if it was the much more expensive Virginian leaf. England's officials were aware of the large volume of tobacco currently being produced in Ukraine; Whitworth himself was a witness to a large shipment of Ukrainian tobacco arriving in Riga on his trip to Moscow. He observed:

> 50 or 60 sleds loaden with Tobacco which is planted in the Ukraine, and I am informed that 2 or 300 of the same usually pass every year; This Tobacco is extreamly bad but not costing above a penny a pound find a considerable vent amongst the poor Peasants of Lithuania, who provided they can have the smoke at a cheap rate are not nice as to the smell.[39]

While the quality did not impress him, the Board of Trade had gathered sufficient evidence to conclude that cheapness overrode a concern for quality in northern Europe. While Russian tobacco habits may have been relatively recent, Whitworth was concerned that they were pleased to 'chop their tobacco with axes on the ground' in order to prepare it, which made both Virginian leaf and the elaborate manufacturing process unnecessary.[40] The English masters brought not only new flavours to disguise the poor quality of Ukrainian leaf but also a cleaner and quicker process for turning raw leaf into rolled cigars. If any part of the factory had been left functioning, the English would have had little to offer the unsophisticated consumers of Russia, who were not willing to pay a premium for the superior Virginian leaf.

Observing Siberian habits

While the arrival of legal tobacco in European Russia was unsuccessful, Siberia continued to thrive as a vibrant tobacco market. Tobacco was so essential to the Siberian economy that tobacco leaves became a substitute for specie among the indigenous communities there. John Bell, an Englishman on Lev Vasilevich Izmailov's embassy to China (1718–1721), frequently commented on the useful-ness of tobacco. Among the Siberian Tatars, he wrote 'They are very hospitable; and desire nothing, in return of their civilities, but a little tobacco to smoke, and a dram of brandy, of which they are very fond'.[41] Shortly thereafter, while traveling among the Ostiaks, he made a similar remark, 'Give them only a little tobacco, and a dram of brandy, and they ask no more, not knowing the use of money.'[42] A prisoner of war taken during the Great Northern War, Philip Johann von Strahlenberg, would make a similar observation in his account from the 1730s.

> If one meets any of them [Ostiaks] upon this River, and only calls out the Word *Quarni-patsch* [Bear's gall], they presently come, with their little Boats, and bring a good Quantity, and at a very cheap Rate; Generally a Gall, well dry'd, may be had for as much *Chinese* Tobacco, as amounts, in Value, to two *Kopeiks*.[43]

While much of the travel in Siberia was through the lands of the Ostiaks, as the travellers neared Lake Baikal, and along the road to China, the local population was primarily the Tungus. The Tungus not only had adopted the tobacco habit but had also begun cultivating tobacco. As Brand observed,

> The next Place we came to, was inhabited by the *Targuts Chinay*, who are Pagans, subject to the *Chineses*; they are good Husband-men, the Countrey abounding in Oats, Barley, Oatmeal and Tobacco; and Salt, we furnished our-selves with as much as we stood in need of.[44]

Bell considered tobacco to be one of the basic necessities of Tungus life, comment-ing 'They are very civil and tractable, and like to smoke tobacco, and drink brandy. About their huts they have generally a good stock of rain-deer, in which all their wealth consists.'[45]

By the time of the Second Kamchatka Expedition (1733–1743), led by Vitus Bering, all of its members travelled with the knowledge that tobacco was essen-tial to facilitate trade throughout Siberia. Johann Georg Gmelin, the naturalist on the expedition, frequently used gifts of tobacco to gain access to local women. In Kuznetsk, between Novosibirsk and Krasnoiarsk, he would observe that:

> These [Siberian] Tartars have several wives. They do not eat pork, but they drink alcohol, and partake often. Their women are not beautiful and almost all smoke tobacco. One of them saw me loading a pipe, pulled hers out of her pocket and asked for a filling. That done, she lit it, swallowed all the smoke, and gave the pipe to another who did the same.[46]

While he suggested that Tatar women had a noted interest in smoking, Tungus women were quite public in their consumption:

> The women and men smoke and make use of Chinese tobacco: each of them had on his or her pants a little leather bag in which they kept tobacco, lighter and a pipe. . . . We invited some of these women onto our boat, but only after promising them tobacco, flour and bread. They felt contentment at receiving these little presents, which gave us the greatest pleasure. They carefully wrapped the tobacco in paper, and the bread and flour, and then took off their stockings and put it in one or the other. We then returned to tell their husbands that we gave such presents to them: we waited some time, but the men never arrived.[47]

While gifts of tobacco facilitated Gmelin's interactions with Siberian women, he followed in the pattern established by earlier travellers and used tobacco as a form of currency to pay his local Tungus (male) guides as well.

> I gave them tobacco and Chinese goods, including a new pipe made of brass, barley, raw meat, so they could cook it in their way, and as much milk as they wanted and so they would be satisfied. They stayed with me ten days.[48]

Though many of Gmelin's observations remain consistent with earlier comments on the popularity of tobacco, he also recorded the development of sophisticated consumers. In Krasnoiarsk, he noted the preferences of the local Tatar community, who 'prefer Chinese tobacco, but the poor among them make use of the Circassian [Ukrainian]: they mix it with small, thin shavings of birch bark, both to save the tobacco and diminish its force'.[49] Gmelin's comments seem to indicate that the Siberian use of Chinese tobacco was not just from its origin nearby, but possibly from a taste preference. This would provide an explanation about the high value of Chinese tobacco in Eastern Siberia, where Ukrainian tobacco held little value despite its presumably greater transportation costs.

Furthermore, Gmelin was the first of the travellers to remark upon the use of tobacco as medicine among different communities in Russia, though as leader of a scientific expedition to Siberia his interests differed from the earlier commercial embassies. He first noticed this unusual action outside of Kazan' among the Chuvashes, where a local healer relied on tobacco as part of his medical services: 'The doctor took smoking tobacco that for some time he rolled between his fingers, then asked the patient's name, and then made a prediction: the patient needed to find a Tatar, who could heal him by reading from the Koran'.[50] Later in the Siberian outpost of Tara, Gmelin once again observed tobacco in use as a local medicine, when it was used to treat a Bashkir.

> A young Bashkir was attacked by a local disease: he felt a hard growth on his face. The usual treatment was to pierce the growth with a needle covered with sal ammoniac and Circassian Tobacco, then cover it with a plaster bandage and not interrupt its work.[51]

Gmelin did not record, however, if the cure was effective, but we have another suggestion that Circassian tobacco was not used in regular consumption as smoke or snuff.

This importance of Chinese tobacco in Siberia, therefore, is confirmed by consumption habits as well as the booming trade.[52] There was sufficient demand for tobacco exports from China that the Chinese government developed, or at least allowed, the establishment of large tobacco plantations along the border to supply the Russian trade. In Ides' account of his embassy in the 1690s, he was rather concerned about the border community: 'These People have very rich manured Lands and all sorts of Garden Fruits, and several Tobacco Plantations; but their Religion is downright Impious and Diabolical; for according to their own report they are all *Schammans*, or *Conjurers*, which invoke the Devil'.[53] While the connection of shamanism and tobacco arrived in Ides's narrative inside the Chinese border, it was probable he was describing the local Buriats rather than Chinese settlers. Two decades later, John Bell was more clear that the Buriats had incorporated tobacco as part of their religious practices.[54] Nor was this limited to those communities along the Chinese border, as the Iakuts along the Pacific coast also included smoking as part of their religious practices, where smoking and singing became an integral part of their healing rituals.[55] While Western observers were likely unreliable on the significance of smoking tobacco in these different rituals, tobacco was an essential component of life for diverse Siberian communities by the early eighteenth century. With different methods of consumption, distinct preferences for type of tobacco, and unique customs attached to smoking, 'Siberians' were not a single group but individual communities revealed by customs and trade networks. Tobacco assisted the naturalists and explorers of the eighteenth century to distinguish the Buriats, Iakuts, Ostiaks, Tatars, and Tungus from each other as much as from Russians.

Lessons of consumption

With the multiple trade policies and the varied regions and trading partners, it is perhaps not surprising that tobacco use varied widely. European Russia initially adopted the English and Dutch preference for pipe-smoking, possibly supplemented by smuggled leaf from Ukraine. Eastern Siberia's indigenous population relied on Middle Eastern blends in their water pipes, while the western Siberia population adopted Chinese sweetened ball tobacco for their pipes. Foreign observers might have confused 'Circassian/Ukrainian' or 'Chinese' tobacco in their observations of the Russian Empire's smoking habits – but if we consider Circassian and Chinese as markers for 'southern' and 'eastern' rather than countries of origin – then consumption did match the region of origin. There was little evidence of Chinese tobacco traversing Siberia to reach Moscow, despite English complaints of illegal Chinese imports, but likely the English merchants were complaining of tobacco transit along the road to China, even if the true origin was the Middle East or the Caucasus.

Across the great span of the Russian Empire, tobacco was consumed as a variety of products, as Western rolled cigars, sweetened Chinese balls, and a mixture of tobacco and henbane for a water pipe. These supplies were produced around the globe, from the Americas to China, arriving in different regional trade networks across the empire. The tremendous variety serves as an excellent introduction to the concept of 'localization,' as the consumption methods followed the supplies, which ultimately reinforced regional differences within the Russian Empire. Even when the Russians became tobacco suppliers, as they did in their Kamchatka expeditions, they failed to foster a 'Russian' consumption habit among the local population, and rather became a conveyance for exporting Chinese customs to the north Pacific, in the form of Chinese ball tobacco and pipes. While it has become a commonplace in the twenty-first century to consider 'globalization' as a means of eradicating local differences as the same products are consumed in different regions, Eurasian tobacco did the opposite – it reinforced cultural distinctions, separating European Russia from both Eastern and Western Siberia. This is not to say that tobacco creates a counter-narrative to the idea of globalization, but rather that the process of building global trade was uneven, intermittent, and could reinforce local diversity as much as (or more than) it unified regions.

Notes and References

1. Jacob M. Price, 'The Tobacco Adventure to Russia: Enterprise, Politics, and Diplomacy in the Quest for a Northern Market for English Colonial Tobacco, 1676–1722,' *Transactions of the American Philosophical Society*, New Series 51:1 (1961), 1–120; A.V. Demkin, *Britanskoe kupechestvo v Rossii XVIII veka* (Moscow: Institut rossiiskoi istorii RAN, 1998), 107–114.
2. A. V. Shapovalov, *Ocherki i kul'tury potrebleniia tabaka v Sibiri: XVII–pervaia polovina XX vv.* (Novosibirsk: Izdatel'skii tsentr 'Progress-Servis,' 2002); Igor Bogdanov, *Dym otechestva, ili kratkaia istoriia tabakokyreniia* (Moscow: Novoe literaturnoe obozrenie, 2007); *Tobacco in Russian History and Culture: From the Seventeenth Century to the Present*, ed. Matthew P. Romaniello and Tricia Starks (New York: Routledge, 2009).
3. Alex Hughes and Suzanne Reimer, 'Introduction,' in *Geographies of Commodity Chains*, ed. Alex Hughes and Suzanne Reimer (London: Routledge, 2004), 4. This idea was supported by Peter Dicken, Philip F. Kelly, Kris Olds, and Henry Wai-Chung Yeung, in 'Chains and Networks, Territories and Scales: Toward a Relational Framework for Analysing the Global Economy,' *Global Networks* 1 (2001): 89–112. For a summary of commodity chains, see: Terence K. Hopkins and Immanuel Wallerstein, 'Commodity Chains in the World-Economy Prior to 1800,' *Review* 10:1 (1986): 157–170; Elaine Hartwick, 'Geographies of Consumption: A Commodity-Chain Approach,' *Environment and Planning D: Society and Space* 16 (1998): 423–437.
4. David Howes, 'Introduction: Commodities and Cultural Borders,' in *Cross-Cultural Consumption: Global Markets, Local Realities*, ed. David Howes (London: Routledge, 1996), 5–7.
5. Isaac Massa, *A Short History of the Beginnings and Origins of these Present Wars in Moscow under the Reign of Various Sovereigns down to the Year 1610*, trans. and ed. G. E. Orchard (Toronto: University of Toronto Press, 1982), 190. For further discussions of the introduction of tobacco in Russia, see: Matthew P. Romaniello, 'Through the Filter of Tobacco: The Limits of Global Trade in the Early Modern World,' *Comparative Studies of Society and History* 49 (2007): 914–937.

6. Arkheograficheskaia kommissiia. *Russkaia istoricheskaia biblioteka* (St. Petersburg, Izda-vaemaia Arkheolograficheskoiu kommissieiu, 1884), vol. 8, 451–452.
7. *The Muscovite Law Code (Ulozhenie) of 1649* ed. and trans. Richard Hellie (Irvine, Cal.: Charles Schlacks, 1988), ch. 25, article 11, 228.
8. Audrey Burton, *The Bukharans: A Dynastic, Diplomatic, and Commercial History, 1550–1702* (New York: St. Martin's Press, 1997), 440, 509, 511–512, 522; Erika Monahan, 'Regulating Virtue and Vice: Controlling Commodities in Early Modern Siberia,' in *Tobacco in Russian History and Culture*, 61–82.
9. *Russia's Conquest of Siberia, 1558–1700*, ed. and trans. Basil Dmytryshyn, E.A.P. Crownhart-Vaughn, and Thomas Vaughn (Portland: Press of the Oregon Historical Society, 1985), #62, 24 August 1642, 195.
10. *Sobranie gosudarstvennykh gramot i dogovorov khraniashchikhsia gosudarstevennoi kollegi inostrannykh del*, vol. 2 (Moscow: Tipografiia N. S. Vsevolozhskago, 1822), #124, 18 March 1646, 422–425; here 424.
11. Dmytryshyn, Crownhart-Vaughn, Vaughn, *Russia's Conquest*, #89, 5 September 1657, 337–339.
12. Dmytryshyn, Crownhart-Vaughn, Vaughn, *Russia's Conquest*, #113, 1680, 430–442, here 437.
13. Dmytryshyn, Crownhart-Vaughn, Vaughn, *Russia's Conquest*, #113, 1680, 430–442, here 438.
14. Henbane is poisonous plant, native to Europe, but believed to have beneficial qualities in Western medieval and Middle Eastern medical practices. See Margery Rowell, 'Russian Medical Botany before the Time of Peter the Great,' *Sudhoffs Archiv* 62:4 (1978), 339–358, here 349. For a discussion of the arrival of tobacco and the nature of early Muslim consumption, Aziz A. Batran, *Tobacco Smoking under Islamic Law: Controversy over its Introduction* (Beltsville, Maryland: Amana, 2003).
15. E. Ysbrant Ides., *Three Years Travels from Moscow over-land to China* (London: W. Freeman, 1705), 21.
16. Some Chinese consumers did also adopt the water-pipe, but it was quite rare until the nineteenth century. See Carol Benedict, *Golden-Silk Smoke: A History of Tobacco in China, 1550–2010* (Berkeley: University of California Press, 2011), 111.
17. M. I. Sladkovskii, *History of the Economic Relations between China and Russia*, trans. M. Roublev (Jerusalem: Israel Program for Scientific Translations, 1966), 18.
18. Ides, *Three Years Travels*, 54.
19. Jarmo Kotilaine, *Russia's Foreign Trade and Economic Expansion in the Seventeenth Century: Windows on the World* (Leiden: Brill, 2005), 382, 401–402.
20. Adam Olearius, *The Travels of Olearius in Seventeenth-Century Russia*, trans. and ed. Samuel H. Baron (Stanford: Stanford University Press, 1967), 230–231.
21. Olearius, *Travels of Olearius*, 146.
22. The National Archives (TNA), Kew, PRO 22/60, English Royal Letters in the Soviet State Archive of Ancient Records, 1557–1655, no. 62, 1634.
23. Serge Konovalov, 'Seven Letters of Tsar Mikhail to King Charles I, 1634–1638,' *Oxford Slavonic Papers* 9 (1960), 52–54.
24. S. P. Orlenko, *Vykhodtsy iz zapadnoi Evropy v Rossii XVII veka* (Moscow: Drevle-khranilishche, 2004), 292–293.
25. TNA, SP 91/3, part 2, State Papers: Russia, ff. 210r–212v., 'Instructions from the Right Woell. the Governor and fellowship of English Merchants for Discovery of New Trades, Usually called the Muscovia Company, unto John Hebdon Esq.,' 16 September 1676.
26. Arkheograficheskaia kommissiia, *Akty iuridicheskie, ili sobranie form starinnago dielo-proidvodstva* (St. Petersburg: Tipografiia Il-go otdieleniia Sobstvennoi E.I.V. Kantseli-arii, 1838), 368–370.
27. *Polnoe sobranie zakonov Rossiiskoi Imperii* (PSZ), Series 1, 45 Vols. (St. Petersburg: Pechatano v tipografii otdieleniia sobstvennoi ego Imperatorskago Velichestva Kantseliarii, 1830), vol. 3, 329; Burton, *Bukharans*, 525–527.

28. PSZ, II, 313–318.
29. TNA, CO 389/15, Board of Trade: Entry Books, ff. 185–189, 'Whitehall to Lords Commission, August 10th 1697, of the state of Trade between Russia and England,' esp. 188–189.
30. Demkin, *Britanskoe kupechestvo*, 107–114.
31. Will F. Ryan, 'Peter the Great's Yacht: Admiral Lord Carmarthen and the Russian Tobacco Monopoly,' *Mariner's Mirror* 69 (1983): 65–87; Bogdanov, *Dym otechestva*, 35–42.
32. TNA, CO 388/6, Board of Trade: Original Correspondence, A12, 'Copy of an Extract of the outward Cargos of Ten England and Ten Foreign Ships to the Dominions of the Northern Crowns, 10 Aug 1696,' and TNA, CO 389/19, ff. 181–297, 'Report to the House of Commons, 1707,' here f. 245.
33. TNA, CO 388/6, B38, 'To the Right Honorable the Lords Commissioners of the Councill of Trade,' 26 November 1697, ff. 3r–v.
34. For a discussion of the numerous protests, see: Lindsey Hughes, *Russia in the Age of Peter the Great* (New Haven: Yale University Press, 2000), esp. 447–451.
35. TNA, CO 389/19, ff. 181–297, 'Report to the House of Commons, 1707,' here ff. 245–246.
36. TNA, SP 104/120, State Papers Foreign: Entry Books, Russia and Poland, ff. ff. 54v–56r, 'Report from the Lord's Commission for Trade and Plantation,' 31 May 1705.
37. TNA, SP 91/4, part 2, ff. 11–12, 'Letter from Charles Whitworth to Secretary Harley,' 25 July 1705.
38. TNA, SP 91/4, part 2, ff. 2–8, 'Letter from Charles Whitworth to Secretary Harley,' 18 July 1705, here ff. 5r–v.
39. TNA, SP 91/4, part 1, ff. 22–25, 'Letter from Charles Whitworth to Secretary Harley,' 18 February 1705, here f. 22v.
40. TNA, SP 91/4, part 2, ff. 2–8, 'Letter from Charles Whitworth to Secretary Harley,' 18 July 1705, here f. 6v.
41. John Bell, *A Journey from St. Petersburg to Pekin, 1718–22* (Edinburgh: University of Edinburgh Press, 1965), 56.
42. Bell, *Journey from St. Petersburg*, 202.
43. One hundred kopeks were the equivalent of one ruble. Philip John von Strahlenberg, *An Historico-Geographical Description of the North and Eastern Parts of Europe and Asia* (London: W. Innys and R. Manby, 1738), 438.
44. Adam Brand, *A Journal of the Embassy from Their Majesties John and Peter Alexievitz, Emperors of Muscovy, Over Land to China* (London: D. Brown, 1698), 67.
45. Bell, *Journey from St. Petersburg*, 65.
46. Johann George Gmelin, *Voyage en Sibérie*, 2 vols. (Paris: Desaint, 1767), vol. 1, 136.
47. Gmelin, *Voyage en Sibérie*, vol. 1, 329.
48. Gmelin, *Voyage en Sibérie*, vol. 1, 417.
49. Gmelin, *Voyage en Sibérie*, vol. 2, 98.
50. Gmelin, *Voyage en Sibérie*, vol. 1, 32.
51. Gmelin, *Voyage en Sibérie*, vol. 2, 204–205.
52. Sladkovskii, *History of the Economic Relations*, 18, 25, 34, 44, 48, 52; Clifford M. Foust, *Muscovite and Mandarin: Russia's Trade with China and Its Setting, 1727–1805* (Chapel Hill: University of North Carolina Press, 1969), 196–199, 201–202.
53. Ides, *Three Years Travel*, 54.
54. Bell, *Journey from St. Petersburg*, 79.
55. Gawrila Sarytschew, *Account of a Voyage of Discovery in the North-East of Siberia, the Frozen Ocean, and the North-East Sea* (London: Richard Phillips, 1806), 13.

9

SUGAR REVISITED

Sweetness and the environment in the early modern world

Urmi Engineer

Scholars have long recognised the centrality of sugar and slavery in shaping early modern Atlantic history. Numerous historians have analysed the wide-ranging impacts of 'sugar revolutions' including the growth of tropical colonialism, the rise of plantation monocultures and the Atlantic slave trade, and changes in European consumption and dietary habits, all of which contributed to the rise of global industrial capitalism.[1] The pioneering work of Sidney Mintz has established the impact of sugar as a global commodity, and demonstrated the social, economic, and cultural significance of its production and consumption.[2] Since the publication of his seminal book in 1985, historians have produced a series of studies that focus on singular commodities as a framework for understanding global patterns and processes. This approach opens doors for thinking about the ways in which non-human agents can shape human history, and is an essential bridge to incorporating environmental perspectives, in which non-living and living things, including minerals, soils, pathogens, plants, insects, primates, and other animals, play a role in determining human history. In this study of the ecological history of sugar, I deliberately foreground the unintended and seemingly unconnected environmental transformations that developed in response to the growth of sugar as a global commodity.

Just as the rise of early modern sugar production and consumption had a global impact in social, economic, and cultural terms, so the ecological changes that resulted from the transition to sugar production on large-scale plantations in the Atlantic had broad consequences. From the sixteenth through to the nineteenth century, these changes were entwined with the rise of early modern capitalism and industrialisation, characterised by the intensification of the use of labour, land, and natural resources. Ecological intensification had several predictable results and some unexpected consequences. For the most part, environmental historians have emphasized the direct ecological impacts of large-scale sugar production, especially soil deterioration (nutrient depletion and erosion) and heavy deforestation, which also contributed to soil erosion.[3] My work assesses broader and less direct effects of these environmental changes, combined with the ecological impacts of water management projects.

Most significantly, my aim is to highlight changes in disease ecology by outlining the impacts of sugar on deforestation, soil deterioration, and water management projects. Deforestation, combined with ecological shifts caused by the intensification of water management projects, including irrigation, canal building, river clearance, and swamp drainage, created a distinct environment that was particularly hospitable to West African diseases, especially yellow fever and malaria. By the nineteenth century, with the industrialization of the sugar milling and refining processes, the environmental impacts of sugar cultivation intensified further due to increasing energy demands. A critical and novel feature of my work is its emphasis on the links between increased sugar consumption, growing markets, and the growth of mosquito habitats and non-immune host populations.

The spread of early modern sugar production can be divided into three phases. The first phase begins with the spread of sugar westward from Asia, and focuses on the development of sugar production in the Mediterranean and eastern Atlantic. The second phase centres on the escalation of production in Brazil and the Caribbean in the seventeenth and eighteenth centuries. The third phase examines how sugar transitioned into an industrial product in the late-eighteenth and nineteenth centuries. While the existing literature adopts a similar chronology, it neglects the ecological alterations that marked each phase. My purpose is not only to distinguish these phases, but to foreground the epidemiological transitions that occurred at each stage. Related processes including transatlantic commerce, pre-industrial development, and the eventual industrialization of sugar production form a crucial part of the narrative of the rise of endemic yellow fever in tropical West Africa and the greater Caribbean, as well as the increase in epidemics across the temperate and tropical Atlantic in the eighteenth and early-nineteenth centuries.[4]

Sugar production in the early modern world

Sugar cane is a tropical grass, native to Southeast Asia, that requires plentiful water and arduous labour to cut and haul its thick, bulky, heavy stalks. Because of its short shelf life, sugar produced for distant markets had to undergo a complex milling and refining process. Cane juice was boiled, and then systematically heated and cooled to make crystallized sugar and molasses. Milling required substantial energy, harnessed by animal, wind, or water power for most of the early modern era, and heating required substantial amounts of wood or charcoal. Because sugar needed to be processed immediately after cultivation, early modern plantations functioned both as fields and factories.[5]

The first phase of sugar production began in Oceania and the Indian Ocean region, possibly in New Guinea. For millennia, peasant cultivators in South Asia grew sugar cane. By 800 BCE, they produced crystallized sugar and developed techniques for its manufacture. Methods of cultivation and manufacturing spread east to China, along Buddhist trade routes, and then west through Persia, reaching the Mediterranean by about 600 CE.[6] In China and India, household and free labour systems dominated production until the nineteenth century. After sugar reached the Mediterranean, production increased gradually and by the fourteenth century developed into a plantation-based industry. The Mediterranean system of sugar cultivation therefore 'can be seen as a school for the colonizers of Madeira, the Canaries, and tropical America.'[7] In both the Mediterranean and China, cultivators processed sugar by using a traditional method known as 'claying,' in which they poured hot sugar into upside-down earthenware cones, placed clay on top of the cones, and repeated this process as the cones dried. The end result was a layer of white sugar at the bottom of the cone, and a spectrum of layers of brown sugars, darkest near the tip of the cone.[8] Technical experiments and innovations included the development of irrigation techniques and animal- and water-powered milling technologies, notably the vertical three-cylinder mill, which upon its transference to the Americas became known as the 'standard mill.'[9] By the fifteenth century, corvée labour, and then slave labour, supplanted previous peasant and tenant labour arrangements in the Mediterranean, while small-scale production continued in China. Simultaneously, sugar entrepreneurs in the Atlantic adopted Mediterranean processing techniques and forced labour systems (see Map 9.1).[10]

In the Atlantic, experiments in growing sugar cane began in Spanish and Portuguese colonies off the coast of Iberia and West Africa, including the Canaries, Madeira, the Azores, the Cape Verde islands, and São Tomé. These experiments mark the beginning of rise of the Atlantic 'plantation complex,' and a subsequent escalation in world sugar production that occurred when Europeans, including Spanish, Portuguese, Dutch, British, and French sugar prospectors, began growing massive amounts of sugar in the Americas in the seventeenth century. The plantation complex, as

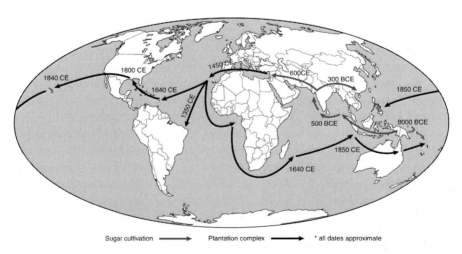

MAP 9.1 Global spread of sugar cultivation and the plantation complex. © 2015 Urmi Engineer

conceived by Philip Curtin, emerged in the Americas as a unique product of European colonialism and African slavery.[11] Ulbe Bosma provides a more inclusive definition of the term 'plantation,' as 'an entity in which the management of the cash crop-growing unit is in complete control of every aspect of the work process, as well as of the applied technologies.'[12] This interpretation distinguishes the plantation system from peasant cultivation and accounts for the continuation of plantation systems after the abolition of slavery. Plantation systems that developed from the fifteenth century onward share a number of vital characteristics including large-scale production, capital investment, reliance on an enslaved, disenfranchised, or low-wage labour force, and the intensification of environmental modification and exploitation.

In the second phase of sugar's global journey, it moved to the Atlantic Americas. The rapid growth of the plantation system in Brazil prompted the decline of the Madeiran sugar industry in the 1580s. The rise of Brazil was sidelined by the rise of the sugar plantation complex in the Lesser Antilles, especially in Barbados and Martinique. As these smaller islands became ecologically expended in terms of their land, soil quality, and timber resources, planters established plantations on the larger islands of Hispaniola, Cuba, Jamaica, and Puerto Rico. Over the course of the eighteenth century, in the western part of Hispaniola, the French colony of Saint-Domingue emerged as the region's largest sugar producer, followed by Cuba. Throughout this period, Asian cultivators, mostly in India and China, produced nearly four times as much sugar as American plantations.[13] Sugar production in the Americas vigorously expanded in the late-eighteenth and nineteenth centuries as a result of the industrialization of the plantation system. After the Haitian Revolution in the last decade of the eighteenth century, Cuba replaced Saint-Domingue as the region's leading sugar producer. At this time, Brazil re-emerged as a regional centre of sugar production, and French Louisiana developed as a sugar plantation zone.

The transition from peasant production to a capital-heavy plantation system necessitated intense ecological transformations, which increased severely as plantations industrialized. The industrialization of the plantation system at the end of the eighteenth century marks the third phase of the global expansion of sugar production. The proliferation of large-scale monocultures contributed to greater land use and the expansion of plantations into diverse landscapes, into wetlands and regions that were not in close proximity to rivers. Such growth required capital investment in the construction of large-scale water management infrastructure. Larger quantities of sugar cane required greater quantities of wood to power mills, and the development of industrial mills in the nineteenth century put a greater strain on forest reserves. This ecological intensification paralleled the intensification of forced labour practices, which escalated in the seventeenth century, and continued through the nineteenth century.

Deforestation and soil deterioration

When mapping the rise and spread of the sugar plantation complex in the Atlantic, a pattern of severe deforestation and soil deterioration emerges. This process was particularly evident in the Atlantic and Caribbean islands. Madeira, the location of the first Portuguese offshore sugar mill, experienced a substantial loss of forest cover by the end of the fifteenth century. In the seventeenth century, a similar process occurred in the sugar islands of the Lesser Antilles; by the close of the eighteenth century, planters in Saint-Domingue and Cuba exhausted much of the islands' indigenous forests. The experience of Brazil provides a contrast to island ecosystems, since the colony could access the vast tropical forests of South America.

Large-scale sugar production caused deforestation in multiple ways. First, the establishment of plantations required the clearing of forests for fields, a common agricultural practice that escalated in the eighteenth and nineteenth centuries with rising demand for sugar. Often, planters cleared forests by setting them on fire. Sugar plantations required land for cane fields as well as sugar mills, which required firewood for fuel, used primarily to boil cane juice and heat syrup. Deforestation was the most conspicuous environmental transformation caused by the growth of sugar plantations, and it triggered numerous residual impacts. The clearing of forests accelerated soil erosion and desiccation, displaced and eradicated indigenous species, and drastically altered landscapes, which encouraged the habitation and proliferation of new species.

Why didn't these processes occur in the Mediterranean during the later middle ages? The lack of adequate forest resources, which had diminished as early as the eighth century, prevented the industry from expanding and precluded the cultivation of sugar in regions that lacked forest resources, such as the irrigable valleys of Morocco. The lack of abundant forest resources was perhaps the ultimate cause of the expense of sugar production in the medieval Mediterranean, which contributed to its status as a luxury good.[14] It was the search for cheap fuel, rather than more land, that led to sugar cultivation in the Atlantic islands. Accounts of the island of Madeira, translated literally as the 'isle of timber,' reveal its renown for rich forests that served as a source of cheap timber.[15] Madeira's dalliance with sugar production was brief, but substantial; by 1450, the island produced sugar for markets in Europe and beyond. Production peaked by about 1510 but already in the 1530s it had declined by as much as 90 percent.[16] Within a few decades sugar production consumed the island's forests, and by the 1560s gave way to the region's wine industry, which did not require large reserves of timber. Similarly, as sugar plantations developed in São Tomé and the Canary Islands, cultivators depleted the islands' forests and soil nutrients, contributing to the relatively quick decline of the eastern Atlantic sugar industry by the end of the sixteenth century.[17]

One of the most salient factors in hastening the decline of production in the Mediterranean and eastern Atlantic islands was the rise of sugar in Brazil. Portuguese entrepreneurs began growing sugar in Brazil by about 1516, shortly after their settlement in forests and fields occupied by Tupi cultivators. Initially, Portuguese and French traders were interested in exploiting forest resources, particularly brazilwood, in addition to jaguar skins and indigenous birds. However by the mid-sixteenth century, with the introduction of the robust variety of sugar cane known as Creole cane, sugar grew as the colony's primary export. By the 1580s, Brazil emerged as the leading producer of sugar in the Atlantic.[18]

The primary cause of Brazil's comparative success as a sugar colony was its rich land and forests. Throughout the seventeenth century, European visitors often referred to the region as a 'forest zone' (*zona da mata*).[19] Two tropical forests, the Atlantic Forest and the Amazonian Forest, converge in Pernambuco. The wonder and amazement expressed in contemporary accounts reveal the comparative wealth and abundance of natural resources, including the density and profusion of trees and wildlife.[20] Sugar planter Ambrósio Fernandes Brandão wrote that, 'the humidity that all the soils of Brazil enjoy makes them produce so abundantly that any kind of stick thrust into the earth will send forth roots and soon bear fruit.'[21] Seemingly 'endless' forests, nutrient-rich soil, and abundant sources of water provided the necessary elements that allowed planters to transform the environment into a lucrative sugar colony.[22] Of course, the productivity of Brazilian planters depended on their reliance on the importation of enslaved African labourers. In fact, the abundance of environmental resources in the region increased demand for labour, and in turn, accelerated the African slave trade.

Due to high rates of production in the seventeenth century, scholars have referred to the period as Brazil's 'golden age' of sugar. High rates of production relied on 'unrestrained exploitation of the Atlantic forests.'[23] By the early-seventeenth century, Pernambuco's sugar fields were already located up to fifty kilometres inland, and as a result, loggers began to delve deeper into the interior forests for timber. Usually they would clear forests along a river, which could then be used to transport sugar to the coast.[24] The Portuguese crown issued land grants, with value based on the amount of available forest.[25] A popular belief that sugar cane flourished in forest soils, which were rich in minerals, stimulated rapid expansion into the interior. Cultivators grew sugar on a plot for fifteen to twenty years, until they depleted the soil and yields declined; they then 'abandoned those cane fields and carved out new ones from burnt and cleared forestlands.' In 1700, cane fields occupied about 120 square kilometres of land; however, between 1550 and 1700, planters had depleted more than 1,000 square kilometres of forests as they abandoned fields and found new ones, and consumed more than 1,200 square kilometres of surrounding forests for fuel.[26]

In the early-seventeenth century, British, French, and Dutch entrepreneurs began establishing small island colonies in Caribbean territories that Spanish and Portuguese settlers had not occupied. British settlements in St. Kitts and Barbados began growing tobacco for export, and by the 1640s, transitioned to sugar.[27] In less than twenty years, Barbadian planters had cleared most of the island's forests, resulting in a severe transformation to the island's soil, climate, flora, and fauna (Figure 9.1). Deforestation displaced and eventually eradicated numerous species that lived in the forest canopy, including land birds and large mammals, and possibly the island's monkeys.[28] The nutrient-rich, tropical soil suffered from leaching, weathering, compaction, erosion, and an overall decline in fertility.[29] By the end of the seventeenth century, Barbadian planters 'complained endlessly of declining crop yields, insect and vermin plagues, drought, barren soil, and rising costs,' which instigated a move from Barbados to the larger territories Jamaica and Hispaniola (Figure 9.2).[30] Jason W. Moore argues that lowered soil quality instigated planters

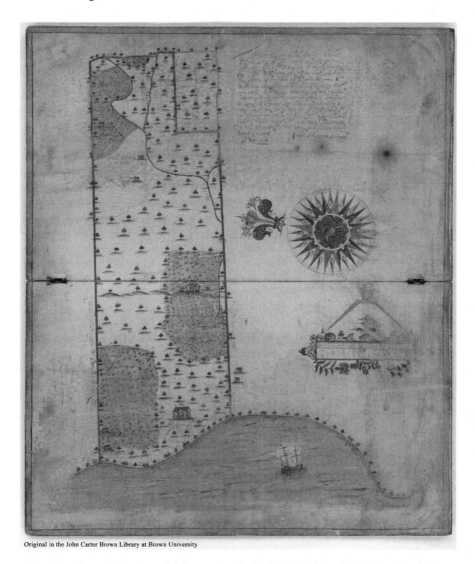

FIGURE 9.1 Representation of deforestation in Barbados. Map of John Hapcott, 'This plott representeth the forme of three hundred acres of land part of a plantation called the Fort Plantation of which 300 acres Cap. Thos. Middleton of London hath purchased'. Watercolour, London, *c*.1646. Courtesy of the John Carter Brown Library.

to purchase more slaves, so that 'the pressures to exploit the soil and the slaves were accordingly intensified.'[31]

In the eighteenth century, as France expanded its colonial territories, prospectors began to establish sugar plantations in the fertile islands of Martinique and Guadeloupe. Rich in mountain, evergreen, and seasonal forests, Martinique gradually developed a plantation-based economy, focused on sugar by the

IMPOVERISHED SUGAR-ESTATES, BARBADOS

FIGURE 9.2 'Impoverished Sugar-Estates, Barbados', in Robert T. Hill, *Cuba and Porto Rico With Other Islands of the West Indies: Their Topography, Climate, Flora, Products, Industries, Cities, People, Political Conditions, Etc.* (New York: The Century Co., 1898), p. 404. Courtesy of www.archive.org.

mid-seventeenth century. Land clearance for plantations, in addition to hardwoods, transformed the coastal forests; planters adopted a system of intensive land use and abandonment that led to high levels of soil erosion, leaving depleted fields for new ones. By 1783, more than fifty percent of the island had been altered substantially, and no longer housed original pre-colonial plant cover.[32]

During this time, the French colony of Saint-Domingue, on the western side of Hispaniola, developed into a highly profitable sugar colony. In previous centuries, the island was largely covered with forests and tropical vegetation; the indigenous Taino referred to the island as Haiti, sometimes translated as 'Green Island.' Spanish settlers had brought cane to Hispaniola as early as Columbus' second voyage in 1493, and exported it to Europe by about 1516. However, after its initial settlement colonists lost interest in the territory and focused on acquiring silver and gold in Peru and Mexico, and the region was inhabited by French pirates, African creoles, and others of mixed European and African descent, who mostly lived as subsistence cultivators. Political developments in Europe, notably the Treaty of Utrecht, led to French immigration, and the growth of the sugar industry after 1713 proceeded rapidly. For much of the eighteenth century, under French colonial rule, the territory of Saint-Domingue served as the world's most productive sugar colony. By the close of the century, most of the island's forest resources had been depleted. Today, only one percent of Haiti remains forested.[33] Figure 9.3 reveals the stark contrast along the border between Haiti and the Dominican Republic.

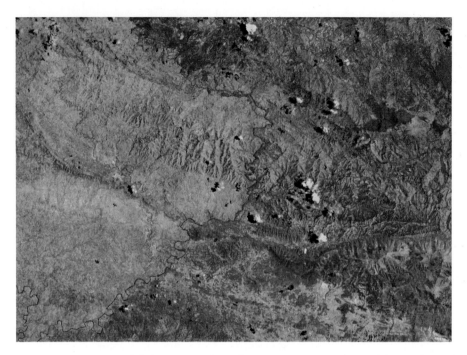

FIGURE 9.3 Erosion and deforestation along the Haiti/Dominican Republic Border. From NASA: http://svs.gsfc.nasa.gov/vis/a000000/a002600/a002640/

The late-eighteenth century also marked the rise of Cuban sugar production. Small-scale cultivators produced sugar for local use in the early sixteenth century, but during the British occupation of Havana during the Seven Years' War, the island saw a rise in slavery and sugar production. After the Haitian Revolution, and the decline of sugar in Haiti, Cuba emerged as the world's most productive sugar colony.

Prior to its rise, Spanish colonists valued Cuba for its precious woods. The Spanish Crown retained ownership of the island's forest resources, and throughout the eighteenth century, guarded the island's forest wealth by enacting a series of laws that made it illegal for landowners to chop down forests. Until the end of the eighteenth century Cuba was an island covered by forests, with many precious woods including mahogany, cedar, ebony, dagame, quebracho, and giant palms. Early observers consistently noted the abundance of trees. One said that a person could walk from one end of the island to the other in the shade provided by the wealth of trees.[34] In 1755, an observer wrote that the island seemed 'entirely covered in a continuous forest of precious woods.'[35] As Cuba's sugar economy expanded in the late-eighteenth century, it developed around new, industrial technologies, including steam-powered sugar mills.[36] New methods of processing required greater amounts of fuel, straining the limits of forest conservation laws. Turn-of-the-century legal battles over the protection of Cuban forests were resolved by 1805, when sugar planters gained what Manuel Moreno Fraginals calls the 'right to destroy the forests.'[37] Cuban sugar technician José Ignacio Echegoyen observed that 'the sugar mill's need for firewood is alarming – and where are the forests that can meet it?'[38] By 1809, sugar mills used twice as much wood as they did in the late-eighteenth century, and the amount of forest depleted for land and fuel increased at an alarming rate over the nineteenth century. Fraginals argues that 'sugar exterminated the forests,' resulting in soil deterioration and erosion, causing water sources to dry.[39]

Since the late-eighteenth century, Cuba had relied on importing additional timber from the United States, particularly pine and cypress from the lower Mississippi Valley in French Louisiana.[40] Before Louisiana began producing sugar, the region's primary exports were timber and fur. Timber traders shipped wood from New Orleans to Havana, which Cuban planters used for fuel, in addition to sugar-boxes to ship granulated sugar to Europe and North America. In the early-nineteenth century, as Cuban sugar planters burned through the island's forest wealth, they were also the primary consumer of wood from Louisiana. Like Cuba, southern Louisiana emerged as a sugar-producing region after the Haitian Revolution, and engaged in a similar process of deforestation and expansion. The major obstacles to building plantations in the lower Mississippi valley were the vast swamps and wetlands that surrounded New Orleans.

Water management projects

As a tropical grass, sugar cane requires a plentiful supply of water. Large-scale cane cultivation necessitated intensive water management systems that structurally altered the ecology and landscape in sugar-producing regions. Specific practices varied across the diverse ecosystems that sugar prospectors transformed into plantation landscapes, resulting in a broad spectrum of water management projects. Most plantations utilized existing river and rainfall patterns to irrigate crops, and supplemented them by building canals, dams, reservoirs, and irrigation ditches. Canals also enabled the transport of processed sugar from plantations to port cities. In marshes and wetlands, common in much of the lowlands of the Caribbean, planters utilized the labour of slaves and indentured servants in land clearance and swamp drainage projects, which enabled the expansion of cane fields. In some cases, planters installed water wheels to power mills, and diverted natural water sources for this purpose.

Earlier models of production in the Mediterranean and Atlantic islands shaped the development of water management projects to support sugar cultivation in the Americas.[41] With the spread of Islamic rule in the eighth through eleventh centuries, the diffusion of Asian crops into Syria, Palestine, Egypt, and into the Mediterranean and Iberia led to the development of intensive irrigation technologies, particularly in subtropical regions that began growing sugar.[42] In the 1430s and 1440s, Portuguese cultivators in Madeira developed a system of irrigation canals known as *levadas*, which formed the island's 'most distinctive geographical feature, extending 2,100 kilometres on an island that runs just 50 kilometres east-to-west.'[43]

Caribbean planters constructed similar projects. In Martinique, plantations relied on dams, reservoirs, and waterwheels to power the mills. Large canals and underground flumes brought water from the rivers to the plantations for irrigation and to power mills.[44] In Saint-Domingue, by 1739, over 350 large sugar estates had been established throughout the colony's 'well-watered, well-drained land.'[45] Over the next twenty years the French Crown invested in large-scale irrigation projects, and sent engineers to oversee the digging of irrigation canals across the region's floodplains, including the Artibonite Plain, the Cul de Sac Plain, and the Plain of Les Cayes. By 1760, sugar plantations occupied 40,000 hectares of irrigated land. This process of expansion and irrigation continued until the eve of the Haitian Revolution.[46]

Similar water management strategies enabled the growth of Louisiana's sugar industry in the nineteenth century. As the sugar industry grew rapidly after 1817, development was characterized by swamp drainage combined with the construction of artificial levees, canals, and waterways in the Mississippi floodplains and delta region. Beyond the rare section of high ground that was the Old City (*Vieux Carré*), the region consisted of mostly swampland (Figure 9.4).[47] Sugar planters drained these regions, and built canals to connect their plantations to the port of New Orleans. Sugar planters relied on drainage canals and ditches to keep their sugar crops from flooding. In his manual on sugar cane cultivation, Benjamin Silliman advised planters that:

> The draining of the land ... merits sugar planters generally ... It is only when the drains are sufficiently frequent and deep, and carried far back into the swamps, that the land can be delivered, with the requisite rapidity, of the water from the rains, and the filtration which takes place through the banks of the river during the spring, when its level is above that of the land. Unless the land is capable of rapid drainage, it is impossible to deprive it of its coldness and clamminess; both of which are hostile to the early budding of cane plants.[48]

Early planters established plantations along natural levees because these elevated regions provided the only well-drained soil in the region, safe from flooding.[49] Plantations occupied land tracts at ninety-degree angles to the rivers and bayous, so each had access to riparian space and could build drainage canals to the backswamp. Because levee land was required for a viable plantation, demand increased as more prospective sugar planters moved to the region in the early decades of the nineteenth century, and 'since the better drained land lay nearest the river, earliest settlement faced the river while latecomers settled farther back.'[50] By 1820, newcomers from the eastern United States established plantations along levees of the Mississippi as well as along bayous Lafourche and Teche.[51] However, even levee sites were susceptible to flood damage, particularly on plantations located along the Mississippi, as 'periodic high water topped the levees damaging crops and buildings and in severe cases, literally wiping out entire plantations.'[52]

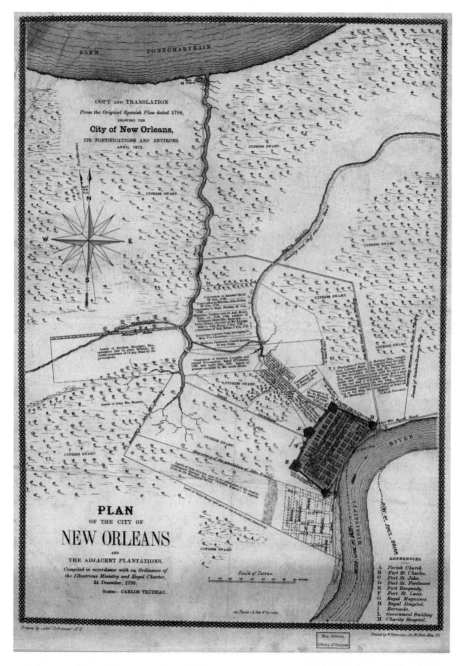

FIGURE 9.4 Plan of the City of New Orleans and adjacent plantations, 1875. Original produced by Charles Laveau Trudeau (*c.*1750–1816). Library of Congress Geography and Map Division Washington, D.C. 20540–4650 USA G4014.N5 1798.T7 1875

Planters responded by ordering slaves and hired labourers to dig ditches and drainage canals, and to reinforce natural levee lands by creating artificial levees. The size and scope of hydraulic engineering projects, characterized by the building of large canals, levees, mechanical drainage systems, and reservoirs, escalated in the Mississippi Delta region in the nineteenth century.[53] Despite these efforts, high water would often generate a breach in the levee, known as a *crevasse*. Breaches caused devastating floods that lasted for weeks, resulting in severe crop damage. Such transformations in aquatic ecosystems had severe consequences, for indigenous wildlife and human populations.

Disease ecology

The growth of large-scale sugar mono-cropping, in the form of the plantation complex, drove the expansion of West African slavery in the tropical Americas and the slave trade in Central and West Africa. As planters demanded increasing numbers of enslaved Africans, West African pathogens, including the yellow fever virus and malarial parasites, together with their host mosquitoes, arrived in the Americas onboard slave ships. The spread of African diseases was more than just a result of the growth of the Atlantic slave trade; their prevalence was directly connected to ecological changes forged by the growing sugar industry.

In the Americas, environmental impacts of the growth of sugar plantations, including changes in the landscape and ecology due to deforestation and water management projects, combined with heightened maritime activity, urbanization, and demographic changes enabled by the productive sugar industry, created an environment that was extremely hospitable to mosquito-borne diseases, especially yellow fever and malaria. The *Aëdes aegypti* (*A. aegypti*) mosquito, which entomologists have described as an 'urban species' that thrives in manmade environments, served as the primary insect host for the yellow fever virus. Various species of *anopheles* mosquitoes, which host malarial *plasmodia*, are more rustic, and thrive in swamps, savannahs, prairies, and forests. Ecological changes stemming from the rise of the sugar plantation complex fashioned niches that favoured the proliferation of both types of mosquitoes.

Deforestation had a dire effect on indigenous animal populations, radically altering island ecosystems. Impacts were especially severe when sugar prospectors elected to burn forests, an acute process that killed more than plant life. The clearing of forests resulted in the eradication or near eradication of numerous animal species, particularly those that lived in the forest canopy, including large mammals, rodents, bats, and birds. Bird and bat communities that resided highest typically fed on insects, and their extermination opened a viable niche for mosquitoes.[54]

Among the larger species whose habitats diminished were indigenous primates, especially those who resided in the forest canopy, such as howler monkeys. For example, David Watts estimates that between 1624 and 1645, ecological changes by settlement populations depleted native monkey populations in St. Kitts and Barbados.[55] It is possible that the introduction of yellow fever contributed to the extinction of indigenous monkeys during the process of felling trees. Like humans, monkeys that had not been previously exposed to the virus had extremely high mortality rates, and combined with the decimation of their habitat, yellow fever may have contributed to their extinction.[56] In Brazil, the introduction of the yellow fever virus had an enduring impact on indigenous monkey and mosquito populations, which served as a reservoir for the virus in the jungles of Amazonia.

Water management infrastructure on plantations, in surrounding areas, and in cities, also encouraged the habitation of mosquitoes. Drainage ditches and artificial waterways created habitats for *anopheles* mosquitoes. During the construction of these projects, a hybrid environment that attracted both species emerged. Ships, harbours, and port cities provided the ideal conditions favoured by *A. aegypti* mosquitoes.

Accounts of deaths among canal construction workers illustrate the process of the creation of new mosquito habitats. For instance in New Orleans, the simultaneous rise of sugar and yellow fever reveal the perilous consequences of canal construction in cane plantation zones. The first epidemic of yellow fever in 1796 coincided with a major canal-building project, aimed to connect the *Vieux Carré* to Lake Pontchartrain and Bayou St. John. In 1795, west of the old city, in the space now occupied by Audubon Park, Etienne de Boré, the son of French immigrants, successfully grew and granulated sugar. In the next year, the governor of Louisiana, the Baron Frances Louis Hector de Carondelet, began construction of the 2.5-kilometre canal project. Sources indicate that 'all of the labourers engaged in the work were carried off by yellow fever, and a violent epidemic ensued.'[57] While most planters relied on African-American slaves for agricultural labour, they usually hired Irish and German immigrants to perform construction-related labour on plantations, including the arduous tasks of digging ditches and drainage canals, as well as clearing swamps, rivers, and bayous.[58] Some Irish immigrants worked for 'local contractors, who hired out teams of immigrants to conduct laborious and hazardous plantation maintenance knee-deep in disease-infested waters.'[59] Malaria-carrying *anopheles* mosquitoes often resided in undeveloped swamps, bogs, and marshes. While the process of developing these swamp and prairie regions disrupted the preferred habitat of *anopheles* mosquitoes, it created a niche for *A. aegypti*. As a result, immigrants who worked as ditchers and delvers encountered both types of mosquitoes, and were exposed to both malaria and yellow fever. Since most European newcomers did not have contact with these fevers prior to their immigration to Louisiana, they were particularly susceptible and subsequently suffered high mortality rates during epidemics.

Anecdotal and empirical evidence reveals a broad connection between the rise of sugar and yellow fever. The earliest recorded epidemics occurred in 1647–48 in the colonies of Barbados, Guadeloupe, and St. Kitts, more than 100 years before the first recorded yellow fever epidemics in West Africa. These epidemics occurred shortly after colonists began planting sugar and importing African slaves to the islands, as sugar production expanded rapidly in the 1640s, when Dutch traders supplied in English sugar planters with slaves and techniques for processing the cane.[60] The first appearance of yellow fever in Barbados was unusual since residents were not familiar with the disease, and it was exceptionally overwhelming because it reached epidemic proportions, killing roughly fifteen percent of the population.[61] The epidemic proved to be so devastating, that in his chronicle of life in mid-seventeenth-century Barbados, Richard Ligon compared it to the plague in England.[62] Similarly in Saint-Domingue, there are no records of yellow fever for more than 150 years after the Spanish claimed the island of Hispaniola. As French colonists established plantations in the mid-eighteenth century, outbreaks of yellow fever appeared among newly arrived military forces. Records show several outbreaks between 1733–1755. By the mid-century, it is likely that yellow fever became endemic in the colony.[63]

On plantations, reservoirs and cisterns, in addition to numerous inadvertent water receptacles, provided ample breeding spaces for *A. aegypti* (Figure 9.5). These mosquitoes seem to have a unique preference for man-made containers, especially those made of wood, cement, or clay.[64] Plantation environments usually had an abundance of cisterns, water-barrels, and clay pots, ideal for *A. aegypti* to lay eggs. Even small plantations needed hundreds of clay pots, used to clarify crystallized sugar.[65] Larger plantations could have more than ten thousand pots in use over the course of one year. Even if these pots were broken or discarded, they could still hold a small amount of rainwater to provide a breeding space for *A. aegypti*.[66]

FIGURE 9.5 'A heap of odd water receptacles, collected out of yards. Barbados, 1909', in Rubert Boyce, *Yellow Fever and its Prevention: A Manual for Medical Students and Practitioners* (New York: E.P. Dutton & Company, 1911), p. 298. Courtesy of Columbia University Library.

Additionally, sugar plantations provided nourishment to *A. aegypti* mosquitoes, in the form of sucrose, found in various forms of unrefined and refined sugar cane. James Goodyear's groundbreaking analysis demonstrates how the emergence of yellow fever was connected with the rise of sugar in Guadeloupe, Barbados, St. Kitts, the Yucatán peninsula, and Cuba, and emphasizes how the material characteristics of sugar facilitated the proliferation of *A. aegypti* mosquitoes.[67] These mosquitoes 'are especially attracted to sweet fluids,' including 'fruits, honey, flowers and sugar.'[68] Though human blood is the primary meal of the female mosquito, it can be supplemented by a diet of sucrose, and adding sucrose to its diet can increase its lifespan. Sucrose was available throughout the year on Caribbean sugar plantations, located in places such as on used cane that was discarded after it had been pressed (*bagasse*), in cooling vats that held boiling cane juice, and in the run-off from the clay pots that held the crystallized sugar.[69] Additionally, sucrose was likely available along docks and harbors, where shippers stored sugar barrels before export (Figure 9.6).

In addition to transforming the landscape, the rise of sugar heightened maritime trade in the Atlantic, triggered economic growth, and enabled rapid urban growth in

LANDING, ST. PIERRE

FIGURE 9.6 'Sugar barrels on the landing dock in St. Pierre, Martinique', from Robert T. Hill, *Cuba and Porto Rico With Other Islands of the West Indies: Their Topography, Climate, Flora, Products, Industries, Cities, People, Political Conditions, Etc.* (New York: The Century Co., 1898), p. 349. Courtesy of www.archive.org

port cities throughout the Caribbean, Gulf Coast, and Brazil. Curtin has argued that the sugar revolution produced a 'new version of the plantation complex' that was 'more specialized [and] more dependent on networks of maritime, intercontinental communication.'[70] Plantations, built in close proximity to river ports or canals, were in close and frequent contact with urban port cities via riverboats. The infrastructure used to move sugar from plantations to port cities also transported infected mosquitoes. Maritime expansion during the seventeenth century played a critical role in inciting early epidemics, and by the eighteenth century yellow fever had become endemic in plantation societies across the Americas. Throughout the early modern period, and into the nineteenth century, observers connected outbreaks of yellow fever with maritime activity. In his study of *A. aegypti*, S.R. Christophers has argued that 'at the dock side and water front of teeming harbours in moist and rainy tropical climates, with miscellaneous collections of water in machinery, country boats and even in the old days in ships, whereby it is spread to other ports and harbours, the species obtains conditions optimal for its proliferation.'[71] In the eighteenth century it was also known as 'yellow jack' because of prevalence on seaborne vessels, which were required to display a yellow quarantine flag (or jack) when carrying infected passengers. Chroniclers of the disease often associated its appearance with ships that appeared to initiate epidemics. Accounts of yellow fever outbreaks in 'healthy' port cities generally traced the onset of epidemics to vessels that apparently contracted the disease when stationed at an infected port. For example, following the first recorded epidemic in Recife, Brazil, in 1685, the Pernambuco region gained a reputation as a source of yellow fever.[72] In an account of the yellow fever that arrived in Martinique in 1690 on the *Oriflamme*, Père Labat wrote that it had picked up the fever when it 'touched at Pernambuco.'[73] In 1866, after the U.S.S. *Jamestown* stopped in Panama, United States Navy Surgeon Delavan Bloodgood reasoned that a subsequent shipboard outbreak was caused by two soldiers who spent eleven days on duty in an 'unhealthy' location, three miles from where the ship was docked.[74]

The links between the growth of large-scale sugar production, maritime trade, and urbanization had numerous indirect and unpredictable impacts. For example, cities in the Caribbean and Gulf Coast adopted common methods of collecting and storing water, which created niches for *A. aegypti* mosquitoes. In Barbados, residents on plantations and cities relied on collecting rainwater for drinking and domestic use. Richard Ligon noted that on plantations, the common practice of building clay ponds to collect water attracted insects, and in cities, Barbadians kept cisterns near their homes to collect rainwater from roofs and gutters.[75] Similarly, M.E. Descourtilz, a French naturalist visiting Haiti after the revolution, noted that mosquitoes were ubiquitous, especially near homes and water sources.[76] Homes in New Orleans had similar features, as rainwater served as the city's primary source of drinking water (Figure 9.7).

The growth of sugar plantations and port cities shaped demographic patterns, through forced and free migrations of Africans and Europeans. The growth of large-scale sugar plantations accelerated the African slave trade, and the burgeoning sugar

A NEW ORLEANS YARD AND CISTERN.

FIGURE 9.7 'A New Orleans yard and cistern', in Eliza Moore Chinn McHatten Ripley, *Social Life in New Orleans: Being Recollections of My Girlhood* (New York and London: D. Appleton and Company, 1912), p. 33. University of North Carolina, Documenting the American South Collection.

industry and subsequent growth of port cities throughout the Greater Caribbean encouraged immigration from Europe. The occurrence of epidemics was only possible because of the continual introduction of a population of newcomers who had not previously encountered the yellow fever virus.

A similar process enabled the virus to become endemic in West African port cities, as they emerged as destinations for enslaved African migrants. Trade and interaction increased between interior forest/savannah zones and slave ports, which developed as centres of maritime trade and urban development. Despite the existence of detailed historical records of yellow fever epidemics in the seventeenth-century Caribbean, the earliest documented outbreaks in West Africa appear more than one hundred years later, in the late-eighteenth century.[77] Epidemics escalated in West Africa after 1816, and by the 1850s yellow fever became endemic in coastal cities in Sierra Leone, Ghana (Gold Coast), and Benin.[78] The rise of endemic yellow fever in West Africa was another indirect and unpredictable outcome of the growth of sugar and slavery in the Americas.

Conclusions

As long as sugar was a luxury good, its production did not cause rapid ecological change. For thousands of years, small-scale cultivators in India and China supplied local and distant markets.[79] Mintz's detailed account of the increase in British consumption, followed by an increase in its colonies, North America, and Europe, demonstrates the 'neatly interdigitated' relationship between patterns of consumption and changing methods of production. The rise of sugar as an item of mass consumption in the eighteenth and nineteenth centuries, along with tea and coffee, marks a turning point in the ecological history of sugar cane.[80] Increasing rates of per capita consumption stimulated the intensification of the plantation system, which necessitated massive environmental transformations.

Similar ecological patterns continued through the modern era, in regions beyond the Atlantic Americas. Dutch production in Java diminished as a result of heavy deforestation and soil deterioration in the late-eighteenth century.[81] The transition from peasant production to plantation monocultures in the late-nineteenth and twentieth centuries was characterized by soil exhaustion and the construction of large-scale irrigation projects, in colonial and postcolonial contexts throughout sugar-producing regions in Mauritius, India, Indonesia, Australia, the Philippines, and beyond. Sugar production ushered numerous other environmental changes that are beyond the scope of this essay, such as increasing the frequency of floods and forest fires. Further, industrial sugar processing in the nineteenth and twentieth centuries polluted the air, contributed to climate change, and affected weather and rainfall patterns.[82] Finally, the ecology of sugar consumption reveals another dimension of sugar cane's far-reaching impacts. Increased rates of consumption had considerable impacts on human health that cut across social and economic classes. As sugar became a significant source of calories, a host of health and dietary problems emerged, ranging from nutritional deficiencies to increased rates of obesity, diabetes, and coronary disease. Nutrient depletion in the soil affected agriculture more broadly. The use of fertile land for sugar production and the depletion of fertile soil exacerbated famines in sugar-producing regions. Sugar alone did not cause these myriad outcomes; the intensification of sugar production and consumption, a process that began in the early modern Atlantic, was interwoven with global movements toward colonial regimes, forced labour migrations, capital investment, and industrialization.

Notes and References

1. See Richard Dunn, *Sugar and Slaves, The Rise of the Planter Class in the English West Indies, 1624–1713* (Chapel Hill, NC: University of North Carolina Press, 1972); Manuel Moreno Fraginals, *El Ingenio. Complejo económico-social cubano del azúcar*, 3 vols. (La Habana: Editorial de Ciencias Sociales, 1978); Rebecca J. Scott, 'Defining the Boundaries of Freedom in the World of Cane: Cuba, Brazil, and Louisiana after Emancipation,' *American Historical Review* 99.1 (1994): 70–102; Dale Tomich, 'Small Islands, Huge Comparisons: Caribbean Plantations, Historical Unevenness, and Capitalist Modernity,' *Social Science History* 18.3 (1994): 339–358; Jason W. Moore, 'Sugar and the Expansion of the Early Modern World-Economy: Commodity Frontiers, Ecological Transformation, and Industrialization,' *Review: A Journal of the Fernand Braudel Center* 23.3 (2000): 409–433; B.W. Higman, 'The Sugar Revolution,' *Economic History Review* 53.2 (2000), 213; Philip D. Curtin, *The Rise and Fall of the Plantation Complex: Essays in Atlantic History* (Cambridge: Cambridge University Press, 2002); Wendy A. Woloson, *Refined Tastes: Sugar, Confectionery, and Consumers in Nineteenth-Century America* (Baltimore: Johns Hopkins University Press, 2002); Russell R. Menard, *Sweet Negotiations: Sugar, Slavery, and Plantation Agriculture in Early Barbados* (Charlottesville: University of Virginia Press, 2006).
2. Sidney Mintz, *Sweetness and Power, The Place of Sugar in Modern History* (London: Penguin, 1985).
3. David Watts, *The West Indies, Patterns of Development, Culture, and Environmental Change since 1492* (Cambridge: Cambridge University Press, 1987); Richard Grove, *Green Imperialism: Colonial Expansion, Tropical Island Edens and the Origins of Environmentalism, 1600–1860* (Cambridge: University Press, 1995); Moore, 'Sugar'; Curtin, *Rise and Fall*; J.R. McNeill, *Mosquito Empires: Ecology and War in the Greater Caribbean, 1620–1914* (Cambridge: Cambridge University Press, 2010).
4. In this sense, my work confirms some of the arguments in McNeill's recent *Mosquito Empires*.
5. See Mintz, *Sweetness and Power*, 50; Mintz argues that this 'land-and-factory' combination necessitated scheduled and disciplined labour regimes.
6. Ulbe Bosma, *The Sugar Plantation in India and Indonesia, Industrial Production, 1770–2010* (Cambridge: Cambridge University Press, 2013), 11; J.H. Galloway, 'Sugar,' in *The Cambridge World History of Food*, ed. Kenneth F. Kiple and Kriemhild Coneè Ornelas (Cambridge University Press, 2000); Candace Goucher, *Congotay! Congotay! A Global History of Caribbean Food* (Armonk, New York: M.E. Sharpe, 2014), 92.
7. J.H. Galloway, 'The Mediterranean Sugar Industry,' *Geographical Review* 67.2 (1977), 177.
8. Galloway, 'Mediterranean Sugar Industry,' 188; Bosma, *Sugar Plantation*, 24–25.
9. Galloway, 'Mediterranean Sugar Industry,' 186; Mintz, *Sweetness and Power*, 27.
10. Mazumdar, *Sugar and Society in China*, 191; Galloway, 'Mediterranean Sugar Industry,' 190.
11. Curtin, *Rise and Fall*, xi.
12. Bosma, *Sugar Plantation*, 26.
13. Note that this figure includes date, palm, and coconut sugar. See Bosma, *Sugar Plantation*, 17–18; W.H. Sykes, 'Contributions to the Statistics of Sugar Produced within the British Dominions in India,' *Journal of the Statistical Society of London* 13.1 (1850), 2; Kenneth Pomeranz, *The Great Divergence, China, Europe, and the Making of the Modern World Economy* (Princeton: Princeton University Press, 2000), 120–121.
14. Galloway, 'Mediterranean Sugar Industry,' 188.
15. Jason W. Moore, 'Madeira, Sugar, and the Conquest of Nature in the "First" Sixteenth Century. Part I: From "Island of Timber" to Sugar Revolution,' *Review: A Journal of the Fernand Braudel Center* 32.4 (2009), 350–351 and 355.
16. Moore, 'Madeira,' 345 and 358; Jason W. Moore, 'Madeira, Sugar, and the Conquest of Nature in the 'First' Sixteenth Century. Part II: From Regional Crisis to Commodity Frontier, 1506–1530,' *Review: A Journal of the Fernand Braudel Center* 33.1 (2010), 2.

17. Stefan Halikowski Smith, 'The Mid-Atlantic Islands, A Theatre of Early Modern Ecocide?' *International Review of Social History* 55 (2010), 67.
18. John F. Richards, *The Unending Frontier. An Environmental History of the Early Modern World* (Berkeley: University of California Press, 2003), 388.
19. Thomas D. Rogers, *The Deepest Wounds, A Labour and Environmental History of Sugar in Northeast Brazil* (Chapel Hill, NC: University of North Carolina Press, 2010), 2.
20. Rogers, *Deepest Wounds*, 23.
21. Ambrósio Fernandes Brandão, *Dialogues of the Great Things of Brazil* (*Diálogos das grandezas do Brasil*), trans. Frederick Holden Hall, William F. Harrison, and Dorothy Winters Welker (Albuquerque: University of New Mexico Press, [1618] 1987), 16; see also Rogers, *Deepest Wounds*, 23.
22. Rogers, *Deepest Wounds*, 28.
23. Rogers, *Deepest Wounds*, 31; Richards, *Unending Frontier*, 392.
24. Rogers, *Deepest Wounds*, 31–33.
25. Rogers, *Deepest Wounds*, 29.
26. Richards, *Unending Frontier*, 392–393.
27. Richards, *Unending Frontier*, 419.
28. While several historians note that the indigenous monkeys of Barbados became extinct in the 17th century, there is no archaeological evidence of indigenous monkeys on the island; see: Watts, *The West Indies*, 156; McNeill, *Mosquito Empires*, 28; Richards, *Unending Frontier*, 421; see also Siobhán Cooke, Alfred L. Rosenberger, and Samuel Turvey, 'An Extinct Monkey from Haiti and the Origins of the Greater Antillean Primates,' *PNAS* 108.7 (2010), 2699; Richard F. Kay *et al.*, 'Preliminary Notes on a Newly Discovered Skull of the Extinct Monkey *Antillothrix* from Hispaniola and the Origin of the Greater Antillean Monkeys,' *Journal of Human Evolution* 60 (2011), 124–128.
29. Richards, *Unending Frontier*, 422.
30. Moore, 'Sugar,' 424.
31. Moore, 'Sugar,' 425.
32. Richards, *Unending Frontier*, 431, 435, and 436–437.
33. Jared Diamond, *Collapse, How Societies Choose to Fail or Succeed* (London: Penguin, 2005), 329.
34. Manuel Moreno Fraginals, *The Sugarmill (El Ingenio): The Socioeconomic Complex of Sugar in Cuba, 1760–1860*, trans. Cedric Belfrage (New York: Monthly Review Press, 1976), 74.
35. Nicolás Joseph de Ribera, quoted in McNeill, *Mosquito Empires*, 30.
36. Fraginals, *Sugarmill*, 38.
37. Fraginals, *Sugarmill*, 74.
38. Fraginals, *Sugarmill*, 17 and 74–6.
39. Fraginals, *Sugarmill*, 76.
40. Fraginals, *Sugarmill*, 76.
41. Galloway, 'Mediterranean Sugar Industry,' 180.
42. Galloway, 'Mediterranean Sugar Industry,' 180.
43. Moore, 'Madeira,' 356.
44. Richards, *Unending Frontier*, 436.
45. Richards, *Unending Frontier*, 438.
46. Richards, *Unending Frontier*, 438.
47. The French 'Old City,' or *Vieux Carré*, now occupies the space that is now commonly known as the 'French Quarter.'
48. Benjamin Silliman, *Manual on the Cultivation of the Sugar Cane and the Fabrication and Refinement of Sugar* (Washington DC: Francis Preston Blair, 1833), 15.
49. Sam B. Hilliard, 'Site Characteristics and Spatial Stability of the Louisiana Sugarcane Industry,' *Agricultural History* 53.1 (1979), 258.
50. Hilliard, 'Site Characteristics,' 258.

51. John Solomon Otto, *The Southern Frontiers, 1607–1860, Agricultural Evolution of the Colonial and Antebellum South* (New York: Greenwood Press, 1989), 120–121.
52. Hilliard, 'Site Characteristics,' 263.
53. L.G. De Russy, *Special Report Relative to the Cost of Draining the Swamp Lands Bordering on Lake Pontchartrain* (Baton Rouge: J.M. Taylor, 1859), 4–10; see also Ari Kelman, *A River and Its City: The Nature of Landscape in New Orleans* (Berkeley: University of California Press, 2003), 81; Craig Colten, *An Unnatural Metropolis: Wresting New Orleans from Nature* (Baton Rouge: Louisiana State University Press, 2005), 202, along with the essays in *Transforming New Orleans and its Environs: Centuries of Change*, ed. Colten (Pittsburgh: University of Pittsburgh Press, 2000).
54. Jason W. Moore, 'Sugar,' 421; McNeill, *Mosquito Empires*, 48; Watts, *West Indies*, 39.
55. Watts, *West Indies*, 168.
56. McNeill suggests that in the period between 1640 and 1690, African monkeys introduced to the Caribbean may have provided a sylvan reservoir for yellow fever. See McNeill, *Mosquito Empires*, 49–50.
57. Gayle Aiken, 'The Medical History of New Orleans,' in *The Standard History of New Orleans, Louisiana*, ed. Henry Rightor (Chicago: The Lewis Publishing Company, 1900), 206.
58. Richard Follett, *The Sugar Masters, Planters and Slaves in Louisiana's Cane World, 1820–1860* (Baton Rouge: Louisiana State University Press, 2005), 10, 39–40, and 85.
59. Follett, *Sugar Masters*, 85.
60. Dunn, *Sugar and Slaves*, 49–62.
61. Sheldon Watts, *Epidemics and History, Disease, Power and Imperialism* (New Haven: Yale University Press, 1997), 228.
62. Richard Ligon, *A True and Exact History of the Island of Barbados* (London: Peter Parker and Thomas Guy, 1673), 21; Dunn, *Sugar and Slaves*, 303–304.
63. McNeill, *Mosquito Empires*, 241. See also Médéric Louis Elie Moreau de Saint-Méry, *Description topographique, physique, civile, politique et historique de la partie française de l'isle Saint-Domingue* (Philadelphia: Chez l'auteur, 1797).
64. Charles Morrow Wilson, *Ambassadors in White: The Story of American Tropical Medicine* (New York: Henry Holt and Company, 1942), 269; James D. Goodyear, 'The Sugar Connection, A New Perspective on the History of Yellow Fever,' *Bulletin of the History of Medicine* 52 (1978), 12; S.R. Christophers, *Aedes Aegypti (L.) The Yellow Fever Mosquito, Its Life History, Bionomics and Structure* (Cambridge: Cambridge University Press, 1960), 57.
65. J.R. McNeill, 'Yellow Jack and Geopolitics, Environment, Epidemics, and the Struggles for Empire in the American Tropics, 1640–1830,' in *Rethinking Environmental History, World-System History and Global Environmental Change*, ed. Alf Hornborg, J.R. McNeill, and Joan Martinez-Alier (Lanham, MD: AltaMira Press, 2007), 205.
66. Goodyear, 'Sugar Connection,' 13.
67. Goodyear, 'Sugar Connection,' 12.
68. Christophers, *Aedes Aegypti*, 468–469.
69. Goodyear, 'Sugar Connection,' 12.
70. Curtin, *Rise and Fall*, 73.
71. Christophers, *Aedes Aegypti*, 54–55.
72. *Bulletin of the Pan American Health Association* 26.4 (1992), 140.
73. Henry Rose Carter, *Yellow Fever, An Epidemiological and Historical Study of its Place of Origin*, ed. Laura Armistead Carter and Wade Hampton Frost (Baltimore: The Williams & Wilkins Company, 1931), 196.
74. Delavan Bloodgood, *An Account of the Yellow Fever which Appeared in December, 1866, and Prevailed On Board the United States Ship Jamestown, Store and Hospital Ship at Panama* (Washington DC: Government Printing Office, 1873), 201.
75. Ligon, *True and Exact History of the Island of Barbados*, 28–9.
76. M.E. Descourtilz, quoted in McNeill, *Mosquito Empires*, 241.

77. See James Lind, *An Essay on Diseases Incidental to Europeans in Hot Climates* (London: T. Becket and P.A. De Hondt, 1768) and Johann P. Schotte, *A Treatise on the Synochus Atrabiolosa, A Contagious Fever which raged at Senegal in the Year 1778* (London: M. Scott, 1782). While Johann Schotte's account of the 1778 epidemic is commonly agreed upon by historians and chroniclers to be the first definitive epidemic, there is some compelling evidence of outbreaks prior to 1778. In addition to Lind's account, Schotte argues that there may have been an earlier outbreak. He notes an epidemic on the French settlement on the Island of Gorée. See also H.R. Carter, *Yellow Fever: An Epidemiological and Historical Study of Its Place of Origin* (Baltimore: The Williams & Wilkins Company, 1931), 257; Natalie Reys, *Saint-Louis du Sénégal a L'Epoque Précoloniale: L'Emergence d'une Société Métisse Originale, 1650–1854* (Paris: Université de Paris, 1982), 3, 69.
78. George Augustin, *History of Yellow Fever* (New Orleans: Searcy & Pfaff Ltd., 1909), 150–151.
79. Bosma, *Sugar Plantation*, 10.
80. Mintz, *Sweetness and Power*, 42; Bosma, *Sugar Plantation*, 17–18.
81. Bosma, *Sugar Plantation*, 16.
82. Moore, 'Madeira,' 375; Moore, 'Sugar,' 418 and 424; Mazumdar, *Sugar and Society*, 381–382.

10

COFFEE, MIND AND BODY

Global material culture and the eighteenth-century Hamburg import trade

Christine Fertig and Ulrich Pfister

Introduction

Long-distance trade was instrumental in globalizing European material culture. This chapter focuses on goods used for dietetic and medical purposes such as cinchona bark, jalapa ('black rhubarb') and asafoetida ('devil's dung'). It argues that the diffusion of such goods cannot be satisfactorily interpreted by adopting the now-traditional framework of the consumer revolution thesis. Rather, this process occurred in the context of an increasing appreciation of the individual and of care of the body in the wake of the Enlightenment movement. The globalization of European material culture involved intellectual efforts to frame how new foreign substances were used in European dietetic and medical practices. This occurred because traded goods enhancing bodily well-being assumed different meanings in the dietetic and medical practices prevailing in different parts of the world. Thus, we consider different strands of learned, practical and public discourses that 'glocalized' these substances related to the care of the self within European practices, connecting globally traded goods with local perceptions.[1]

Standard accounts that link early globalization with the eighteenth-century consumer revolution build on the relationship between the diversity of supply and the utility of consumption.[2] From the late seventeenth century, the growth in long-distance trade contributed to a differentiation of the supply of consumer goods. Consequently, goods acquired new functions, which in turn increased their utility. First, dressing fashionably acted as a source of prestige and, hence, could advance social status. Second, an increasing variety of consumer items such as plates, cutlery, furnishings, clocks and, possibly, books to be found within the household created utility by contributing to the construction of individual identity, often marking the acquisition and cultivation of personal taste.[3]

The spread of material objects that occupied and stimulated the minds of consumers was flanked, on the one hand, by colonial groceries such as sugar, coffee, tea, cacao and tobacco and, on the other hand, by substances contributing to bodily well-being through their dietetic or medical application such as cinchona or jalapa. To be sure, some colonial groceries such as tobacco and coffee had been used in early modern Europe as medicaments or substances with a dietetic connotation.[4] But a drastic reduction in their relative price made possible by an expansion of supply and improvements in product-specific transaction and transportation methods turned these goods into objects of mass consumption during the late-seventeenth and early-eighteenth centuries.[5] Hot beverages in particular, by combining bitter substances with sugar, created a welcome addition to the dull diet of the European lower classes heavily centred on carbohydrates derived from foods based on grain.[6] It was their capacity to complement existing diets – rather than product differentiation as in the case of consumer goods in the narrow sense – that lay at the heart of the rise of colonial groceries to the single most important category of intercontinental trade by the mid-eighteenth century.[7]

Substances that remained confined to dietetic and medical purposes also followed a history of their own: whereas their magnitude of trade in the eighteenth century was small, their growth was above average and comparable to the products and manufactured commodities at the centre of the consumer revolution. Whereas the inflow of these substances into Europe multiplied and improved consumers' options to care for their bodily well-being, the growth of this trade cannot be accounted for by the standard utility-of-consumption argument discussed above. Rather, access of European consumers to information relative to the use of specific substances must be considered a crucial factor contributing to their dissemination. Thus, the growth of European import trade in dietetic and medicinal substances went hand in hand with processes of classification, creation of meaning and accumulation of knowledge. These intellectual processes 'glocalized' the substances in question: they separated substances from the ritual and dietetic practices associated with them in non-European societies and reconfigured them for uses in a European context.[8] At the same time, information regarding these substances became detached from tacit knowledge and turned increasingly formal and classificatory.[9] The development of scientific botany, which was closely linked to colonial and economic interests, was instrumental for developing methods of systematizing and classifying medicinal plants originating in other continents.[10] Pharmaceutical handbooks destined for apothecaries described the dietetic or medical properties of plants and parts of animal bodies and sometimes included medical advice.

In this study we document the diffusion of exotic substances serving as expedients for bodily well-being on the basis of eighteenth-century Hamburg toll ledgers and contemporary German treatises. Thus, our research also contributes to the debate concerning the geographical extension of the late-seventeenth- and eighteenth-century consumer revolution. The salient features of this phenomenon have been studied primarily for north-western Europe so far; to what extent it occurred in other parts of the European mainland remains an open issue. This is particularly the case for Germany: since real wages were low compared to north-western Europe and actually fell after the 1730s until the early 1800s, it is difficult to see where mass demand for consumer goods and colonial commodities came from.[11] In addition, evidence from Württemberg suggests that state regulation of consumption held out longer than elsewhere and that craft guilds limited access of outsiders, particularly of women, to labour markets. This curtailed the articulation of consumer demand and an outward shift of labour supply.[12] It remains uncertain whether this result can be generalized to other regions of Germany characterized by different institutional characteristics, particularly an absence of rural guilds. It is important, therefore, to embed the spread of traded goods with dietetic and medical applications into the larger context of consumption practices in eighteenth-century Germany. Below we demonstrate, again on the basis of toll ledgers documenting import trade in Hamburg, the selective presence of elements of a consumer revolution, which qualifies the pessimistic picture drawn above in important respects. Still, there was no tendency of household goods to become necessities within the framework of a new middle-class life style as appears to have been the case in north-western Europe.

The remainder of this chapter is organized as follows: the first part contextualizes the trade in dietetic and medicinal substances by exploring the extent to which the volume and structure of imports reflect changes in the culture of consumption. This part rests on a preliminary analysis of toll ledgers that document the Hamburg overseas import trade from 1733 to 1798. In the second part, we use the same source to identify traded substances used for dietetic and medical purposes. We draw on merchant manuals, handbooks for apothecaries and encyclopaedias published in the eighteenth and early nineteenth centuries to track processes of classification, creation of meaning and accumulation of knowledge that served to glocalize these exotic goods to dietetic and medical practices prevailing in Germany.

Was there a consumer revolution in eighteenth-century Germany?

At first sight, eighteenth-century Germany was not propitious ground for a consumer revolution. Between the five-year periods 1728–1732 and 1788–1792 the real day wage of unskilled urban construction workers (measured as the fraction of an annual consumer basket that could be purchased with a single day wage) was about 25 percent lower than in southern England. Over the same period it fell by 30 percent. Increases in the work effort per capita and revenues from other sources seem to have compensated for the fall in the real day-wage as GDP per capita appears to have remained constant during the second half of the eighteenth century.[13] What is sure is that there was no income increase that could be spent on new consumer goods. Moreover, tight regulation of consumption, which persisted into the second half of the century in at least some parts of Germany, inhibited the spread of novel consumer goods.[14]

There were however encouraging signs to this otherwise sombre picture. The share of the population living in towns exceeding 5,000 inhabitants increased during the entire eighteenth century and by 1800 surpassed ten percent for the first time in modern German history. Likewise, the second half of the eighteenth century saw an expansion of the share of the rural population engaged in non-agricultural activities.[15] In addition, some sort of industrious revolution based on intensification of labour was achieved thanks to the use of seasonal agricultural slack time for non-agricultural activities, especially textile production carried out by women and children, and a reduction of free days. Evidence is thin; nevertheless it is significant that authorities in Catholic territories – on the background of a perception of economic backwardness – staged a campaign for a reduction of feast days during the third quarter of the eighteenth century that resulted in a potential lengthening of the work year at the order of magnitude of 30 to 50 days.[16]

The expansion of the non-agricultural sectors also implies an increased weight of traded goods in the economy. At least some part of the manufactures produced by rural industries was exported to international markets and the proceeds rendered it possible to increase the variety of the supply of consumer goods. Indeed, by drawing on a preliminary analysis of the Hamburg toll ledgers this chapter shows that the openness of the German economy increased between the late 1730s and the early 1790s. Likewise, the evolution of the structure of imports documents a sort of consumer revolution, albeit with important modifications relative to the patterns prevailing in the parts of north-western Europe that enjoyed higher levels of income and faster economic growth.

From the mid-seventeenth century, Hamburg rose to a prominent position in the trading network of northern Europe both as a gateway between a large hinterland and maritime trade in the North Sea and the Eastern Atlantic, and as an emporium serving a larger area including Scandinavia and the Baltic.[17] A major feature that distinguishes eighteenth-century Hamburg from other major seaports of Western Europe is that it lacked direct access to non-European markets. Thus, the western Mediterranean and European seaports of the eastern Atlantic were Hamburg's main trading partners in south-westerly directions. Over time two major shifts in overseas import trade occurred: first, Hamburg progressively emancipated itself from the Dutch staple market and received the majority of its imports from other European countries; second, within two decades after the end of the War of Spanish Succession (1701–1713) the sea ports situated on the French Atlantic rose to a dominant position among Hamburg's trading partners. Between the 1730s and the French Revolution, roughly half of all recorded overseas imports from west of the Schelde estuary originated from France.[18] In many respects Hamburg, together with other Hanseatic port cities, functioned as an appendix to the distribution network of French colonial trade.

The location on the estuary of the Elbe provided Hamburg with a large hinterland extending into northern Bohemia, and the construction of the Müllrose channel between the Spree and Oder rivers (1668) established a direct waterway between Hamburg and Silesia. While no region that specialized in the production of non-agricultural exportables existed in Hamburg's neighbourhood, this sea-port was well placed to handle the external trade of major manufacturing regions, namely, the linen districts of Saxony, Lusatia, Northern Bohemia and Silesia, and the metallurgical complexes in the Harz mountains and some parts of Saxony. Whereas Bremen handled the majority of Westphalian linen exports, a minor share also seems to have been channelled through Hamburg. Since river transport on the Rhine was burdened by many tolls, even a part of the overseas trade of South Germany may have taken the route through Hamburg.[19]

Given its large hinterland, trade statistics for Hamburg allow a rough estimate of Germany's imports. According to Pierre Jeannin, during the second half of the eighteenth century Hamburg handled about 60 percent of the trade flowing through the three Hanseatic seaports, the other two being Bremen and Lübeck.[20] Dutch trade with the German hinterland, mostly via the Rhine, was of similar magnitude, at least before 1795. In the latter years of the century, French occupation of the United Provinces dealt a fatal blow to Dutch trade. Dislocation of trade to alternative routes boosted Hamburg's position as a seaport of primary importance: from 1790/94 to 1795/98 alone, recorded imports increased by 41 percent in real terms.[21]

What follows rests on a preliminary analysis of the ledgers of the Admiralty and Convoy Tolls of Hamburg.[22] They consist of roughly 180,000 individual declara-tions of import values covering 36 entire years between 1733 and 1798.[23] Whereas the import toll ledgers provide a wealth of information they also suffer from sev-eral shortcomings.[24] The most important one in the present context relates to the absence of a system of commodity classification. Thus, in the database imported goods are described with almost 2300 different terms. To be sure, from the per-spective of the history of consumption this is an interesting fact since it allows identification of highly differentiated fashion and home goods, such as individual cloth types, mirrors and chairs. However, the lack of a system of classification might mean that goods were sometimes lumped together to summary designations, such as retail goods or diverse merchandise. In the context of the present study, the most important summary category concerns drugs and *Materialwaren*, vague contemporary terms that relate to dyestuffs, chemicals and medicaments constituting 0.6 percent of the recorded import value. In total, summary categories as 'colonial goods', 'manufactures', or 'retail goods' made up close to 6 percent of recorded import values, which is substantial given the fact that only about a dozen commodities and industrial products (cotton goods, woollens and worsteds) comprised more than one percent of recorded imports over the entire period. Consequently, information on import values of goods with minor weight in the import bill, such as those of goods used for dietetic and medical purposes, are subject to a wide margin of error.

Three results derived from Hamburg's import toll ledgers suggest a change in consumption patterns in eighteenth-century Germany, which differs markedly with respect to patterns observed in north-western Europe.

First, openness of the economy increased as overseas import trade grew faster than population. This is a non-trivial finding given that aggregate income per capita remained stable. Thus a shift of demand from domestic goods to tradeables occurred. The population of Hamburg's hinterland between Westphalia and Silesia increased at an annual rate of 0.5 percent between 1740 and 1790. By contrast, quantities of overseas imports in Hamburg grew at 0.9 percent annually between 1736 and 1798. At the same time Dutch exports to Germany by overland and river transport doubled every forty to fifty years in the decades preceding 1790, which makes for an annual growth rate of about 1.5 percent.[25] Thus, it seems reasonable to conclude that between the 1730s and the 1790s German imports via the North Sea grew at about one percent per year on average, which was double the rate of increase of population.

Some indications suggest that the shift from domestic to traded goods occurred at a slower pace than in the leading economies of Western Europe. A case in point is the cotton sector, which constituted a salient element of the consumer revolution.[26] In Hamburg, the share of cotton goods in total recorded imports fell from 13.8 percent in 1733–1742 to 0.9 percent during the 1780s. This was caused by import substitution through the development of specialized regional industries, most notably in western Saxony and parts of the lower Rhineland and adjacent Westphalia. Conversely, imports of raw cotton and particularly of dyes increased: import quantities of raw cotton flowing through Amsterdam and Hamburg combined expanded at an annual rate of one percent between 1753 and 1789–1792. Yet, this figure remains far below the growth rates observed in France and Britain: the raw cotton imports of Marseille from the Levant grew at two percent annually during the three decades preceding the French Revolution and they were increasingly complemented with raw cotton from the New World. British imports of raw cotton increased at an exponential trend of three percent a year already in 1740–1779, that is to say before the rise of the cotton industry in the 1780s.[27] Germany obviously participated less than other parts of western Europe in the cotton boom of the second half of the eighteenth century and the concomitant rise of market goods production.

The second development that points to changes in consumption patterns is the spectacular expansion of imports of colonial goods. This category of merchandise constituted the single most important commodity group in Hamburg's overseas imports: already in 1733–1742 their value amounted to 46.9 percent of total recorded imports, and from 1769 their share exceeded 70 percent on average. Sugar and coffee alone accounted for more than 60 percent of total import value in the second half of the period under study. This implied faster than average growth: during the 1790s real import quantities of colonial groceries were almost 140 percent higher than in 1736 which corresponds to a growth rate of 1.6 percent per year (Table 10.1). Since the present estimate does not take into account the shift of white sugar to (cheaper) muscovado, the actual growth rate of import quantities may have been a little bit higher. This implies that German imports of New World goods through Hamburg grew at a pace that fell little short of the expansion of Europe's American trade as a whole, namely, about two percent a year.[28]

TABLE 10.1 Real import quantities of colonial commodities through Hamburg (yearly average of index values, 1736–1742=100)

	1753, 1755	1756–63	1769–73	1781–89	1790–98
All colonial goods	132.7	99.3	158.0	187.5	237.3
Individual commodities					
Coffee	187.0	156.8	324.6	462.7	747.4
Sugar	129.6	82.3	144.5	151.7	145.6
Tobacco	120.7	104.5	129.9	148.4	246.1

Sources: Own calculation on the basis of *Statistik des Hamburger Seewärtigen Einfuhrhandles in 18 Jahrhundert,* and *Preise in vor-und frühindustriellen Deutschland;* see Pfister, 'Great Divergence'.

Whereas all colonial goods showed import growth rates above average, coffee stands out as the major commodity whose trade grew particularly strongly between 1736 and the 1790s the coffee imports of Hamburg increased more than tenfold in real terms, with an annual growth rate of 3.7 percent. Dutch coffee exports to Germany via overland and river transport expanded at a similar pace. Assuming that all coffee entered Germany through the Netherlands, Hamburg and Bremen yields a figure of coffee consumption of about 0.8 kg per capita in 1790. In 1841–1845 per capita consumption in the *Zollverein* area had risen to 1.25 kg, and in 1911–1913 average annual coffee consumption amounted to 2.6 kg.[29] It thus appears that already in the course of the eighteenth century coffee had made significant inroads into the everyday consumption patterns of the German population.[30] By contrast, the increase in imported quantities of sugar and tobacco, the two other major colonial goods in Hamburg's import bill, was much less spectacular, while tea and cocoa were only of marginal importance. Consumption of tea in particular seems to have been largely confined to the coastal areas of northern Germany.[31]

By comparison with other imported groceries, coffee was characterized by a low price elasticity, namely, −0.4 to −0.5.[32] This supports the idea that coffee had entered the everyday consumption habits of large segments of the German population already by the late eighteenth century. Qualitative accounts suggest that coffee consumption became particularly widespread among outworkers in the emerging regional export industries, at least in those regions where there was no rural guild to restrict access to labour markets. Given the higher participation of women in the labour force, the fast preparation of dishes became highly desirable. In addition, work in textile manufactures was physically less demanding than work in agriculture; hence, textile workers tended to consume less grain and protein-rich foods than the agricultural population. They consumed instead more items that today we would define as 'junk food'. Apart from the rapidity with which it could be prepared, coffee aided concentration to sustain long hours of monotonous work and to suppress hunger. In addition, the spread of coffee consumption among proto-industrial outworkers was facilitated by the fact that many merchants engaged in the organization of textile exports were also dealing with coffee as a countertrade and often used coffee to pay outworkers.[33] Finally, two pieces of evidence from Hamburg's import toll ledgers can be linked to a consumer revolution within Germany, albeit on a modest scale. On the one hand, a marked increase in the diversity of traded goods over time is visible: after standardizing spelling and excluding composite items, toll registers record 653 different items in 1733–1742; by 1790–98 the number of items had risen to 983. The finding is all the more remarkable given the growing concentration of imports on few relatively homogeneous commodities such as coffee and sugar as noted earlier. Obviously, the increase of import commodity concentration at the top hides a trend towards greater differentiation of other goods with lower total import values. Already this finding alone indicates the presence of a consumer revolution based on the diversification of consumer culture. On the other hand, the import value of goods normally associated with an emerging consumer culture experienced vigorous growth, at least if one excludes textiles. Over the whole period 1733–1798 import values of household goods, which include pottery, furniture, clocks and the like, expanded at a rate of 2.9 percent per year. Similarly, imports of plated goods, mats and straw goods grew at 2.3 percent annually. Since the import price index increased at 0.7 percent per year during the same period, these figures probably imply a growth rate in real import values that exceeded the one of total imports. The absolute magnitude of the import values of these consumer goods remained modest, however, even if their share in total recorded trade increased. Taken together, home goods, plated goods, mats and straw goods as well as soap constituted only 0.25 percent of the total value of recorded imports in 1733–1742 and 0.51 percent on average in 1781–1798. This suggests that in Germany changes in consumption patterns beyond the spread of colonial groceries were confined to narrow elite circles, and this in turn was perhaps in part due to the absence of major metropolitan centres in Hamburg's hinterland. A consumer revolution deriving from increased diversity of traded goods and a corresponding rise in the utility of their consumption was happening in eighteenth century Germany, but it remained a socially marginal phenomenon.

Global substances and local diets

The import value of goods to be used for dietetic and medicinal purposes recorded in the Hamburg toll ledgers increased at a high growth rate of 1.9 percent per year between 1733 and 1798. This diffusion does not fit within a traditional narrative of a consumer revolution nor did it contribute to shaping a new diet as in the case of colonial groceries. Rather, the expansion of trade in medicinal substances is evidence of a growing awareness in European societies of the care of the self and one's body.[34] The interest paid by the eighteenth-century bourgeoisie to drugs and spices was quite new: it was directed towards a notion of physical well-being, instead of the medieval and early modern habit of using spices to connote status.[35]

The adoption of these substances in eighteenth- and early nineteenth-century Europe resulted from blending medical pluralism with a pattern of knowledge creation that emphasised an open access culture within the scientific and (second) commercial revolutions emerging in the seventeenth century. Medical pluralism was closely linked to a multi-causal conception of morbidity: bodily malfunctions and ailments could result from physical, social, mental and spiritual disorder; hence, a multitude of practices had the potential to restore health and wellbeing, the application of natural substances being only one of them.[36]

Within a concept of medical pluralism, exotic substances – an outside force intervening in a disorder on a local scale – appeared highly attractive. This notion was already present in the middle ages: Hildegard von Bingen, a twelfth-century Benedictine scholar produced two compendia on nature and medical matters and recommended pepper, ginger and galangal against gastric disorders.[37] The search for dietetic and medicinal substances was continued by early modern discoverers and trading companies by screening the natural diversity of foreign continents for profitable ventures. Trading companies instructed pharmacists and physicians like Leonhart Rauwolf – who was the first European to describe the ceremony of coffee drinking in the late sixteenth century – to look out for effective and profitable medicinal plants. Physicians of the English East India Company used local substances to cure tropical diseases, and at the end of the seventeenth century they started to send medicinal plants to London.[38]

Appreciation of the therapeutic value of particular substances was not based on knowledge of their pharmacological effect. Present-day ethno-pharmacological research in non-European contexts shows that the non-existence of formal knowledge concerning the processes underlying particular diseases and the mode of action of therapeutic substances implies both a low degree of consensus among informants relative to the substance that should be used to cure a particular ailment and a broad range of medical indications attributed to a given plant.[39] In the context of early modern Europe this meant that there existed a broad continuum between the use of a particular substance for therapeutic purposes and its use as a spice or recreational drug. Major examples include tobacco, coffee and tea. Moreover, it is symptomatic that in many early modern European villages and towns retail trade of both spices and drugs was in the hands of the same groups of merchants and retailers.[40] Finally, as we show below, many exotic substances were considered effective for a bewildering range of medical indications.

An exception is South American cinchona, which was universally considered the most effective means against high fever until the early nineteenth century and remained the basis of most therapies designed to combat infection with malaria down to the 1930s. Its relevance and success in eighteenth-century Germany is testified to by the fact that in Hamburg imports of cinchona bark recorded a higher value than any other medicinal substance, and imports expanded with a massive growth rate of 4.8 percent between 1733 and 1798. The high consensus concerning the therapeutic value of cinchona and its widespread application help to explain why it was the first substance whose extraction became industrialized from 1820.[41]

A major feature of the 'glocalization' of medicinal substances in eighteenth- and early nineteenth-century Europe relates to the fact that knowledge transfer between continents was apparently thin and that expertise concerning the pharmacological value of substances imported from other continents was established in Europe as part of an emerging scientific and commercial culture. Efforts by Europeans travelling to other continents to learn about local plants and substances were often limited by language barriers and the unwillingness of locals to share their knowledge. In many cases, knowledge was tightly associated with religious and spiritual beliefs, and indigenous people were not eager to share this kind of knowledge.[42] It is no wonder, therefore, that European knowledge of pharmacological substances of exotic origin was mostly constructed from within the old continent. Influential treatises on medical matters were written by authors who had never left Europe. Nicolás Monardes (1508–1588), for instance, a Seville physician, published a *materia medica* on New World substances, becoming the foremost European authority on this topic for a long time. However, he had never travelled to the Americas, but gathered information on substances from soldiers and other travellers returning from the New World and experimented with them in Seville. Monardes explained the effectiveness of New World *materia medica* in terms of European theories using Galenic and Hippocratic conceptions.[43] Thus, these goods were largely dissociated from the meanings and religious practices surrounding them in their sixteenth- and seventeenth-century contexts.[44]

The early development of European knowledge of the pharmacological properties of exotic plants as epitomized by the work of Monardes, from the late seventeenth century was followed by the parallel accumulation of knowledge in fields as diverse as botany, commerce and pharmaceutics. A distinctive feature of this system of knowledge creation was the accessibility of scientific and commercial communities.[45] This led to the proliferation of handbooks destined for the use of practitioners and, over time, led to an increasing specialization of the medical properties associated with particular substances and hence, in a sense, to a reduction of medical pluralism.

What follows explores the evolution of discourses relating to three substances whose import values in Hamburg show a clear rise during the period under study. We thereby hope to track the formation and dissemination of knowledge of these substances and of their effects on bodily well-being. During the eighteenth and early nineteenth century handbooks and encyclopaedias paid increasing attention to substances with medical and dietetic uses, discussing their characteristics as objects of long-distance trade as well as their use in the kitchen and the pharmacy.

The global trade in substances originating in different parts of the world needed to be connected to European dietetic, medical and business practices. These in turn were closely related to culturally specific perceptions of the body. Merchants needed to be able to judge the authenticity, quality, and characteristics of the material they wished to trade. Whereas stimulating substances like coffee, tobacco or tea were often regarded as threats to the moral order, especially by religious movements such as Puritanism and Pietism, the substances considered here served to keep the consumer's body in good order and promote its healthy functioning. Hence their integration into a modern diet accommodated bourgeois notions of the care of the self.

The first case study relates to jalapa and rhubarb roots. Both substances were used to treat constipation and were reputed to be effective but rather mild purgative agents. Jalapa and rhubarb originate from very different parts of the world, but due to their almost identical properties and similar physical appearance, they were considered potential substitutes. Jalapa was gathered in southern Mexico and was sometimes called 'black rhubarb'. Rhubarb, by contrast, originated from China and arrived at Hamburg in larger quantities, with an annual growth rate of 6.2 percent in 1733–1798. Since ancient times Europeans knew rhubarb although they encountered difficulties with accessing the plant. In the late sixteenth century, missionary priests in China reported that rhubarb was cultivated only in the country's western and north-western regions, from where it was traded to coastal China. Most rhubarb was traded via Russia, and during the sixteenth and seventeenth centuries the Russian state was eager to keep quantities low and prices high. After 1700 the English East India Company participated in the rhubarb trade, bringing increasing quantities of this plant to London. In the late eighteenth and early nineteenth centuries, rhubarb imports from Russia made up only a small market share in London, although it kept its good reputation – and considerably higher price – due to the Russian quality controls.[46]

Mexican jalapa had been known in Europe since the sixteenth century, but its import into Hamburg became substantial only in the last quarter of the eighteenth century.[47] Jalapa was also known as 'black rhubarb', or 'purging bindweed'. It is noteworthy that systematic analysis of the plant occurred relatively late in the early nineteenth century. At the time it was believed that these roots had been imported into Europe since the beginning of the seventeenth century, yet the earliest known documentation of its purgative effect dates back to 1552.[48] Since that time jalapa had been 'the most ordinary drastic purgative'. Overdose could lead to painful adverse reactions, yet an adequate application was considered highly effective.[49]

Testimonies concerning Chinese rhubarb can be found from an earlier time than descriptions of jalapa. Rhubarb was already part of many medicinal compounds in Johann Schroeder's dispensatory of 1693. Rhubarb was believed to be helpful against dropsy, worms as well as disorders of liver, spleen and stomach, and was a popular purgative agent.[50] Half a century later, Zedler's *Universallexikon* devoted 20 pages to a detailed description of the root, its physical appearance, geographical origin, methods of harvesting and its medical indication.[51] Obviously merchants, but also a wider readership was to be informed about this interesting root from the Far East. However, although the author(s) refer to several scholarly works, knowledge seems to have been rather restricted at that time. The major part of the article actually reproduces another treatise, published only four years earlier, on plants in medical use from 'all four parts of the world'. The author, Peter Hotton, claimed that the people harvesting the roots had no idea of their medical value, excavating them just for the money, although rhubarb is well-known in traditional Chinese medicine.[52] In 1758, a treatise on rhubarb, published in Jacobi's journal of economic and physical treatises, threw light on the ways rhubarb was brought to Europe and discussed the effect of different forms of transport on the quality of the roots.[53] These examples show how experts in the first half of the eighteenth century started to provide a basis of systematic knowledge about a foreign product.

During the 1780s several publications began to explore the opportunities and potential benefits of cultivating Chinese rhubarb in Europe and Germany in particular. The first issue of the *Handelszeitung*, published in Gotha in 1784, reported successful cultivation of rhubarb roots in England and Sweden. Only a year later, Germershausen's *Hausvater* promoted the cultivation of rhubarb in Germany, and reported several trials not only in Scotland and near London, but also in the surroundings of Dresden, Hamburg, Insterburg (Eastern Prussia, today part of Kaliningrad Oblast) and Mannheim. Early attempts to cultivate rhubarb in Europe seem to date back to the late 1760s, and the author praised these successful pioneers as examples to be followed by others.[54] The evolution of European knowledge of rhubarb roots had covered a long distance from very vague and scattered information to systematic expertise, moving from pharmacists and medical exports to merchants and an informed bourgeois readership.

The second case study concerns asafoetida or devil's dung. Well-known in many parts of Asia, it is part of traditional diets as well as an important medicament. Medical practitioners prescribed it against gastrointestinal and nervous disorders as well as respiratory problems.[55] In present-day Nepal, asafoetida is part of the daily diet, with quantities usually larger than those of treatment formulas.[56] In present-day Germany its application is limited to the use as spice in Indian cuisine. In the early eighteenth century, by contrast, asafoetida had a reputation as an anticonvulsant medicinal substance. It consists of gum resin, obtained from the roots of ferula plants growing in the region of present-day India, Afghanistan and Pakistan, often mixed with flour or other media. Hotton's *Kräuter-Schatz* characterized the substance as warming, softening, dissipating, opening and healing. Readers were advised to apply it against cough, dyspnoea, and other respiratory illnesses. Pelvic complaints should be alleviated, childbirths facilitated after taking asafoetida. Horses and humans could be relieved from worms, and if poisonous stings were bandaged with asafoetida, the substance would extricate the poison.[57]

Regardless of its effectiveness in a wide range of indications, the substance was not popular: in its raw state, it smells bad, losing its stench only after cooking. In Hotton's book and in the Zedler's *Universallexikon* (published from 1731 onwards), there is some astonishment with respect to the popularity of the spice in the ancient world. Eighteenth-century experts believed that devil's dung was identical with a plant named *silphium* or *laserpitium*, originating from northern Africa and very popular in ancient Greece and Rome. They were also convinced that asafoetida originated from North Africa, Armenia and Persia. As a matter of fact, the ancient silphium had become extinct by the first century CE, and was substituted by asafoetida in Roman cuisine. After the end of the Roman era Europeans rarely used it in meals, and they only considered it as a medicine.[58] The *Zedler* contains many examples of its healing power, explaining in detail how to prepare it, mix it with other substances and ingest the mixture.

Half a century later authors began to wonder why and when people lost taste for this allegedly ancient spice. Some speculated that possibly in ancient times it was used only for reaming bowls and for serving meals, as Indians would do some-times.[59] In the late eighteenth century asafoetida was mentioned in many phar-macological treatises. Obviously it was a well-established medicament dispensed both to humans and farm animals; only sometimes is there a hint at its property as spice. In 1787, Gleditsch's introduction to raw and basic drugs categorized it as 'spice-like' medicine. The same holds for Kolbány in his compendium on poison-ous drugs, where it is characterized as arousing nausea, fear and fierce headaches.[60] Trade routes mostly ran through Italy, but Marseille was of some importance as well. Asafoetida also appears in the toll registers of eighteenth-century Hamburg, although not continuously and with strongly fluctuating values.[61]

This section concludes with castoreum ('Bibergeil'), which has long been known in Europe. The substance is a secretion of a gland, which beavers use for groom-ing and to mark their territory. Europeans had known and used it as a medicinal substance since ancient times. Unfortunately, there is no information as to whether and for what purpose it might have been used in the producing regions. In 1780 Höpfner's *Deutsche Enzyklopädie* claims that already Hippocrates of Kos knew of and applied it.[62] During the first three quarters of the eighteenth century the sub-stance is frequently mentioned in the context of beekeeping. The earliest reference to castoreum in German treatises dates back to 1597: Johann Coler, a Protestant clergyman and important contributor to the paterfamilias literature, advised readers to mix it with several other substances and to rub both the inside and the entrance of the beehive with this concoction, so that the bees would like to live there.[63] Apparently castoreum had a very favourable effect on bees, so recommendations to apply it followed over and again. In volume 64 of Zedler's *Universal-Lexikon*, pub-lished in 1750, castoreum is recommended to help against tongue disease in horses; a guidebook for hunters gave several recipes for fish lure.[64]

In Höpfner's *Deutsche Enzyklopädie* we find both a long description of beavers and a separate article on castoreum. The article describes a number of compounds, such as 'Bibergeilbolus' (*Bolus e castoro*), 'Bibergeilessenz' or '-tinktur' (*Essentia castorei, Tinctura castorei*), 'Bibergeilgeist' (*Spiritus castorei compositus*), 'Bibergeilöl' (*Oleum castorei*), 'Bibergeilschmalz' (*Axungia castorei*), and 'Bibergeilwasser' (*Aqua castorei*). However, the author consistently discussed questions of effectiveness, pointing at a broad range of different opinions on the usefulness of castoreum regarding different diseases. In another volume of this encyclopaedia the substance is also mentioned as part of every military pharmacy.[65]

In the late eighteenth century authors endeavoured to become more specific about indications and began to produce systematic knowledge about the charac-teristics of castoreum as a merchandise. In Krünitz's *Ökonomisch-technologische[r] Encyclopädie* almost four pages discussed the origin, manufacturing, quality and adulteration of castoreum in trade. In 1797 another *Kaufmannslexikon* reports the same level of knowledge, mostly copying the earlier text, just adding a few words about medical applications.[66] The question of authenticity was crucial for pharmacists, who seem to have been the key buyers of castoreum in the market, probably because castoreum was applied mostly in the form of compounds with other substances. Ebermaier published in 1815 a volume about the authenticity and quality, confusion, adulteration of castoreum and how to test different substances.[67]

A significant characteristic of castoreum as a medicinal substance was its product differentiation. Beavers in different parts of the world delivered castoreum in strongly varying qualities, and deceitful attempts to dilute the valuable substance intensified the problem. Buyers and users of rhubarb faced a similar problem. The Chinese root was traded on very different routes, overland through Russia or via the seaborne trade through Mediterranean or North Sea ports. Methods of handling and transport had strong effects on the quality of the substance, so questions of transport and quality control were discussed at large in many publications. In contrast, jalapa and asafoetida were relatively new to the Old World, and authors endeavoured to inform their readers on the substances themselves and their benefits to European consumers. However, establishing systematic knowledge on substances from very different parts of the world was a project pursued by many authors in the eighteenth and nineteenth centuries, no matter whether the substances had clear indications, as jalapa and rhubarb, or were used for many different disorders, as asafoetida and castoreum. We observe a parallel development of growing demand for global substances and growing interest in accurate knowledge on these substances, glocalizing them as medicinal substances and merchandise. This process ended with pharmaceutical industrialization in the late nineteenth century.

Conclusion

Overseas trade grew faster than aggregate income over much of the eighteenth century, even in a relatively poor and landlocked country such as Germany. Since imports consisted largely of consumer goods, trade contributed to a globalization of material culture. This constituted a multifaceted process comprising at least three distinct histories. At the end of the eighteenth century Hamburg's overseas imports consisted mainly of colonial goods with the coffee trade having experienced the most spectacular expansion over the previous decades. Colonial groceries were commodities characterized by a low degree of differentiation; growth of trade in these goods cannot be associated with the conventional concept of a consumer revolution. Rather, the expansion of coffee consumption in eighteenth-century Germany, which took place despite stagnant per capita incomes, occurred in connection with the concomitant development of handicraft industries: textile work required less physical force than concentration, and given the strong involvement of women in the production of market goods, meals had to be prepared quickly. Furthermore, merchants that organized exports of manufactures were frequently also involved in the coffee trade and offered coffee and sugar to outworkers as part of the truck system. Coffee was thus well suited to become an ingredient of the everyday diet of the emerging industrial working class.

To be sure, the paraphernalia of an emerging consumer culture, fashion and home goods, are also present in Hamburg's toll ledgers. As differentiated goods they stimulated consumers' minds by contributing to fashionable appearance as well as to identity construction through the tasteful decoration of interiors. Their spread fits well into the standard account of the consumer revolution that links the growth of long-distance trade with an increase in the variety of supply, which in turn increased the utility of consumption given love-of-variety preferences. Nevertheless, the share of fashion and home goods that can be associated with an emerging consumer culture remained marginal in total trade even at the end of the eighteenth century. This suggests that in Germany the consumer revolution remained confined to a small elite. There are no signs of a conversion of luxuries into necessities as it took place in the leading economies of north-western Europe.

This chapter placed a focus on a third history linked with the globalization of material culture, namely, on the increasingly global character of goods contributing to bodily well-being through their dietetic and medical application. Although small in absolute magnitude, trade with substances of this kind expanded at a more rapid pace than imports in general according to the toll ledgers of eighteenth-century Hamburg. As with colonial groceries, however, the relatively low degree of product differentiation and the irrelevance of aesthetic qualities preclude an interpretation of their diffusion in the framework of the familiar consumer revolution thesis. And in contrast to goods like cacao, coffee and tobacco, which also began their career in early modern European consumption in the framework of dietetic and medical applications, many other substances did not become groceries firmly embedded in patterns of everyday diet. This contrasts sharply with at least some of these substances, for instance asafoetida, which was used both as a medicament and a common ingredient of everyday meals in many parts of South Asia. Rather, the increasing willingness during the eighteenth century to acquire substances with dietetic and medical uses must be seen in the context of the growing valuation of the individual in the wake of the Enlightenment movement. The human body, neatly separated from its physical surroundings, became both an element of individual identity and an object for the care of the self. In the framework of a concept of medical pluralism any substance from anywhere having the potential to contribute to bodily well-being could be helpful in such a context.

Glocalizing substances originating in other continents were key to dietetic and medical practices emerging in Germany and formed an important concomitant of expanding import trade. This stemmed from the fact that substances applied to bodily well-being assumed different meanings in dietetic and medical practices in different parts of the world. From the sixteenth century, medical practitioners and herbalists had collected information on plants from other continents with a potential for medical applications. Physicians accompanying war and merchant vessels, missionaries, soldiers, but also pharmacists and botanists were instructed to collect foreign knowledge. However, their efforts were often doomed to fail not only due to language problems, but also because of the religious and magical secrets surrounding these substances. An important result of these obstacles to obtaining indigenous knowledge is a distinct glocalization of knowledge about these global plants and animal substances, and a fast integration of these new remedies and dietary supplements into the European systems of thought. With reference to Germany we observe that between the second quarter of the eighteenth and the first half of the nineteenth century the production and dissemination of knowledge of medicinal and dietetic substances became much more multifaceted and involved a broader set of actors. The emerging science of botany and the proliferating genre of merchant manuals joined forces in classifying substances with respect to morphology, product quality and origin. Authors of pharmacological manuals increasingly sought to identify and isolate active substances in plants or parts of animal bodies, and medical practitioners became progressively more specific about indications. All this provided the basis for an at times elaborate discussion of foreign substances in encyclopaedias published for a wider educated readership. The circulation of multifaceted knowledge of goods with dietetic and medical uses in turn offered guidance with respect to their application to the physical aspects of the care of the self.

Seen in longer perspective these developments proved to be a temporary phenomenon, however. From the second quarter of the nineteenth century there emerged a bifurcation between popular medicine that continued to be grounded in the application of natural substances and academic medicine supported by an increasingly professionalized medical personnel applying more and more industrially manufactured medicaments. The ascendency of the latter type of health care implied a progressive disjunction between traded goods and drugs dispensed to patients, which in turn led to a de-globalization of material culture with respect to goods applied to the physical aspects of the care of the self. The global history of material culture followed anything but a uniform trend.

Notes and References

1. See for instance Roland Robertson and Kathleen E. White, 'What is Globalization?,' in *The Blackwell Companion to Globalization*, ed. John Ritzer (Molden, MA: Blackwell, 2007), 54–66.
2. Neil McKendrick, John Brewer and J.H. Plumb, *The Birth of a Consumer Society: The Commercialization of Eighteenth-Century England* (London: Europa, 1982); Daniel Roche, *The Culture of Clothing: Dress and Fashion in the "Ancien Régime"* (Cambridge: Cambridge University Press, 1994); Maxine Berg, *Luxury and Pleasure in Eighteenth-Century Britain* (Oxford: Oxford University Press, 2005); *Consumers and Luxury: Consumer Culture in Europe, 1650–1850*, ed. Maxine Berg and Helen Clifford (Manchester: Manchester University Press, 1999); *Luxury in the Eighteenth Century: Debates, Desires and Delectable Goods*, ed. Maxine Berg and Elizabeth Eger (Basingstoke: Palgrave Macmillan, 2003); and most notably Jan de Vries, 'Between Purchasing Power and the World of Goods: Understanding the Household Economy in Early Modern Europe,' in *Consumption and the World of Goods*, ed. John Brewer and Roy Porter (London: Routledge, 1993), 85–132; Id., 'The Industrial Revolution and the Industrious Revolution,' *Journal of Economic History* 54 (1994): 249–270; Id., *The Industrious Revolution: Consumer Behavior and the Household Economy, 1650 to the Present* (Cambridge: Cambridge University Press, 2008).
3. Lorna M. Weatherill, *Consumer Behavior and Material Culture in Britain, 1660–1760* (London: Routledge, 1988); *Luxury in the Eighteenth Century*, esp. ch. 8.

4. Annerose Menninger, *Genuss im Wandel: Tabak, Kaffee, Tee und Schokolade in Europa (16.–19. Jahrhundert)* (Stuttgart: Steiner, 2004), 237–263; Marcy Norton, *Sacred Gifts, Profane Pleasures: A History of Tobacco and Chocolate in the Atlantic World* (Ithaca: Cornell University Press, 2008).
5. For tobacco, see Russell R. Menard, 'Transport Costs and Long-range Trade: Was There a European "Transport Revolution" in the Early Modern Era?,' in *The Political Economy of Merchant Empires*, ed. James D. Tracy (Cambridge: Cambridge University Press, 1991), 253–264; for the case of coffee, see: Kristof Glamann, *Dutch–Asiatic Trade, 1620–1740* (s'Gravenhage: Nijhoff, 1958), 201–211, 285–286; Steven C. Topik, 'The Integration of the World Coffee Market,' in *The Global Coffee Economy in Africa, Asia and Latin America, 1500–1989,* ed. William G. Clarence-Smith and Steven C. Topik (Cambridge: Cambridge University Press, 2003), 27–30.
6. Sidney Mintz, *Sweetness and Power: The Place of Sugar in Modern History* (New York: Viking, 1985), 18, 137, 148–150.
7. Niels Steensgaard, 'The Growth and Composition of Long-distance Trade of England and the Dutch Republic before 1750,' in *The Rise of Merchant Empires: Long-distance Trade in the Early Modern World, 1350–1750*, ed. James D. Tracy (Cambridge: Cambridge University Press, 1990), 102–152.
8. For tobacco, see Norton, *Sacred Gifts*.
9. Pamela Smith, *Making Knowledge in Early Modern Europe: Practices, Objects and Texts, 1400–1800* (Chicago: University of Chicago Press, 2007); for a similar process in the case of dyes, see Alexander Engel, *Farben der Globalisierung: die Entstehung moderner Märkte für Farbstoffe 1500–1900* (Frankfurt a. M.: Campus, 2009), 37–95.
10. *Colonial Botany: Science, Commerce and Politics in the Early Modern World*, ed. Londa Schiebinger and Claudia Swan (Philadelphia: University of Pennsylvania Press, 2005).
11. See below, footnote 13.
12. Sheilagh Ogilvie, 'Consumption, Social Capital, and the "Industrious Revolution" in Early Modern Germany,' *Journal of Economic History* 70 (2010): 287–325.
13. Ulrich Pfister, 'Economic Growth in Germany, 1500–1850,' unpublished contribution to Quantifying long run economic development conference, University of Warwick in Venice, 22–24 March 2011, 15; Id., 'The Timing and Pattern of Real Wage Divergence in Pre-industrial Europe: Evidence from Germany, c.1500–1850' (unpublished manuscript, 2014).
14. In addition to Ogilvie, 'Consumption,' see Michael Stolleis, 'Luxusverbote und Luxussteuern in der frühen Neuzeit,' in *Pecunia Nervus Rerum: Zur Staatsfinanzierung in der frühen Neuzeit*, ed. Michael Stolleis (Frankfurt a. M.: Klostermann, 1983), 9–61, see 15, 51–3; Peter Albrecht, 'Es geht doch nicht an, dass all und jeder Kaffee trinkt! Kaffeeverbote in der frühen Neuzeit,' in *Am Limit: Kaffeegenuss als Grenzerfahrung*, ed. Eva Dietrich and Roman Rossfeld (Zürich: Johann Jacobs Museum, 2002), 22–35.
15. Pfister, 'Economic Growth,' 5; cf. also Sheilagh C. Ogilvie, 'The Beginnings of Industrialization,' in *Germany: A New Social and Economic History. Vol. 2: 1630–1800*, ed. Sheilagh C. Ogilvie (London: Arnold, 1996), 263–308.
16. Peter Hersche, *Muße und Verschwendung: europäische Gesellschaft und Kultur im Barockzeitalter, 3 vols.* (Freiburg: Herder, 2006), vol. 1, 618–28.
17. Pierre Jeannin, 'Die Hansestädte im europäischen Handel des 18. Jahrhunderts,' *Hansische Geschichtsblätter* 89 (1971): 41–73; Karin Newman, 'Hamburg and the European Economy, 1650–1750,' *Journal of European Economic History* 14.1 (1985): 57–94; Michael North, 'Hamburg: "The Continent's Most English City",' in *From the North Sea to the Baltic*, ed. Michael North (Aldershot: Variorum, 1996), ch. 6; Klaus Weber, *Deutsche Kaufleute im Atlantikhandel 1680–1830: Unternehmen und Familien in Hamburg, Cádiz und Bordeaux* (München: Beck, 2004), 37–86, 225–39; Toshiaki Tamaki, 'Hamburg as a Gateway: The Economic Connections between the Atlantic and the Baltic in the Long Eighteenth Century with Special Reference to French Colonial Goods,' in *The Rise of the Atlantic Economy and the North Sea/Baltic Trades, 1500–1800*, ed. Leos Müller, Philipp Robinson Rössner and Toshiaki Tamaki (Stuttgart: Steiner, 2011), 61–80; Yuta Kikuchi,

Hamburgs Handel mit dem Ostseeraum und dem mitteleuropäischen Binnenland vom 17. bis zum Beginn des 19. Jahrhunderts: Warendistribution und Hinterlandnetzwerke auf See-, Fluss- und Landwegen (Unpublished Ph.D Thesis, University of Greifswald, 2013).

18. This excludes imports from the Netherlands and the period 1756–1763, which suffered from an adverse shock during the Seven Years' War.

19. Newman, 'Hamburg,' 63–77.

20. Jeannin, 'Hansestädte,' 56–8, 72.

21. Ulrich Pfister, 'Great Divergence, Consumer Revolution and the Reorganization of Textile Markets: Evidence from Hamburg's Import Trade, Eighteenth Century' (unpublished manuscript, 2012; download from http://www.wiwi.uni-muenster.de/wisoge/organisation/personen/pfister/forschung/Hamburg-trade-2012–06.pdf, 32–34).

22. *Admiralitätszoll und Convoygeld*, published and digitized by Jürgen Schneider, Otto-Ernst Krawehl and Markus A. Denzel ed., *Statistik des Hamburger seewärtigen Einfuhrhandels im 18. Jahrhundert nach den Admiralitäts- und Convoygeld-Einnahmebüchern* (St. Katharinen, Scripta-Mercaturae, 2001); Pfister, 'Great Divergence'.

23. Import quantities of 44 commodities, which comprise the bulk of reported imports, were derived by deflating import values by annual averages of prices quoted at the Hamburg stock exchange from 1736. *Preise im vor- und frühindustriellen Deutschland*, ed. Hans-Jürgen Gerhard and Karl Heinrich Kaufhold (Stuttgart: Steiner, 2001); for details, see Pfister, 'Great Divergence,' 25–29.

24. Pfister, 'Great Divergence,' 10–16.

25. Jan de Vries and Ad van der Woude, *The First Modern Economy: Success, Failure, and Perseverance of the Dutch Economy, 1500–1815* (Cambridge: Cambridge University Press, 1997), 489–490.

26. Beverly Lemire, *Fashion's Favourite: The Cotton Trade and the Consumer in Britain, 1660–1800* (Oxford: Oxford University Press, 1991); *The Spinning World: A Global History of Cotton Textiles, 1200–1850*, ed. Giorgio Riello and Prasannan Parthasarathi (Oxford: Oxford University Press, 2009).

27. Pfister, 'Great Divergence,' 48–9.

28. Jan de Vries, 'The Limits of Globalization in the Early Modern World,' *Economic History Review* 63. 3 (2010), 710–733, see 718–20.

29. Pfister, 'Great divergence,' 43–4.

30. Michael North, *Material Delight and the Joy of Living: Cultural Consumption in the Age of Enlightenment in Germany* (Aldershot: Ashgate, 2008), 159.

31. Christian Hochmuth, *Globale Güter – lokale Aneignung: Kaffee, Tee, Schokolade und Tabak im frühneuzeitlichen Dresden* (Konstanz: UVK, 2008), 88; North, *Material Delight*, 158–160. In Hamburg during the 1780s and 1780s, in Prussia in 1795/6 and in trade between Amsterdam and Germany import values of tea amounted to only 2 to 4 percent relative to those of coffee; Otto Behre, *Geschichte der Statistik in Brandenburg-Preußen* (Berlin: Heymann, 1905), 256–257; Leonie van Nierop, 'Uit de bakermat der amsterdamsche handelsstatistiek,' *Jaarboek van het Genootschap Amstelodamum* 13 (1915), 104–172 (quantities multiplied with prices from Hamburg).

32. Pfister, 'Great Divergence,' 39.

33. Peter Kriedte, Hans Medick and Jürgen Schlumbohm, *Industrialization before Industrialization: Rural Industry and the Genesis of Capitalism* (Cambridge and Paris: Cambridge University Press and Maison des Sciences de l'Homme, 1981), 148–149; Rudolf Braun, *Industrialisation and Everyday Life* (Cambridge: Cambridge University Press, 1990), 64–66; Gregory Clark, Michael Huberman and Peter H. Lindert, 'A British Food Puzzle, 1770–1850,' *Economic History Review* 58.2 (1995): 215–237, see 226–8; Weber, *Deutsche Kaufleute*, 42–45, 277–280; evidence on proto-industrial regions in Germany: Peter Kriedte, *Taufgesinnte und großes Kapital: die niederrheinisch-bergischen Mennoniten und der Aufstieg des Krefelder Seidengewerbes (Mitte des 17. Jahrhunderts–1815)* (Göttingen: Vandenhoeck und Ruprecht, 2007), 546; Hochmuth, *Globale Güter*, 184; for similar practices in England, see: Beverly Lemire, *The Business of Everyday Life* (Manchester: Manchester University Press, 2005), 89–102.

34. Philipp Sarasin, *Reizbare Maschinen: eine Geschichte des Körpers 1765–1914* (Frankfurt a. M.: Suhrkamp, 2001); Philipp Sarasin, 'The Body as Medium: Nineteenth-Century European Hygiene Discourse,' *Grey Room* 28 (2008): 48–65. The notion of the care of the self draws on Michel Foucault, *The History of Sexuality. Vol. 3: The Care of the Self* (New York: Vintage, 1990).

35. Wilhelm Schivelbusch, *Tastes of Paradise: A Social History of Spices, Stimulants, and Intoxicants* (New York: Pantheon Books, 1992).

36. *Medical Pluralism. Past – Present – Future*, ed. Robert Jütte (Stuttgart: Steiner 2013).

37. Annerose Menninger, 'Tabak, Zimt und Schokolade. Europa und die fremden Genüsse (16–19. Jahrhundert),' *Das Eigene und das Fremde. Festschrift für Urs Bitterli*, ed. Urs Faes (Zürich: NZZ Verlag, 2000), 232–262.

38. Reinhard Wendt, 'Globalisierung von Pflanzen und neue Nahrungsgewohnheiten: Zur Funktion botanischer Gärten bei der Erschließung natürlicher Ressourcen der überseeischen Welt,' *Überseegeschichte. Beiträge der jüngeren Forschung*, ed. Thomas Beck, Horst Gründer, Horst Pietschmann and Roderich Ptak (Stuttgart: Steiner, 1999), 206–222; T.J.S. Patterson, 'Indian and European Practitioners of Medicine from the Sixteenth Century,' *Studies on Indian Medical History*, ed. G. Jan Meulenbeld and Peter Das Rahul (Delhi: Motilal Barnarsidass, 2001), 111–120; Annerose Menninger, 'Drogen aus der neuen Welt. Tabak und Schokolade als Paradigmen für Interkultur- und Medizingeschichte,' *Lateinamerika 1942–1850/70*, ed. Friedrich Edelmayer, Bernd Hausberger and Barbara Potthast (Wien: Promedia 2005), 115–136.

39. For a typical example, see N. Rajakumar and M.B. Shivanna, 'Ethno-medicinal Application of Plants in the Eastern Region of Shimoga District, Karnataka, India,' *Journal of Ethnopharmacology* 126 (2009): 64–73.

40. Hans-Jürgen Gerhard, 'Gewürzpreise in europäischen Handelszentren im 18. Jahrhundert,' *Gewürze: Produktion, Handel und Konsum in der frühen Neuzeit*, ed. Markus A. Denzel (St. Katharinen: Scripta-Mercaturae-Verlag, 1999), 149–185; Anne Radeff, 'Gewürzhandel en detail am Ende des Ancien Regime: Handel und Wandern,' *Gewürze: Produktion, Handel und Konsum in der frühen Neuzeit*, ed. Markus A. Denzel (St. Katharinen: Scripta-Mercaturae-Verlag, 1999), 187–204.

41. Felipe Fernandez-Armesto and Benjamin Sacks, 'The Global Exchange of Food and Drugs,' *The Oxford Handbook of the History of Consumption*, ed. Frank Trentmann (Oxford: Oxford University Press, 2012), 127–144.

42. Londa Schiebinger, 'Prospecting for Drugs: European Naturalists in the West Indies,' *Colonial Botany: Science, Commerce, and Politics in the Early Modern World*, ed. Londa Schiebinger and Claudia Swan (Philadelphia: University of Pennsylvania Press, 2005), 119–133; see again Rajakumar and Shivanna, 'Ethno-medicinal Application,' 71-2, f. 41.

43. Daniela Bleichmar, 'Books, Bodies, and Fields: Sixteenth-Century Transatlantic Encounters with New World Materia Medica,' *Colonial Botany*, 83–99.

44. Hilary Marland, '"The Diffusion of Useful Information": Household Practice, Domestic Medical Guides and Medical Pluralism in Nineteenth-Century Britain,' *Medical Pluralism*, 81–100; Robert Frank and Gunnar Stollberg, 'Conceptualising Hybridisation – on the Diffusion of Asian Medical Knowledge to Germany,' *International Sociology* 19.1 (2004): 71–88; Ivone Manzali de Sa and Elaine Elisabetsky, 'Medical Knowledge Exchanges between Brazil and Portugal: An Ethnopharmacological Perspective,' *Journal of Ethnopharmacology* 142 (2012): 762–768.

45. On patterns of communication in the emerging community of scientists, see: Anne Goldgar, *Impolite Learning: Conduct and Community in the Republic of Letters, 1680–1750* (New Haven: Yale University Press, 1995); David Lux and Harold Cook, 'Closed Circles or Open Networks: Communicating at a Distance during the Scientific Revolution,' *History of Science* 6 (1998): 179–211. On the growing openness of access to information concerning business practices and information concerning market conditions, see John J. McCusker, 'The Demise of Distance: The Business Press and the Origins of the Information Revolution in the Early Modern Atlantic World,' *American Historical Review* 110 (2005): 295–321; Markus A. Denzel, 'Handelspraktiken als wirtschaftshistorische

Quellengattung vom Mittelalter bis in das frühe 20. Jahrhundert: eine Einführung,' *Kauf-mannsbücher und Handelspraktiken vom Spätmittelalter bis zum beginnenden 20. Jahrhundert / Merchant's Books and Mercantile Practice from the Late Middle Ages to the Beginning of the 20th Century*, ed. Markus A. Denzel (Stuttgart: Steiner, 2002), 11–45.

46. Clifford M. Foust, *Rhubarb: The Wondrous Drug* (Princeton: Princeton University Press, 1992).

47. During the 1730s, annual imports of jalapa roots arriving at Hamburg hovered around values of 5000 *Mark banco* and fell to a mean of 2400 *Mark banco* in the 1760s and 1770s. In the early 1780s imports suddenly jumped to an average of 9173 *Mark banco* (1784–1798).

48. Eduard Winkler, *Vollständiges Real-Lexikon der medicinisch-pharmaceutischen Naturgeschichte und Rohwaarenkunde* (Leipzig: F.A. Brockhaus, 1840), 833–837.

49. Friedrich Gottlob Hayne, *Darstellung und Beschreibung der Arzneygewächse welche in die neue Preussische Pharmakopöe aufgenommen sind* (Berlin: Friedrich Gottlob Hayne, 1834), 65.

50. D. Johannis Schroeder, *Vollständige und Nutzreiche Apotheke* (Nürnberg: Johann Hoffmans, 1693).

51. Johann Heinrich Zedler, *Großes vollständiges Universal-Lexikon aller Wissenschaften und Künste* (Leipzig/Halle: Johann Heinrich Zedler, 1742), 1028–1048.

52. Peter Hotton, *Thesaurus Phytologicus. Neu-eröffneter und reichlich-versehener Kräuter-Schatz* (Nürnberg: Johann Andreas Seitz, 1738), 355–360.

53. D. Joh. Bernhards von Fischer, 'Bhandlung von der Rhabarber,' in *Oeconomisch-physikalische Abhandlungen. Dreizehnter Teil*, ed. Carl Ludwig Jacobi (Leipzig: Carl Ludwig Jacobi, 1758), 62–68.

54. Christian Friedrich Germershausen, *Der Hausvater: in systematischer Ordnung, Band 4* (Leipzig: Johann Friedrich Junius, 1785), 87–91.

55. Milad Iranshahy and Mehrdad Iranshahy, 'Traditional Uses, Phytochemistry and Pharmacology of Asafoetida (Ferula Asa-Foetida Oleo-Gum-Resin) – A Review,' *Journal of Ethnopharmacology* 134 (2011): 1–10.

56. D. Eigner and D. Scholz, 'Ferula Asa-Foetida and Curcuma Longa in Traditional Medical Treatment and Diet in Nepal,' *Journal of Ethnopharmacology* 67 (1999): 1–6.

57. Hotton, *Thesaurus Phytologicus*, 567–569.

58. Andrew Dalby, *Dangerous Tastes: The Story of Spices* (London: British Museum Press, 2002), 110–112.

59. Georg August Langguth, *Neuer Schauplatz der Natur: nach den richtigsten Beobachtungen und Versuchen in alphabetischer Ordnung durch eine Gesellschaft von Gelehrten, Band 1* (Leipzig: M.G. Weidmanns Erben und Reich, 1775), 406–409.

60. Johann Gottlieb Gleditsch and Carl E. Schröder, *Einleitung in die Wissenschaft der rohen und einfachen Arzeneymittel nach physikalisch-chemischen und medizinisch-praktischen Gründen, vol. 3* (Berlin and Leipzig: Georg Jacob Decker, 1787), 310–313; Pál Kolbány, *Gift-geschichte des Thier- Pflanzen- und Mineralreichs nebst den Gegengiften und der medizinischen Anwendung der Gifte* (Wien: Aloys Doll, 1793), 91.

61. Gottfried Christian Bohn, *Gottfried Christian Bohns Waarenlager, oder Wörterbuch der Produkten- und Waarenkunde, vol. 1* (Hamburg: Carl Ernst Bohm, 1805), 57–58.

62. Ludwig Julius Friedrich Höpfner, ed., *Deutsche Enzyklopädie oder Allgemeines Real-Wörterbuch aller Künste* (Frankfurt a. M.: Varrentrapp Sohn und Wenner, 1778–1804), 652–653.

63. Johann Coler, *Oeconomia ruralis et domestica, vol. 4* (Mainz: Paul Helwigs, 1597).

64. Henrich Wilhelm Döbel, *Jäger-Practica oder Der wohlgeübte und erfahrene Jäger, Bd. 3* (Leipzig: Johann Samuel Heinius, 1746), 235.

65. Höpfner, *Deutsche Enzyklopädie*, 637.

66. Carl Günther Ludovici and Johann Christian Schedel, *Neu eröffnete Academie der Kaufleute, oder encyclopädisches Kaufmannslexikon* (Leipzig: Breitkopf und Härtel, 1797), 1829–1832.

67. Johann Christoph Ebermaier, *Tabellarische Übersicht der Kennzeichen der Ächtheit und Güte so wie der fehlerhaften Beschaffenheit, der Verwechslungen und Verfälschungen sämmtlicher bis jetzt gebräuchlichen einfachen, zubereiteten und zusammengesetzten Arzneymittel* (Leipzig: Johann Ambrosius Barth, 3rd edn 1815), 32–33.

AFTERWORD:
HOW (EARLY MODERN)
THINGS TRAVEL

Paula Findlen

> "But what!" someone will now say, "when will you stop dwelling on your parrot, which does not concern us?"
>
> Jean de Léry, 1578[1]

In January 1558 a small French merchant ship transported a group of marooned Huguenots from the Brazilian coast across the Atlantic to the shores of Brittany. The initial voyage had been difficult, fraught with unexpected disasters that left these prospective colonists shipwrecked, and beholden to the native Tupinambá for their survival for almost a year, but the trip home was equally arduous. Despite their eagerness to leave America behind, the French did not depart without taking home a cargo of precious goods, loading their ship with 'brazilwood, long peppers, cotton, apes, marmosets, parrots, and other things, rare over here, which most of us had acquired earlier'.[2]

Terra do Brasil, as readers may recall, earned its name from a much desired South-east Asian and Malaysian commodity which Europeans sought long before their arrival in the New World: a hardwood known as *lignum brasilium*, or Sappanwood, from which red dye was extracted.[3] When European explorers and traders found a South American wood that not only resembled this medieval import but produced a richer and brighter red, they began to harvest it for export back to Western Europe. Well before the French planned this ill-fated expedition to Brazil, shipments of brazilwood provided Norman and Breton cloth-makers with a less expensive method for achieving a much desired colour than awaiting costly shipments of a similar Asian commodity.[4] The lure of brazilwood encouraged the French to cross the Atlantic and compete with the Portuguese in depleting the coastal forests with the labour of the Tupinamba. But it was Portuguese merchants who gave Brazil its name in the first decade of the sixteenth century, making it the first part of the Americas to be visibly identified with its ability to generate a major commodity.

Even prior to the emergence of the sugar plantations, Brazil already contributed to the new political economy of the first global age.[5] And yet the point, however, is not about discovery but rediscovery and reorientation. 'Brazil' already existed on late medieval maps which located an island, known as *insula brasil*, somewhere in the Atlantic, with no reference to this particular commodity.[6] In the sixteenth century the greater ease of acquiring red, dye-producing wood in the Americas rather than in Asia finally gave this geographic orphan a home. It no longer articulated a longing for a place but a location for a desired artefact.

Brazilwood was not the commodity that mattered most on this ill-fated voyage of 1556–1558, at least not for its most articulate eyewitness, a French Huguenot named Jean de Léry (1534–1611). He nonetheless observed that the land was named after this wood, and he lamented having to wear a brightly coloured shirt after efforts to clean dirty clothing with a soap made from lye and brazilwood ashes produced this unanticipated effect.[7] Léry's 1578 account of the failed Brazilian expedition is one of the most important records of French efforts to establish a colony and observe the region and its people. When Léry boarded the ship home, the most precious thing he brought with him was a living talisman of the New World: a Brazilian parrot. As he would later tell readers of his adventures, he treasured the parrot not only for its striking plumage, but because it preserved the Tupinamba's speech. It brokered these two worlds.

During his eight months in Brazil, Léry observed how readily the Tupinambá traded monkeys, parrots, and other local commodities valued by Europeans for clothes and trinkets. He devoted an entire chapter to the dazzlingly colourful birds of the Americas, appraising their appearance like someone used to assessing the quality of good cloth – 'a fine scarlet', blue like 'lapis lazuli', yellow like 'fine gold'. Their sumptuous colours evoked social hierarchies as well as material worth. Of the blue-throated macaw, Léry wrote: 'You would think that he was dressed in a golden cloth below, and clad in a mantle of violet damask above'.[8] Léry observed how the Tupinambá used feathers as a currency of exchange as well as decorative and ceremonial objects, even dying the feathers of some birds to alter their appearance. He collected samples to bring back to France. Fundamentally, Léry reminds us that Brazil was also known as the 'land of parrots', almost from the moment of the Portuguese arrival in 1500. Martin Waldseemüller put these words on his 1516 map; his disciple, the Nuremberg mathematician, printer, and instrument-maker Johann Schöner, subsequently expanded this description into an even longer phrase that did not force a choice, writing *America vel Brasilia sive pappagalli terra* (America or Brazil or the land of parrots) on his 1520 globe.[9]

Above all, Léry delighted in a parrot trained by an interpreter to mimic the sounds of Tupinambá and French which he received as a gift. Surely this was the bird that he carefully preserved as long as possible on the voyage home. Supplies were already low by the time they neared Cape São Roque on the northeast Brazilian coast. Rather than risk a landing, the crew resolved to commence eating 'monkeys and parrots'. Pilot error led the ship further off course and they ran out of food by the end of April 1558, resulting in the inevitable sacrifice of the rest of the living cargo. 'Those who still had monkeys and parrots (for several had already eaten theirs long before), which they had kept so long as to teach them to speak a language that they did not yet know, now put them in the cabinet of their memory, and made them serve as food.' Léry, however, resisted. Unlike the Spanish bureaucrat and naturalist Gonzalo Fernández de Oviedo, who shipped an iguana across the Atlantic in a large barrel of dirt to Giovanni Battista Ramusio, the famed Venetian compiler of global travels, believing erroneously that it needed no other sustenance, Léry knew that his parrot would not survive without food and water.[10] Fearful that others would devour his large, beautiful, talkative bird, he kept it hidden – and presumably resisted his own cravings to eat this wonder of nature that he hoped to give to his French patron, Admiral Coligny. The men were by then softening shoe leather, killing mice and rats, and foraging in refuse piles for anything that might provide sustenance. Recalling the delirium of one shipmate's hunger, Léry described watching the man 'eat the raw guts of a parrot'.[11] In light of Léry's famous meditation on whether eating people was so wrong, one has to wonder how he felt about this evisceration of everything that made the parrot worth taking home.

Finally, when there was nothing left to scrape, boil or forage, Léry reluctantly sacrificed his own parrot. It was consumed so thoroughly that nothing but the feathers remained. Léry no longer had enough of his parrot to stuff and preserve, which would have permitted him to keep it as a kind of natural curiosity that filled many a Wunderkammer. If there were any toucan beaks on board, so greatly admired by Renaissance naturalists, they had long been consumed as well. Specimens that survived such voyages often ended up in aristocratic and royal aviaries as well as cabinets of curiosities. The Bolognese naturalist and collector Ulisse Aldrovandi (1522–1605), who never travelled to Brazil, nonetheless had a parrot and a monkey in his possession while Léry did not.[12] His bird had been silenced, its body reduced down to nothing but brilliant colour. Léry mournfully placed his precious parrot in the cabinet of his memory. Five days later they sighted land. Recognizing that some of his readers might wonder why he wrote at length about a bird, Léry joked of his uncommon passion for this singular memento of his Brazilian adventures. He claimed to have drafted his memoirs in brazilwood ink to retain something of the intimacy of his encounter with a foreign land.[13] Some of the more ravenous crew members tried to eat the wood but, unlike the monkeys and eventually the parrots, it did not digest well. As a result, Léry returned with feathers and ink, making both tangible by writing them into his book, and presumably writing the book with them. Eventually he parted with many of his feathers at the insistence of a member of the king's entourage. They were indeed objects transformed in the course of an encounter.

There are many different ways to consider Léry's parrot. It was yet another artefact on the move that did not quite survive the voyage. It belongs to the classic story of European curiosity, collecting, and ethnography in which objects often stood in for people, and words about imaginary islands became attached to concrete places and things.[14] For Léry, the parrot was a curious and multifaceted creature, emblematic of a world he encountered and wished to remember and share with others. The parrot as an especially rich example of an artefact belonging to a local network within the Americas that subsequently became part of long-distance trading networks while also having individual, even affective meaning for those who possessed it. In the context of this volume, however, I especially want to deposit Léry's parrot in an endless ocean of goods on the move in many different directions. There is really nothing unusual about this parrot, save for the afterlife – and epitaph – it enjoyed in Léry's history of his voyage to Brazil where he gave it a biography. In the end, however, this sixteenth-century parrot was one more transitory object that reveals the emerging contours of an increasingly connected world.[15]

Anne Gerritsen's and Giorgio Riello's *The Global Lives of Things* offers a number of itineraries shaped by the material cultures of the early modern world. Rather than creating a universal chain of commodities, unfolding uniformly and almost mechanically in an age of empires, the essays in this volume trace the specific patterns of things.[16] They create what we might call *material microhistories* whose underlying premise might be summed up as follows: small things can tell big stories.[17] In the process, they raise an important question – how exactly do things become global? Every artefact has a specific point of origin, even if the ingredients are not purely local. Certain taxonomies of objects have so many intermediary steps, like the ramifications of a tree branching outward, that eventually the relationship to the original is lost. The global can lie *within* objects, interwoven into the very fabric of a thing, shaped by craft, knowledge, and materials that migrate over time from one place to another. The global is also about the misperception of objects, including efforts to simulate but not entirely replicate something observed elsewhere. Things – and the ability to make them – travel but they do not remain the same. Recapturing the dynamic nature of these transformations is an important aspect of current work at the intersection of material culture and global history.

The 'global lives' recounted in this stimulating set of essays do not happen everywhere all at once. They are not unidirectional, moving centripetally towards to a single centre – Europe or China, for example. Nor are they driven by a single impulse such as profit, curiosity, wonder, a desire for the exotic, luxury, or even utility. Instead, the global lives of things emerge within and at the interstices between local, regional, and long-distance trading networks. Much like the compass roses on a medieval portolan, networks only exist when a connection is made – no line touches another without a node that creates the point of contact which is also the moment of exchange. Each exchange becomes an opportunity to observe how things metamorphose from one society to another. The networks through which goods move are no more stable than the meaning of the things themselves. They can be redirected, extended, contracted, or even break down. They not only shape social relations and cultural preoccupations but tangibly transform the physical environment. When historians recreate how and why objects matter to a particular society, they also need to attend to questions of human agency and material exigency in order to move beyond an overly simplified view of commodities as simply a fulfilment of consumer desire.

The past decade of new work on subjects such as consumption, collecting, and material culture has built upon an earlier generation of scholarship that initiated this research, often around tightly organized debates about the abundant, self-conscious materialism of a particular society or its moment of consumer revolution. Such work is increasingly informed by recent developments in economic history and by a new sense of this subject as geographically unbounded in its agenda. We need to be open to understanding all the potential itineraries that set the world and its things in motion between the fifteenth and eighteenth centuries. What began as a largely British and European subject, has become one of the most exciting testing grounds for understanding global early modernity not only at the level of macro-analysis but also by immersing ourselves in its micro-processes.

To be certain, at times we run the risk of losing ourselves in the act of contemplating the fabulously interwoven textiles, consuming habits, delightful curiosities, and material hybridity of the early modern world. The wealth of descriptive detail is fascinating and seductive but cannot answer our questions without careful interrogation. The answer to this problem, as this group of essays illustrates well, is to make each case study contribute something specific to the larger task of defining the nature of early modern globalization, while also refining what we mean by material culture. Each object becomes a *material interface*, a repository of social and economic exchange as well as a bearer of cultural meaning that can also be subject to physical inspection and analysis. It demands all of these different methodologies, to one degree or another, depending on the nature of the documentation that survives, and of course the properties inherent to an object as a bearer of historical meaning.

By insisting that historians have much to learn from curators, Gerritsen and Riello have done an important service. They remind us that the feathers on a cape in a modern museum once belonged to a parrot that, dead or alive, crossed the Atlantic on a ship after being selected in a local market for export. Let us turn the globe yet another quarter of a rotation. We discover ceramic parrots in Pondicherry, their colours now realized in a fine glaze. Much like the passion for Mediterranean red coral at the early Qing court, the parrot can be remade, more than once. The paper history of things – described by travellers, enumerated in manifests, toll registers, household inventories, and lush depictions of ceremony and ritual – tells one part of the story. The physical presence of surviving artefacts in modern collections reveals another dimension. When combined with their artistic representations and undergirded by an understanding of economic value and exchange, our material microhistories no longer look particularly small or simple.

Following the itinerary of important artefacts across time and space, we find ourselves curiously replicating the kind of voyage that Jean de Léry once made. But we cannot consider what transpired from his perspective alone, valuable as it is. Our task is also to attempt a reconstruction of what the Tupinambá thought of the European mania for parrots, of the uses of parrots in their own lives before and after this encounter, even contemplating what an early modern parrot network looked like. Whom did it connect and how? What kinds of relations formed around these birds and their feathers? What happened to them as they migrated from one place to another? As the coastal forests disappeared and hunters captured birds in ever greater quantities, how did this transform the local environment? Since the bird can no longer tell us what we want to know, it is up to the historian to reconstruct everything but its speech.

Notes and References

1. Jean de Léry, *History of a Voyage to the Land of Brazil, Otherwise Called America*, ed. and trans. Janet Whatley (Berkeley: University of California Press, 1990), 213. For the broader context of this expedition, see especially Frank Lestringant, *Le Huguenot et le sauvage. La controverse coloniale en France, au temps des guerres de Religion (1555–1589)* (Paris: Klincksieck, rev. ed. 1999).
2. Léry, *History of a Voyage*, 196–197.
3. Laura de Mello e Souza, 'O nome do Brasil', *Revista de História* 145 (2001): 61–86. On the ongoing evolution of the quest for natural commodities that produced variations of this colour, see: Amy Butler Greenfield, *A Perfect Red: Empire, Espionage, and the Quest for the Color of Desire* (New York: HarperCollins, 2005).
4. Surekha Davies, 'Depictions of Brazilians on French Maps, 1542–1555', *Historical Journal* 55/2 (2012): 321. On the role of geography in globalization, see most recently Benjamin Schmidt, *Inventing Exoticism: Geography, Globalism, and Europe's Early Modern World* (Philadelphia: University of Pennsylvania Press, 2015).
5. Stuart B. Schwartz, *Sugar Plantations in the Formation of Brazilian Society: Bahia 1550–1835* (Cambridge, U.K.: Cambridge University Press, 1985).
6. Mello e Souza, 'O nome do Brasil', 66.
7. Léry, *History of a Voyage*, 100–1.
8. Léry, *History of a Voyage*, 87–88. On the fascination with birds, see Marcy Norton, 'Going to the Birds: Animals as Things and Beings in Early Modernity', in *Early Modern Things: Objects and Their Histories, 1500–1800*, ed. Paula Findlen (London: Routledge, 2013), 53–83.
9. Mello e Souza, 'O nome do Brasil', 67. See John W. Hessler and Chet van Duzer, *Seeing the World Anew: The Radical Vision of Martin Waldseemuller's 1507 and 1516 World Maps* (Washington DC: Library of Congress, 2012); Id., *A Renaissance Globemaker's Toolbox: Johannes Schöner and the Revolution in Science, 1455–1550* (London: Giles, 2013).
10. Antonello Gerbi, *Nature in the New World: From Christopher Columbus to Gonzalo Fernández de Oviedo*, trans. Jeremy Moyle (Pittsburgh: University of Pittsburgh Press, 1985), 169.
11. Léry, *History of a Voyage*, 201, 208, and 210.
12. Findlen, *Possessing Nature: Museums, Collecting and Scientific Culture in Early Modern Italy* (Berkeley: University of California Press, 1994), 313.
13. Davies, 'Depictions of Brazilians', 340.
14. Daniela Bleichmar and Peter C. Mancall, eds., *Collecting Across Cultures: Material Exchanges in the Early Modern Atlantic World* (Philadelphia: University of Pennsylvania Press, 2011).
15. Sanjay Subrahmanyam, 'Connecting Histories: Notes towards a Reconfiguration of Early Modern Eurasia', *Modern Asian History* 31/3 (1997): 735–762.
16. For an especially stimulating reflection on calibrating the economic dimensions of globalization, see: Jan de Vries, 'The Limits of Globalization in the Early Modern World', *Economic History Review* 63/3 (2010): 710–733.
17. My suggestion here is partly inspired by Francesca Trivellato, 'Is There a Future for Italian Microhistory in the Age of Global Studies?', *California Italian Studies* 2/1 (2011) ismrg_cisj_9025. Retrieved from: https://escholarship.org/uc/item/0z94n9hq (accessed 22 June 2015).

AFTERWORD: OBJECTS AND THEIR WORLDS

Suraiya Faroqhi

We live in a world of massive inequalities between rich and poor; but at the same time in quite a few countries such as South Korea, India or Turkey, we observe that the sums of money available for non-subsistence purposes among people of middle-level income have grown substantially. Men and women with resources significant enough to permit the enjoyment of certain luxuries may well wish to show this fact in public. Unless it is a palace in Portugal like that of Duke Teodosio studied by Nuno Senos, the major luxuries of the 1600s such as silk scarves from India or silver ornaments from Mexico or South-east Asia, are all reasonably accessible in, for instance, today's Istanbul. Moreover as middle-income people appreciate and highlight the luxuries at their disposal, certain scholars, historians included, will consider it legitimate to make the acquisition and use of such items into an object of study. Books on luxury objects, including the present one, presumably reflect this situation; be that as it may, scholars in recent years have become more and more interested in beautiful, unique and luxurious things.

Such items often have no practical use and thus are acquired only for enjoyment and display; arguably this superfluity even adds to their charm. Gaining access to luxury goods is part of consumption; and consumption studies have gained in legitimacy since the 1980s, once a sizeable number of customers not only in the western world but also in other places could choose between a variety of goods both domestically produced and imported. After all, while import-substitution strategies were in place, consumers could decide to do without certain goods altogether or buy inferior items from local producers. These were the only alternatives available to the consumers. But once an economy geared to export – admittedly more vulnerable to the ups and downs of the world market – was in place, a broader spectrum of goods became available and consumers could make certain choices. Sometimes this meant that domestic producers suffered, but by no means always.[1]

Elite women and precious objects

Gender history also plays a role in drawing scholars into the study of consumption. While in many societies, women have spun, woven, embroidered and otherwise contributed to the production of high-value goods, in early modern times, women of the elite were even less likely to be producers than their menfolk, who – apart from a few spectacular exceptions such as Leone Leoni of Milan (1509–1590) or Leonardo da Vinci (1452–1519) – consisted of warriors, courtiers, high officials and rich merchants. Thus when historians study 'women and the arts' they typically focus on female patrons especially of Renaissance painting and architecture; and such patronage, which we can consider as an aspect of conspicuous consumption, is part of the status competition among members of the elite in general.[2] It thus makes sense to assume that the growing interest in consumption has permitted the highlighting of elite women, but sometimes also of middle-income urban females. In this context it is surely of interest that one of the few humorous compositions of Johann Sebastian Bach (1685–1750) is the 'Kaffee-Kantate', which ends with the statement that women cannot be prevented from enjoying their coffee.[3] Thus the study by Christine Fertig and Ulrich Pfister, who have shown that throughout the eighteenth century the importation of coffee into Hamburg increased while real wages fell quite significantly, possesses an unexpected gender aspect.

Moreover a growing interest in the activities of women has contributed to the liveliness and differentiation observable in consumption studies today. Thus among the illustrations of her article on Brazilian feather-work, Mariana Françozo has accorded the portrait of Sophia of the Palatinate (1630–1714, painting from 1644) a rather prominent place. Wearing a 'royal' coat of red feathers, Sophia poses for her sister Louise Hollandine; the sitter's silk dress and the string of pearls around her neck suggest wealth and high rank.

In a way this claim was not wrong; for on their mother's side, both women were granddaughters of King James I of England and Scotland, while their father Frederick of the Palatinate was the Protestant 'winter king' that the estates of Bohemia had elected in place of the Catholic Habsburgs. But there was a problem: for the defeat of the Bohemian forces in the Battle of the White Mountain (1620) meant that Sophia's family had to take refuge in the Netherlands, where its members lived as guests of the Dutch Republic. Here Louise Hollandine honed her skills as a painter, assimilating the style of Gerard van Honthorst (1592–1656) the leading light of the Utrecht Caravaggists.[4] The acquisition and use of a coat made of Brazilian feathers thus united two elite women, one in the traditional role of subject to a painting and the other in the more novel identity of a practising artist. Moreover, while the coat and the jewellery 'sign-posted' the advantages of a match with young Sophia, potential suitors needed to consider her modest resources and the fact that not only her parents but also her other British relatives were in exile; after all, Louise Hollandine painted this portrait while the English Civil War was at its height.

Succumbing to – or resisting – the charms of exotic objects

Long-distance trade and accumulated wealth thus form the background of this book, which focuses on items which by gift, purchase, conquest, or mixtures of all three procedures came to be owned by people in places often remote from the site of cultivation or manufacture. Thus, as Christine Guth has shown, shagreen, or to be exact, objects covered in shagreen, might travel from Japan to the Mediterranean world or north-western Europe, along a route to which economic historians have been accustomed for quite some time. But once in north-western Europe, shagreen acquired a novel quality: it was regarded as especially suitable for covering instruments and other items connected with science; thus using shagreen connoted a gentleman's scientific interests, even if this meant 'stretching the truth' as far as it could possibly go.

But moves in the opposite direction were possible as well: Pippa Lacey has demonstrated that the Qing emperors of China were interested in possessing a supply of red coral suitable for fashioning into courtly ornaments or gifts to high-level dignitaries; and to satisfy this demand, English merchants purchased these items in Mediterranean ports and carried them to Whampoa Island, where they were taken over by Chinese merchants and/or officials who conveyed them to the imperial court. Thus even though Chinese demand for western goods was strictly limited and the emperors prided themselves upon the fact that no imports were indispensable to the well-being of their empire, a few exotic luxury goods such as red coral were exceptions proving the rule. We may well conclude that even the Qing emperors, at the centre of the known world, were not immune to the charm of exotic goods.

While not central at all, but rather marginal to the world they inhabited, the French merchants and other sojourners in eighteenth-century Pondicherry were also not much inclined to accept 'foreign' goods, in this instance, items available in the Indian environment. As Kévin Le Doudic has shown, especially goods with a 'demonstration effect' such as furniture for the *salon* were ordered from Indian artisans but resembled fashionable French furniture as closely as feasible in the hot climate of southern India. Interestingly this attitude was not limited to Frenchmen in India, but can be observed among at least some of their counterparts in the Ottoman world as well.[5]

People might also oscillate between acceptance and rejection of exotic objects: thus for most of the seventeenth century, tobacco was strictly forbidden in European Russia though not in Siberia. When Peter I (1672–1725) abolished the prohibition, largely for fiscal reasons, smoking continued to arouse widespread disapproval, as one of the impious novelties practised by his westernizing court. As Matthew P. Romaniello has shown, this reticence upset the calculations of certain British merchants, who had hoped that given significant smuggling under previous tsars, their tobacco would find eager buyers as soon as the official prohibition had been lifted. But perhaps tobacco was most enticing when it was forbidden?

Relating the body to exotic objects

Some of the luxuries treated here were desirable because they had a direct effect upon the body of the consumer: this applied most obviously to tobacco, coffee, and sugar. Spices had a comparable effect; and something similar can be said about perfumes and other cosmetics, which do not feature in the present volume although they might have done so. Thus a careful study of the goods imported through the eighteenth-century port of Hamburg has shown that a myriad plants and drugs, including for instance Chinese rhubarb, reached this city and its hinterland, although the latter was inhabited by poor and rural folk. While the individual quantities may have been small, together they 'added up' to a substantial trade.

As a historian of science, Pamela Smith has traced the movement of vermilion, a dyestuff in which mercury and sulphur figure prominently; after a laborious process of manufacture, vermilion (or cinnabar) produces a bright red, which in the age of alchemy was associated with blood. As mercury is poisonous, the bodies of people producing this dyestuff often showed signs of poisoning. But at least in sixteenth-century Germany, the impact of metal-working was even more radical where lizards were concerned; for perhaps following the teachings of Arab alchemists, these reptiles were killed and burned in an effort to find a way of turning base metals into gold.

Many metal-working processes were originally Chinese inventions; and in this culture a mixture of pounded lizards and cinnabar was also in use, supposedly indicating whether or not the concubines of an emperor had engaged in illicit sex. It is unlikely that this combination was invented independently in China and thirteenth-century Cologne, where the scholar and alchemist Albertus Magnus (around 1200–1280) used to teach. Rather, it makes more sense to assume that through the physical practices of workshops all over Eurasia, metal-workers of different places and cultures passed on this set of beliefs. After all, they bore the imprint of their work upon their very bodies.

In quite a different sense, the cultivation of cane sugar in large quantities has had an impact on human bodies, both directly through the diseases caused by excessive consumption and indirectly, through the illnesses that arise from attempts at water management and other enterprises connected with sugar cultivation. Urmi Engineer has thus expanded the literature on the negative ecological consequences of massive sugar cultivation, and also emphasized the connections between slavery, soil exhaustion and sicknesses such as yellow fever, once more highlighting the fragility of the well-being which many people currently enjoy.

Reinterpretations

When goods and substances travelled, people in their new contexts normally used them in ways that differed, often sharply, from those customary in the regions of origin. Sometimes the newly arrived items might even embody novel meanings and purposes; and these reinterpretations are a principal topic of the present volume.

Thus certain peoples of Siberia used tobacco in religious ceremonies – while the Catholic Church explicitly forbade priests to smoke when officiating. Often mixing the new substance with henbane, Siberian peoples valued tobacco because it induced trance-like conditions. As for tobacco consumption in European Russia, many people – as noted – associated it with the impious ways of non-Orthodox foreigners.

In a different vein, the cargo remains of stranded ships once belonging to the Dutch East India Company (often very mundane articles for daily use) which were retrieved during the late 1800s and the twentieth century, are so important to the Dutch that a treaty between the Netherlands and Australia stipulates that they should belong to the government in The Hague. But as Susan Broomhall has pointed out, Native Australians also value these remnants; and when people of the latter community do not obtain sufficient recognition for their share in locating relics of this kind, there are energetic protests. Moreover Australians of European background also consider these items significant to their history and identity, as apparent from the fact that governmental rewards are available not only to people that the law calls 'primary finders', but also to those involved in the retrieval in a 'secondary' fashion.

Other reinterpretations are at issue when Indian artisans worked for French patrons: thus a torch-bearing angel, obviously intended for use in Catholic worship, appears in a posture unknown to European imagery but that recalls statues made in the Dravidian context. Furthermore the artefact features a garland of flowers of the kind used in Indian ceremonial, to say nothing of the lotus-shaped pedestal upon which it stands; the latter is common in Buddhist-inspired imagery but unknown to European makers and patrons of Catholic statues. While Kévin Le Doudic is quite correct in stating that the mass, as it was celebrated in Pondicherry, conformed exactly to the requirements of the French Church, we may still assume that for the maker at least, the angel belonged to the world of Indian art.

Thus not only the articles in this volume, but also the images it contains, may help the reader reflect on the changes that objects supposedly familiar to us have undergone – and still undergo – in the course of their travels throughout the world.

Notes and References

1. Although imported bananas are widely available in Istanbul, the growers of bananas on the Mediterranean coast continue their activities and recently have taken to transporting their produce by cable car: http://www.yenialanya.com/m/?id=11234 (consulted on 5 May 2015).
2. Jonathan K. Nelson and Richard J. Zeckhauser, *The Patron's Payoff: Conspicuous Commissions in Italian Renaissance Art* (Princeton: Princeton University Press, 2008). To these authors, I owe the terms 'sign-posting' and 'stretching'. The former term means emphasizing the desirable qualities of a person or thing while leaving the less attractive ones deliberately in the shadow; as for the latter, it quite literally means 'stretching the truth', as commonly practised in advertising and politics.
3. http://www.almut-fingerle.de/projekte_kaffeekante.htm (consulted on 5 May 2015; the typo in the word *Kaffeekantate* is part of the address).

4. See the article by Susan Broomhall, also a contributor to this volume, in: https://www. academia.edu/9215993/The_Queen_of_Bohemia_s_daughter_Managing_rumour_ and_reputation_in_a_seventeenth-century_dynasty. On Honthorst compare: 'Gerrit van Honthorst,' in *The Oxford Dictionary of Art and Artists*, ed. Ian Chilvers (Oxford: Oxford University Press, 2009) Oxford Reference Online (accessed on 7 May 2015).
5. Suraiya Faroqhi, 'Representing France in the Peloponnesus: A Wealthy French Dwelling in 1770,' in *The Illuminated Table, the Prosperous House, Food and Shelter in Ottoman Material Culture*, ed. Suraiya Faroqhi and Christoph Neumann (Istanbul: Orient-Institut, 2003), 255–273.

AFTERWORD: THINGS IN GLOBAL HISTORY

Maxine Berg

Where does a history focused on objects and things fit within wider global history? Hitherto, economic historians studied trade flows, the data on exports and imports and trade balances, with their main interest in exports. Even Eric Hobsbawm in the 1960s set his *Industry and Empire* within the context of trade and empire; his main interest too was the export of goods. Those goods were first and foremost textiles, generically identified as wool or cotton.[1] During this earlier generation the appearance, use and cultural attributes of those objects and goods were left to anthropologists and art and curatorial historians. But those studying such objects from an art historical perspective focused on provenance and collections and on individual aesthetic characteristics.

The 'things' researched in this new volume raise issues such as the materials of nature ranging from precious stones and woods to the coral studied here by Pippa Lacey and the feathers studied by Mariana Françoso. They extend further to the crafted objects or substances made from such materials as the shagreen studied by Christine Guth, the vermilion by Pamela Smith or the colonial furnishings by Kévin Le Doudic. *The Global Lives of Things* takes us into the relatively new field of material culture, and provides us with studies that range from Latin America and the Caribbean to Australia, from China to the Mediterranean, and from India to Central Europe.

New questions encircle objects and substances that once appeared only in trade statistics, probate inventories and museum collections. Separate histories of objects in museums, once confined to the 'decontextualised material culture of elites' are now a part of our wider histories. The Newberry Collection in the Ashmolean Museum, Oxford, is formed of 12,000 textile fragments dating back to the tenth century CE, made in Gujarat and excavated in Egypt. This collection now forms part of a large history of Indian Ocean trade extending back to the ancient world.[2] Porcelain shards found in East Africa or the cargo of fine porcelain found in the early seventeenth-century Dutch East India Company shipwreck of the vessel 'Witte Leeuw' off St. Helena in 1977 are no longer curious finds and incidents added to the labels of museum collections and auction catalogues. They are part of a large global story of early modern China's manufacturing, its technological achievements and the large scale of its trade with the rest of the world in exportable commodities like porcelain and silk.[3]

Historians now ask questions about the uses and meanings of goods, not just at the time and place where they were produced, but as they were traded and eventually collected. One classic example is the Chinese green-glazed porcelain bowl produced in Jingdezhen in the mid-sixteenth century, arriving through various stages of trade in Germany where it was fitted with gold and silver mountings. Gerritsen and Riello emphasise the different meanings that objects acquired as they were moved over vast areas of the world.[4] Objects became goods, acquiring value as they became part of consumer cultures; consumer cultures in turn were reshaped by incorporating substances and objects once viewed as exotic into the routines of everyday life. The material culture of these goods is about their reception or refusal in Europe, the Pacific, the Indian Ocean or East Asia as much as it is about their materials or aesthetics. Gerritsen and Riello's new volume builds on themes they explored in *Writing Material Culture History* (London: Bloomsbury, 2015). Their material culture approach set in a global context takes us beyond earlier perspectives on European encounters with wider world cultures and precious cargoes into the networks and connections forged through objects that were collected or traded.

Making and trading

Material culture analysis forces us to ask the kind of questions about objects, foodstuffs and substances that open ways to understanding connections among different parts of the world. But goods that are consumed, becoming part of any society's material culture must first be made and traded. The vital production process, understanding skills, tools and craftsmanship must lie at the heart of any serious study of material culture. Dagmar Schäfer in her *Crafting Ten Thousand Things* tells us of the convergence of theoretical and practical knowledge in Ming China, where scholars paid close attention to craft processes.[5] Larry (S.R.) Epstein's research on early modern European technologies gave priority to Europe's skilled workforce; profound changes in European technology were achieved by small incremental improvements made by anonymous craftsmen. Experiential and collective knowledge and its spatial transfer through texts and patents, but above all through its skilled technicians provided the key to a whole range of new products and techniques that developed across wide areas of Europe. Artisans took cotton weaving and printing techniques, papermaking, glass and ceramics manufacturing, and all manner of metalworking from the Mediterranean to Northern Europe moving through different technological frontiers over the course of the thirteenth to the eighteenth centuries. From the east-central Mediterranean and Northern Italy in the thirteenth century, regional technological leadership shifted to southern Germany and central Europe in the late fifteenth century, and on to the southern Low Countries in the sixteenth century. It reached the Dutch Republic in the seventeenth century and Britain in the eighteenth century. A highly mobile and well-informed artisan workforce deployed tacit knowledge, often only codified much later. They moved, adapted and transformed Europe's technologies as they themselves transferred techniques 'in the flesh'.[6]

This process of making was vital to all the objects discussed in this volume. This was not about individual artists or craftsmen; it was about complex production processes, key skills, and knowledge deployed and passed on through manual practices. Pamela Smith's 'Itineraries of Matter and Knowledge' connects workshop practices to the human body. She connects early modern understandings of the human senses to the tacit knowledge of making and crafting. Her case study of the making of vermilion from combining sulphur and mercury, and its use by artists to imitate blood, shows the very early development of the technique among craftspeople. Their long practice in making vermilion spread across Eurasia from at least the eighth century. Associated with wonders and medicinal virtues, it entered into alchemical theory. Smith argues that this craft manufacture of vermilion provided the knowledge later codified into the sulphur-mercury theory of metals.

Craft practices were also vital in the appeal of other special goods such as shagreen, a type of leather made from ray and sharkskin in specific communities in Japan, but also developed for export through its use in Japanese lacquerwares brought to Europe by the Portuguese in the sixteenth century. Christine Guth here gives us details of production processes, sourcing of materials, and aesthetic appeal in different parts of the world which provide real depth to the material culture of this exotic material.

These detailed accounts of the making of objects and the craft skills that inform our knowledge of materials and resources demonstrate the fundamental significance of the deep study of technology to any material culture analysis. As these objects become goods traded through the global economy, so too we must understand the commercial economy and the levels and organization of trade. Vermilion, shagreen and feathers may not have been commodities traded in large quantities in the early modern world, but their trade and that of other high-level luxury goods provided the stimulus for the great expansion of transoceanic trade from the sixteenth century. This trade in what Immanuel Wallerstein dismissed as one in 'preciosities' brought with it what became major world commodities: sugar, tobacco, tea, coffee, cocoa, opium, pepper and spices, silk and silver, cotton textiles and porcelain. None of these were basic necessities, but spread into the consumption patterns of ordinary people in Europe and elsewhere. Many of these were addictive or fashion goods – they were goods that people could be induced to work longer and harder for after their basic needs were met – the goods that led to what Jan de Vries called 'the industrious revolution' – they had the effect of changing work and consumer cultures.[7]

We must remind ourselves of the size of this Asia trade to Europe. Tea, textiles, porcelain, lacquerware, furnishings, drugs and dyestuffs made for a systematic global trade carried in quantities which by the later eighteenth century came to 50,000 tons a year, as estimated by Jan de Vries. This made for just over one pound of Asian goods per person for a European population of roughly 100 million.[8] If we look to textiles and porcelain alone, we see the prodigious amounts of these goods reaching Europe from the seventeenth century. Riello's recent estimates show 1.3 million pieces of cotton textiles a year reaching Europe by the late 1680s, and 24.3 million pieces over the period 1665–1799.[9] The indicators for porcelain are similar. By the early eighteenth century, the British alone imported between 1 and 2 million pieces of Chinese porcelain a year. The Dutch East India Company (VOC) imported 43 million pieces from the beginning of the seventeenth century to the end of the eighteenth century.[10]

The trade, not just in textiles and porcelain, but also in such specialist goods as shagreen and coral relied from the seventeenth century on an integration of monopoly companies and private trade. Competing European East India companies complemented private traders in the intra-Asian trade. They also competed back in Europe, selling goods at auction to foreign and domestic merchants. Belief in the fabulous wealth to be gained by this trade induced shareholders to invest huge wealth in these companies and states, and to send sometimes significant parts of their populations to the Indies. The VOC greatly expanded the capital it invested in the trade from 1630–70 to 1680–1730, while returns fell between the first and second periods from 6 percent to 3.4 percent. And it sent 4,000 recruits a year to Asia by 1700–20, a time of declining population growth.[11]

Consumption

Global history has deeply affected our recent histories of consumer culture. Those histories that once mainly concentrated on Europe now emphasize the significance of the global trade in colonial groceries and the transfers of foods and seeds across different parts of the world. They focus now on how manufactured goods such as textiles and porcelain became embedded in European consumer cultures. They look to the encounters, misconceptions and new appropriations of European goods in other parts of the world, as indicated in Susan Broomhall's chapter on the goods brought by the VOC to the indigenous peoples of Australia. We seek to understand the cultural and political role of elite cabinets of curiosities such as conveyed in Nuno Senos's chapter, 'The Empire in the Duke's Palace'. But we now also want to know just how deeply those goods from around the world penetrated into European societies. Some markets were about courts, elites and luxury display, but much wider and more significant markets might be developed among middling and even lower class consumers seeking fashion, civility, status and respectability.

Collections in museums give us access to material artefacts, but these need to be integrated with the kinds of sources historians use such as the inventories of the Amsterdam Orphanage or the identifying marks in the form of textile tokens of the London Foundling Hospital. Though such textile tokens are also artefacts, they are not like the individually-displayed object of traditional museum collections. Other historians are making use of sources such as English pauper letters and inventories of the English Poor Laws, and the records of theft recorded in the archives of the Old Bailey.[12]

Just how extensive was this 'global' consumption in Europe? As we have seen, the trading companies landed one pound of Asian goods per person in Europe in the 1770s, equivalent to a week's earnings for a manual worker. Of course this was unevenly distributed across the social structure, but detailed analysis of probate inventories in the Southern Netherlands and of the inventories of the Amsterdam Orphanage show the depth of penetration. Jan de Vries shows clear evidence of a widespread 'breakable' material culture, of objects such as decorated ceramics, chipped, broken and quickly replaced, or fashion textiles and clothing, changed with the season. Equally Anne McCants has shown the deep penetration of Chinese porcelain and Indian textiles in the Dutch Republic.[13]

Yet was this experience of global objects and goods so widespread beyond Northwest Europe? Britain and the Dutch Republic had large East India Companies and extensive Atlantic mercantile trade. What was it like for Southern Europe and for other parts of Northern and Central Europe? These regions are new frontiers of research addressed by two chapters here, Matthew Romaniello's 'Russians and their Global Tobacco Habits', and Christine Fertig and Ulrich Pfister's 'Coffee, Mind and Body . . . Hamburg in the Eighteenth Century'. While tobacco spread quickly across Russia after the seventeenth century, it was consumed in very different European and Chinese ways, reinforcing regional differences within the Russian Empire. The entry of wider-world goods into Hamburg's consumer culture tells us more about extremes in the distribution of income and the food cultures of work and poverty than about the greater riches of a broad consumer culture. The Sound Toll records reveal little change in consumption patterns beyond a narrow elite, apart from colonial groceries such as sugar and coffee. And coffee and sugar consumption was as much a source of fast energy, and indeed went with lower grain rations for a large protoindustrial workforce.

The objects and substances discussed in this volume include some which seem rarified or exotic to us today, such as shagreen, coral or featherwork. Others seem unfashionably antique, such as ebony furnishings, and some just very ordinary, such as coffee, sugar and tobacco. But as we look at them, we ask questions about their histories and their production, now as in the past. We want to know how they were discovered, why they were sought out, and how they entered into European, Pacific, Asian and African cultures. These objects and substances crossed borders and regions of the world, and connected cultures in new ways. Their afterlife in museum collections, on Renaissance paintings, or in cafés or kitchen cupboards conceals great global histories of production, trade, distribution and consumption. They also open a new curiosity we have in social uses for these things, their meanings as gifts and markers of status, and their symbolism in our mental universe. These too have a global history, for the material culture of these objects and substances developed as they were made and moved across the regions of the world.

Notes and References

1. See Ralph Davis, *The Industrial Revolution and English Overseas Trade* (Leicester: Leicester University Press, 1979); Eric Hobsbawm, *Industry and Empire: From 1750 to the Present Day* (Harmondsworth: Penguin, 1969).
2. Ruth Barnes, *Indian Block-Printed Textiles in Egypt: The Newberry Collection in the Ashmolean Museum Oxford* (Oxford: The Clarendon Press, 1997); Giorgio Riello, *Cotton: the Fabric that Made the Modern World* (Cambridge: Cambridge University Press, 2013).
3. Anne Gerritsen and Giorgio Riello, 'The Global Lives of Things: Material Culture, Commodities and History,' this volume, p. 25; Anne Gerritsen, 'Global Jingdezhen: Local Manufactures and Early Modern Global Connections,' AHRC Project 2009–2011 http://www2.warwick.ac.uk/fac/arts/history/ghcc/research/globalporcelain; Anne Gerritsen, 'Fragments of a Global Past: Ceramics Manufacture in Song-Yuan-Ming Jingdezhen,' *Journal of the Economic and Social History of the Orient* 52 (2009): 117–152.
4. Anne Gerritsen and Giorgio Riello, 'Spaces of Global Interaction: The Material Landscapes of Global History,' in *Writing Material Culture History*, ed. Anne Gerritsen and Giorgio Riello (London: Bloomsbury, 2015), 111–133, esp. 113–115.
5. Dagmar Schäfer, *The Crafting of 10,000 Things: Knowledge and Technology in Seventeenth-Century China* (Chicago: University of Chicago Press, 2011).
6. S.R. Epstein, 'Transferring Technical Knowledge and Innovating in Europe,' in *Technology, Skills and the Pre-Modern Economy in the East and the West*, ed. Maarten Prak and Jan Luiten van Zanden (Leiden: Brill, 2013), 25–68.
7. Jan de Vries, *The Industrious Revolution: Consumer Behaviour and the Household Economy 1650 to the Present* (Cambridge: Cambridge University Press, 2008).
8. Jan de Vries, 'The Limits of Globalization in the Early Modern World,' *Economic History Review* 63. 4 (2010), 718.
9. Riello, *Cotton*, 93.
10. Robert Finlay, 'The Pilgrim Art: the Culture of Porcelain in World History,' *Journal of World History*, 9.2 (1998), 168; also Robert Finlay, *The Pilgrim Art: Cultures of Porcelain in World History* (Berkeley: University of California Press, 2010).
11. Jan de Vries and Ad van der Woude, *The First Modern Economy: Success, Failure and Perseverance of the Dutch Economy* (Cambridge: Cambridge University Press, 1997), pp. 437, 447.
12. Anne McCants, 'Poor Consumers as Global Consumers: The Diffusion of Tea and Coffee Drinking in the Eighteenth Century,' *Economic History Review*, 61, S1 (2008) 172–200; John Styles, *The Dress of the People: Everyday Fashion in Eighteenth-Century England* (New Haven: Yale University Press, 2008); John Styles, *Threads of Feeling: The London Foundling Museum's Textile Tokens, 1740–1770* (London: The Foundling Museum, 2010).
13. de Vries, *Industrious Revolution*; McCants, 'Poor Consumers'.

INDEX

Note: 'N' after a page number indicates a note; 'f' indicates a figure; 't' indicates a table.

Ablin, Seitkul 184
Aboriginal people. *See* indigenous people
Abu-Lughod, Janet 3
Adams, John 92
Africa 133–134
agriculture: and geographic movement of knowledge 44; international exchange of, after New World discovery 6. *See also* specific crops
Ahmed, Sarah 146
Albertus Magnus 42–43, 58n42
alchemy 42–43, 51–52, 54–55. *See also* knowledge, geographic movement of; science
Aldrovandi, Ulisse 243
Allsen, Thomas 49
al-Majusi, Ali b. 'Abbas 52
al-Rāzī, Abū Bakr 53f, 54, 55
al-Zahrawi, Abulcasis 52
Amerindian cosmologies 111
ammonium chloride 52, 52f
angels 173, 174f, 251
anthropology, approach to artefacts 10–11
Appadurai, Arjun 2
Arabia, medical knowledge in 51–52
archaeology 10–11
architecture 166, 167f
Aristotelian elements 33, 40
Aristotle 42
artefacts. *See* objects; specific items
asafoetida (devil's dung) 232–233, 234

astronomical clock 14–15, 15f
Atul, Esin 65
Australia: and Dutch East India Company 147–158; indigenous people of 149–150, 153–155, 156–157; Swan River Colony 152–155

ballet 118, 119
Barbados 203–204, 204f, 205f, 212, 212f, 214. *See also* Caribbean
Bartholomew, Terese Tse 96
beavers 233–234
Bell, John 192, 194
Belon, Pierre 64
Bennett, Jane 146
Berg, Maxine 12
Bering, Vitus 192
beverages 222
birds 44, 45f, 172f, 173, 242
Biringuccio, Vannoccio 33
Bjaaland Welch, Patricia 96
blood: of dragons 59n57; and gold 40; of Jesus 39f; and metal 35; and red colour 38–40; and red coral 86; significance of 38–39; uses of, for metalworkers/jewelers 39–40
Bloodgood, Delavan 214
bodies. *See* humans
Bogdanov, Martin 188
Boré, Etienne de 211
Bosma, Ulbe 201

Brand, Adam 192
Brandão, Ambrósio Fernandes 203
Brazil: featherwork production in 109–111; naming of 241–242; sugar production in 202–203; and Teodósio I collection 134; yellow fever in 211, 214. *See also* Tupinambá people
brazilwood 241–242
Breton, André 113
Brewer, John 11
Broomhall, Susan 18
Bujok, Elke 115, 119, 121
Buono, Amy 111, 112
Buvelot, Quentin 127n71

cabinet of curiosities 10, 72; and featherwork 107, 115–116, 121–122; mobility of 119
Canton System 89
Caribbean 212f, 213f; deforestation 204f, 205f, 206f; and disease 211–214; sugar production in 203–207; and Teodósio I collection 134; water management projects 208
Carondelet, Frances Louis Hector de 211
carpets 136
Carstenszoon, Jan 149, 151
Cartwright, John 187
castoreum 233–234
Catherine de Medici 117
Cennini, Cennino 40, 49
ceramics 4–5, 72
Charles I (King of England) 187
China: Canton System 89; Imperial officials 49, 50f; imperial workshops 93–95; medicinal uses of cinnabar in 49–51; and palace presentation lists 89–92; red colour's significance in 49, 97; red coral's significance in 81–82, 82f, 83f, 84–85, 90–91, 95–97; and Teodósio I collection 134–135; as terminology 132; and tobacco trade 185–186, 194, 195; trade in 89; tributary system 92–93; view of natural world 59n69
chocolate 6
Christophers, S.R. 214
cinchona bark 229
cinnabar 38, 49–51, 51f, 58n42, 58n48, 250. *See also* vermilion
clothing: French adaptation of Indian 168–170, 169f. *See also* feathers and featherwork; textiles
cochineal 38
coconut 132

coffee 22; as dietetic object 222; gender aspect of 227, 234, 248; trade in Germany 227, 227t, 234
Coffy, Phillip 187
Coler, Johann 233
collections and collecting, scholarship on 10–11
Collet, Dominik 122
colonialism: and Dutch East India Company in Australia 147–152; and featherwork 112–115; and possessive meaning of objects 151–152
Columbian exchange 6, 21
Columbus, Christopher 117
commodities: and consumption 21–22; Kopytoff on 63. *See also* specific commodities
commodity network 183–184
connectivity, global, and objects 16–19
constipation 231
consumer revolution, in Germany 223–228
consumption: as field of study 11–12, 19; French vs. Indian 174–176, 175f; and global history 256–257; of luxury goods 247–251; and trade, in Europe 22; voluntary vs. imposed 166
coral 16. *See also* red coral
costume 28n69. *See also* clothing; feathers and featherwork
Cotton, John 88
Crosby, Alfred 6, 21
crystal objects 131
Cuba 206–207
Culpeper, Edmund 71
Curtin, Philip 201, 214
cutlery 71, 72f

Davies, Surekha 113, 118
decorative arts, porcelain objects 8, 9f, 10–11
deforestation 201–207, 204f, 205f, 206f, 216
de Pereda, Antonio 1–2, 2f, 4–6
Descourtilz, M.E. 214
Desprez, François 113
dietetic objects: asafoetida (devil's dung) 232–233; castoreum 233–234; cinchona bark 229; colonial groceries 222; European adoption of global 228–234; jalapa roots 231; rhubarb roots 231–232. *See also* medicine
disease 250; and medical pluralism 229; and sugar production 199, 210–216. *See also* dietetic objects; medicine; specific disease
Dutch East India Company 10, 251; and Australia 147–158; as colonisers in

Australia 147–152; Dirck Hartogh plate 145, 146f; material culture of 147, 152–155; power dynamics and material culture of 155–158

early modern period, trade during 3–4

Echegoyen, José Ignacio 207
Encounters (museum exhibition) 12
Engineer, Urmi 21, 22
England, shagreen in 71–73
English East India Company (EEIC) 87–89, 98, 229
English Tobacco Company 190–191
epidemics. *See* disease
Epstein, Larry 254
Eremeev, Ivan 184
Eurasia, itineraries of material complexes in 43–49
Europe: shagreen in 64, 71–73; 'shagreen' terminology in 65–66
Europeans: adaptations of, to Pondicherry 165–170; adoption of global dietetic/medicinal objects 228–234; in Pondicherry 163–165

Fathonreckt, Thomas 188
feathers and featherwork 18, 248; and Amerindian cosmologies 111; and colonial encounter 112–115; in curiosity cabinets 107, 115–116, 121–122; European collecting of 115–116; and performance 116–121; in *Portrait of Sophie of the Palatinate* 105, 106f; printed representations of 113, 113f, 114f, 115, 116; production of, in colonial Brazil 109–111; as symbol of America 117; *tapirage* 110, 124n18; Tupinambá cape 107, 108f, 112, 120
Ferdinand II 119
Fertig, Christine 22
festivals 116–118
Feuchtwanger, Lewis 87
fish skin. *See* shagreen
folk tales 48–49, 60n75
food crops. *See* agriculture
Fraginals, Manuel Moreno 206–207
France, shagreen in 71–73
Françoso, Mariana 18
Frederick I 119
French people: adaptations of, to Pondicherry 165–170; Indian interest in 171–172; interest of, in Indians 173; and parrot statuettes 172f, 173; in Pondicherry 163–165

Frischlin, M.J. 119
furniture 249; French adaptation of Indian 166–168, 168f

galuchat (French shagreen) 65
Galuchat, Jean-Claudie 73
Ge Hong 49–50
geographic movement of knowledge. *See* knowledge, geographic movement of
George III (King of Britain) 93
Germany: coffee consumption in 227–228, 227t, 234; colonial commodity trade in 227t; consumer revolution in 223–228
Gerritsen, Anne 13
globality, of objects 2–3
glocalization 229
Gmelin, Johann Georg 192–194
gold: and blood 40; and red colour 49–50. *See also* red/gold/lizard complex
Gonzaga, Anne 119
good luck symbols: in Chinese culture 102n81; red coral 96
Goodyear, James 213
Greece, view of natural world 59n69
Grey, John Henry 91
Guth, Christine 16

Hajstrup, Peter Hansen 113, 115
Halleux, Robert 55
handstein 33, 34f
Hardinge, Charles Edmund 15
Harris, Oliver T.J. 146
Hartogh, Dirck 145, 156
Hartwell, Robert 47
health 33; objects for 222
Henry II 117, 118
Hippocratic-Aristotelian-Galenic view of nature 40
history, field of: approach to artefacts 11–14; global turn in 12–13
'A History of the World in 100 Objects' (radio programme) 13
Hobsbawm, Eric 253
Holland, shagreen in 71–73
Hollandine, Louise 105, 248
Hotton, Peter 231
Huff, Toby 14
humans: bodies of, as tools 32–33; health of 33, 222, 235–236; and materials 31–37; migration of, and knowledge transfer 47; and mining/metalworking 35–43; as source of manufacturing materials 32
hunting 44, 45f

Ides, Evert Ysbrant 186, 194
India 60n74; Pondicherry 162–176; as
    source of 'wonders' 48, 59–60n70;
    and Teodósio I collection 136–137; as
    terminology 132
Indians: French interest in 173; interest of,
    in French 171–172; in Pondicherry 164
indigenous people: in Australia 149–150,
    153–155, 156–157; and tobacco use
    184–186
Industrial Revolution 12
'Interwoven Globe' (museum exhibition)
    13
ivory 133–134
Izmailov, Lev Vasilevich 192

Jābir ibn Hayyan 54, 55
Jackson, Beverly 91
jalapa roots 231, 234
Japan: appeal of shagreen in 64; lacquerware
    produced in 66–68, 67f; shagreen
    manufacture in 68; shagreen's value in
    75; sword and daggers in 70, 70f, 75
Jeannin, Pierre 225
jewelry making, and uses of blood 39–40
jewels. See precious gems
Jonston, Joannes 36–37
Joosten, Willem 149

Kalmyk people 184–185, 185f
kamaboko-bako 66, 67f
kermes beetles 38
Ketelaar, Eric 146
Keyser, Jacob de 92
knives, as objects of global connection
    16–18, 17f
knowledge: creation of, and objects 14–16.
    See also science
knowledge, geographic movement of
    84; agriculture 44; between China
    and Arabia 51–52, 54–55; lizards and
    salamanders 43–44, 49; luxury goods
    44, 46–47; and migration 47; multi-
    focal origins of proto-chemistry 54f;
    vermilion 49–55; weapons technology
    44; 'wonders' 48–49
Kopytoff, Igor 63
Korber, Ulrike 68
Krizhanich, Iurii 185–186
Kunstkammer (cabinet of curiosity).
    See cabinet of curiosities

Lacey, Pippa 16
Las Casas, Bartholomé de 117

Laufer, Berthold 59–60n70, 60n75
Le Doudic, Kévin 19
Leinberger, Hans, altarpiece relief of mine
    accident 37f
Léry, Jean de 110, 111, 241, 242–244
Ligon, Richard 212, 214
Li Shiyao 91
lizards and salamanders: and geographic
    movement of knowledge 43–44, 49;
    and metalworking 40, 41f; and modern
    science 57n37. *See also* red/gold/lizard
    complex
localization 184, 195
Louisiana 207, 208, 209f, 210, 211, 214,
    215f
Louis XIV (King of France) 118
Lu Lengja 84–85
luxury goods: and Chinese imperial
    workshops 94–95; consumption of
    247–251; and geographic movement of
    knowledge 44, 46–47; in *Interior of a shop*
    (painting) 6–8; red coral as 84; shagreen
    as 66; and women 248

madder root 38
Madeira 201–202
maize 44
malaria 210, 211, 229
manufacturing, and human bodies 32
Mao Keming 91
maps: coral network 86f; and indigenous
    people 113; Pondicherry, India 164f;
    trading zones between China and
    Central Asia 53f
Marcgraf, George 111
Mary Stuart 120
Mason, Peter 118–119
material complexes: itineraries of, in Eurasia
    43–49; itinerary of, for vermilion 49–55;
    use of term 31
material culture: approach of, to objects
    162; of Dutch East India Company 147,
    152–155; globality of 254; and power
    dynamics 155–158
materials: as capable of growth 33–34; and
    humans 31–37; transformation of 31.
    See also objects
Maurits, Johan 115, 120–121, 122, 127n71
McGowan, Margaret 118
McGregor, Neil 13
McKendrick, Neil 11
medical pluralism 228–229
medicine: and Chinese and Arabic
    alchemy 51–53; European adoption of

global 228–234; 'glocalization' of 229; migration of, and knowledge transfer 48. *See also* dietetic objects
Meier, Michael 187
mercury 16, 38, 41–43, 51, 54, 55. *See also* vermilion
metal: and blood 35; as capable of growth 33–34. *See also* mining and metalworking; specific types
migration, and knowledge transfer 47
Mikhail Fedorovich 184, 187
Miller, Daniel 11
mining and metalworking: altarpiece relief of mine accident 37f; and lizards 40, 41f; reciprocal effect of, between workers and materials 35–37; and uses of blood 39–40; vermilion 37–43
Mintz, Sidney 22, 198, 216
Misenor, John 89
mobility, of curiosity cabinets 119
Mocarto, Abraham 87
Molino Ewer 46, 46f
Monardes, Nicolás 230
monkeys 210–211
Moore, George Fletcher 153
Moore, Jason W. 203–204
Morinaka, Kanako 65
mosquitoes 210–211, 212

natural world, Chinese vs. Greek views of 59n69
Newberry Collection 253
New Orleans 209f, 211, 214, 215f
Newton, Isaac 71
Nieuhof, Johannes 92
Norton, Marcy 111, 115, 121–122

objects: archaeological and anthropological approach to 10–11; and connectivity 16–19; function of 221; globality of 2–3, 12–13, 244; historians' approach to 11–14; and knowledge creation 14–16; making of 254–255; material culture approach to 162; possessive meaning of 151–152; scholarly interest in 2. *See also* luxury goods; material culture; materials; specific objects
Olearius, Adam 187
otherness, symbols signifying 117

Paludanus, Bernardus 107
paper making 47, 59n61
parrots 126n53, 245–246; Columbus' display of 117; exchange of 113, 115;
French interest in 172f, 173; and Léry's voyage to Brazil 242–244
peanuts 44
pearls: mother-of-pearl casket 131, 131f; necklace in Teodósio I collection 130–131
Pepper, Tom 156–157
performance, and featherwork 116–121
Peter the Great (Tsar of Russia) 183, 188
Pfister, Ulrich 22
philosopher's stone 42
Pillai, Ananda Ranga 170, 172
Pincon, Abel 65–66
pineapples: global impact of 20–21; *Pineapple* (White) 20, 20f
plantation complex 200–201, 214, 216
plates, Dirck Hartogh plate 145, 146f
Playford, Phillip 157
Pondicherry, India: commercial networks in 170–171; demographic overview of 163–165, 178n10; in 18th century 164f; French adaptations to 165–170; study methodology 174–176; as trade hub 162, 165
porcelain objects 8, 9f, 10–11, 46, 82f, 132, 134, 135f, 136
Portugal: trading practices of 130. *See also* Teodósio I
Portuguese trade, and shagreen 66–70
power dynamics, and material culture 147, 155–158
precious, as concept 96–97
precious gems 59–60n70, 134. *See also* jewelry making; specific gems
prisoners 47, 59n61
proto-chemistry 54f

Rauwolf, Leonhart 229
Rawski, Evelyn 93
rayskin. *See* shagreen
red, colour: and blood 38–40; in Chinese culture 49, 97; and gold 49–50. *See also* gold; vermilion
red coral 38, 50, 87f, 249; in Chinese culture 81–82, 82f, 83f, 84–85, 90–91, 95–97; and Chinese imperial workshops 93–95; *Foreigners Presenting Coral Trees to an Arhat* (Lu Lengja) 85f; as foreign tribute 92–93; as good luck symbol 96; in Greek mythology 86; links in trade network 81; as luxury good 84; and palace presentation lists 89–92; trade in 87–89; trade route of 86–89, 86f, 97–98

red/gold/lizard complex 40, 43–44, 51, 60n76
Rein, J.J. 64
religious syncretism 173, 174f, 251
rhubarb roots 231–232, 234, 250
Riello, Giorgio 13
Roger II 47
Romaniello, Matt 21–22
Russia: ban on tobacco 184–187; pipe-smoking 194; tobacco habits 187–191, 189f; tobacco imports into 188–190; tobacco legalization in 188; tobacco's history in 21–22, 183

Saikaku, Ihara 75
sal ammoniac 52, 52f, 54
Sang Hongyang 84
Schäfer, Dagmar 254
Schmalkalden, Caspar 115
Schongauer, Martin, *The Flight into Egypt* 41f
Schroeder, Johann 231
science: astronomical clock 14–15, 15f; modern, and lizards 57n37; reconceptualization of 14; vernacular 57n38
scientific instruments, shagreen's use for 71
Senos, Nuno 18
senses: and manufacturing 32–33. *See also* humans
shagreen 16, 249, 255; cultural meanings of 63, 77; cutlery 71, 72f; dinnerware 72; and Dutch traders in 62–63; in Europe 64, 71–73; galuchat (French shagreen) 65; Japanese production of 68; and lacquer coffers 66–67, 67f; as luxury good 66; origins of term 65–66; and Portuguese trade 66–70; preparation of 64; properties of 62, 63–64; rayskin shield 68, 69f, 70; scientific instruments 71; shark species used for 64–65; sword and dagger hilts 70, 70f, 75; trade in 73–76; in United States 72–73
shanhu. See red coral
shark, species of, used for shagreen 64–65
sharkskin. *See* shagreen
Sherley, Anthony 65
shipwrecks 10
Siberia: tobacco habits 192–194; tobacco in 184–186. *See also* Russia
'Silk Road' 47–48
silver: as capable of growth 34, 36f; in *Still Life with an Ebony Chest* (de Pereda) 4
slavery 133, 137, 200, 201, 203, 210, 211, 214, 215–216

Smith, George Vinal 74
Smith, Pamela 15–16
soil deterioration 201–207, 206f, 216
Sophie of the Palatinate 105, 106f, 120, 248
Sørensen, Tim Flohr 146
Sousa, Gabriel Soares de 110
South Lands 158n2. *See also* Australia
Speculum metallorum 33, 35f
Stevenson, Charles 64
stingray skin. *See* shagreen
sugar: effects of, on human health 216; as global commodity 22; as international commodity 6; trade in Germany 227t
sugar production 250; in Brazil 202–203; in Caribbean 203–207; deforestation and soil deterioration 201–207, 204f, 205f, 206f, 216; and disease 199, 210–216; in early modern world 199–201; in Louisiana 207, 208, 209f, 210; in Madeira 201–202; plantation complex 200–201, 200f, 214, 216; and water management projects 207–210, 211
sulphur 16, 38, 41–43, 46, 51, 55. *See also* vermilion
sweet potatoes 44
syncretism 173, 174f

tapirage 110, 124n18
Tasman, Abel 150–151
Tavernier, Jean-Baptiste 87
temper, as concept 33
Teodósio I 129f; access to global products 130; ducal palace 129f
Teodósio I, inventory of possessions: carpets 132; coconut carvings 132; crystal objects 131; as expression of duke's interests 140–141; extent of 128, 132–133; mother-of-pearl casket 131, 131f; pearl necklace 130–131; porcelain objects 132, 134, 135f, 136; problems of interpretation 130–132; slaves 133, 137; spatial distribution of 137–140; terminology of 132; tortoiseshell 138f
textiles: French adaptation of Indian 168–170, 169f; in *Still Life with an Ebony Chest* (de Pereda) 5–6; in Teodósio I collection 136–137. *See also* clothing
Thevet, André 109, 110
things. *See* objects
tobacco 249, 251; China's trade in 185–186, 194, 195; as dietetic object 222; history of, in Russia 183; import of, into Russia 188–190; and indigenous people 184–186; legalization of, in Russia 188; Russian ban of 184–187; Russian habits

189f; in 17th-century Russia 21–22; in Siberia 184–186; Siberian usage 192–194; smuggling 187; trade in Germany 227t
tortoiseshell 138f
trade: in China 89; and consumption, in Europe 22; during early modern period 3–4; practices of 255–256
trade routes: for red coral 86–89, 86f, 97–98. *See also* knowledge, geographic movement of
Tret'iakov, Ivan 184
Tsūryū, Inaba 64, 76
Tupinambá people 111, 113f, 116, 117–118, 123n2, 242
'Turks' (museum exhibition) 13

Uichi, Shimizu 72
United East India Company (VOC). *See* VOC (United East India Company)
United States, shagreen in 72–73

van Dyke, Paul 90
van Goyer, Pieter 92
verandas 166, 167f
Verberckmoes, Johan 116, 119
vermilion 250; case study 37–43; itinerary of material complex for 49–55; and Jesus' blood 38–39, 39f; production of 38, 41–43
Vlamingh, Willem de 145
VOC (United East India Company) 73–74, 79n40, 145. *See also* Dutch East India Company
Vollmer, John E. 84

von Bingen, Hildegard 229
von Strahlenberg, Philip Johann 192

Wagener, Zacharias 110, 111, 115
Waldseemüller, Martin 242
Wallerstein, Immanuel 255
water management projects 207–210, 211
Watts, David 210
weapons technology, and geographic movement of knowledge 44
Wedgwood 72
White, John, *Pineapple* 20–21, 20f
Whitehead, Peter James Palmer 65
Whitworth, Charles 190–191
Willemsen, Mathieu 74
William III (King of England) 188
Wintroub, Michael 117
women, and luxury goods 248
'wonders': and geographic movement of knowledge 48–49; as originating in India 48, 59–60n70
wood: cultivation and management 31–32; in *Still Life with an Ebony Chest* (de Pereda) 4
wunderkammer (display) 137. *See also* cabinet of curiosities

Yang Boda 93–94
Yang Yongbin 91
yellow fever 210–211, 212, 213, 214, 216
Yuan Cai 46

Zhang Hua 43
Zheng Wusai 91
Zuytdorp shipwreck 157